Bresnahan and Tuttle's

Track and field
athletics

Bresnahan and Tuttle's

Track and field athletics

FRANCIS X. CRETZMEYER, M.A.

Track Coach, University of Iowa, Iowa City

LOUIS E. ALLEY, Ph.D.

Head, Physical Education for Men, University of Iowa, Iowa City

CHARLES M. TIPTON, Ph.D.

Associate Professor, Physiology and Biophysics, University of Iowa, Iowa City

Seventh edition

With 181 illustrations

The C. V. Mosby Company

Saint Louis 1969

Preface

George W. Bresnahan (deceased) and W. W. Tuttle were pioneers in the application of scientific research to performances in track and field athletics. Their book, *Track and Field Athletics,* served as a bible for track coaches and physical educators both in the United States and abroad for over 30 years.

This seventh edition, now titled *Bresnahan and Tuttle's Track and Field Athletics,* represents the efforts of the current authors to retain the many valid aspects of previous editions and to revise those parts of the book that no longer apply to modern programs in track and field athletics. A major portion of such a task consists of bringing the record performances listed in the book up to date, revising the comparative marks for scholastic competitors in keeping with the improved performances of high school athletes, and correlating rules in the text with recent changes in the rules for track and field athletics.

The details on techniques of vaulting with a fiber glass pole are expanded considerably and new illustrations are provided. The diagrams for the lay out of quarter-mile tracks are modified to conform with current rules and practices.

Information concerning the physiology of training is updated and a table for determining the normal weight of athletes is provided. Recent research, pertinent to track and field athletics, is added whenever possible.

The current edition provides both the coach and the athlete with a functional guide toward improving performance in track and field athletics.

Francis X. Cretzmeyer
Louis E. Alley
Charles M. Tipton

Contents

Bresnahan and Tuttle's

Track and field athletics

Introduction

Methods of instruction in track and field athletics have continued to change markedly in the last quarter century. These innovations have resulted in improved styles of executing track and field events.

Scientists have contributed immeasurably to the fund of knowledge of both athletes and instructors. Experts in the areas of cardiology, chemistry, dietetics, medicine, physics, physiology, orthopedics, and surgery have reported the results of numerous laboratory experiments that are directly related to track and field activities.

We have discussed and interpreted in this book the results of many of these laboratory experiments. In addition, we have continued to supervise controlled laboratory studies on our own campus.

Throughout the world the number of individuals participating in this sport has increased steadily. It is interesting to note that athletes from some of the less populous nations have surpassed the track and field performances of competitors from the larger and richer countries.

Although a women's section of track and field athletics has been included in the Olympic games since 1928, some nations have refrained from entering female contestants, possibly for the reason that they believed the physical demands were too strenuous.

During the past 10 years, the attitude of women physical educators in the United States toward interscholastic competition for girls has shifted rather markedly in the direction of favoring such competition under proper guidance and control. The Division of Girls and Women's Sports, American Association for Health, Physical Education and Recreation published in 1963 a *Statement of Policies for Competition in Girls and Women's Sports* and in 1965, *Guidelines for Interscholastic Athletic Programs for High School Girls.* As a result of the increased interest and leadership in girl's athletics, the participation of girls in track and field athletics is increasing rapidly; for example, over 18,000 girls were members of interscholastic track and field teams in Iowa during the school year of 1967-68.*

The literature on track and field techniques has gained additional distribution, as evidenced by the material from sources other than the United States that has crossed our desks. Among the countries from which we have noted recent treatises are Australia, Czechoslovakia, Esthonia, Germany, Great Britain, Hungary, Italy, Japan, New Zealand, Russia, and South Africa. These exchanges of ideas should prove to be rewarding.

*Personal communication from Wayne Cooley, Executive Secretary, Iowa Girl's High School Athletic Union.

Chapter 1

Preliminary season preparations

W hen the track and field squad is assembled to discuss the approaching season of training and competition, the topics usually considered first are the personal equipment requirements of the individual candidates, the importance of warming up, and the schedules of practice that are to be followed. In order that we may know what the requirements are, they are discussed in some detail in this chapter.

PERSONAL EQUIPMENT

The desires of the competitor, weather conditions, the condition of the runway, and available funds determine largely the selection of personal equipment. The major items to be considered in the track and field athlete's personal equipment are hose, jersey, supporter, shoes, trunks or pants, and warm-up suit.

Hose. Cotton half hose, light woolen half hose, or chamois-skin pushers are used commonly. They give protection against chafing, act as pads in loose-fitting shoes, and can be cleaned easily. Many athletes whose feet are toughened sufficiently require no foot covering; some are able to wear shoes on bare feet. However, a covering for the feet is recommended for sanitary reasons and for protection against injury. The use of white hose eliminates the possibility of dye poisoning.

It has been shown by Folk and Peary[1] that the type of footwear is unimportant in the production of sweat. However, the amount of perspiration absorbed by the hose varies directly with their thickness.

Jerseys. Jerseys are made of cotton, wool, or synthetic fibers. Here, again, the type of material is one of personal choice. The jerseys should fit so as to permit freedom of chest and arm movements. Some athletes prefer a jersey which has a quarter-length sleeve.

Supporter. The selection of a supporter is usually made by the individual competitor, who can judge its snugness, feeling of comfort, and freedom from binding and chafing. Types of supporters include those of all cotton, elastic cotton, and web pouch.

Shoes. The importance of shoes in track and field competition warrants considerable emphasis. For events requiring special shoe adjustments, the reader should refer to the chapter dealing with the event in question.

Since runways and tracks vary in texture, adjustment of spike length is desirable. In order to avoid the necessity of having several pairs of shoes, there are types available which permit the interchanging of threaded-head spikes of varying degrees of length and sharpness. These are usually designated as detachable spikes.

The fitting of the shoe is extremely important, and because of this the athlete should never be content to try on only one shoe and trust to luck that the other will fit. Both shoes should be drawn on the bare feet (if new shoes) and laced snugly. One should stand on a wood floor, rise on the toe tips, and jab downward and forward with the force approximating that which will be experienced in running and jumping. Under this force, if the shoe fits, the great toe of each foot should exert no more than comfortable pressure on the soft leather toe tip. A shoe that causes discomfort to the great toe is a possible source of nail injury because it is too short. On the other hand, a shoe that curls up is fraught with danger because it is too long.

Too little attention is given to the width of shoes even though the length is correct. Comfortable pressure on the first joint of the great toe and the second joint of the little toe is experienced when the shoe is fitted correctly. Track and field shoes can be fitted a little more snugly than street shoes since they are worn only for a short period. Some qualities of shoes, after a period of use, stretch more than others, and allowance for stretching should be made at the outset. In breaking in new shoes, they should be worn for only a brief period each day to avoid discomfort. If a shoe, when laced, permits the eyelets to meet, it is obviously too loose and may be cast at an inopportune moment. A competitor who removes his shoes without first untying them stretches the upper leather and courts the trouble of shying his moccasin-like footwear.

The care of the shoes should not be overlooked. Loose stitching should be repaired immediately. Broken shoestrings should never be knotted but should be replaced by new ones. The life of a leather shoe may be prolonged and the shoe made more resistant to moisture by the application of saddle soap, harness oil, neats'-foot oil, or graphite dressing.

Trunks or pants. Trunks or pants are made of duck, muslin, satin, or synthetic material. The type of fabric is relatively unimportant and is a matter of personal choice. Whatever the material may be, the trunks should fit comfortably at the waist and the crotch. Above all, there should be freedom of thigh action. A V notch at the lower end of the outer thigh seam gives full coverage as well as ample room for thigh action. Waist bands of elastic or with either elastic backs or elastic sides are preferable to those of nonresilient material.

Warm-up suit. The warm-up suit, sometimes called the sweat or training suit, ranges from the inexpensive cotton fleece-lined, two-piece shirt and pants to the zipper-fitted suit of wool or synthetic material. The purpose of this suit is twofold: (1) to hasten the warm-up when the athlete takes preliminary exercises and (2) to retain body heat between practices or competitions.

PHYSICAL ADJUSTMENTS FOR COMPETITION

At this point it seems advisable to consider briefly those factors related to the functional activity of muscles which should be familiar to every competitor.

An isolated muscle serves as a good example to illustrate the most important effects of exercise on muscle activity. Excised muscle, when stimulated directly at regular intervals with stimuli of uniform intensity, from the beginning of activity to complete fatigue, illustrates what goes on in the athlete's muscles through a similar period of exercise. These phenomena indicate the type of activity exhibited when the muscle is first stimulated and the changes in performance as activity continues. From them, we may suggest explanations of certain factors that affect the achievement of every competitor and that will help him to

prepare himself intelligently to function most efficiently.

Effect of exercise on muscle activity. In making comparisons between isolated and intact muscle, it should be remembered always that the isolated tissue is devoid of nerve and blood supply. This results in an exaggeration of the phenomena which make their appearance. A record of the behavior of excised muscle tissue is shown in Fig. 1-1. The phenomena that are of interest to the athlete are as follows.

Introductory contractions. The first responses at the beginning of activity are irregular and indicate erratic performance. These are sometimes hard to demonstrate in excised tissue and are not shown in Fig. 1-1. The reason for these irregular contractions is believed to be the lack of an optimum cellular environment within the muscle. By warming up it is believed that the increase in temperature, blood flow, and oxygen availability will improve the ability of the muscle to respond to a neural

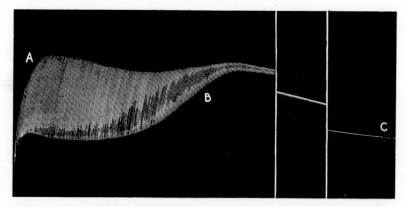

Fig. 1-1. This is the response of the excised gastrocnemius muscle of the frog from the beginning of activity to complete fatigue. At the beginning, **A**, of the record, the contractions gradually get higher, showing an increased irritability due to functional activity. This is the staircase phenomenon. Well along in the record, the muscle fails to relax completely (fails to come down to the baseline), **B**. Then, it relaxes only slightly. This is contracture and parallels the common cramp. Finally the muscle fails to contract due to fatigue, **C**. This is an exaggerated picture of what occurs in intact human muscle.

stimuli. Moreover, it has been shown that reflex time (patellar) becomes faster after a period of light physical activity. For these reasons one can recommend a practice of warming up.

Staircase phenomenon (period of better performance). Soon after a muscle contracts there is a period during which the height of the response increases in a steplike manner until a plateau occurs. This characteristic of muscle is known as the staircase phenomenon and can be seen in Fig. 1-1. Surprisingly, the precise reasons for this phenomenon are not clearly understood. Most authorities believe that it is closely associated with the initial chemical and thermal events within the muscle. One effect is an increase in temperature and a decrease in viscosity. This change will increase the efficiency of muscle contraction.

The major application of this phenomenon to the athlete is to be certain that adequate warm-up period occurs before competing. It would be extremely desirable for an athlete to know when his muscles had achieved the staircase effect because he would then know when to provide a maximum effort. Unfortunately, this feeling can only be acquired from trial-and-error methods used during the practice sessions.

Contracture. Contracture, a phenomenon of muscle activity, is described as retarded relaxation. A similar condition is that of a cramp which occurs in the untrained individual. For excised muscle, this is shown in Fig. 1-1, *B*. Contracture is closely associated with fatigue since, for the most part, they make their appearance simultaneously. It is believed that the reason for contracture is the presence of chemical products which interfere with the cellular process that promotes relaxation. Pain and/or an inadequate blood supply to a working muscle will also promote this condition.

Fatigue. The onset of fatigue occurs soon after the end of the staircase effect. After fatigue appears, it progresses until there is a total loss of response in excised muscle (Fig. 1-1, *C*). Fatigue, as far as is known, is caused by the accumulation of the chemical products resulting from contraction. The severity of the fatigue depends on the rate of accumulation of these products, whereas their rate of formation in turn depends on the amount of work which the muscle performs.

PHYSICAL TRAINING

Experiments by Bock and associates[2] showed that from the standpoint of the efficiency of the body as a machine physical training was of great advantage to the organism. The superiority of the athlete is due to his ability to meet demands for oxygen. This enables him to maintain a cellular environment that is not disrupted during severe muscular work. As emphasized earlier, the increased metabolism resulting from muscular work is met more efficiently by trained subjects than by nontrained subjects.

In the case of the intact muscle the situation is somewhat different. Here, since circulation is intact, the onset and the persistence of fatigue depend not only on the rate of formation of chemical products of contraction but also on the adequacy of the circulation to remove these products.

Training is the chief factor to be considered here. In order to enhance performance it is desirable to delay the symptoms that are collectively known as fatigue. Since it has been repeatedly demonstrated that the individual in good physical condition is capable of completing a given work task with less fatigue symptoms than a poorly conditioned individual, the process of training is important in improving performance.

Training has been shown to increase muscular strength, endurance, and coordination. The ability to utilize fats and carbohydrates for the energy requirements of the muscle is improved by training. By increasing the amount of red blood cells, the number of capillaries, the blood volume, the amount of myoglobin, and the distribution of blood flow to active from inactive parts, training causes more oxygen to be delivered and utilized by the working cells. Not only are waste products more effectively eliminated but also, apparently, training results in lower concentrations of lactic acid, a fatigue substance found within the blood. Some data suggest that trained individuals can tolerate higher concentrations of waste products than nontrained subjects.

Warm-up. Although there are some who tend to de-emphasize the warm-up, evidence exists that the majority of authorities make it obligatory as a part of the athletic program.[3] Experience and observation support this view. In addition, laboratory experiments[4] have shown that in an exercise such as riding a bicycle ergometer significantly more work was done when the subject warmed up previous to the exercise than when he did not.

The warm-up is, however, an individual matter, depending on the condition and response of the athlete. A well-trained athlete soon learns to know when he is warmed up sufficiently, hence ready for competition.

Relaxation. It is a well-known fact that, for the most part, the groups of muscles which the athlete uses in the track and field events are arranged in pairs, one antagonistic to the other. While one group is contracting, the other is relaxing. Physiologic evidence points out that any factor that alters the activity of muscle affects the phase of relaxation more pronouncedly than the period of contraction. It is obvious, then, that a muscle which is warmed up as far as its contracting phase is concerned may not be physiologically able to relax effectively. This fact may explain why the sprinter frequently pulls muscles during the early stages of the race. Examination of the injury may reveal the fact that it is the relaxing muscles which suffer rather than the contracting ones.

It is important to note that after the muscles have been warmed up properly they must not be exposed to sudden changes in temperature during the event. There are cases in which a runner suffered muscle injury by merely running from a practice stretch out into a cold environment. Examination showed that it was a relaxing muscle that suffered. These instances of injury emphasize not only the importance of warming up but also of protection against chilling.

Respiration. It has been shown conclusively that unrestricted breathing follows a reflex pattern, depending on the demands of the situation at hand.[5,6] The situations that alter the breathing patterns are (1) attention, (2) demand for elimination of carbon dioxide resulting from strenuous exercise, and (3) muscle fixation in static work.

It is generally accepted that whatever the situation may be the respiratory adjustment is automatic. However, there is considerable discussion within scientific circles that the pattern of breathing during running and swimming may be influenced by the movement of the arms. Since the evidence is lacking it seems wise to refrain from suggesting any pattern of breathing to the track and field athlete except in the case where overventilation may be an advantage in breath holding.

Second wind. Almost every athlete who has been running or swimming vigorously has experienced breathlessness, general distress, nausea, muscle pains, and combinations thereof. However, as exercise continues the symptoms disappear and one experiences a second wind. The explanation for this change is obscure. The concensus of most investigators is that neural circulatory, respiratory, and heat production adjustments are involved and are in some way determined by metabolic requirements of the working muscle. The end result is that an adequate blood flow is maintained to the working tissue with a minimum of accumulated waste products.

It remains to be determined whether a well-trained athlete acquires a second wind more readily or is more tolerant to the condition of breathlessness than a poorly conditioned individual.

Cooling off. This discussion would not be complete if the cooling period were not considered. After a contest the athlete should make use of such protective equipment as a sweat suit or a blanket. During the cooling period, light exercise involving especially the musculature used in the event should be continued. Sometimes massage by the athlete himself is beneficial. This will avoid stiffness and will facilitate a future warm-up if it is required. The individual should not cool off by lying or sitting on the ground.

DAILY SCHEDULES OF PRACTICE

The purpose of the daily schedule of practice is the attainment of proper physical condition and mental poise. By engaging in a series of graded exercises, which will point the athlete toward proficiency in his event, this can be attained. The successive stages of conditioning an individual are presented in the following plan:

Preliminary	
season	March 15 to April 1
Early season	April 2 to April 15
Midseason	April 16 to May 15
Late season	May 16 to June 17

The dates suggested for each division of the schedule are adapted only for institutions located in the north temperate zone. However, these dates may be adjusted to fit the climatic conditions in any part of the world.

Due to the fact that during the preliminary season the squad may be drilled as a group, a detailed schedule of practice can be prescribed for this period for the whole squad. Because at the beginning of the early season the candidates are separated and grouped according to events, the daily training schedules are necessarily different.

Throughout the schedules of practice it is necessary to prescribe effort distribution in the various sections of a race. The same thing is true in recommending a pace which is less than full effort. Degrees of effort assigned, beginning with the least, are as follows: walking, jogging, running at $\frac{1}{2}$, $\frac{2}{3}$, $\frac{3}{4}$, $\frac{7}{8}$, $\frac{9}{10}$, and $\frac{95}{100}$ effort, and sprinting. Obviously, these are not absolute values but are expressions employed to designate various degrees of energy expenditure. However, as the coach becomes familiar with the ability of his men, fractional parts of effort may be supplanted by exact stop watch time values.

Preliminary season. The objective of the preliminary season schedule of practice, as well as all others, is not confined merely to the attainment of basic physical condition. Poise, relaxation, grace of movement, and agility in action are the aims of the training schedules. The acquisition of these qualities, valuable in both current daily habits and those of future years, is ample reward for the time spent in practice. Track and field candidates obtain physical and mental benefits from their practice, even though they may not be fortunate enough to break into the scoring column.

Fartlek system of training. The Fartlek system, meaning "speed play," consists in acquiring an acceptable physical condition through a program of running. Those who use this system recommend that the running be done over a cross-country course which provides a soft, spongy surface. Where such a course is not available, a running track covered with sawdust serves the purpose. Distances and speeds are optional, depending on both the capacity and judgment of the individual runner. A sample practice schedule is as follows:

1. Warm up by running easily for 5 to 10 minutes.
2. Run at a fast, steady speed over a distance of $\frac{3}{4}$ to $1\frac{1}{4}$ miles.
3. Walk rapidly for 5 minutes.
4. Practice easy running, broken by sprints of 65 to 75 yards, repeating until fatigue becomes evident.

5. Run easily, injecting 3 or 4 swift steps occasionally.
6. Run at full speed up hill for 175 to 200 yards.
7. Run at a fast pace for 1 minute.
8. Finish the routine by running 1 to 5 laps around the track, depending on the distance run in competition.

Those who use the Fartlek system recommend that the practice session last for 1 to 2 hours and that it be repeated 3 to 5 times a week. It is said that if the schedule is followed properly the athlete should feel stimulated rather than tired.

Attention is called to the fact that some coaches who employ the Fartlek system for middle distance and distance runners are reluctant to use the full series of activities for competitors in the sprints, hurdles, jumps, and weights.

Interval running. Interval running consists of running repeatedly sectors of 110, 220, 330, 440, 660, or 880 yards interspersed with jogging. Careful consideration should be given to the intervals between the sectors. The athlete should establish either an objective in minutes for each interval of jogging or an objective of a fixed distance covered in each interval. For example, at first he may elect to jog 440 yards between each sector of running. As soon as his physical condition improves, he may choose either to increase the speed of the jog or to reduce the distance of the jog. If he chooses the "minutes" objective plan for the early practices, he may jog for a period of 4 minutes during the intervals. As soon as he becomes more proficient, he may decide rightfully to reduce the jogging time to 3 minutes, 2 minutes, or possibly 1 minute. He should strive to keep moving, even though the movement is reduced to a slow shuffle.

Interval running activities may be repeated as many times as the physical condition of the athlete warrants.

Progressive resistance exercises—weight training. There are differences of opinion regarding the advisability of including weight training in the conditioning program of the track and field athlete. The fact that progressive weight training will increase muscular strength quite rapidly cannot be denied. In addition to increasing strength, the advocates of weight training claim that it imparts a feeling of well-being and improves an athlete's ability in his favorite sport by increasing both strength and endurance. In addition, the use of resistance exercises is advocated as a means of strengthening weaknesses in various parts of the body and as a corrective measure for rehabilitating muscles that have been impaired by injury.

One should not confuse weight training with weight lifting. The objectives of a weight-training schedule are to provide exercises of graded intensity, designed to develop muscular strength, to meet the requirements of individual competitors. Weight lifting is commonly applied to those activities in which the athlete seeks to lift a maximum number of pounds in competition with others in the same body-weight class.

Favorable results obtained from the use of weight-training exercises have been reported by prominent competitors in running, jumping, middle distance running, and weight events in the track and field program.

Although it is pointed out that the so-called muscle-bound effect does not occur as the result of practicing lifting heavy weights, it is emphasized that weight-training exercises should be selected judiciously so as to be suited to the activity in which the athlete desires to excel. In most cases weight-training exercises are scheduled either on alternate days or not more than 3 times per week. Some coaches recommend that weight training be eliminated at the beginning of the season of competition, whereas others use it throughout the competitive season.

Weight-training exercises (concentric-type muscle contractions) have been embodied in the conditioning programs of notable competitors in various sports, and their value appears to be recognized. In kindred studies by Chui[7] and Capen,[8] favorable results from weight-training exercises were reported. The increase in strength is explained by the principle of overload. A muscle develops in size and strength only as it is overloaded, that is, as it is required to exert force against progressively greater resistance than it normally does. This development occurs because of an increase in the cross-sectional area of individual muscle fibers.

For the convenience of the coach and the athlete, a series of weight-training routines is included here. Some of these exercises do not apply to all track and field events. Reference is made to the appropriate exercise in the schedules of practice as the subject matter is developed.

The number of weight-training exercises included in the conditioning program and the frequency of their repetition in the schedule of practice is left to the discretion of the coach and the athlete. It is recommended by leading coaches who advocate weight-training exercises that they not be performed more than once a day, 3 days a week, during the preliminary season and not more than 2 days a week during the competitive season.

In addition, it is recommended, as in the case of any activity, that the athlete warm up before engaging in weight-training exercises. As an example of the routine that may be employed for this purpose, the following is suggested:

1. Squat from a standing position to the position of half squat, on the toes. Return to the standing position and bend forward with the arms stretching toward the floor; then bounce several times.

2. Stride stand, with the hands on the hips, circumduct the trunk, first to the right, and then to the left. Repeat several times.

3. Finish the warm-up with stationary running, bringing the knees up to the level of the hips.

After the warm-up, the appropriate exercises may be performed. The number of repetitions and the poundage of weights employed depend on the strength and endurance of the individual athlete. Ordinarily a 40-pound bar bell and a 10 to 15-pound dumbbell are adequate for beginners.

The following is a description of a representative group of weight-training exercises referred to by number in the following discussion.

1. In a seated or squat position, with the forearms resting along the thighs, with palms up, grasp a bar bell, just beyond the knees. Flex the hands upward. Repeat with palms down, flexing the hands backward and upward.

2. Stand and hold the bar bell in front of the thighs, palms forward. Flex the forearms completely or until the bar bell is just in front of the shoulders.

3. Stand and hold the bar bell just in front of the shoulders, palms forward. Press or thrust the bar bell upward to arm's length, over the head.

4. Rest the bar bell on the shoulders, behind the neck. Execute half squats, flatfooted. The weight of the bar bell used depends on the strength of the athlete.

5. Stand and rest the bar bell on the shoulders, behind the neck or hold in the hand in front of the thighs. Rise up on the toes.

6. Stand with dumbbells in the hands beside the thighs, and then lift the dumbbells sideward to a position about 45 degrees above the shoulders. Repeat, using progressively heavier dumbbells.

7. Stand with dumbbells beside the thighs and then raise the weights

forward to a position about 45 degrees above the level of the shoulders. Repeat several times.

8. Lie on a bench, face up, with the arms at right angles to the trunk above the shoulders. Swing the dumbbells from this position to a position out to the side and as near to the floor as possible.

9. In a supine position (with the aid of an assistant) lift a heavy bar bell in front of the shoulders until it is at arm's length. Keep the arms straight; raise the bar bell up as far as possible.

10. Lie on a slanting abdominal board with the feet upward, or lie on the floor with the feet held down. Hold a weight as heavy as can be managed and execute sit-ups.

11. Lie on the floor without weights and perform abdominal "curls." Lying face up, hands on front of the thighs, lower the back until it contacts the floor. Curl the trunk forward, pushing the hands down the thighs, and attempt to touch the knees.

12. Stand with the bar bell behind the neck, step forward a foot or so with one foot, and then squat on the rear heel. Upon rising, stride forward with the opposite foot and repeat the procedure.

13. Stand with the bar bell in front of the thighs and bend forward, with the knees almost straight, until the bar bell rests on the floor. Assume the original position.

14. Execute one of the following exercises:
    a. With dumbbells in the hands,
    jump in the air and swing one foot forward and the other backward. Bend the forward leg so that the leg and thigh form a right angle. Jump to a reverse position without coming to an erect position.
    b. With the bar bell on the floor and with the knees bent, bend over and put the bar bell upward to arm's length over the head, extending one leg forward and the other backward as in *a*.

15. With the bar bell behind the neck and the knees straight, bend forward and downward. Bounce 3 times.

16. With the feet in a stride-stand position and the dumbbells in the hands, bend the trunk forward to a right angle. Rotate the trunk to the left and bounce. Repeat in the opposite direction.

17. Seated, with the legs hanging down, select weights and adjust them to the feet. Extend first one leg and then the other.

18. Stand on a box and permit one leg to hang free. Fasten a weight to the foot and then swing the leg backward and forward as far as possible.

19. With a light dumbbell or bar bell held above the head, swing the implement forward and downward and then forward and upward to a position above the head.

Those who wish to introduce weight training into the conditioning program should refer to other sources.[9-12]

To facilitate the use of these weight-training exercises, those that apply to the various events are as follows:

Running 2, 3, 4, 5, 6, 7, 8, 10, 11, 12, 17, 18, 19
Hurdling 2, 3, 4, 5, 6, 7, 8, 10, 11, 12, 14, 16, 17, 18, 19
High jumping 1, 2, 3, 4, 5, 6, 7, 8, 10, 11, 12, 14, 17, 18, 19
Long jumping 2, 3, 4, 5, 6, 7, 8, 10, 11, 12, 17, 18, 19
Shot-putting and discus throwing 1, 2, 3, 4, 5, 6, 7, 8, 9, 10, 11, 12, 13, 17, 18, 19
Pole vaulting 1, 2, 3, 4, 5, 6, 10, 11, 12, 19

Gymnastic exercises and calisthenics. A person starting the performance of a physical activity new to him is frequently confronted with difficulties in its mastery due to stiffness, weakness, or clumsiness. Therefore, it is desirable when training for an event to practice exercises and calisthenics that are pointed toward the development of flexibility, strength, and coordination. Each event requires that emphasis be directed to some specific part of the body. Since space prohibits a detailed description of the most suitable exercises and calisthenics for each given case and since excellent treatises are available which provide adequate description, exercises are suggested in the schedules of practice but are not fully described.

Tension exercises (static-type or isometric muscle contractions). For a number of years physical educators have employed the concentric type of muscle contraction as exemplified in weight-training exercises. Hettinger and Müller[13] published the results of a study focusing attention on the effects of static-type contractions for the development of strength. They reported that 1 practice session per day, in which the muscles were held in static contraction for a period of 6 seconds, resulted in as much increase in strength as longer periods of muscle contraction (up to 45 seconds) and more frequent practices (up to 7 per day).

Wolbers and Sills[14] concluded that for muscle groups tested in an experiment, static muscle contractions of 6 seconds' duration will cause significant gains in strength. For the convenience of those who wish to include tension exercises in their programs, a list of those applicable to track and field athletes is included. The number of repetitions of any one exercise depends on the need of the athlete in question. The quantity of tension exercises employed in the training schedule is left to the discretion of the coach and the athlete.

A list of representative tension exercises is presented. They should be repeated. The number of times is dependent on the physical status of the athlete.

1. Press the hands together over the head.
2. Press the hands together in front of the chest.
3. Pull the hands apart in front of the chest.
4. Press backward vigorously either on front of the thighs (standing) or against the floor (lying on the back).
5. Either in a half-squat position or lying on the back with the knees in front of the hips, pull forward and upward against the backs of the knees.
6. Either from a half-squat position or sitting in a chair, pull up with the hands against the thighs behind the knees.
7. Either from a half-squat position or sitting in a chair, push downward and backward with the hands against the knees.
8. Push downward with the hands against the knees.
9. Lunge to a side position. Push down forcefully with the hands first against one bent knee and then against the other.
10. In a half-squat position, pull up with hands crossed between the knees.
11. Perform a three-quarter squat, first on one leg and then on the other.
12. Push up on the ball of first one foot and then the other.
13. Press the legs together.
14. Hook the feet and pull them apart.
15. Pull with the heel of the partially flexed leg against the sole of the opposite foot. Repeat with the opposite leg.

Since some of the exercises included do not apply to all track events, the ones appropriate for each event are tabulated as shown on page 12.

Schedules of practice, preliminary season (entire squad). Adjustments are obligatory if the athlete is on a 7-day rather than a 6-day routine. In presenting schedules of practice for preliminary season conditioning, the idea is to provide adequate activities for all members of the track and field squad.

We are cognizant of the fact that in European countries the preliminary season of practice is markedly altered, especially for middle distance and distance running. These alterations are taken into account in the appropriate places in the text.

Monday

1. Review the experiments dealing with the importance of the warm-up (see p. 6). Record your body weight before and after each day's activity (see p. 23).
2. Warm up with easy alternate jogging and walking distances of 50 yards each. Repeat 4 or 5 times.
3. Perform 5 minutes of general calisthenics, including trunk twisting and push-ups from the front leaning rest position.
4. Spend 10 to 15 minutes alternately jogging 25 yards, running 50 yards at ½ effort, and walking 50 yards. Repeat.
5. Warm up for weight-training exercises and then engage in those designed for your track or field event (see p. 8).
6. Terminate the day's activities with a jog of 440 yards, followed by a tepid shower bath. Record your body weight.

Tuesday

1. Consider the factors aiding injury prevention. Study the recommended diets presented on p. 16.
2. Make use of tension exercises suggested on p. 11.
3. Jog (preferably on turf) for a period of 5 minutes.
4. Execute 4 or 5 trials of the standing long jump for the purpose of developing the spring.
5. Engage in the Fartlek system of exercises (see p. 7) and adjust both their duration and intensity to your capabilities. (Possible exceptions might be required for individuals competing in the sprint, hurdle, and field events.)

Wednesday

1. Warm up with a jog of 440 to 660 yards, execute 10 minutes of calisthenics, and stride 80 to 100 yards at gradually increasing speed. Emphasize relaxation.
2. Execute 3 minutes of inverted running as an aid in perfecting the striding actions. (For a description of inverted running, see Glossary.)
3. Alternately jog 25 yards, run 50 yards at ⅔ effort, walk 25 yards. Repeat 7 or 8 times.
4. Utilize the warm-up schedule for weight-training exercises and follow with those weight-training activities that have been found effective in developing other athletes (see p. 9).
5. Conclude with a jog of 880 yards, emphasizing the optimum length of stride and acceptable arm action, as well as relaxation. Take a tepid shower bath and record your body weight.

Thursday

1. Participate for 10 to 15 minutes in gymnasium activities which may include the use of parallel bars, horizontal bar, flying rings, and tumbling mats. Jumpers and vaulters especially should be interested in the knack of falling, a skill which may be learned on mats.
2. Spend 2 or 3 minutes on executing inverted running.
3. Select all or a portion of the Fartlek system of exercises as the concluding assignment for the day. (Possible exceptions might be required for individuals competing in sprint, hurdle, and field events)

Friday

1. Warm up by jogging and running alternately for a period of 5 minutes.
2. Engage in general calisthenics for an optional length of time.
3. Hop and bound 60 to 80 yards, employing alternate feet.
4. Run 440 yards, alternating the speed of the 40-yard segments (the first at $\frac{1}{2}$ effort and the second at $\frac{7}{8}$ effort).
5. Spend 5 to 10 minutes executing those tension exercises that are recommended for your track or field event.
6. Run 150 yards at a rate of speed gradually increasing (up to $\frac{7}{8}$ your best effort). Begin to establish a warm-up plan which will be the most effective for you.
7. Jog 440 yards, take a tepid shower bath, and record your body weight.

Saturday

1. Study and discuss the rules covering track and field events. Observe the photographs and charts displayed on the bulletin board.
2. Spend 10 minutes on gymnastic apparatus (under supervision).
3. Jog for a period of 5 minutes.
4. Spend 10 minutes alternately jogging 25 yards, running 50 yards at $\frac{3}{4}$ effort, and walking 25 yards.
5. Jog 440 yards or more and follow the exercise with a tepid shower bath.
6. Analyze the fluctuations in your chart of body weight (which you have recorded both before and after practice). For an interpretation of changes in weight, see pp. 23 and 24.

It is obvious that the preliminary season schedule of practice is built around the idea of developing endurance, speed, strength, and coordination. Furthermore, the athlete should know the methods of preventing injury, the most effective type of warm-up, and the official rules governing his event.

SCHEDULES FOR SEASONS OF COMPETITION

Early season. During early season training, much time is spent in perfecting form and the proper execution of the event. The practice periods are longer and more intensive during this season than during any other season. Ordinarily there are no important meets scheduled during this time.

The early season schedule of practice points the competitor toward proficiency in executing his special event. The emphasis is placed on skill and ability to endure repetition. This plan also provides an opportunity for an athlete to discover latent ability in events other than his first choice.

Midseason. By the time midseason arrives, the athlete is presumably in proper condition and has a fair mastery of the execution of his event. The purpose of the midseason schedule of practice is to maintain physical condition and to improve form and technique. During this season more attention is given to the development of the proper mental attitude toward the event. This includes confidence in self, yet respect for the ability of one's opponents, and mental poise during competition. This phase of training is pointed toward a further development of skill and endurance.

It is here that the athlete passes from the elementary to the advanced stage of instruction.

Late season. The purpose of the late season schedule of practice must be somewhat altered since the athlete is at the peak of his physical condition and has perfected the execution of his event. Fewer technical corrections are indicated at this period of the year. The athlete should refrain from making any fundamental changes in his form. For example, he should not shift from the stride-in-air to the knee-tuck type of flight in the long jump. Such changes as these should have already been made.

In general the time allotted for practice is shorter and the work less intensive, since competition is of higher caliber. More emphasis must be placed on the contest. At this time participation in events other than his specialty should be less and less emphasized in order to permit concentration. Competition in numerous events tends to detract from one's best performance.

The late season schedule of practice is arranged for the purpose of perfecting the athlete on such phases as the correct amount of rest, the warm-up, and pace judgment. By this time the athlete should know definitely the amount of physical effort necessary for the maintenance of condition.

BODY WEIGHTS, SHOWER BATHS, AND MASSAGE

In the schedules of practice for the various events, no uniformity is adhered to in finishing the practice. In some instances body weight, shower baths, and massage are mentioned, whereas many times they are omitted. The reason for mentioning these items here is to make the athlete conscious that such points are to be considered.

Body weight should be recorded both before and after each day of practice and competition (see pp. 23 and 24).

A tepid shower is recommended after each exercise period.

Since massage is opposed by some and because competent masseurs are not available to all, massage may be used at the discretion of the coach.

REFERENCES

1. Folk, G. E., Jr., and Peary, R. E.: Report #37 (Quartermaster Climatic Research Laboratory), Environmental Project Section, 1950, Lawrence, Mass., Office of Quartermaster General.
2. Bock, A. V., Vancaulaert, C., Dill, D. B., Folling, A., and Hurxthal, L. M.: Studies in muscular activity. III. Dynamic changes occurring in man at work, J. Physiol. **66**:136, 1928.
3. Morehouse, L. E., and Miller, A. T.: Physiology of exercise, ed. 5, St. Louis, 1967, The C. V. Mosby Co.
4. Tuttle, W. W., and Bresnahan, G. T.: Unpublished data.
5. Schudel, H.: A study of the respiration of golfers during the drive and the putt, Res. Quart., Am. A. Health, Phys. Ed. & Rec. **5**:62, 1934.
6. Felkner, A. H.: A study of the respiratory habits of sprinters in starting a run, Res. Quart., Am. A. Health, Phys. Ed., & Rec. **5** (supp. 1):20, 1934.
7. Chui, E.: The effect of systematic weight training on athletic power, Res. Quart., Am. A. Health, Phys. Ed. and Rec. **21**:188, 1950.
8. Capen, E.: The effect of systematic weight training on power, strength, and endurance, Res. Quart., Am. A. Health, Phys. Ed. & Rec. **21**:83, 1950.
9. Murray, J.: Weight lifting and progressive resistance exercise, New York, 1954, A. S. Barnes & Co.
10. The Iowa Program of Physical Education for Boys, Secondary Schools, Des Moines, Iowa, 1945, the State of Iowa Department of Public Instruction, p. 66.
11. Physical reconditioning, War Department Technical Manual T.M. 8-292, Washington, D. C., 1944, U. S. Government Printing Office, p. 136.
12. Counsilman, J. E.: Does weight training belong in the program? J. Health, Phys. Ed. & Rec. **26**:17, 1955.
13. Hettinger, T., and Müller, E. A.: Muskelleistung und Muskeltrainung, Arbeitphysiol. **15**:111, 1953.
14. Wolbers, C. P., and Sills, F. D.: Development of strength in high school boys by static muscle contractions, Res. Quart., Am. A. Health, Phys. Ed. & Rec. **27**:446, 1956.

Chapter 2

Conditioning for track and field events

Before attempting to carry out a program of conditioning, the athlete should submit to a physical examination by a physician. This examination will point out any organic or anatomic disturbances which may exist.

The term "conditioning" is a rather broad one. However, in this discussion it is limited to those more pertinent things which go to build and maintain physical and mental states that are most conducive to acceptable performance. The topics discussed are diet, elimination, exercise, weight chart, rest, sleep, staleness, alcoholic beverages, and use of tobacco. The process of conditioning rests chiefly in the hands of the individual. Therefore, it is necessary for him not only to know how to proceed to get into condition but also to be familiar with the criteria for judging his status at various times throughout the season of competition.

DIET

An adequate diet supplies materials which not only yield energy but also serve for the construction and reconstruction of the body tissues. Protein, found in such foodstuffs as lean meat, peas, and beans, is chiefly responsible for tissue building and repair. Research during the past 10 years has clearly established that carbohydrates (essentially glucose) and fats (fatty acids) are the principal energy-yielding substances at rest and during exercise.

In addition to energy-yielding and body-building materials, the diet must also contain salts such as sodium chloride, calcium chloride, and potassium chloride, which are necessary for the maintenance of the proper environment of the cell. Vitamins are essential for efficient body function, although the exact way in which they operate is not well understood. It must be emphasized, however, that an excess of vitamins within the diet will not increase or enhance athletic performance.

The athlete who comes from the average American home is usually provided with a diet which is adequate for ordinary purposes. However, since most athletes are not privileged to eat at home every day, they often find it necessary to select their own food. In order to do this, they should know something of the constituents of an adequate diet. This requires a knowledge of the nature of the diet, time of meals, kinds of foods, menus, amount of food, the training table, fluids, and concentrates.

Nature of the diet. The general nature of the diet depends almost entirely on the type of activity in which one is engaged. In general, one needs to give special attention to his diet when his routine includes hard manual labor, strenuous mental effort, and relaxation. These are the states of mind and body which must be considered in order to avoid physical disturbances from a dietary cause.

For hard manual labor. It is customary in many places for the athlete to indulge in hard manual labor during the off season of practice and competition. During such activity there must be an increase in the amount of energy-yielding food that is consumed. With increased physical effort there is a natural increase in appetite. The appetite serves quite well as the guide in the amount of food required by an individual. The weight loss or gain must also be considered. During a period of manual labor, diet restrictions can be practically eliminated.

For strenuous mental effort. In the ordinary course of events, the athlete returns to school after this period of hard manual labor. At this time his activities are changed to strenuous mental effort in his academic pursuits. This occupational change should

be accompanied by an adjustment in the diet. Often the tendency is to continue the heavy diet after the cessation of the hard manual labor, the result being a sudden gain in weight, chiefly caused by the storage of fat. Many times the athlete comes to school in good physical condition but quickly eats himself into poor condition.

Any occupation change should be accompanied by a careful observation of weight as the best criterion. Such a change can be overcome by balancing the diet against the work to avoid a handicap due to excessive poundage at the beginning of the training season. One also must bear in mind that when a change is made from an active to a sedentary occupation the processes of digestion and assimilation are altered, and heavy energy-yielding foods may cause rather severe digestive disturbances as well as mental and physical lethargy.

For periods of relaxation. The school year is usually broken up by vacation periods during which the athlete does neither strenuous physical nor mental work. It is during these periods that he is prone to overeat, to select improper food, to underexercise, and to reduce his level of conditioning. The habits of eating must not be broken during periods of relaxation, since the maintenance of condition is less difficult than the acquisition of it.

Time of meals. Most individuals have well-established habits as to the time their meals are eaten. Although these may vary in different parts of the world, the principle is recognized as valid. Therefore, since athletics is usually an extracurricular activity, the daily schedule of practice and competition should be arranged so as not to interfere with the customary eating plan of the participant.

Breakfast is the meal that is omitted most frequently. This omission occurs in many instances because the individual fails to allot sufficient time for the morning routine, including eating breakfast. Research[1] has shown that a substantial breakfast is conducive to both the well-being and the efficiency of the athlete. Competitors are urged to provide sufficient time in the morning to eat a nourishing breakfast in a leisurely manner. A well-planned breakfast should contain approximately one-fourth the total daily caloric requirement and protein allowance.

Persons who indulge in strenuous exercise, regardless of condition and diet, must not fail to consider the relationship between the time of eating and the period of exercise. It should be remembered that when the process of digestion is at its height, the stomach and intestines are making strong demands on the heart and circulation. Moreover, when one is performing strenuous exercise, the skeletal muscles are making a similar demand on the circulatory system.

It is reasonable to assume that if exercise is performed while digestion is occurring there is an increased demand upon the circulatory system. This demand causes an adjustment to be made in the amount of blood being distributed to the working muscles and to the digestive system. In order to avoid this problem, food should be consumed several hours before muscular exercise begins.

Kinds of foods. Plain, wholesome, well-cooked foods will suffice for track and field athletes. Each man is familiar with his personal desires and reactions toward various foods. Each individual has idiosyncrasies in the matter of eating. In training diets, each individual should choose the diet that agrees with him and that he relishes.

Most of the time that the athlete is in training his contacts with the event in which he competes are during the practice schedule. He competes 1 day and practices 6 days each week. Since this is true, we believe that considerable leeway must be allowed in the matter of eating. From this point of view, foodstuffs are classified as those that are acceptable and those that are questionable. The following lists will serve the athlete in selecting his food for all occasions.

Acceptable foods. In presenting a list of acceptable foods from which the athlete may select his menu, those items are included that, in our experience, have proved to be agreeable to the majority of athletes.

Beverages: cocoa (moderately), coffee (mornings), hot water, milk, tea

Breads (enriched): dry toast, French, graham, rolls (hard), Vienna, rye, whole wheat; butter as desired

Cereals: any cooked or ready-to-eat cereals

Cheese: soft cheese freely, others in small quantities

Desserts: custards, fruit salad, ice cream, puddings (rice, raisin, tapioca), sponge cake, candy (chocolate or sugar)

Eggs: boiled (soft), omelet, poached, scrambled, shirred

Fruit: apples (baked, raw), grapefruit, oranges, pears, pineapples, raisins, dates, peaches

Juices: fruit juices, vegetable juices except sauerkraut

Meats and fish: bacon (crisp at breakfast), beef (roast, stew, steak), fowl, lamb, mutton, fresh fish

Nutmeats: very sparingly; not to exceed ½ ounce at a meal

Preserves: jams, jellies, marmalade

Sugar: use in abundant quantities at mealtime with cereals, deserts, fruits, juices; honey

Vegetables: asparagus, beans (green, baked), cabbage (raw), carrots, celery, corn, hominy, lettuce, spinach, parsnips, peas, potatoes (baked, boiled, creamed, scalloped, mashed, riced), tomatoes, squash

No doubt there are other foods which could be added to the list, but it is hoped that the items included will serve as a guide to the acceptable types of foods which may be eaten by an athlete who is striving toward condition for an event.

Something should be said here regarding questionable foods.

Questionable foods. Under this heading are included those items which have proved to be a source of annoyance and difficulty at various times. Many of them are prone to cause gastric disturbances such as cramps, nausea, gas, and diarrhea. Others cause excessive thirst which is satisfied only by the intake of too much fluid. Perhaps some of the items listed as questionable do not interfere with the digestive system of some individuals. On the other hand, in our experience, when digestive difficulties have arisen, they could be traced directly to some item included in the following list of questionable foods.

Beverages: coffee and tea; liquids shortly after exercise

Bread: freshly baked breads, biscuits, pancakes, waffles

Condiments: catsup, chili sauce, meat sauces, spices

Fruits: berries with seeds

Meats and fish: chopped meats, most fried meats, pork (except bacon, ham, and roast loin of pork), veal, salt fish

Pastry: heavy cake, pie, other pastries which are digested slowly

Relishes: olives, pickles

Vegetables: cooked cabbage, cucumbers, heavy dressings, raw onions, radishes, turnips, fried vegetables

Other items may be added in accordance with the personal experience of the athlete if he finds other foods that interfere with his digestion. From the list of acceptable foods presented, menus are suggested for training and competition days.

Menus. From the list of acceptable foods the athlete may select a wholesome menu for any occasion and at the same time avoid repetition, which causes one to lose taste for certain foods. Through the course of the week of training previous to the day of competition, the athlete should be free to select widely but with care in order that the diet contains the necessary items for balance. As an aid in selection, the following menus are suggested.

For noncompetition days. The following menus, based on the list of acceptable foods, provide a choice under each heading and meet the demands of a single competitor as well as the requirements of different competitors over a period of time.

Breakfast

Fruits: ½ grapefruit, stewed prunes, baked apple, orange juice, grape juice, tomato juice; choice of 1 item

Cereals: one serving either of cooked or ready-to-eat cereal; cream and sugar as desired

Meat and eggs: crisp bacon, poached, soft-boiled, shirred, or soft scrambled eggs, jelly omelet; choice of bacon and 1 other item

Bread (enriched): dry toast, whole wheat, toasted sweet rolls, Vienna rolls, milk toast, raisin-nut; choice of 1 item

Spreads: butter, jam, marmalade, jelly

Beverages: milk, cocoa, hot water with cream and sugar; choice of 1 item

Noon luncheon

Soups: vegetable, celery, potato, tomato, barley, or meat (stock); choice of 1 item

Main course: lamb chops, baked macaroni and cheese, creamed tuna fish, salmon loaf; choice of 1 item

Vegetables: scalloped potatoes, spinach, green beans, buttered carrots, asparagus, stewed tomatoes; potatoes and choice of 2 other items

Bread: see Breakfast

Spreads: see Breakfast

Beverages: see Breakfast

Desserts: rice pudding, custard, tapioca pudding, prune whip, sliced peaches, applesauce; choice of 1 item

Evening dinner

Soups (with meat stock): see Luncheon

Main course: roast chicken, roast beef, roast loin of pork, broiled steak, roast lamb, baked fish, boiled dinner; choice of 1 item

Vegetables: baked, boiled, or mashed potatoes, candied sweet potatoes, baked squash, creamed corn, buttered peas, buttered hominy, lima beans; choose potatoes and 2 other items

Salads: lettuce and tomato, celery and apple, grapefruit and lettuce, head lettuce, cottage cheese, pear and lettuce, stuffed tomatoes, cabbage; dressings as desired; choose 1 item

Bread: see Breakfast

Spreads: see Breakfast

Beverages: see Breakfast

Desserts: preserved fruits (peaches, pears, apricots, plums, cherries, pineapple, etc.), ice cream and sponge cake, rice-raisin custard, baked apple with cream; choose 1 item.

An examination of these menus makes it evident that the diet restrictions of an athlete during the noncompetitive days are few. In fact, almost every type of food is included. The menus are presented not only from the standpoint of showing the athlete the types of foods that are acceptable, but also to point out how they should be grouped throughout the day.

Meal planning is an important phase of the training program, and therefore the basic principles involved should be well understood by both trainers and coaches so that they are in a position to advise their team members, and thus reduce the nutrition difficulties that may arise.

We recognize the impracticability of recommending rigid menus for every athlete, yet we believe that a day's menu which can be used as a guide will serve a useful purpose. With this idea in mind a sample meal plan is included.*

For competition days. Certainly the total

*Food values from Church, C. F., and Church, H. N.: Food values of portion's commonly used, ed. 9, Philadelphia, 1963, J. B. Lippincott Co.

Breakfast

Let us assume that an athlete needs approximately 3,600 calories and 100 grams of protein to meet his nutritional requirements. Since sound nutritional principles require that he eat approximately one-fourth of his daily caloric requirement and one-fourth his protein allowance at breakfast, this means that the morning meal should contain approximately 900 calories and not less than 25 grams of protein. The following breakfast menu meets these requirements.

Food item	Amount	Cal.	Protein (gm.)	Fat (gm.)	Carbohydrates (gm.)
Grapefruit	½ large	100	1.3	0.5	25.6
Sugar	2 tbsp.	96	—	—	24.0
Cereal, cooked	1 cup	148	5.4	2.8	26.0
Egg, poached	1	77	6.1	5.5	0.3
Milk, whole	8 oz.	166	8.5	9.5	12.0
Cream	2 oz.	122	1.8	12.0	2.4
Toast, enriched	2 slices	126	4.0	1.4	23.8
Butter	1 pat	72	0.1	8.5	—
Total		907	27.2	40.2	114.1

Noon luncheon

It is essential to provide the competitor with sufficient food to ensure an energetic performance, without including items that may be prone to result in his discomfort. The following luncheon menu will meet the desired needs:

Food item	Amount	Cal.	Protein (gm.)	Fat (gm.)	Carbohydrates (gm.)
Orange juice, fresh	¾ cup	81	1.5	0.4	20.3
Cereal, ready-to-eat	1 oz.	108	3.1	0.6	22.0
Roast beef	3 oz.	280	21.6	19.8	—
Toast, enriched	2 slices	126	4.1	1.4	23.8
Butter	2 pats	144	0.2	17.0	—
Sugar	1 tbsp.	48	—	—	24.0
Cream	2 oz.	122	1.8	12.0	2.4
Total		909	32.3	51.2	92.5

Evening dinner

Dinner must provide the remaining nutritional requirements of the day. The problem at this meal is to satisfy the athlete since he is invariably hungry after strenuous activity and will eat his food with relish. The meal should contain approximately the remaining daily requirements. The following is a suggested dinner menu:

Food item	Amount	Cal.	Protein (gm.)	Fat (gm.)	Carbohydrates (gm.)
Soup, chicken noodle	¾ cup	65	2.1	1.7	6.0
Chicken, roast	8 oz.	350	35.3	22.0	———
Potatoes, baked	2 medium	196	4.8	0.2	4.5
Butter	4 pats	288	0.4	32.4	———
Beans, green	¾ cup	21	1.4	0.2	4.5
Carrots	¾ cup	35	0.8	0.6	7.2
Bread, enriched	2 slices	126	4.1	1.4	23.8
Salad, lettuce, tomato	liberal serving	37	2.0	0.6	7.4
Dressing, french	1 tbsp.	60	———	0.6	2.0
Milk, whole	1 cup	166	8.5	9.5	12.0
Ice cream	½ pt.	293	5.5	17.2	30.4
Sauce, chocolate	1 oz.	69	0.7	0.3	16.5
Total		1,706	65.6	86.7	114.3

Evening snack

Some athletes feel the need for food in the evening before retiring. If, for example, the day's menu presented has proved adequate, an evening snack amounting to 244 calories can be provided for by omitting one potato and one-half the dessert from the dinner menu. This caloric discrepancy can be met by eating 1 ounce of cereal with ¾ cup of milk and 1 teaspoon of sugar.

daily food consumption on competition days should not be reduced. The chief problem to take into account is to space luncheon far enough ahead of competition to ensure ample time so that the athlete will be assured of a relatively empty stomach. The importance of eating an adequate breakfast should be stressed since it has been shown conclusively that either omitting or eating an inadequate breakfast results in decreased physical and mental efficiency in the late morning hours. In the case of the nervous type of athlete, whose digestive system is interfered with by the thought of approaching competition, exceptions may need to be made by increasing the elapsed time between luncheon and competition.

The dinner menu on competition days need not be different from that of any other day. An athlete who insists on a light lunch in the late morning hours before competition will, no doubt, be extremely hungry. In fact it may be that a reasonable amount of food will fail to satisfy his hunger. In such instances there are no objections to allowing a late evening lunch consisting of acceptable food items.

Amount of food. The amount of food which one should eat depends on a number of things, such as age, personal tendencies to accumulate fat, and the amount of exercise which one performs. The menus which were suggested may be varied both as to the kind and the amount of food. The chief guiding factor is the appetite. One should always observe the principle of the balanced diet. The types of foods that yield energy, vitamins, and roughage should be included.

If a competitor demands either more or less food than that suggested in the dinner after competition, adjustments in quantity as well as in items can be made. By substituting 8 ounces of sirloin steak for 6 ounces of chicken, the caloric value of the meal is increased by 360 calories. The addition or omission of bread and butter provides an easy way of adjusting the menu. Another convenient way of increasing the caloric value of the day's menu is to include an evening snack.

Training table. The provision of a training table has precipitated considerable discussion in the various college conferences. In some sections of the country it is maintained, while in others it is rejected.

The purposes of the training table, obviously, have been to provide sufficient energy-yielding food, properly prepared, for the athletes who are in training for competition and to have it served regularly and at the proper time relative to the training schedule and contest.

Perhaps the training table is of little advantage to an athlete who has access to adequate food at home during the season of training and competition. However, the athlete on a limited income who must depend on public eating places would no doubt be benefited by the training table. At the present time there is available ample material dealing with foods for the athlete so that he can, if he gives the problem some attention, manage his own diet satisfactorily.

Those who reject the training table do so because of the difficulties that it presents. In some instances abuses have been practiced that made it difficult to maintain amateur standards. Because there are arguments that favor both sides, the use of the training table is an open question.

Fluids. Some coaches and trainers tend to withhold fluids from competitors for a considerable time before competition. Findings from numerous laboratories during the past few years have shown dramatically that the consumption of fluids will not hinder one's performance. In fact, the consumption of fluids when the temperature exceeds 80° F. or higher may even enhance performance. However, it is quite possible that the rapid ingestion of fluid immediately before competing in an event could prove troublesome and should be avoided.

Precaution must always be taken to prevent excessive dehydration of the tissues. The water content of the various body compartments must be maintained in order for the heat-regulatory mechanisms to function effectively and efficiently.

Concentrates and supplements. Some trainers and coaches have followed the practice of supplementing the diet with vitamins, minerals, and liquid supplements. If the diet is balanced and sufficient in quantity, these additions are unnecessary. On the other hand, if the athlete has an inadequate diet, these substances should be considered, particularly the latter item. One advantage of the liquid supplement is to ease the hunger pains when time does not permit the consumption of a meal. Moreover, liquid supplement may be of value to an athlete who has a nervous stomach. However, coaches and athletes must be aware of the fact that there is at present no convincing scientific evidence to prove conclusively that liquid supplement per se will enhance or improve performance.

ELIMINATION

Ordinarily the elimination of body wastes is not a serious problem for active individuals. However, there are a number of points worthy of consideration which may aid not only in the maintenance of health but also in the establishment of habits which make for convenience in carrying out the processes of elimination.

The body rids itself of waste materials, including water, through defecation, urination, perspiration, and respiration. The feces contain such substances as undigested food, indigestible materials, products of putrefaction, inorganic salts, bacteria, and sometimes parasites. The urine consists chiefly of water in which is dissolved some inorganic salts and nitrogenous products. Sweat is mostly water in which is dissolved small amounts of sodium chloride and nitrogenous substances. The only products eliminated through the process of respiration are water and carbon dioxide. Little need be said of perspiration and respiration as processes of elimination since they work automatically, depending on the temperature of the environment and the rigor of exercise. Whenever a considerable amount of fluid is lost through the process of perspiration, an appreciable amount of salt (sodium chloride) is eliminated and must be replaced. This is done best by adding a small amount of salt to either the food or drinking water.

The secretion of urine requires only little attention on the part of the athlete since it is an automatic function capable of caring for the elimination of water and substances dissolved in it. It might be added that before the beginning of a contest the athlete may have a tendency toward frequent urination because of nervous excitement. This can be overcome only by reducing the nervousness due to excitement, although frequent urination seems to have no influence on either health or performance.

The elimination of the fecal material through the process of defecation is perhaps the most important of all. This is true because constipation may lead to ill health and because defecation depends to some extent on factors that are under voluntary control.

The process of defecation deserves special attention. The healthy athlete who is in training should void fecal matter regularly. This act should be habitually established by associating it with some event which occurs regularly in the routine of daily living. Defecation may be associated with rising in the morning, drinking a glass of water on arising, the ingestion of food at regular mealtime, or with the beginning of the practice period. By conditioning this response, constipation is avoided, and the desire comes at a time which is convenient.

Constipation can be avoided in many cases by a properly selected diet. In the diet schedules presented elsewhere, allowances were made for a sufficient amount of roughage and other food materials conducive to proper elimination.

Dysentery is another digestive disorder which has caused athletes and coaches much concern, especially during trips to distant contests. This disturbance is usually characterized by cramps and diarrhea. In past years, because some thought that water was the source of this difficulty, athletic teams have carried their water supply with them. However, interest in public health has resulted in pure water supply almost everywhere, and the necessity for carrying water has been lessened. In order to avoid dysentery, the athlete should eat properly cooked food. Milk which has not been pasteurized should be avoided. When the athlete is away from home, he tends to select foods to which he is not accustomed, which may lead to gastrointestinal disturbances, and therefore, care should be taken in choosing foods.

Athletes who have stubborn cases of constipation which fail to yield to exercise and diet should not take cathartics except as prescribed by a physician.

EXERCISE

If the athlete is in school, he is required to be active in carrying out his daily routine. However, exercise thus obtained, although not pointed toward any sport event, must be given some consideration. When an individual has no responsibilities demanding exercise except those required in pursuit of the academic schedule, the problem of exercise outside of the event needs but little attention. In some instances, however, the athlete may be faced with the responsibility of manual labor at home or in the pursuit of a livelihood while in school. In such cases there exists the danger of overfatigue, especially when the work required by the event is added. If proficiency in any sport is to be acquired, overwork must be avoided.

The ideal situation is one in which the athlete has no responsibilities requiring strenuous exercise other than the prescribed work in his event. When such a condition does not exist, the individual will have to be the judge in controlling his exercise to make it fall within the bounds of his endurance. The problem of conditioning, through exercise in his chosen event, is discussed where the weekly training schedules are presented.

WEIGHT CHART

Although a steady, consistent drop in body weight is a danger signal, a competitor must expect fluctuations from day to day. Fig. 2-1 shows a typical weight record of a trained athlete for a period of 2 weeks. At the beginning of the preliminary training season the weight of this man was 163 pounds, and at the beginning of the competition season it was 157 pounds, a loss of 10 percent.

In order to guard against an excessive loss of weight, the competitor should have some idea of what his normal weight should be and must keep a regular check on his current weight. To accomplish the latter purpose, it is recommended that a chart similar to one shown in Fig. 2-1 be kept accurately. It should be noted that the weight is recorded daily, before and after practice or competition.

The weight is taken stripped, just before the track suit is put on. After practice or competition, the weight is taken at the termination of the bath, with the body thoroughly dry. The reason for stripped weight is obvious, since perspiration in varying amounts is retained by the clothing. The perspiration excreted accounts

for most of the weight change. The dry weight is necessary since either bath water or perspiration to the amount of $\frac{1}{2}$ pound or more may cling to the body.

An examination of the chart presented shows that periods of exercise lower the body weight, the amount depending on the severity of the work. This loss of weight amounted to as much as $3\frac{1}{2}$ pounds due to competition. During days of rest, except Friday, the weight lost is gained back, sometimes going beyond the precompetition level.

It is of interest to note that on the day (Friday) previous to competition there was a weight loss, even though practice had been curtailed or entirely eliminated. This may have been due partly to emotional stress resulting in a reduction in the desire for food and partly to a voluntary effort by the athlete to reduce the amount of food and liquids ingested.

The weight chart serves as a guide for the coach in determining the intensity and amount of physical effort to be prescribed. He is interested in obtaining the weight reaction to a well-defined workout so that future schedules may be planned accordingly. Above all else, he is vitally interested in determining the length of time required to replenish weight lost during a day of strenuous competition.

Weight charts are worthless if entries are made aimlessly and irregularly. They can be made valuable if the record is kept accurately and interpreted correctly. The conscientious, ambitious athlete will make his contribution to the end that his schedules of practice may be prescribed more intelligently.

Desirable weight. One may record fluctuations in body weight and have no idea about how much one should weigh. It is most important that the normal weight of the athlete be known because weight losses in excess of 10 percent of the normal weight are associated with impaired performance levels and undesirable health changes. Although there are

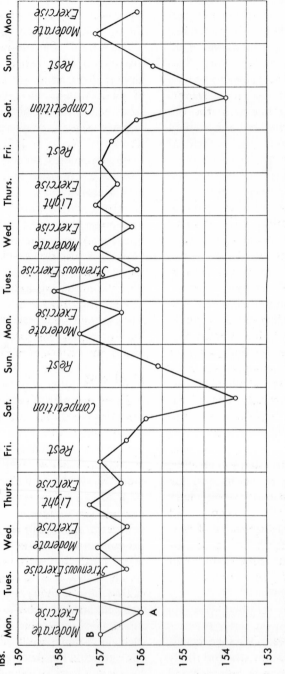

Fig. 2-1. The fluctuation in body weight of a trained athlete during a two-week period of training and competition.

numerous procedures for predicting desirable weights, most of them are complicated, time consuming, require expensive equipment, and are impractical for the coach to administer. One procedure that is suitable for high school athletes is the Hall method (see Chapter 15). This method evolved from the testing of more than 40,000 boys and girls in Illinois and has been demonstrated to be an effective means of objectively determining the desirable weights of junior or senior high school students.

REST

Although rest and sleep are often thought of as more or less synonymous, rest, here, means relaxation. Much is to be gained by proper relaxation during the working hours. The amount of rest, either during competition or outside of competition, depends on the amount of work which the person is required to do. Fatigue calls for rest, just as hunger is a signal for food. In the case of the athlete, it is unusual to experience a daily routine which prohibits a few minutes' rest from time to time when the sensation of fatigue arises. Even if there are only a few minutes available, through a process of training oneself, it is possible to acquire the ability to relax for brief periods and thereby gain much from such procedures. The "wonder man" who seems to have the stamina to work almost continuously over long periods of time is able to keep fit and efficient by observing short periods of rest. To acquire and maintain a condition suitable for proficient performance in any event, rest and fatigue must be well balanced.

SLEEP

It has been truly stated that inadequate sleep contributes more to mental and physical dullness in normal man than any other single factor. The amount of sleep required for proficiency in performance is a matter for the athlete to decide for himself. His criteria are the feeling of well-being, the absence of fatigue, and the amount of energy he possesses to carry on his work. Sufficient sleep should be acquired at the expense of everything else.

Since the student who competes in athletics is usually called upon to make a careful distribution of his time, he should be familiar with the conditions that are most conducive to sleep so that he may become efficient in sleeping as well as in his event. When he is tired, it is easier to sleep, since fatigue diminishes the readiness of the nervous system to respond to stimuli. In any case, if one wishes to sleep efficiently, he should lie in a comfortable, well-ventilated room, free from noise. Freedom from noise is especially important, since sound is the last disturbing factor to disappear as sleep comes on and is the first to be realized on awakening. Let it be remembered that there is nothing more conducive to attaining and maintaining the proper condition for track and field events than the optimum amount of sleep.

STALENESS

There are many factors related to staleness. Among them we find loss of appetite, sleeplessness, worry, excessive fatigue, excessive loss of weight, attitude toward the event, and illness. Whatever the reason, the athletes—and particularly the coach—must be constantly on the alert for the numerous symptoms.

Loss of appetite. When an athlete is in condition for his event, he looks forward to his meals and relishes them. Conditions which cause loss of appetite are undesirable because they result in poor nutrition. An athlete who continually fails to consume the proper amount of energy-yielding food is unfit for competition. It is quite common for a good athlete to experience a loss of appetite on the day of competition. The use of liquid supplements for these individuals during the day of competition may help to overcome this condition.

Sleeplessness. The condition of sleeplessness may be nothing more than an undesirable health habit. On the other hand, there may be some physical factors involved. Sleeplessness deprives the athlete of the physical and mental rest so necessary for creditable performance in competition. It is usually occasioned by some type of nervous overstimulation for which there are innumerable reasons such as worry and anxiety. Since the nervous make-up of the individual is a determining factor, it may be necessary to resort to self-analysis to determine the cause before the condition can be corrected.

Worry. The reasons for worry are countless, and the results are disastrous to the performance of the athlete. Worry is one of the most difficult problems with which we have to deal. There is no cure-all for it. Each case must be considered individually.

Excessive fatigue. A man may become stale because of overwork. The signal of this type of staleness is a more or less continuous feeling of fatigue. The individual lacks zest. The remedy is either a reduction in the amount of work which the athlete does or a change in the type of practice schedule. Moreover, he may become stale from excess physical exertion in activities unrelated to track and field events. As an example, we have known men who suffered from staleness in the long jump because unknown to us they participated each night in other sports. A shift in the type and quantity of our schedule of practice failed to correct fully the condition. It was necessary to discontinue the outside activities.

Excessive loss of weight. The athlete's weight fluctuates, depending on the strenuousness of the practice and the competition. A consistent loss of poundage after the athlete has reached his peak in training is a definite sign that the individual is becoming stale. The remedy for such a condition is a reduction in the quantity and intensity of the practice. In extreme cases, complete rest, including absence from the practice field, is recommended. The application of the principles of mental hygiene may be a remedy for the contributing causes of loss of weight.

Attitude toward the event. Occasionally an athlete tends to lose interest in his event. Every athlete must fortify himself against this type of reaction by learning in the beginning that a day will come when he fails to achieve a goal equal to past performances. One must also realize that an opponent, or perhaps a teammate, will, on some occasion, be named the winner. There may be a time when the athlete will come to a point in his training where the rate of progress seems slow. It may even appear that he is not in the class with the other performers. If one does not recognize these eventualities and fortify himself accordingly, he may acquire a defeatist attitude.

Illness. The onset of illness is often a contributing factor to poor performance. Even though the inroads of illness may not be apparent, its progress may produce a condition of debility resulting in poor performance which the athlete cannot explain. Sometimes an examination of the teeth, the tonsils, and other possible sources of infection will account for inferior performance. The correction of any existing defect may solve his problem.

ALCOHOLIC BEVERAGES

Needless to say, alcoholic beverages have no place in the menus of the athlete, either during or out of season. It is believed that their use should be prohibited and that it is unnecessary to defend such a position.

TOBACCO[2]

It is a well-known fact that the inhalation of tobacco smoke irritates the delicate membranes of the respiratory passages. This irritation tends to lead to a chronic cough. In addition, surveys appear to have proved quite conclusively that the incidence of lung cancer is greater among smokers than nonsmokers.

The physiologic effects of tobacco smoking must not be overlooked. Tobacco smoke contains gases which unite with the red corpuscles of the blood, as does oxygen, thus decreasing the capacity of the blood to transport oxygen. Furthermore, the physiologic effects of nicotine must be considered. In addition to increasing blood pressure and heart rate, there is considerable evidence to support the idea that nicotine in the amount found in cigarettes reduces the blood flow through muscle significantly. It has been recently shown that the nicotine level in cigarettes will significantly reduce the reflex times (knee jerk) of both habitual smokers and nonsmokers. All in all, there is sufficient evidence at hand to indicate that tobacco decreases physical efficiency, and thus the athlete should abstain from its use.

REFERENCES

1. A summary of the Iowa breakfast studies, Cereal Institute, Inc., 135 S. La Salle St., Chicago 3, Ill., 1957.
2. Smoking and health. A summary and report of the Royal College of Physicians of London, New York, 1962, Pitman Publishing Corp.

Chapter 3

Physical aids for the track and field athlete

There are a number of physical aids at the disposal of the athlete during the season of training and competition which may be used to advantage in acquiring and maintaining efficiency. When there is definite injury or infection, a physician should be consulted, since he is the only one who can safely and legitimately assume the responsibility for the health of the athlete. However, there are a number of protective devices that the individual may employ as aids in overcoming some of the conditions that detract from his efficiency. They are discussed as follows: bath, care of the feet, athlete's foot, plantar warts, sore muscles, care of pulled muscles, use of liniment, massage, blisters, irritations, calluses, heel protection, and athletic injuries.

BATH

In discussing the bath, we must remember that it may be employed for two purposes. As ordinarily used, the object of the bath is to remove perspiration and other substances that have accumulated on the body during exercise. In addition, the bath is widely used to alter physiologic functions, its effect depending on the temperature of the water and the duration of exposure. Unless the athlete is familiar with the physiologic changes which may be caused by the bath, he may produce conditions which are wholly undesirable and unsuited to his needs.

When the paramount purpose of the bath is that of cleansing the body, extremes in water temperature and long exposure, which materially alter physiologic conditions, should be avoided. Exposure to water at a temperature of approximately 95° F. for 2 or 3 minutes is sufficient. A nonirritating soap should be used. The body should be dried thoroughly, especially the feet. Authorities are not agreed on the value of finishing off with a cold shower.

There are instances when it might be

advantageous for an athlete to employ the bath as a therapeutic measure. In this instance, then, the type of bath depends on the effect one wishes to accomplish. Although the shower may be used to advantage in this respect, experience has shown that the tub bath is more effective.

Immersion in cold water, 60° to 65° F., for a period of 10 minutes or longer causes a depression of body functions as exhibited by the fact that there is a significant decrease in heart rate.[1] The cold bath should be regarded as restful and invigorating. Those who have experienced a cold bath know that it produces a feeling of bettered condition.

Immersion in hot water, 100° to 110° F., for a period of 10 minutes or longer, speeds up bodily functions, as indicated by a marked increase in heart rate.[2] The hot bath should be regarded as fatiguing. Those who have experienced the hot bath know that it is relaxing and, although conducive to sleep, is as wearing as strenuous exercise.

The altered physiologic functions produced by the hot and cold bath make it obvious why a shower of moderate temperature, 90° to 95° F., for a short duration is recommended for the athlete.

MASSAGE

The art of massage has been practiced all over the world for many centuries, and practically everyone has at least a general idea of the technique employed and the apparent results.

Massage can be administered most effectively by one who has been trained in its practice. Massage consists in rubbing, kneading, thumping, and slapping various parts of the body. Although the manipulations are applied to the surface of the body, they affect the skin, the musculature, the subcutaneous tissues, the superficial cutaneous vessels, the superficial nerve endings, and the superficial lymphatic ducts and spaces.

Massage is used either for bettering performance or facilitating the repair of injured tissue. Although considerable experimentation has been done concerning the effect of massage on athletic performance, there is a lack of uniformity in the results.

The use of massage for aiding the repair of injured tissue must be employed with discretion, since the type of injury is the determining factor. In cases of soreness and stiffness, beneficial results are usually attained. Where hemorrhage is in evidence, massage may prove definitely detrimental to the athlete. In cases in which immobilization is indicated, massage is not recommended.

The variation in the extent of the use of massage is as great as the diversity of opinions among coaches and trainers as to its benefits. Some say that it has practically no value; other substitute massage for a part of the warming-up exercise; and there are numerous intermediate opinions.

The fact that massage is relaxing, restful, and conducive to sleep and to a feeling of well-being can scarcely be denied. Its therapeutic use in athletic injury is the responsibility of the trainer or the physician.

CARE OF FEET AND HANDS

Since the track and field athlete's feet, especially those of the jumper, are subject to considerable jarring, they must receive special attention. Even though a properly fitting shoe is worn, blisters are likely to occur in the early training season.

A thickening of the skin on the soles of the feet usually occurs during the training season. This is nature's way of compensating for the added amount of friction on the skin due to the additional strain placed upon the feet. One can aid nature in this toughening process by bathing the feet frequently in saturated salt solution. Another aid in the toughening process is that of swabbing the feet daily with compound tincture of benzoin during the early training period.

Athlete's foot. The incidence of athlete's foot is becoming less and less as our knowledge of prevention becomes more complete.

Generally, athlete's foot, which is caused by a fungus, makes its initial appearance in the third or fourth interdigital space. It is characterized by itching and redness, accompanied by scaling. As soon as symptoms appear, one of the many available products known to be effective should be applied until a cure is effected. It is important to know that this infection is more prevalent in hot weather than in cool weather and is aggravated by moist footwear.

It must be remembered that untreated athlete's foot finally may become chronic and troublesome. Should this occur, the team physician should be consulted as to treatment.

Plantar warts.[3] Ordinary warts that appear on the surface of the body usually present no serious problems to athletes. However, that type known as plantar warts, because they appear on the plantar surface of the foot, may require attention. Plantar warts may increase in size to the extent that they interfere with athletic activity because of pain resulting from pressure. A plantar wart is caused by a recognized virus that is capable of spreading rapidly. Those individuals suspected of being infected should avoid contaminating others, because plantar warts are considered to be contagious. The treatment of plantar warts should not be undertaken by the athlete himself because of the wide variety of accepted treatments. Furthermore, some plantar warts are extremely resistant to treatment, and their care should be considered within the realm of the medical profession.

Blisters. A blister consists of the separation of the superficial layer of skin from the true skin, accompanied by an accumulation of fluid between the layers. Any skin surface subject to friction or heat be-

yond that to which it is accustomed may become blistered. Blisters most commonly occur on the hands and feet. It is in these regions that track and field events call for the greatest amount of friction. The grasping of equipment, especially during early season, frequently causes blisters on the hands. Perhaps ill-fitting shoes are the most common cause of blisters on the feet. This latter point is discussed elsewhere in this text whenever equipment is described.

Blisters may be classified as simple or infected. The former includes those in which the skin separation is filled with a clear, watery fluid and usually is not painful. The latter refers to those which become infected and are characterized by the presence of pus, pain, and tenderness in an inflamed skin area. The danger of a blister lies in the fact that it is prone to become infected, especially if the skin is broken and the fluid lost.

One can aid in preventing blisters by the proper care of the skin. Since the skin is capable of developing thickness as compensation against friction, the gradual use of the part involved brings this about without blistering until, finally, the added skin is sufficient to prevent blistering. Frequent bathing of the friction-exposed areas in a saturated saline solution aids in toughening the skin. It is recommended that compound tincture of benzoin be utilized daily both during preseason and early season practices. This may be applied by swabbing it on the exposed skin area.

Calluses. Calluses are the natural result of friction on the skin and are protective in nature. They develop principally on the hands and feet. Sometimes difficulty results when they become so thick and lacking in elasticity that cracking or separation from the active skin layer results. Much difficulty will be avoided if a gradual toughening of the skin is encouraged. The early season prophylaxis for blisters as previously suggested is an aid in establishing a tough skin. Thick and unwieldly calluses should never be treated by the athlete. When they become troublesome, the physician is the only one capable of treating them.

Heel protection. In track and field contests such as the hurdle races, long jump, running high jump, and pole vault, the heel of the take-off foot is required to contact the ground forcefully. Heel protection is necessary if the athlete is to avoid bruising the heel.

The insertion of pads made of resilient material, such as sponge rubber, felt, or coiled rubber tubing, in the heel of the shoe has served to prevent injury. The athlete is better served by the use of the heel cup.

Since the heel cup is constructed of a hard and durable material, its value lies not in a cushionlike quality, but rather in its efficacy in distributing the effect of the shock over the entire heel. Frequently the athlete is provided with either 1 or 2 extra heel cups as an assurance that he will be equipped adequately at all times.

SORE MUSCLES

One of the problems confronting the athlete during early season is sore muscles. In order to avoid them, it is important to understand their causes.

Types. There are two types of muscular soreness that are generally recognized.

Soreness accompanying exercise. This type of muscle soreness makes its appearance during work and continues for a few hours afterward. It is evidently the result of the accumulation of waste products produced by muscular contraction, and it is associated with the phenomenon of fatigue. Generally, muscular soreness of this type occurs following the awareness of fatigue. For this reason it is argued that the soreness is due to a further piling up of fatigue products in the sarcolemma and later in the interstitial muscular lymph sacs, beyond the point of the occurrence of fatigue.

The disappearance of this type of soreness depends on the elimination of the ac-cumulated waste products by the circulatory system.

The sensation of soreness in this case is a result of pressure on the sensory nerve endings due to swollen muscle tissue or to chemical stimulation of these endings by waste products. It has been demonstrated that after severe muscular work, muscle tissue may contain an excess of fluid equal to 20 percent of its original weight. The presence of this excess fluid may account for soreness and stiffness after exercise.

Postexercise soreness. In this type of muscle soreness the pain and discomfort do not make their appearance during the period of exercise but are noticeable some hours after the workout.

It is reasonable to suppose that the muscle fibers which are less frequently used are more susceptible to strain than those which are in training. The persistence of the soreness may also be a result of the breaking up of adhesions during use. This type of soreness is associated with an injury to the muscle tissue. This aspect has been demonstrated histologically in experimental animals. Experiments with human beings have demonstrated that postexercise muscle soreness is associated with the performance of negative work and the spasms of tired muscles.

Relation of training to soreness. Every individual who participates in training for track and field events undoubtedly will experience both types of soreness. By proper training, athletes can eliminate these conditions.

Unfortunately the mechanism responsible for this change as a result of training is unknown. It is known that muscle fibers become stronger and more efficient with use. Experimental results with animals have shown that ligaments become stronger with use and that trained ligaments show more elongation when subjected to a given force than nontrained ligaments. Coordination improves during training, as does the blood supply to a working muscle. Also, with an improved circulation the metabolic end products are removed, thus reducing the accumulation of substances which might exert a pressure on nerve endings located in muscles, tendons, or ligaments.

Often, inquiry is made of the coach as to the effect of muscular soreness on prospective accomplishments. It should be noted that the injury occurring in postexercise soreness, whatever its nature may be, involves no harm to the athlete, either temporary or permanent.

Treatment. In either type of soreness complete rest is not recommended. The athlete should continue training by doing a limited amount of exercise, resulting in the contraction of the muscle fibers involved.

In a case of soreness accompanying exercise, alternate contraction and relaxation of the sore muscle materially facilitates the elimination of the waste products by aiding in bringing fresh blood to the affected region. Perhaps the best exercise to recommend is a continuation of practice of the event in which the soreness occurred, except that there should be a reduction in the amount of muscular activity.

In cases of postexercise soreness greater care must be taken in recommending exercise. It rightly may include mild performance in the event in which the soreness occurred. The exercise in this type of soreness is recommended to aid circulation in the sore muscle and to prevent and break up adhesions resulting from the repair of injured fibers.

Since postexercise soreness is conceived to be caused by fiber injury, the application of heat is an aid in the repair process.

Pulled muscles. Severe muscle injury immediately terminates the participation of the athlete in either a track or field event. However, in mild cases, pulled muscles can be supported so that the athlete may execute his event without danger or much discomfort. Support not only is useful for protecting mild cases but also in preventing

recurrence of injury after a severe case has apparently healed. The type of support to be employed depends on the nature and location of the injury; thus no specific instructions can be given in this respect. Both the coach and the athlete must depend on the physician or trainer in charge for advice as to the type of support to be applied and the extent to which the muscle can be used.

Use of liniment

Liniment may be used to advantage on the muscles of the legs and thighs before exercise. A liniment consisting of 45 percent arnica, 45 percent witch hazel, and 10 percent methylsalicylate is frequently used. The irritating quality of this liniment may be controlled by varying the amount of methylsalicylate. For use on cold days the prescription should contain a greater amount of the methylsalicylate and on warm days a lesser amount. There are many proprietary products available which are satisfactory.

GYM ITCH

Gym itch is an infection that occurs among track and field athletes. Gym itch is caused by a fungus similar to that which causes athlete's foot. It usually infects the lower portion of the abdomen, the groin, the buttocks, and the axilla, but it may occur on the thighs and adjacent skin. It has been known to infect the toes, fingers, elbows, knees, and flat surfaces of the body. However, it is usually associated with those parts of the body that are in contact with one another.

This infection begins as a flat, reddish pimple. In the course of a few days a ring-like patch is formed, the center of which is pink or red. The margin of the sore is sharply defined, slightly elevated, actively inflamed, and scaly in appearance. A slight itching and burning are usually associated with the infection.

One of the chief means of spread of this

disease is by the supporter, although it may be picked up from benches and other furniture upon which the athlete sits. Because of the important part the supporter plays in spreading gym itch, it deserves special attention. First of all, each athlete should wear only his own supporter. When it becomes soiled or infected, it should be boiled for 15 minutes or burned.

The athlete should be familiar enough with this infection to recognize it as soon as it makes its appearance. However, let us emphasize again that he should not attempt treatment but should consult a physician immediately.

IRRITATIONS

Irritation occurs where the surface of the skin is in contact with other skin surfaces or with foreign objects. The skin-to-skin irritations usually occur in the crotch as the result of contact between the scrotum and the thighs and, in the heavier individuals, contact of thigh with thigh. Irritations of this nature also occur between the toes, especially in persons whose feet perspire profusely. Ill-fitting shoes and defective shoelaces also take their toll. Where contact is unavoidable, personal hygiene and suitable protection alleviate the irritation. The remedy for poorly fitting equipment is self-evident.

Thigh irritations due to unavoidable skin contacts can be remedied by washing the surfaces with a neutral soap, carefully drying them, and then applying talc or other dusting powder. For the feet, lathering with a neutral soap and pulling on the socks without removing the lather are recommended. Another method quite commonly practiced is dusting freely with a powder. In cases in which previous difficulty with foot irritation has been experienced, a few

weeks of preseason treatment as suggested under the discussion of blisters is effective. Perhaps a routine prophylactic measure against foot irritation as well as blisters will prove profitable for the entire squad.

Upon the first appearance of an irritation, suitable protection should be provided. Proper cleansing and drying followed by dusting powder, chiefly talc, furnish sufficient protection in many cases. Where constant irritation cannot be avoided, the use of a gauze covering may prove necessary. Cleansing and constant dryness are important. The dryness may be maintained by absorbent cotton pads which are frequently changed. A dusting powder is usually effective, although some athletes prefer mild ointments or cold cream. In the case of the feet, a pair of shoes which do not irritate will probably alleviate the difficulty. Clean white socks are a further aid in combating irritations.

ATHLETIC INJURIES

Serious athletic injuries are purposely omitted from this discussion. The reason for this is that both the coach and the athletes owe it to themselves to shift the responsibility for treating injuries to the team physician, who is the only one who can safely and legitimately assume this responsibility.

REFERENCES

1. Tuttle, W. W., and Corleaux, J. F.: The response of the heart to swimming pool temperatures, Res. Quart., Am. A. Health, Phys. Ed. & Rec. 6:24, 1935.
2. Wells, G.: A study of the effect of temperature changes on physiologic functions, Res. Quart., Am. A. Health, Phys. Ed. & Rec. 3:108, 1932.
3. Pillsbury, B. S., Skelley, W. B., and Klingman, A. M.: Dermatology, Philadelphia, 1956, W. B. Saunders Co.

Chapter 4

The sprints

Sprints are defined in this discussion as including all races in which the contestant runs at full speed over the entire distance on the flat. Although the running distances vary, the upper limit is usually considered 300 yards. Outdoor meets ordinarily include only two sprint races: the 100-yard and the 220-yard dashes. One finds distances of 40 yards, 50 yards, 60 yards, 70 yards, and 80 yards on the indoor program. The determining factor in the indoor distances is usually the amount of space available.

There are two sprint races on the program of the Olympic games. They are the 100-meter race, comparable to the 100-yard dash and the 200-meter race, paralleling the 220-yard dash.

The universality of running and the apparent simplicity of sprinting requirements are no doubt responsible for the fact that there is usually no dearth of candidates for the sprint events. Although it is true that almost anyone can run, it is another matter to run fast. It is indeed a surprise to many when they learn that running sprint races involves techniques that are equally as difficult as those required for many of the other events on the track and field program.

A study of the records of champions during the past half century reveals the fact that more than 1 second has been cut from the time required to run the 100-yard dash. The records show also that the 220-yard dash is now run more than 3 seconds faster than in early contests.

It is the purpose of this discussion to point out the methods that are believed to be responsible for improvement in sprinting time.

GENERAL CONSIDERATIONS

Types of competitors. Sprinters do not readily conform to a classification by types since athletes having a wide range of characteristics are listed as champions. Top-flight sprinters who weigh less than 130 pounds or more than 170 pounds are seldom found. They range in height from 5 feet 7 inches to 6 feet 3 inches. Sprinting has been termed a young man's event, a statement borne out by the fact that rarely has an American sprinter maintained championship form after the age of 25 years.

The tall sprinter is characterized by long lower extremities, equipped with long powerful muscles. The short sprinter compensates for muscle length found in his taller opponent by possessing strong thick muscles. Since driving force is the chief prerequisite for fast sprinting, it matters little whether it is derived from a long slender muscle or a short thick one.

Qualifications. If an athlete is to become a fast sprinter, there are a number of inherent qualities which he must possess. Among these are short reaction time, short reflex time, pure dominance, motor-mindedness, and strong power of inhibition.

Reaction time. Since many of the adjustments required of a sprinter are voluntary in nature, the athlete who can make them quickly and efficiently is at a distinct advantage. It has been proved that there is a high correlation between sprinting ability and reaction time. (See Chapter 15 and reference 1.)

Reflex time. In view of the fact that it is generally agreed that a fast start is conducive to a fast race, the sprinter possessing a short reflex time is obviously at an advantage. This means that the athlete profits by having a short reflex time and is well on his way before his slower opponent is off his mark. Actual measurements have shown that champion sprinters have a shorter reflex time than those requiring a longer interval to cover an equal distance. (See Chapter 15 and reference 2.)

Dominance. When manual acts such as starting the sprints are performed, lead preference is usually given to one side of the body. There is good evidence that dominance is an inherited characteristic. Individuals who give lead preference to the right side of the body are said to be right dominant. Those who show preference to the left side are designated as left dominant, whereas those who show no preference lack dominance (ambidextrous).

In starting the sprint, the right-dominant athlete places his right foot back, and when he leaves the mark, a definite sequence of movements is executed. The left-dominant individual places the left foot back and likewise performs a definite sequence of movements. (See Chapter 15 under Movement pattern of the sprinter in starting from the mark; also Bresnahan.[3])

It has been demonstrated that an individual who shows no preference in body lead is likely to execute a mixed movement pattern in leaving the mark, regardless of the foot placed back. Such a situation interferes with coordination in getting into the first stride.

Advising hurdlers to reverse the feet at the start of a race, for the purpose of approach adjustment, no doubt causes an interference in coordination in getting into the first strides (see the chapter on hurdles). However, it is believed that in some instances the loss in time in getting into stride is overbalanced by the benefit derived by the change in number of strides.

Motor-mindedness. Through practice, the athlete must be able to reduce all of the acts of skill in any event to a reflex pattern; that is, he must be able to do them without thinking. Whenever an athlete is able to execute his event automatically, he can rest assured that he has the technique truly mastered. The sprinter is not to be criticized for driving off his mark at the click of a pistol, the cough of an official, or at any other clear-cut stimulus. Such a response by a sprinter is evidence that his attention is fixed on the act of starting (motor-mindedness) rather than on the report of the pistol (sensory-mindedness).

Inhibition. When an athlete is participating in any event, his attention must be focused on the task at hand. This means that when a sprinter is running a race he is literally deaf to everything around him. A well-trained competitor is able to inhibit response to any distraction, whether it is the cheering of the spectators, the derogatory remarks of a bystander, or the advice of a teammate.

Comparative marks in competition. In order that the schoolboy sprinter may be guided in his ambition to become a point winner at the various levels of competition, an estimate of the time required for placing is indicated in Table 4-1. Attention is called to the fact that the times presented are not the anticipated requirements for winning first places. Since the times listed in Table 4-1 represent average performances, the individual will be obliged to adjust his evaluation in case the performances of his opponents deviate from the average. This means that each sprinter should become familiar with the current competitive marks made by athletes in his conference, state, province, or nation.

Equipment. The shoe, which is the most important piece of the sprinter's equipment, together with other apparel, is discussed on p. 3.

During the first few weeks of the preliminary season the athlete may find it advantageous to use rubber-soled shoes in order to avoid shin-splints. On hard tracks, sharper spikes, shorter in length, are desirable, whereas, on a loose or wet course, longer spikes serve best.

TECHNIQUE OF THE SPRINTS

In attempting to master the technique of sprinting, the beginner must recognize the fact that this event involves something more than being able to run rapidly. There are physical, physiologic, and psychologic adjustments which must be made and with which he must be familiar. For the sake of clarity in presentation, the sprints are broken up into the following components: the start, the running strides, the coast, and the finish.

Start

It is generally recognized that a good start is a prerequisite to a winning performance. Ways for reducing the starting time of the sprinter have been considered for many years. One of the most outstanding changes in the start which reduced the time in getting under way was the adoption of the crouch some 80 years ago. In 1927 an advantage was given the sprinter by the addition of starting blocks.* In the discussion which follows, items of technique which the sprinter must consider if he is to become efficient are presented.

Foot support. The essential requirements of any starting blocks are that they may be quickly placed, easily adjusted to suit the

*Patents granted George T. Bresnahan: U. S. A. No. 1701026 (1929) and No. 2144962 (1937); Dominion of Canada No. 294077 (1929).

Table 4-1. Comparative marks for scholastic competitors in the sprints

Meet	No. of places scored	100 yards (sec.)	220 yards (sec.)
Dual high school	3	10.0-10.5	22.0-23.0
Qualifying—state	3	9.8-10.2	21.7-22.2
State, province	5	9.6-10.0	21.3-21.9

angles of the feet, firmly fastened to the track, and speedily removed from the course.

The recommended adjustment for the foot-supporting surfaces of the starting blocks is 90 degrees for the back block and 45 degrees for the front block, but it may be shifted to suit the competitor.

Types. A study of the starting positions assumed by trained sprinters reveals the fact that there is a rather wide variation in the distances at which they space their

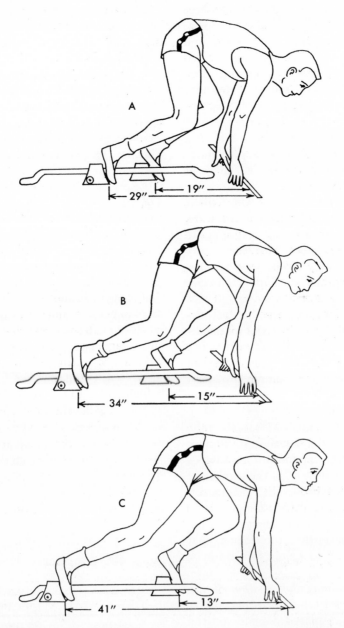

Fig. 4-1. The sprinter in the "set" position. **A,** Bunch spacing. **B,** Medium spacing. **C,** Elongated spacing.

feet. The sprinter is advised to experiment with the various patterns of foot spacing and to select the one that best suits his requirements. The more commonly used positions are as follows:

Bunch spacing (Fig. 4-1, *A*). This position is defined as one in which the toe of the back foot is placed opposite the heel of the front foot while in a standing position. This start represents the one extreme in foot spacing since sprinters seldom place the feet closer together than described in the bunch spacing. (See Chapter 15 under Physical measurements and foot spacing; also Dickinson.[4])

Medium spacing (Fig. 4-1, *B*). In this start the knee of the back leg is placed opposite the front of the arch of the front foot, in a kneeling position.

Elongated spacing (Fig. 4-1, *C*). This is a position in which, in a kneeling position, the knee of the back leg is placed opposite the heel of the front foot. This start represents the other extreme in foot spacing since sprinters rarely ever employ a longer foot spread.

Although the positions of the feet described represent the extremes in foot spacing, together with one that falls between them, there are many variations practiced among sprinters. Even though excellent sprinters who employ a rather long foot spread are found, there appears to be a tendency among competitors to favor the use of bunch spacing because it is more conducive to a high hip elevation, provides better for the forward lean of the trunk, and is conducive to speedier leg movement. Those who prefer a foot spread longer than that provided by bunch spacing do so because they believe that the longer foot spread is conducive to a more forceful back leg drive.

Factors determining the position of the feet. The distance from the starting line at which the feet are placed depends on the height of the man and the type of start employed. In general, the taller the man,

the farther the feet should be placed from the starting line. The man of average height (5 feet 10½ inches) locates his feet at approximately the distances (from the face of the support to the back edge of the scratch line) given in Table 4-2 (see also Fig. 4-1).

Although the distances presented are subject to variations by the athlete, they represent those employed by men of average height, possessing arm and leg lengths proportionate to their height, who are well-trained sprinters. The proper position of the feet in relation to the starting line is a question that can be answered only through practice by each individual sprinter. (See Chapter 15 under Physical measurements and foot spacing; also Dickinson.[4])

Effect of foot spacing on starting time. Dickinson[4] conducted a study to determine the effectiveness of the various types of spacing the feet. In advance, the subjects were instructed in the use of each of the commonly accepted methods of foot spacing. These included the bunch, medium, and elongated methods.

Twenty-six trained sprinters served as subjects, and each executed 32 starts upon three occasions, totalling 96 starts for each subject. The grand total of starts timed was 2,496.

The conclusions reached were as follows: (1) the use of the bunch foot spacing resulted in significantly faster starting times; (2) the use of the elongated foot spacing resulted in the slowest starting times; (3) the use of the medium foot spacing resulted in starting times that fell between those of the bunch and the elongated methods.

Table 4-2. Comparative distances in various foot spacings

	Front foot	Back foot
Bunch spacing	19 inches	29 inches
Medium spacing	15 inches	34 inches
Elongated spacing	13 inches	41 inches

The following questions immediately arose. "What method of foot spacing yields the shortest interval to reach the finish yarn? Is the fastest clearance of the starting blocks likewise conducive to faster running time when covering a distance after the start?"

Using a procedure similar to that previously described, Dickinson[4] compared the time elapsed between the pistol shot and the breasting of a yarn placed 7½ feet distant for ten trained sprinters using the elongated, the medium, and the bunch methods. This phase of the experiment indicated that the use of the bunch foot spacing yielded the fastest sprinting time, the use of the elongated foot spacing resulted in the slowest sprinting time, and the use of the medium foot spacing resulted in a time that fell between those of the elongated and the bunch methods.

Relationship of sprinting velocities to starting time. A study of the velocities of nine university sprinters, from the instant of leaving the starting blocks to distances up to 35 yards, was undertaken by Sills and Pennybaker.[5] They utilized microswitches attached to strings stretched across the running track at 5-yard intervals and a cathode ray oscillograph to provide a photographic record of readings at each 5-yard interval.

Repeated experiments indicated that no increases in velocities occurred beyond a distance of 30 yards.

Among the conclusions of Sills and Pennybaker were the following:

1. The mean time at the end of the first 5 yards was 1.05 seconds.
2. The mean time of the total time (for 35 yards) was 4.23 seconds.
3. Two of the three subjects who had recorded the fastest total time (for 35 yards) were below (faster than) the mean time at the end of the first 5 yards.
4. The three subjects who had recorded the slowest total time (for 35 yards) were above (slower than) the mean

time at the end of the first 5 yards.
5. One of the nine subjects attained maximum velocity between 25 and 30 yards.
6. Three of the nine subjects attained maximum velocity between 20 and 25 yards.
7. Five of the nine subjects attained maximum velocity between 15 and 20 yards.

Sills and Pennybaker's experiment indicates that there is a close relationship between fast sprinting times and fast starting times.

In a second experiment, Sills and Carter[6] (see Chapter 15) studied the velocities of sprinters utilizing three types of foot spacing. The techniques used were similar to those of Sills and Pennybaker. Nine varsity sprinters were employed as subjects. The foot positions were the bunch spacing, the free-choice spacing, and the medium spacing. The data showed the following:

1. Sprinters used as subjects attained their maximum velocities between the 20-yard distance and the 25-yard distance from the starting line.
2. Maximum velocity at each 5-yard interval, up to 30 yards, was obtained more frequently with the bunch spacing than with the medium spacing.
3. The sprinters participating in the experiment covered 30 yards faster when they used the bunch spacing than when they used the medium spacing.
4. The correlation is high between the velocity obtained by these sprinters during the first and second 5-yard intervals. There is a low correlation among the velocities attained by sprinters for the first 5 yards and successive 5-yard intervals beyond 10 yards.
5. There is a high correlation between the velocities for the first 5 yards and the cumulative velocities at 10, 15, 20, and 25 yards.

Sills and Carter's conclusions support further the idea that the type of foot spacing that yielded the fastest starting time also yielded the fastest sprinting time.

Running velocity: body rise and stride length. Rapp[7] studied the effects that changes in running velocities have on both the length of the strides and the body rise. (For a fuller discussion of this experiment, see Chapter 15.) The results of his study led to the conclusion that in changing from a slow pace to a moderate pace the runner increased his stride length and decreased his body rise. When the runner increased from a moderate pace to a sprinting pace, a further decrease in body rise was noted.

He stressed the importance of requiring the sprinter to master the technique of exerting maximum force in a near-horizonal direction. In addition to assuring efficiency of movement, the degree of body rise is then kept to a minimum.

Position of the hands and arms. An acceptable position of the hands and arms is shown in Fig. 4-2. In the figure the hands are placed so that the weight rests on the thumbs and fingers. Some sprinters prefer to place the weight on the thumb and second joint of the fingers, whereas others throw their weight on the thumb and knuckles. The guiding factor is the comfort of the sprinter. Care should be taken always so that the hands are back of the starting line.

In the position "on the mark" the arms should be fully extended and not flexed at the elbow. They should be far enough apart to ensure free knee action in getting set. The sprinter should remember that the arms and hands are so placed that there is no feeling of discomfort. He should be in a state of sharply defined balance.

Position of the hips. The height to which a sprinter elevates the hips in relation to

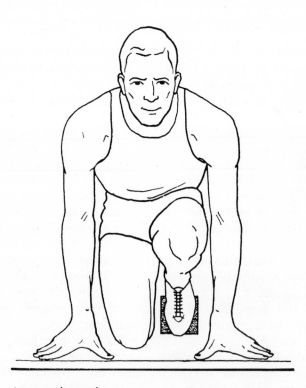

Fig. 4-2. The sprinter on the mark.

the shoulders in the set position depends on the type of foot spacing employed. As a rule, the shorter the longitudinal spacing, the higher are the hips elevated. In bunch spacing the hips are usually about 25 degrees higher than the shoulders. This angle becomes less for medium spacing and still less for the elongated position (Fig. 4-1). Many good competitors favor a hip position which is as high as possible and yet consistent with the type of foot spacing employed. (See Chapter 15 under Effect of the position of the hips on starting time; also White.[8])

Position of the head and eyes. In the set position the sprinter looks down the track as far as is consistent with his body position (Fig. 4-1). If a sprinter starts from a position in which the trunk is parallel with the track, he can see some distance without cramping his neck. However, when the high hip position is employed, the distance of vision is reduced. In any event a sprinter should raise his head high enough so that he can see far enough ahead to guide the direction of his body.

After the start the eyes are focused in the direction of the run. Imbalance and loss of stride may result if a runner turns his head to see what is going on around him. The sprinter should gain whatever information he desires through peripheral vision and sound, just as in hurdling.

Position of the trunk. When the sprinter is on his mark, waiting for the command "set" the position of the body may vary from one in which the center of weight is well behind the knee on the ground to one in which the center of weight is well in front of it. This depends on the type of foot spacing employed and the forward tilt of the trunk. The points to bear in mind are the comfort of the contestant and the efficiency with which the hips are raised to the set position. If the trunk is tilted to its backward limit, there is but little weight on the arms, and when the command "set" is given, the sprinter must move his trunk

forward and upward. If the body position is too far forward, the athlete is conscious of undue strain on the arms and hands. A short foot spacing (bunch spacing) is more conducive to extreme forward trunk tilt than the longer foot spacing (elongated spacing). For any given spacing, the determining factor in the degree of trunk tilt is the amount of leg bend and hip elevation. If the forward lean is too extreme, the back leg is likely to be too straight and thus detract from its drive. An on-the-mark position which permits the sprinter to set merely by raising the hips is the most desirable.

Breathing. There is a lack of uniformity among authorities as to the most effective breathing habits which should be established in sprint racing. The point which a sprinter must consider in any type of breathing habit is that sufficient air must be provided for his race.

A common procedure followed by many sprinters is to breathe forcefully before getting on the mark. Scientific evidence supports this procedure, since by so doing the carbon dioxide in the blood is reduced and the tendency toward labored breathing is postponed.

It has been demonstrated that when the sprinter is in the on-the-mark position, breathing is normal. The breathing habits of the sprinter in the set position are reflex, that is, involuntary. As soon as the command "set" is given, the sprinter takes a deep breath and then holds it until the pistol is fired. The breathing habits of the sprinter in the set position are paralleled by the golfer concentrating on a putt or the marksman aiming at the target. (See Chapter 15 under Respiratory habits of sprinters during the start; also Felkner.[9])

No set rule is laid down to govern the breathing of a sprinter after he leaves his mark. Here again it is a question of supplying the body with sufficient oxygen and eliminating sufficient carbon dioxide to ward off fatigue as long as possible. There are insufficient scientific data at hand to support any set practice in the matter of breathing during the actual running of sprint races.

The sprinter should always bear in mind that the better the physical condition and the more efficient the warm-up, the less will be the air requirements during the course of a sprint.

Attention. When the sprinter is notified by the official that his race is about to start, he must give his undivided attention voluntarily to the preliminary preparations which are necessary so that he will be ready to take his mark when the command is given. As soon as the sprinter takes his mark, his attention is then turned to the finer bodily adjustments in preparation for the command "set." Competent officials allow an interval of 10 to 15 seconds between these commands.

According to the official rules (N.F.S.H.-S.A.A., N.C.A.A., and A.A.U.), the pistol employed in starting races should be no less than a 32 caliber. The powder in the shells must yield a distinct flash that provides a clear-cut stimulus for the timers. For the sake of economy in the cost of blank shells, the 22 caliber is used not only for practice but also for competitive starting in numerous areas. A discussion of the effect of the caliber of the pistol on starting time is found in Chapter 15.

When the command "set" is given, the sprinter assumes the set position, in which the driving muscles become tense, breathing ceases, and extraneous stimuli are shut out. Attention is focused on the act of starting rather than the report of the pistol. Starting is a reflex phenomenon that is set off by the sound of the pistol.*

The sprinter must remember that attention is a fluctuating phenomenon, reaching its peak, then subsiding, and then coming back to its peak again. If the sprinter is to get the best start, the peak of attention and the firing of the pistol must coincide.

Since attention fluctuation is involuntary, the coincidence of attention and the sound of the pistol lies largely in the hands of the official. If the pistol is fired too soon, the peak of attention may not yet be reached, and if the sprinter is held too long in the "set" position, attention may have reached its peak and may be in the subsiding phase when the pistol is fired. Walker and Hayden[10] demonstrated that the peak of attention and the report of the pistol are closest together when the holding time is 1.5 seconds.* This is about 2 seconds after the command "set" is given. (See Chapter 15 under Optimum time for holding a sprinter on his mark.)

Force exerted by the legs. When the sprinter leaves his mark, he should execute a vicious drive with both legs. The amount of force exerted and the distribution of this force depend on the spacing of the feet. When the feet are close together as in bunch spacing, the greatest drive is executed by the front foot. As the foot spacing is increased the tendency is toward an equalization of the force exerted by the legs. In what has been defined as medium spacing the force exerted by the legs is approximately equal. As the foot spacing is increased still further the force exerted by the back leg exceeds that applied by the front leg, as is the case in which the elongated foot spacing is assumed at the start of the race.

Kistler[11] found that the force applied by the front leg is independent of foot spacing, remaining constant in all the spacings described. However, as the longitudinal space between the feet is increased, so also is the force exerted by the back leg increased. Since this is true, then as the foot

---

*Refer to Landis, C., and Hunt, W. A.: The startle pattern, New York, 1939, Farrar & Rinehart, Inc. The startle pattern concept is generally accepted at present.

*"Holding time" is defined as the interval elapsing between the position of momentary steadiness after the command "set" has been given and the firing of the pistol.

spacing is increased, the total force exerted by the legs is increased. As a matter of general information, it may be stated that the average sprinter exerts a force represented as 195 pounds with the front foot. When the feet are close together, as in bunch spacing, the average sprinter exerts a pressure of 150 pounds with the back foot. As the foot spacing is increased, the pressure exerted by the back foot increases, reaching 195 pounds in the medium position and 210 pounds in the elongated spacings. (See Chapter 15 under Distribution of the force exerted by the legs in driving off the mark.)

Sequence of movements in leaving the mark. The sequence of the movements which a sprinter follows when he leaves his mark depends on his dominance (footedness or handedness). The right-dominant individual places his right foot back. The movement pattern employed in leaving the mark is reflex, similar to the hand-foot relationship when walking. The order of movements of the right-dominant individual is left hand, right hand, right foot, and left foot. For the left-dominant sprinter the movement sequence is right hand, left hand, left foot, and right foot. (See Chapter 15 under Time relationships in the sequence of movement in starting from the mark; also Bresnahan.[3])

It is of interest to note that a well-trained sprinter requires from 0.3 to 0.4 second to leave his mark after the pistol is fired.

Response to the pistol. Through practice the sprinter should learn to respond automatically to the firing of the pistol, that is, without giving it any thought. An individual who is able to start in such a manner is said to be motor-minded. The sprinter who finds it necessary first to think about the report of the pistol before he starts is described as sensory-minded and loses valuable time at the start of the race. (See Chapter 15 under Effect of the caliber of the pistol on starting time; also Carson.[12])

Commands. When the stage is set, the official notifies the contestants that the race is about to begin. After preliminary instruction, each sprinter assumes a position in such proximity to his foot supports that little time is lost in getting placed when the command to do so is given. As soon as the sprinters are ready, the official gives the commands as follows:

Get on your mark (Fig. 4-2). Sufficient time is allowed for the contestants to get settled on the mark. During this interval of 10 to 15 seconds, he completes his body adjustments and makes sure that he is ready to assume a position quickly from which he can drive viciously.

Set (Fig. 4-1). The position on the mark is such that most of the body weight is on the right knee. When the command "set" is given, the hips are raised into starting position by contracting the extensor muscles of both legs and thighs. This action throws the body weight on the feet and arms. The sprinter must remember that because a vicious drive is to be executed by both legs the back leg must bear its share of the body weight if the drive is to be most effective. In the set position the arms are used for balance and support.

The degree of inclination of the trunk, the elevation of the hips, the direction of the head and eyes, and the placement of the hands and arms have been previously determined by the athlete himself. Through practice he must learn to assume quickly the desired body position when the command "set" is given. When the contestant has assumed this position and becomes steady, he is said to be set. All musculature involved in driving off the mark is tense, ready to execute quick, powerful movements.

The mental attitude of the sprinter in the set position has been discussed under attention. To achieve the most effective start the contestant must become an automatic (reflex) organism.

Pistol. The sprinter must be ready to go any instant after he is set. Of course, it must be realized that the interval which the contestant is held in the set position is entirely in the hands of the official. The sprinter who is physically and mentally poised may be likened to powder in a shell that is about to be fired. When the spark contacts the powder, it explodes with great force; likewise, when the pistol is fired, the sprinter's energy is automatically released and he springs forward with a vicious drive.

Running strides

During the running strides the body is propelled forward by the pushing action of the driving leg. The function of the recovery leg is to get into position for the next stride as expeditiously as possible with a minimum waste of energy.*

The arms constitute the balancing mechanism for keeping the body aligned, and they also act as a part of the reflex movement pattern developed naturally through walking and running.

The way in which force is applied to the body by the legs and the adjustments of the arms for balance depend on the striding action. A study of sprinting justifies the breaking of it into the component parts of the starting strides, the transitional strides, and the full-speed strides. The movements described are based on the assumption that the sprinter places his right foot back in the starting position.

Starting strides. The two starting strides are defined as beginning when the right foot first applies force against the back block and ending the instant before it leaves the ground the second time. They are illustrated in Fig. 4-3, A and B.

Forward propulsion at the beginning of

---

*The term "leg" is loosely used in this discussion to include both the leg and thigh. During a stride, while one leg is pushing the body forward, the opposite leg is being swung into position to push the body forward during the succeeding stride. The leg that is pushing the body forward is designated as the "driving leg," and the swinging leg is called the "recovery leg."

the first stride is initiated by the back leg. The beginning of the back leg drive is followed very quickly (approximately 0.01 second) by the driving action of the front leg. For a time, both legs are applying force to the body simultaneously. The application of front leg force to the forward propulsion of the body lasts considerably longer (more than twice as long for the average sprinter) than the application of back leg force.[13]

As the force is applied by the legs, the shoulders are raised somewhat higher than the hips. Simultaneously the hands leave the ground in their natural sequence. The hip-shoulder change is the beginning of the straightening of the trunk lean. This straightening process continues until the sprinter reaches full speed.

At the conclusion of the push-off, the back leg starts forward. A combination of the pushing force of the left leg and the backward reaction to the forward swing of the right leg tends to swing the right hip backward. This disalignment is overcome by the compensating reaction force of the swinging of the arms. The right arm swings backward and the left arm forward. The right arm is swung back slightly bent, while the bent left arm is swung forward somewhat toward the midline of the body (Fig. 4-3, A). Although the height of arm swing varies, the hands usually come up to about the shoulder level. The force of the arm swing is proportional to the force of the leg drive. Since the drive off the blocks is vicious, the arm swing is powerful.

The right foot is brought forward and placed on the ground, the knee forming almost a right angle. The length of the first stride depends on both the length of the legs and the type of foot spacing used. This is the shortest stride of the sprint (18 inches to 28 inches in front of the starting line), since the necessarily low body position limits its length.

Almost instantaneously after the right foot hits the ground, the left foot leaves its

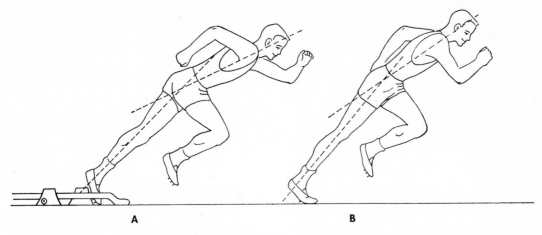

Fig. 4-3. The starting strides in the sprint. **A,** The first stride. **B,** The second stride.

support. It is brought forward in the same manner as described for the right foot except this stride is slightly longer than the first and the trunk is slightly more erect. With the moving of the left foot forward, the arms execute a forceful action, opposite in direction to their movement when the right foot moved forward. Here again, the forceful arm action serves to align the body with the direction of the run.

The paramount point to be remembered is that during the first 2 strides, terrific force must be applied by both legs accompanied by a forceful swing of both arms. It is the force of the leg drive that brings about the achievement of maximum acceleration. This completes the first two-stride section of the sprint.

Transitional strides. During the first 6 to 9 strides there is a gradual transition from what we have called the starting strides to the strides characteristic of full speed. Throughout the transitional period there is a progressive lengthening of the strides and a gradual straightening of the trunk angle. As the trunk becomes more erect the recovery knee becomes straighter as the foot contacts the ground.

The principle involved in this section of the sprint is that since the trunk lean is greater the center of weight is closer to the ground, and of necessity, the strides are shorter than the full-speed strides. During this phase of the sprint, the knee bend of the recovery leg, when the foot contacts the track, varies among different athletes (the bend is greatest in the first stride and becomes less and less until it becomes constant at full speed). From the beginning of the sprint through the period of acceleration, the driving leg executes a terrific backward thrust by extending both the knee and ankle. To this force is added a powerful backward extension of the hip. As full speed is approached and the knee becomes straighter when the foot contacts the ground, the backward knee thrust becomes less, almost vanishing as an effective forward propelling force.

During the transitional strides, when the foot touches the ground, it must be moving backward with an adequate amount of speed. The principle involved here is discussed under full-speed strides.

Full-speed strides (Fig. 4-4). The sprinter is said to be at full speed when he ceases to accelerate. When full speed is attained, there is no further change (decrease) in trunk angle, and the strides become uniform in length. Full-speed strides differ in character from the transitional strides.

A single stride is defined as the distance

A   B   C

Fig. 4-4. The full-speed sprint stride. **A,** The right leg is shown in its driving phase and the left in its recovery phase of the stride. **B,** The double float. During this time both feet are off the ground. As the body moves forward, the left leg moves backward so that the foot touches the ground directly under the center of weight. **C,** The landing.

between the toe of the right shoe and the toe of the left shoe. In other words, it is only one step. However, for the purpose of this discussion a complete cycle (two steps) is described. This cycle is defined as beginning when the right foot leaves the ground and ending when it leaves the ground a second time. A full-speed cycle is divided into the recovery phase and the driving phase.*

Recovery phase. The problem involved in the recovery phase is twofold: (1) to move the leg forward as expeditiously as possible with the minimum waste of energy and (2) to place it in the optimum position for the execution of the drive following the recovery.

In order to achieve recovery in the most

---

*For a thorough technical discussion of the mechanics of the human gait, refer to Steindler, A.: Mechanics of normal and pathological locomotion in man, Springfield, Ill., 1935, Charles C Thomas, Publisher, chap. 27.

economical fashion, the knee is flexed so that when the leg is brought forward the heel is carried high under the buttock. As the thigh swings out forward to a position almost horizontal with the ground, the foot is moved forward and then downward and backward in a pawing motion (Fig. 4-4, *B*). The foot contacts the ground almost directly under the center of weight, with the right knee bent only slightly (Fig. 4-4, *C*).

As has been previously stated, the backward rate of movement of the foot when it contacts the ground must be adequate. It should be moving backward, relative to the center of weight of the body, at a rate of speed which is as great or slightly greater than the forward speed of the body relative to the track.

Driving phase. As the recovery leg comes forward, the toe of the shoe contacts the track, the knee is very slightly bent, and the heel sinks until it almost touches the ground. The driving forces of the leg are

spikes of the shoe. The front block should be set at an angle of approximately 45 degrees or in a position so that it likewise engages all the spikes of the front shoe. Assume a position so that you may respond to the commands, "starters ready," "go to your mark," "set," and "go" (or the pistol). Take 4 or 5 trials without the pistol, driving off your mark for a distance of 15 to 20 yards.

5. Retain or vary the foot spacing longitudinally until, with the aid of a coach or an observer, you arrive at the most effective distance.

6. Pass the baton 3 or 4 times.

7. End the practice with a jog of 150 yards, a walk of 25 yards, and a run of 150 yards at ¾ effort.

Tuesday

1. Record mentally after each day of practice your reaction to the various types of warm-up so that by the time midseason arrives you will have a definite idea of the quantity and type of exercise best suited to your needs. Begin by jogging 100 yards, walking 10 yards, jogging 50 yards, and running 100 yards at gradually increasing speed.

2. Engage in those tension exercises that have been designated for runners (see p. 10).

3. Set the starting blocks and take 4 or 5 trials without the starting pistol. Pay particular attention to these phases of starting when you are on the mark: (1) body relaxation, (2) body weight distribution, (3) the position of the hands on the starting line, (4) the degree of spread of the arms (their relation to the shoulders), (5) the relation of the right hip to the right knee (is it directly above the knee, back of the knee, or forward of the knee?), and (6) the height to which the hips are elevated.

4. Take 3 or 4 starts with the pistol, going 30 yards in case you are sufficiently advanced in your training program to withstand the expenditure of full effort; otherwise postpone this phase of practice. In each case, pay particular attention to the breathing activities just before coming to the mark. Relaxing movements, such as a few seconds of scarecrow or skeleton dancing, have proved beneficial to many athletes. These are performed in a loose-jointed and somewhat aimless manner.

5. Join the long jumpers, adjust the checkmarks, and take 2 or 3 trials for form. In addition to developing leg drive for sprinting, potential long jumping ability may be uncovered.

6. Run 75 yards at ¾ effort, and walk 10 yards; repeat twice.

7. End the practice with a jog of 300 yards, increasing the speed toward the end so that the last 20 yards are run at 9/10 effort.

Wednesday

1. Start the workout with jogging, running, and foot-stretching exercises performed as follows: From a position seated on a bench, throw the right leg over the left, and grasp the right toe with the left hand. By use of the hand, resist the rotary movement of the toe.

2. Set the starting blocks and take 3 starts without the pistol and 3 with the pistol, going 40 yards at top speed, ease up 5 yards, and then run 10 yards at full effort. This exercise is designed to provide drill on coasting or the freewheeling period midway in the 220-yard dash. See the effort distribution chart, Fig. 4-5.

3. Join the hurdlers for a period of 5 or 6 minutes, practicing on mat hurdling Obviously this is for the purpose of

stretching and conditioning the muscles and preventing injury to the hamstring group. The novice is advised to apply only moderate effort to begin with and to increase the vigor of the exercise gradually.

4. Adjust yourself physically and mentally for a pistol start, running a total distance of 200 yards, the first 50 yards at full effort and the last 150 yards at $9/10$ effort. Properly ventilate the body before coming to the mark by deep-breathing exercises and then relax the entire musculature by use of the shimmy or skeleton dance. When once assuming the on-the-mark position, fix the attention on your start. This means focusing the eyes down the course and inhibiting all sounds, awaiting only the report of the pistol. Refrain from coming too rapidly to the set position. Have a stop watch held so that you can retain poise in the set position for a period of at least 1.8 seconds (this is an overhold, 1.5 being the optimum) after the moment of steadiness. In common parlance this is termed the ability to wait for the pistol and to refrain from breaking or false starting. The training should be such that at the instant of the pistol shot you automatically release all forces of propulsion. (See Chapter 15 under Optimum time for holding a sprinter on his mark; also Walker and Hayden.[10])

5. Participate in weight-training exercises for a period of 10 to 15 minutes (see pp. 9 and 10).

6. Conclude the practice with 2 or 3 minutes of hopping and bounding (springing high in the air from alternate feet) followed by a jog of 440 yards.

Thursday

1. Begin with jogging, walking, running, and sprinting.

2. Perform 2 or 3 minutes of rope skipping.

3. Set the starting blocks and take 4 or 5 starts without the pistol, sprinting 20 yards at full effort. Emphasize the forward-upward jab of the left arm and the backward drive of the right elbow with the arm partially bent. Experiment with a first stride of varying lengths but of maximum force, and note the effectiveness of the different styles.

4. Spend 3 or 4 minutes on exercises designed to strengthen the muscles of the thighs, ankles, and feet. An acceptable drill consists of kneeling on the ground with the heels close together and vertical to the toes. Gradually incline the trunk backward until the buttocks touch the heels. Vary the exercise with the toes extended.

5. Run 330 yards as follows: 110 yards at $9/10$ effort, 110 yards at $7/8$ effort, and 110 yards at $9/10$ effort.

6. Rest 5 to 10 minutes and then finish with an easy jog of 660 yards on the grass.

Friday

1. Jog, walk, and run approximately 300 yards to prepare yourself for practice.

2. Set the starting blocks, and incline the face of the back foot support from the 90-degree angle suggested. Likewise, increase the angle of the front foot support from the 45 degrees. Take 5 or 6 starts with the pistol, noting the effect of the changed position. Either accept or reject the new angle adjustment in the light of your experimentation.

3. Attach the finish yarn at breast height to posts placed 40 yards from the start. Brush the track so that your spike marks can be identified. Take 3 or 4 pistol starts and, at top speed, drive through the finish. Use a measuring tape and record the length of

the various strides. How far did you run before you attained the most effective sprinting stride?

4. Engage in weight-training exercises. Adjust their duration and intensity to meet your needs.

5. Ease up Friday's practice because of time trials Saturday over the 100-yard and 220-yard distances. Jog 220 yards.

Saturday

1. Begin this day's practice as though you were preparing for important competition. Fix a definite limit on each activity, such as jogging, walking, running, sprinting, and free exercise. Remember exactly how you warmed up so that if your time trial is creditable you may repeat the procedure at a future date. In case your time trial is not creditable and the cause of slow time can be traced to the warming-up routine, obviously, changes in the type and quantity of its exercise are necessary.

2. Make use of your practice experience in making adjustments for the time trial. Consider such items as the spacing of the starting blocks, the proper mental poise, the most effective breathing practice, the elevation of the hips, the tension of the body when set, and the fixation of attention on the act of starting.

3. Run the 100-yard time trial at full effort, carrying through 10 yards beyond the finish line. Remember that races must be run even though the track is soggy or the wind is from the front, so that occasional trials should be run in spite of unfavorable weather conditions.

4. Walk or jog slowly for 2 or 3 minutes, dry off body perspiration, and rest until it is time to warm up for the 220-yard time trial. The interval between these two sprint races varies

in different meets, the range being from 30 to 70 minutes.

5. Place 2 markers on the track 105 and 115 yards, respectively, from the starting line. These represent the guideposts between which the coast for the 220-yard dash may be taken. The novice will bear in mind that these are but practice devices, which may be moved either forward or backward, and that the distance between them may be lengthened or shortened to meet personal requirements. However, they represent definite objectives around which to construct a plan of running the furlong race. Run the 220-yard time trial.

6. Prepare for the relay by a short spasmotic warm-up 25 to 30 minutes after the 220-yard time trial. Since the emphasis is chiefly on the art of baton passing, the distance may be reduced to 100 yards per man or even to 50 yards. Run the relay time trial.

7. Finish the workout for Saturday in early season with a 300-yard jog, a shower bath, and a massage. Analyze your weight chart for the week.

Midseason. Schedules for this season are arranged to meet conditions in which competition is scheduled for Saturday. The most vigorous exercise of the week is laid out for Tuesday on the theory that with rest or jogging on Sunday and longer running practice on Monday (overdistance at underspeed), the contestant will then be fit for a dress rehearsal of Saturday's events. Again, with progressively lighter activities prescribed for Wednesday, Thursday, and Friday, the athlete should come to Saturday's meet with an abundance of zest and relish for competition. Furthermore, this schedule prepares the individual who is called on to compete on Friday, since many scholastic contests are held then instead of Saturday. He has had a fair degree of freedom from strenuous early week practice even though he is required to compete in preliminary heats Friday afternoon or Saturday morning.

An alternate plan is one in which the types of practice for Tuesday and Wednesday are reversed. However, this substitute is not recommended in those weeks having Friday or Friday-Saturday contests on the schedule, because the rest or build-up period from Wednesday to Friday is too brief.

The sprinter is presumed to compete in the 100-yard and 220-yard dashes as well as the sprint relays. If the 1-mile relay rather than the sprint relay is in his assignment, slightly more endurance running should be included.

Frequently the sprinter is called on to take part in one or more field events in addition to his customary tasks. Provided the athlete has the physical ability, such events as the long jump, the shot-put, or the javelin throw fit in satisfactorily with the sprints. It is conceivable that competitors can warm up for any of these field events, make a supreme effort in one trial, and if the performance was sufficiently meritorius, pass up further trials. It should be evident to the novice that those events requiring but a single effort permit energy conservation not possible in other events such as the pole vault or the running high jump.

The beginner will note that starting with the pistol is not indicated after arduous sprint practice or strenuous exercise. The reasons are twofold: (1) because, in meets, starts are executed in the absence of fatigue and (2) because starting injuries occur more frequently to fatigued than to rested muscles. Starts with the pistol should never be taken until the sprinter is warmed up thoroughly.

Monday

1. Make use of photographs, diagrams, or, if possible, motion pictures of your recent competition in the analysis of your running form.
2. Adjustments in the various flexible phases of starting technique should be mastered prior to the first important meet in midseason. The novice is referred to the discussion of the start earlier in this chapter.
3. Follow the routines of both weight-training and tension exercises suggested for runners (see pp. 10 and 12).
4. Join the relay group and pass the baton 2 or 3 times at top speed. Utilize the nonvisual method of exchange if you compete in the sprint relay only or the visual method if your oncoming teammate runs 440 yards or more.
5. Set the starting blocks and take 2 or 3 starts from the mark without the pistol and then 2 or 3 starts with the pistol, sprinting to a finish yarn set 30 yards away. If the track has been brushed, your spike marks will provide a record of your stride action from the first step through the yarn-breasting drive.
6. Run through 300 yards as follows: 30 yards at full effort, 70 yards at $7/8$ effort, 100 yards at $3/4$ effort, and 100 yards at $7/8$ effort. The objectives of this practice are speed at the start, reduced speed for 70 yards, a coast for 100 yards, and a pick-up of speed (but less than racing effort) for the last 100 yards, thus calling on sprinting endurance. However, the workout should not be so strenuous as to detract from the storehouse of energy needed in possible trials on Tuesday.
7. Terminate the practice with a jog of 300 yards, finishing with a top-speed burst over the last 5 yards.

Tuesday

1. Start the day with the customary jogging, bounding, and running.
2. Prepare for trials in the 100-yard dash. Some coaches prefer to eliminate time trial competition among their top performers. Should you de-

sire more motivation in your practice, station a less proficient sprinter a distance of 5 to 15 yards in front of the starting line, so that you will be required to exert a driving finish to overtake him. Maintain the focus of the eyes on the finish yarn and only incidentally, through peripheral vision, be cognizant of the running positions of the other competitors.

3. Walk or jog easily for 2 or 3 minutes and then dress warmly and rest for the next event, 20 minutes later.

4. Warm up for a 220-yard time trial, noting the efficacy of the preparation. If you have not achieved results by running 105 yards at full effort, coasting 10 yards, and finishing at full effort, alter your pace by spreading your energy evenly over the 220-yard time trial. Move the start so that you can practice running against the wind. Have your elapsed time recorded by a stop watch at 102.5 yards. This represents half the total elapsed time.

5. Jog, walk, and then rest until relay practice is called; this will take an interval of 15 to 20 minutes.

6. Run 1 sector of either a 440-yard relay (110 yards) or the 880-yard relay (220 yards). An alternative drill consists in shortening the running distance of each sector of the relay to 50 or even 30 yards and repeating once. Make use of the nonvisual method of baton transfer. If you are preparing for participation in the 1-mile relay, 1 or 2 visual passes of the baton followed by a run of 330 yards at 7/8 effort are suggested. The majority of authorities believe that the sprinter called upon to run 440-yards in a relay will compete creditably if he has built up a reserve of energy and seldom, if ever, practiced over the full 1/4-mile distance at top effort.

Perhaps the ideal situation occurs when the sprinter has no responsibilities other than the two sprints. Frequently occasions arise when he is required to run the relay, and he should be prepared for this task. However, arduous tests of endurance in the midweek schedule are not recommended since they tend to detract from that fine fettle so highly desired by sprinters. Just as one cannot expect a first-class shave from a razor employed to sharpen pencils, he need not look for excellent results from a sprinter who has dulled his edge by overdistance time trials.

7. Finish the workout with an easy 220-yard jog.

Wednesday

1. Jog and walk alternately distances of 50 yards until 400 yards have been covered.

2. Take a sun bath for 5 to 10 minutes if the weather permits.

3. Spend 10 to 15 minutes on one of your secondary events, for example, the long jump or the javelin throw. Refer to the midseason schedules of practice as indicated for the event under consideration.

4. Prepare for starting practice and take 3 or 4 starts with the pistol, going 25 yards at full effort.

5. Execute 3 or 4 trials of baton passing at full speed, utilizing all sprinters.

6. Conclude the day's practice with six sprints of 120 to 140 yards at 7/8 speed, concentrating on relaxation.

Thursday

1. Jog 200 yards, walk 50 yards, and run 150 yards.

2. Execute 3 nonvisual passes of the baton. Unlimited baton transfer practice tends toward indifferent timing and handling.

3. Engage in 2 to 3 minutes of leg-stretching exercises. These may include vigorous leg swinging, high

kicking, and mat hurdling (see glossary).

4. Take 20 seconds of inverted running at gradually increasing cadence. Repeat twice.
5. Spend 10 to 15 minutes on the field event in which you may be required to participate Saturday.
6. Engage in weight-training exercises applicable to runners. Are they more effective when scheduled toward the end of practice? Are they more beneficial 2 days per week rather than 1 day?

Friday

This daily schedule is based on there being neither trial heats nor competition on Friday.

1. Jog 200 yards, run 50 yards at ⅔ effort, and then run 100 yards at ¾ effort.
2. Investigate the condition of the track so that you may anticipate possible changes in the type of running spikes.
3. Ascertain the exact time of starting each of your events and, if trials are required, the number of your heat and lane, together with the number of qualifiers to be selected.
4. Spend 3 to 4 minutes on varied exercises such as high kicking, trunk bending, push-ups from the front leaning rest position, and medicine ball tossing.
5. Jog 440 yards on the grass.

Saturday

Note the temperature of the day and the direction and velocity of the wind. An optimistic attitude is an asset, especially in the face of adverse conditions.

1. Warm up according to your definite routine.
2. Employ those previously determined phases of starting form which have been tested and proved. Among these are the foot spacing, the degree of

body tension, the breathing, the height of the hips, and the attention to the act of starting.

3. Make the final adjustments and run the 100-yard dash, carrying through well beyond the finish line. The novice will remember that the finish yarn is merely an aid to the judges and timers. First place is awarded the runner whose torso first reaches the nearest edge of the finish line which is marked on the ground. Emphasis is placed on the word "torso" and thus excludes from consideration any other parts of the body.
4. Jog and walk until partially recovered, dry off body perspiration, and keep off the feet.
5. Warm up for the 220-yard dash. Do not make the error of insufficient preparation, even though you have adequately warmed up for the 100-yard dash.
6. Complete the usual mental and physical preparations for the event and sprint the 220-yard distance.
7. Walk and jog until composure is regained, awaiting the call for the relay.
8. Make use of your previous experience in employing racing tactics and run the relay. Frequently an athlete runs his fastest race of the day in the relay, even though at its start he may have felt out of sorts or partially fatigued.
9. Conclude this important day in midseason with an easy jog. Analyze the daily fluctuations in body weight.

Late season. The characteristics of late season schedules of practice are a reduction in the intensity of the practices and the elimination of preparation for secondary events (those in which your competitive marks are inadequate to place in top-flight competition). In case the sprinter has been running 440 yards in the 1-mile relay, those practices pointed toward ¼-mile proficiency are omitted, thus avoiding loss of sprinting tone and cadence. Such a change in the plan does not mean that the sprinter is ill prepared for the relay but rather indicates that emphasis is placed primarily on the two sprint races and, after they are run, on the relay.

Earlier in the discussion the beginner was cautioned to beware of strains occasioned by a track which is wet in spots. However, he should become accustomed to a soggy cinder path so that he will not be a stranger to heavy footing. Some of the time trials should be run in the face of retarding winds. In running the 220-yard dash into a head wind, it is well to know how to distribute one's energy to best advantage.

In late season particularly and sometimes during midseason, the athlete participates in meets calling for both preliminary heats and semifinal rounds before he reaches the final race. The general rule is to forget the quality of opposition when competing in a final event. On the other hand, in trial heats the athlete may be permitted to conserve energy provided he has outstanding racing qualifications and a definite knowledge of both his own and his opponents' capabilities.

Conservation of effort is seldom made either at the start or in the first third of the trial heats. In the 100-yard dash especially, some first-ranking competitors attempt no energy saving. Instead they run the distance at optimum effort. On the contrary, in the 220-yard dash, they may, after obtaining a commanding position, aim to maintain this advantage without running at full effort.

It should be evident to the novice that he should know the regulations of the games committee pertaining to the number of places in each heat that will qualify him to participate in the advanced stage of the competition. Therefore, if three men in each preliminary heat qualify for the semifinals, he is taking chances when he lays back in

fourth position during the body of the sprint.

Although authorities are generally agreed that in midseason the degree of intensity of the practices should be reduced, there are several theories on the amount of starting drill with the pistol. Some believe that a number (5 to 8) of starts from the mark, stimulated by the pistol, should be taken after a thorough warm-up. They believe that such close contact with the event is necessary so that the athlete will maintain his sense of rhythm. They cite the daily practice of golfers, pianists, and billiard players to substantiate their claims.

Others believe that pistol starts should be reduced to a minimum, possibly 2 or 3 on only 1 day early in the week. Their objective is the conservation of both nervous and physical energy.

However, the majority of coaches favor a plan calling for starts, 4 to 6 in number, on either 2 or 3 days a week during late season. Certainly, individual differences must be recognized, and thus the solution lies with the competitor and the coach.

Monday

1. Review the correct as well as the incorrect phases of strategy and execution as manifested in your most recent competition. Snapshots or the reports of your observers are beneficial in case motion pictures are not available.
2. Limber up with 2 to 3 minutes of jogging and stretching exercises.
3. Execute 30 seconds of inverted running, noting your balance, rhythm, and parallel foot action and the path of the heel on the recovery step.
4. Warm up thoroughly and prepare for starting practice. Take 2 starts without the pistol and 2 with the pistol and sprint 30 yards.
5. Participate in an endless relay while carrying the baton. The distance run by each athlete may be either 55 or

110 yards. Repeat three or four times.
6. End the practice with 2 to 3 minutes of calisthenics and a jog of 220 yards.

Tuesday

1. Begin the practice with jogging, walking, running, and stretching.
2. Prepare for time trials of 80 yards and 200 yards, respectively, by completing your usual warm-up routine.
3. Set the starting blocks and make the necessary mental and physical adjustments. Run the 80-yard time trial (corresponding to 100 yards) at full effort.
4. Walk 440 yards, jog 100 yards, and then rest until the time trial of the 200-yard race (reduced from 220 yards) is called.
5. Warm up and run 200 yards at full speed, either spreading your effort evenly over the course or utilizing the coast during that section of the race which you have learned by experience is most beneficial. Many coaches believe that the coast is ideally executed when the athlete takes a semirest and to outward appearances makes no alteration in either running form or speed.
6. Conclude the workout with a jog of 250 yards.

Wednesday

1. Start the day with jogging, walking, stretching, and running exercises for a period of 5 to 10 minutes.
2. Practice inverted running for 2 intervals of 20 seconds each.
3. Set the starting blocks, warm up, take 2 starts without the pistol and 2 starts with the pistol. In each trial, travel a distance of 50 yards, running as follows: 30 yards at full speed, ease up 10 yards, then a burst of speed for the 10 yards to the finish yarn. Emphasize steadiness while in the set position so that you will be able to main-

tain an effective poise for a period of 1.5 seconds after the hips become steady. This interval represents the optimum holding time after the moment of steadiness. The interpretation of the track and field rules states that the holding interval should be approximately 2 seconds after the command "set" has been given. (See Chapter 15 under Optimum time for holding a sprinter on his mark; also Walker and Hayden.[10])
4. Take 6 to 8 sprints of 120 to 140 yards at 7/8 speed.
5. Terminate the practice with 2 to 3 minutes of free exercises and a jog of 300 yards.

Thursday

This day offers more freedom in the type and quantity of exercise. During late season, practice in the jump and weight events is omitted unless the sprinter has outstanding ability in them. Should he be called on to compete in a jump or weight contest, he will be required to alter both the Tuesday and Wednesday schedules to provide for them. No field event practice is prescribed for Thursday if trials are conducted on Friday.

1. Jog 150 yards, walk 50 yards, and run 100 yards.
2. Spend 4 or 5 minutes on varied exercises, such as stretching, bending, and leg flexing.
3. Take a sun bath for 10 minutes.
4. Jog 440 yards on the grass.
5. Divert the attention from things athletic by reading, studying, or attending an entertainment which is relaxing in nature.

Friday

Adjust your day's program so that you can carry on your routine affairs without undue fatigue, either mental or physical.

1. Ascertain the number of men to qualify, the number of your heat and lane,

and the exact hour of starting the sprint races.

2. Prepare for preliminary heats in the 100-yard dash by utilizing the knowledge gained from previous trials, which includes the timing, type, and duration of warm-up exercises. (For specific suggestions see early season, Saturday's schedule of practice.)

3. Run the trial heat in the 100 yards. Walk 100 yards, jog 100 yards, and then rest, awaiting the start of the 220-yard dash.

4. Learn the capabilities of your rivals in the trial heat of the 220-yard dash. If you have drawn a lane toward the outside, it is obvious that the first half of your race must be run at a speed approximating your best effort. When you reach the straightaway, you can then decide how to run the balance of the race.

5. Warm up and get in readiness for the trial heat in the 220-yard dash.

6. Walk 200 yards, and rest a few minutes before completing Friday's trials with a 220-yard jog, a shower, and a massage. Until Saturday's final contests, your main consideration is relaxation and the diversion of your thoughts from racing.

Saturday

1. Reassure yourself of the hour of starting your events and the lanes drawn. In the light of your experience in Friday's races, retain or substitute any equipment needed, such as the spikes or the shoes themselves.

2. Set the starting blocks, warm up, and conclude those adjustments of both mind and body which prepare one for an important race.

3. Think only of yourself, fix the attention on the act of starting, and sprint the 100-yard dash to the best of your ability.

4. Regain body composure by walking

or jogging and then rest in a place free from extremes in temperature. Massage is helpful to some sprinters before the first race, between races, and after the last race. Your personal desire is the guiding factor. The athlete is cautioned to drink water sparingly between races.

5. Follow your proved procedure in the time, type, and duration of the warmup for your second race of the day, the 220-yard dash.

6. Gain that degree of poise and balance so necessary at the start, and then race the 220 yards with a definite plan for distributing your energy.

7. Provided there is no relay race to run, walk 440 yards and then jog 200 yards to complete the day's activity.

REFERENCES

1. Westerlund, J. H., and Tuttle, W. W.: Relationship between running events in track and reaction time, Res. Quart., Am. A. Health, Phys. Ed. & Rec. 2:95, 1931.
2. Lautenbach, R., and Tuttle, W. W.: Relation between reflex time and running events in track, Res. Quart., Am. A. Health, Phys. Ed. & Rec. 3:138, 1932.
3. Bresnahan, G. T.: A study of the movement pattern in starting the race from the crouch position, Res. Quart., Am. A. Health, Phys. Ed. & Rec. 5 (supp. 1):5, 1934.
4. Dickinson, A. D.: The effect of foot spacing on starting time and speed in sprinting and the relation of physical measurements to foot spacing, Res. Quart., Am. A. Health, Phys. Ed. & Rec. 5 (supp. 1):12, 1934.
5. Sills, F. D., and Pennybaker, D. A.: A method of measuring the velocity of speed of movement with a cathode ray oscillograph, Proc. Twenty-Second Annual Convention, Central District Association for Health, Physical Education and Recreation, p. 24, 1956.
6. Sills, F. D., and Carter, J. E. L.: Measurement of velocity for sprint start, Proc. Seventy-Fourth Annual Convention, American Association for Health, Physical Education and Recreation, Research Section, 1959.
7. Rapp., K. E.: Running-velocity: body-rise and stride-length, M.A. Thesis, State University of Iowa, 1963.
8. White, Ray A.: The effect of hip elevation on starting time in the sprint, Res. Quart., Am.

A. Health, Phys. Ed. & Rec. **5** (supp. 1):128, 1935.

9. Felkner, A. H.: A study of the respiratory habits of sprinters in starting a race, Res. Quart., Am. A. Health, Phys. Ed. & Rec. **5** (supp. 1):20, 1934.
10. Walker, G. A., and Hayden, T. C.: The optimum time for holding a sprinter between the "set" and the stimulus (gun shot), Res. Quart., Am. A. Health, Phys. Ed. & Rec. 4:124, 1933.
11. Kistler, J. W.: A study of the distribution of force exerted upon the blocks in the starting of the sprint from various starting positions, Res. Quart., Am. A. Health, Phys. Ed. & Rec. **5** (supp. 1):27, 1934.
12. Carson, G.: The effect of the intensity of the stimulus on starting time, Athletic J. **15**:13, 1935.
13. Tuttle, W. W., and Bresnahan, G. T.: The relation and duration of the application of force to the body by the legs at the start of the sprint (unpublished data).

Chapter 5

The middle distance runs

For the purpose of this discussion, middle distance races include any running event which falls between 300 yards and 1,000 yards. The distances most frequently run are 440 yards and 880 yards. The metric equivalents to these middle distance runs used in Olympic and international competition are the 400-meter (437.45-yard) and the 800-meter (874.90-yard) races. Although a sharp line cannot be drawn between sprinting and middle distance running, there are differences which demand special consideration. The same thing holds true in separating the longer middle distance events from the distance runs.

There are numerous ways of laying out the course for the middle distance runs. The chief factor which determines the plan is the amount of space available. The most common variations in types of courses are as follows:

Outdoor oval track
1. 440 yards (1 complete circuit)
2. 880 yards (2 complete circuits)

Outdoor straightaway and oval track
1. 440 yards (1 straightaway and 1 turn)
2. 880 yards (1 straightaway and 3 turns)

Indoor track (6 to 16 laps per mile)

GENERAL CONSIDERATIONS

Types of competitors. Since the 440-yard run is primarily a sprint and the 880-yard event approximates distance running, one finds almost all sizes and types of runners in these events. For the most part, however, they vary in height from 5 feet 8 inches to 6 feet 2 inches and in weight from 145 pounds to 180 pounds.

Qualifications. An ideal middle distance runner is one who possesses the speed of a sprinter and the endurance of a distance runner. It seems logical to suppose that sprinters entering the middle distance events experience little difficulty in adjusting themselves, since in the acquisition of speed they have developed some degree of endurance as well. It must be recognized, however, that many distance runners have developed into successful middle distance performers. As one changes from a sprinter to a middle distance runner, it must be borne in mind that nearly the same emphasis must be placed on speed, and additional weight must be given endurance.

Whenever a race is long enough to demand special emphasis on endurance, the problem of energy distribution immediately becomes an important factor. This requires that the middle distance runner know how to spread his effort over the entire course, not only in the light of his own energy capacity but also on the basis of the way in which the opponent distributes his effort.

A successful middle distance runner must possess rhythmic striding action. The ability to synchronize leg and arm action is fully as important in this style of running as in sprinting.

Endurance involves the development of strong muscles and hardy vital organs. Through systematic training a condition must be developed in which the cardiorespiratory system is capable of adjusting adequately to the added strain brought about by an increase in distance. The longer distances should not be regarded as harmful if the contestant is physically ready for prolonged exertion.

Regardless of the physical condition acquired by a middle distance runner and regardless of the fact that he is able to run a race without experiencing a sensation of extreme fatigue, he may be called on to run when he is conscious of being tired. Even though a runner has a definite plan of effort distribution, his method of attack may, of necessity, have to be altered since an opponent may place him at a disadvantage by employing an unexpected type of strategy. A change of energy distribution which brings about a sensation of fatigue calls for mental as well as physical adjustments. A tired runner, by sheer determination, may save his race.

Comparative marks in competition. Similar to the plans for other events discussed in this book, comparative marks for scholastic competitors in the middle distance runs are shown in Table 5-1.

Attention is directed to the fact that the times listed are suggested placing times and not winning times. Furthermore, it is recognized that the times in the performance table will not apply to areas where the caliber of the competition is either very high or very low.

Equipment. The middle distance runner must give special attention to footwear. The ordinary sprinting shoe is commonly worn. Because a constant strain is placed

Table 5-1. Comparative marks for scholastic competitors in the middle distance runs

Meet	No. of places scored	440 yards (sec.)	880 yards (min.:sec.)
Dual high school	3	50.0-52.0	2:00-2:04
Qualifying—state	3	49.0-50.5	1:58-2:00
State—province	5	48.5-49.7	1:56-1:59

on the shoe, the contestant in middle distance races, as well as in all other running events, should reassure himself of its fit, strength, and reliability.

TECHNIQUE OF THE MIDDLE DISTANCE RUNS

Since the shorter middle distance runs border on sprinting and the longer middle distance events take on more of the aspects of distance competition, it seems logical that middle distance running technique falls somewhat between sprinting and distance running.

As previously suggested, endurance becomes more and more a problem as the distance covered becomes longer. Furthermore, the increased importance of endurance necessitates a more careful consideration of judgment of pace.

Since middle distance races may be started from a crouch position with the aid of starting blocks, the discussion of the start of the sprint applies here. Similarly, the principles involved in the starting and the transitional strides for sprint races are essentially the same for middle distance running.

Full-speed strides. The middle distance full-speed stride is varied somewhat since the conservation of energy, as well as the distribution of effort, is a factor to be considered. As contrasted to sprinting, the following differences and similarities are pointed out.

Cadence. The cadence is slower in middle distance running.

Stride length. There is a conscious effort to maintain an optimum length stride. (Normally the optimum stride is somewhat shorter than in sprinting.)

Trunk angle. The trunk angle (from a vertical position) is less. It averages approximately 15 degrees (Fig. 5-1, A) as contrasted to 25 degrees in sprinting (Fig. 4-4, A).

Knee lift. The knee lift of the recovery leg is less pronounced (Fig. 5-1, A).

Driving leg. The extension of the driving leg is less vicious.

Arm action. The arm action is less tense, and the arms may rightfully be carried lower.

Landing. The runner has a greater tendency toward a ball-heel landing of the recovery leg in the middle distance runs.

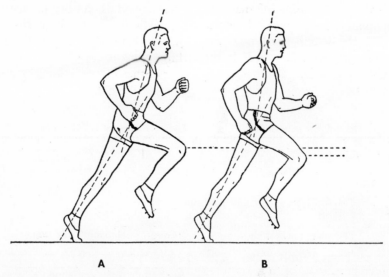

Fig. 5-1. The full-speed stride in middle distance and distance running. **A,** Middle distance. **B,** Distance.

Although he lands on the ball of the foot, he lets down on the heel to the extent that the heel touches the ground.

Hands. The hands are cupped in a relaxed manner.

Breathing. Breathing is through both the mouth and nose, the same as in sprinting.

Shoulder girdle. Shoulder girdle muscular fixation is less tense during middle distance races.

Finish. At the finish of the stride, there is a higher lift of the heel in middle distance running.

Obviously the adjustments in the full-speed strides, which the middle distance runner makes, are designed to permit him to function as a smooth, efficient mechanism and at the same time to develop the optimum amount of speed. In meeting the challenges of opponents, the middle distance runner alters the form of the full-speed stride in the direction of sprinting form, reverting back again after the challenges has been met.

Coast. As previously pointed out in the races of 220 yards or more, a period in which the runner gains a semirest through further muscular relaxation is designated as the coast. By practice the athlete is able to coast for a time without loss of form and without apparent loss of speed. By referring to Fig. 5-2, the beginner will note that coasting is indicated after 225 yards in the

440-yard run and after 450 yards in the 880-yard event. It must be recognized that such factors as maneuvering for position at the start or meeting challenges of opponents make a shifting of the coast necessary. The runner must coast somewhere in the race, and he must learn by experience how to adjust its place of execution in the light of the requirements of any given event.

Finish. When the middle distance runner reaches the last 25 percent or 20 percent of his race, striding at full effort is begun and continued until the finish yarn is reached. An ideal race is one in which the energy has been so spread that when the runner reaches the finish yarn his resources are well spent. Nature in her goodness provides recuperative powers as well as protective mechanisms so that no harm can come to the middle distance runner who is endowed with a normal, well-trained body.

RACING FUNDAMENTALS

If one is to be more than an average middle distance runner, he must not only be well trained and in condition but must also be grounded thoroughly in racing fundamentals. Ability to size up situations quickly and correctly as they arise and to conduct one's race on fundamentally sound principles are assets to any runner. Some of

440 yard run

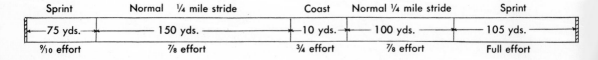

Sprint	Normal ¼ mile stride	Coast	Normal ¼ mile stride	Sprint
75 yds.	150 yds.	10 yds.	100 yds.	105 yds.
$^9/_{10}$ effort	$^7/_8$ effort	¾ effort	$^7/_8$ effort	Full effort

Start

880 yard run

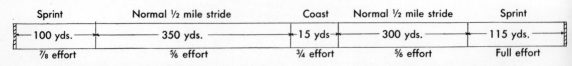

Sprint	Normal ½ mile stride	Coast	Normal ½ mile stride	Sprint
100 yds.	350 yds.	15 yds	300 yds.	115 yds.
$^7/_8$ effort	$^5/_6$ effort	¾ effort	$^5/_6$ effort	Full effort

Fig. 5-2. An effort distribution chart for beginners in the 440-yard and 880-yard runs.

the points which must be considered are discussed.

Knowledge of opponents. Although worry over the ability of one's rivals should be dispensed with, a healthy respect for them is desirable. There is a happy medium between overconfidence and underconfidence. It is well to have a fairly accurate knowledge of the sprinting ability, the amount of endurance, and the customary racing procedure followed by one's opponents. This information is of special importance when the athlete accepts an assignment to run two races. It is possible frequently to complete the first task staying well within the limit of endurance, thereby holding something in reserve for the second contest. However, should the rival show unusual improvement in his race, the athlete should be in readiness to accept the challenge even if it is necessary to draw on reserve energy.

Some of the questions concerning a rival that should be considered are as follows:

1. How many yards does he sprint at the start?
2. Does he run better when leading? When trailing?
3. When will he respond to a challenge? At the start, in the middle, or toward the end of the race?
4. How far can he carry the final sprint? 100 yards? 150 yards? 200 yards?

Shape of the course. The most commonly used track plans employed for middle distance running are as follows (see also Chapter 17, Fig. 17-1):

Straightaway and oval track
1. Occasionally competitors are placed abreast on the starting line at the head of the straightaway (Chapter 17, Fig. 17-1); individual lanes not employed

Oval track only
1. Competitors placed abreast on the starting line (Chapter 17, Fig. 17-1); individual lanes not employed
2. Competitors staggered on the starting line; individual lanes employed around the first turn only
3. Competitors staggered on the starting line; individual lanes employed for the entire distance (880 yards excepted)

Energy distribution and pace judgment. Whenever a race is run in lanes, a competitor's chief concern is with his energy distribution and the pace adjustment of his rivals. Where a lane for each athlete is not provided, the competitor must give attention not only to his distribution of energy and the opponents' spread of speed but also to the direction of his path. He should bear in mind that there are a number of conditions which will require alterations in the predetermined spread of energy. Changes in the plan of the race are necessary if an opponent does as follows:

1. Carries a prolonged sprint at the start. This means that if the danger line is observed speed must be increased in spite of a plan to the contrary. The runner is cautioned against accepting a pace at the start which is out of proportion to sound racing fundamentals. He should not be pulled away too fast by either an exceptional runner or one who is inexperienced in the distribution of effort.
2. Obtains the lead and pole position. Should the opponent in front appreciably reduce the pace, the runner must either do likewise or run around him.
3. Gets directly in front and another opponent gets directly at the runner's right. This requires that he either accept the rate of speed set by the leader or drop back and attempt to run around all opponents. This is known as being boxed in.

Speed at beginning of race. The rate of speed at the beginning of a race depends on the following.

Athlete's ability. The athlete must observe a speed at the beginning of the race which falls within his ability to carry out his plan of attack. A prolonged burst of speed by an opponent usually need not be met, since the rival will experience the necessity of adopting a slower pace somewhere else in the race unless he has exceptional ability.

Staggered or abreast start. If the start is staggered, the athlete must run the beginning of the race according to a predetermined plan, avoiding the danger line as best he can.

Position drawn. When running abreast, if a position is drawn near the pole, the objective is to retain his advantage. If a position toward the outside of the track is drawn, the athlete should run straight ahead at his optimum pace, and then through peripheral vision locate the field so that he may legitimately (refrain from interfering with the opponent's stride) cut to the inside.

Distance to the first turn. The shorter the distance to the first turn, the faster must be the initial speed.

Behavior of opponents. The runner must be ready for emergencies such as body contact with competitors at his right when they are in the act of cutting for the pole position and meeting the challenge of an opponent who speeds up his initial sprint in his determination to get the lead. Through experience a runner learns how to meet these, as well as other, exigencies.

Maneuvering for position. Maneuvering for position depends on the price a runner is willing to pay to obtain either the lead or a desirable running order. As a general rule, he relinquishes the try if the continued sprint taxes his reserve strength so necessary in the later stages of the contest. He cannot be branded as a quitter if he refuses to squander valuable reserve energy in the early stages of the race.

Danger line. Frequently it is neither possible nor desirable to be out in front all through a race. However, it must be remembered that, if two quarter-milers have approximately the same ability, one must not permit the other to lead by more than 6 or 7 yards if he expects to win the race. This is commonly called the danger line. For the 880-yard race this distance ranges from 12 to 15 yards. The closer one runs to an opponent, the better able he is to apprehend any changes in racing tactics. Obviously, the smaller the lead allowed an opponent, the less will be the handicap to overcome when making the final bid for victory.

Passing an opponent. The problem of passing an opponent must be solved in the light of both the stage of the race and whether it is to be done on either a straight stretch or on a curve. It is not considered poor strategy to run around an opponent even on a curve when this act can be accomplished by expending no more than normal effort. The element of surprise is important when overtaking and passing a rival.

In the middle of a race the athlete may be required to speed up beyond his predetermined rate, run around the rival, and then resume his customary pace.

In the late stages of the race, the runner, in order to gain his objective, is frequently required to increase his cadence, to be prepared for a counterchallenge, and then to maintain a dash to the finish at a rate considerably faster than that originally planned. Passing is costly, and the runner must be prepared to pay the price. In case the athlete in attempting to pass an opponent does not succeed in getting around him, he should remain outside the opponent's right shoulder so as to be in readiness for another bid for the lead. Should he drop directly behind his opponent, he may be vulnerable to being boxed in.

An athlete is said to use good judgment when in the act of reducing a lead he closes the gap gradually and initiates his passing spurt at the beginning of a straight stretch.

This permits the maximum distance in which to challenge and meet a counterchallenge before reaching the next curve.

Meeting a challenge. The first challenge to which a middle distance runner is exposed is at the start of the race. He is then challenged by a majority of his opponents, since the common objective consists of gaining either the lead or a desirable running place. Being with the leaders in the early stages of the contest demands that the runner carry the pace. On the other hand, an athlete who plans his race so as to conserve his energy at the start will elect to reject the challenge and adopt a slower cadence.

The next potential challenge may occur anywhere in the body of the race. Ordinarily after about one-fourth of the race has been run, the passing tactics of a rival may be ignored if the athlete is running at his optimum rate of speed. By meeting such a challenge, a runner's plans may be disrupted completely, since it might require him to expend an excessive amount of energy. The disastrous effects of such a move will be manifest in the closing moments of the race. The athlete must increase his pace to keep ahead of or abreast of an opponent, provided the pace does not exceed his most effective running style. Again, extra energy may have to be expended so as to ward off the oncoming rival, especially if the challenge occurs just before a curve. An opponent who gets the lead just before a curve is reached may elect immediately to reduce his cadence to a coasting effort. Since this may not fit with the athlete's plan of running, he will either have to accept this condition or pass his rival on the curve. Moreover, failure to speed up may result in his being pinched off by two or more rivals as the field swings around the curve.

The general plan is for the athlete to accept all challenges in the last one-fourth of the race if he expects to win.

A well-trained runner must know how to distribute his energy most economically, and he must not let this distribution be disrupted by meeting challenges at inopportune moments.

Maintaining the stride. The maintenance of smooth running form throughout the contest is obviously a laudable ambition. If this is to be accomplished, the runner must be ready for those emergencies which tend to throw him out of stride. For example, if the runners start abreast and scramble for the first curve, unavoidable contact with rivals should be anticipated. A better defensive body balance is provided if the strides are short and rapid.

During the body of the race it may be advantageous for the athlete to run to the outside of one or more opponents who are carrying an uneven or uncertain pace, thus leaving him free to proceed at an even rate. In some instances, during the body of a race, the runner may correctly decide to "ride" at an opponent's outside shoulder, even when running around a curve. He elects this alternative in preference to breaking his stride by dropping in behind the opponent on the pole. An outside position may also be an advantage to a third-position runner since he can see better and judge the activities of the leader. Toward the end of the contest, smart racing tactics may demand that the athlete cover the entire last curve to the outside of an opponent so that an even stride and full speed may be maintained. In the closing yards of a race, the axiom, "Any old port in a storm," must be remembered if the runner is to have any hopes of winning. Once he has started his final sprint for the finish line, maximum effort should be continued without easing up until the finish line has been crossed. He cannot take for granted that the opponent he has recently passed no longer offers a threat. Good running form is as important toward the end of the race as it is during the early stages.

Distribution of energy. Perhaps the ideal way to run a middle distance race would be to maintain a uniform cadence and length of stride over the entire distance once the body has been accelerated from the crouch start to optimum speed. However, this ideal is seldom, if ever, attained, because of both the physical limitations of the athlete and the counterplans of the opponents.

On the basis of physical limitations, Fig. 5-2 is presented for the beginner. This shows in general how the energy may be distributed effectively for both the 440-yard and the 880-yard runs. This chart is designed for the novice who has never run the distance and who has no background for determining how fast he can run. After he has become more experienced and knows, for example, what a 60-second quarter-mile means, he may then make use of Table 5-2 for the 440-yard race and Table 5-3 for the 880-yard race. We recognize the difficulty of acquiring scientific data upon which to base recommendations for the most economic distribution of energy. The elapsed times presented are based on stop watch readings made on runners of varying ability competing under a variety of conditions. We believe that the plans presented provide at least a temporary structure around which a runner can build permanently.

It must be remembered that a rival may cause a runner to alter any energy distribution plan which he may adopt. Nevertheless, a runner need not be "run off his feet" by the extra rapid pace of an opponent, nor need he accept an unusually slow gait.

The athlete must bear in mind that he should carry out the plan that is most effective. The repeated challenging of opponents, necessitating changing rates of speed, detracts from rhythmic running and brings on fatigue prematurely.

SCHEDULES OF PRACTICE

In presenting suggested schedules of practice for middle distance running, exercises for developing speed are stressed al-

Table 5-2. The 440-yard run showing the elapsed time at specified division points of the race*

At 110 yards		At 220 yards		
Proportional time (sec.)	Elapsed time (sec.)	Proportional time (sec.)	Elapsed time (sec.)	Total time (sec.)
15.0	14.2	30	28.0	60
14.5	13.7	29	27.2	58
14.0	13.3	28	26.3	56
13.5	12.8	27	25.4	54
13.0	12.3	26	24.5	52
12.5	11.8	25	23.6	50
12.0	11.4	24	22.6	48
11.5	11.1	23	21.7	46
11.25	10.7	22.5	21.3	45
11.0	10.6	22.0	21.0	44

*The competitor's objective speed is shown in the last column.
Proportional time, as indicated in Tables 5-2 and 5-3, is defined as that interval required to reach a designated point should the runner's rate of speed be uniform from the start to the finish. For example, the athlete setting his goal at a 60-second 440-yard race, and running at an even speed would pass the 110-yard post in 15 seconds and the 220-yard post in 30 seconds. However, in reality, races are seldom run according to such a plan. The runner setting out to run 440 yards in 60 seconds distributes his energy so that his time at 110 yards is 14.2 seconds (elapsed time), and at 220 yards it is 28 seconds.

most as much as in sprinting. However, more work is included for the purpose of developing endurance. It is recognized also that pace judgment is more important than in the sprints because the element of fatigue must be met.

The reader is advised that the schedules of practice herewith presented are designed as guides and may be altered to fit individual needs. For example, some runners may require more endurance work than that suggested, whereas others may profit by more speed work.

Some coaches believe that their athletes benefit by the use of at least certain sections of the Fartlek system (speed play). This system has been employed by athletes in certain European countries as a basic schedule of practice. A sample program conforming to this system is found in Chapter 1, p. 7. The Fartlek schedule of practice may be established by the athlete himself, and since it is optional in nature, he determines the distance, speed, and duration of practice sessions. Many European athletes are self-taught, especially in areas where a coach is not available. A few American middle distance runners of prominence have adopted the system in its entirety, and others have made use of certain of its selected phases.

There is much that can be said in commendation of the self-taught athlete who is willing to pay the price for success and adheres faithfully to the Fartlek system. Frequently he is obliged to practice either alone or with a limited number of teammates at an unusual location and at odd hours, in case he is gainfully employed during the day. If he desires to obtain the benefit of a stop watch to aid in developing judgment of pace, he is required to carry it with him.

There is abundant evidence that the Fartlek system has proved beneficial to many athletes, and for that reason it is discussed.

The optional feature of the Fartlek system has been applied for years by coaches

Table 5-3. The 880-yard run showing the elapsed time at specified division points of the race*

At 220 yards		At 440 yards		At 660 yards		
Proportional time (sec.)	Elapsed time (sec.)	Proportional time (sec.)	Elapsed time (sec.)	Proportional time (min.:sec.)	Elapsed time (min.:sec.)	Total time (min.:sec.)
35.0	32.0	70.0	68.0	1:45.0	1:44.0	2:20
34.0	31.0	68.0	66.0	1:42.0	1:41.0	2:16
32.5	29.5	65.0	63.0	1:37.5	1:36.6	2:10
31.0	28.0	62.0	60.0	1:33.0	1:32.2	2:04
30.0	27.0	60.0	58.0	1:30.0	1:29.3	2:00
29.5	26.6	59.0	57.0	1:28.5	1:27.9	1:58
29.0	26.2	58.0	56.1	1:27.0	1:26.5	1:56
28.5	25.8	57.0	55.2	1:25.5	1:25.1	1:54
28.0	25.6	56.0	54.3	1:24.0	1:23.6	1:52
27.5	25.4	55.0	53.4	1:22.5	1:22.1	1:50
27.25	25.0	54.5	53.0	1:21.75	1:21.6	1:49
27.0	24.7	54.0	52.5	1:21.0	1:20.7	1:48
26.5	24.4	53.0	51.4	1:19.5	1:18.9	1:46
26.0	24.3	52.0	50.9	1:18.0	1:17.2	1:44

*The competitor's objective speed is shown in the last column. (For an interpretation, see footnote to Table 5-2.)

the world over, and in America especially, it is incorporated frequently in the schedule of practice for the Monday or Tuesday following week-end competition. A lesser number of American coaches have permitted the athletes a voice in setting both the amount and intensity of their practice activities on the Thursday (or Wednesday) preceding week-end contests.

Some American coaches who favor the Fartlek system for 1-mile and 2-mile runners hesitate to recommend it for athletes specializing in the 880-yard run. Other coaches who make use of the system for longer races do not prescribe it for 440-yard specialists, possibly because they fear an adverse effect on the speed of the athlete.

The Fartlek system emphasizes periods of walking and jogging between the vigorous sections of the workout. This semirest feature has been approved generally by coaches for many years. A turf running course, because of its springy nature, is recommended in the Fartlek system, and again this feature is considered desirable by the majority of coaches.

Athletes in American schools and colleges encounter difficulty in adopting the Fartlek system in its entirety for several reasons. The path or terrain recommended for the system is not readily available, especially in metropolitan areas. In addition, the limited period of time permitted the average American athlete for daily practice may prevent him from completing the Fartlek routine.

The desire of the runner to practice with other athletes rather than alone is an additional factor. It appears that only a limited number of athletes possess the emotional or temperamental qualities necessary to extend oneself in solo practice, a time when other stimuli are lacking.

Some European coaches who favor the Fartlek system have "rejected the American opinion that the runners should have a fixed distance to run in their daily training sched-ule," and contend that the American plan does not "give the boys a feeling of self-creating . . . and training according to their own individuality." "American opinion" is difficult to isolate when one reviews the varied methods successfully employed in developing runners, some of which recognize the wishes of the competitor when arranging a daily workout.

Even though schedules of practice prescribed by American coaches indicate definite distances to be run, they are not as inflexible as some critics think. Very few coaches enforce practice plans that are out of harmony with the wishes of their athletes.

Referring to the criticism of fixed distances, perhaps American coaches advocate the use of the stop watch more frequently than do European coaches; hence they record elapsed time at definite distances. This does not mean that on each occasion when a stop watch is held on a runner during practice he is obliged to run at full effort. Instead, the purpose is to aid the runner's judgment of pace and distribution of energy, even though interval running is employed.

There are days when no stop watch readings are taken and the runner is free to concentrate on those phases of his event which he selects. Nevertheless, on the day of competition the distance of the race he runs is definitely fixed, such as 440 yards, 880 yards, 1 mile, 2, or 3 miles.

Early season. This follows the preliminary season schedule (see p. 12). Early season practices are planned for 6 days of the week on the presumption that no contests have been scheduled for the week end. Further changes are obligatory whenever the athlete is on a 5-day schedule. Ordinarily, speed and endurance are stressed on alternate days. Stop watch readings may be taken during both types of practice so that the athlete may learn to gauge accurately his running time over fractional parts of the total distance, such as 110 yards, 220 yards,

440 yards, and 660 yards (Tables 5-2 and 5-3).

The athlete should determine the most effective warm-up for his use—one that will be applicable to each day's practice in early season, midseason, and late season for the middle distance runs. The following typical warm-up can be adjusted so as to meet the needs of each athlete:

1. Jog 660 to 880 yards.
2. For a period of 5 to 10 minutes engage in bending and stretching exercises.
3. Run a distance of approximately 150 yards and increase the physical output to about $7/8$ effort. Repeat 4 to 6 times. Stress relaxation and running form.

In subsequent daily schedules of practice, it is expected that the middle distance runner will have prepared himself, through the warm-up, for the specific activities suggested.

At the end of each day's practice, all track athletes should spend 5 to 10 minutes in slow jogging and gradually reduce the amount of effort expended.

Whenever one engages in interval running, careful consideration should be given to the intervals between the sectors of running. The athlete should establish either a "minutes" objective for each interval of jogging or a fixed distance to cover in each interval of jogging. For example, the athlete at first may elect to jog 440 yards between each sector of running. As soon as his physical condition improves, he may choose either to increase the speed of the jog or to reduce the distance of the jog. If he chooses the "minutes" objective plan for the early practices, he may jog for a period of 4 minutes during the intervals. As soon as he becomes more proficient, he may decide to reduce the jogging time to 3 minutes, 2 minutes, or possibly 1 minute. He should strive to keep moving, even though this movement is simply a slow shuffle. The interval running activities should be repeated as many times as the condition of the athlete requires.

Monday

1. Record the body weight both before and after each day's practice.
2. Engage in either the Fartlek system of exercises for a period of 20 to 30 minutes (see p. 7) and/or interval running that consists in running 4 to 6 sectors of 440 yards each, timed at 75 seconds, and interspersed with 3-minute to 4-minute intervals of jogging.
3. Practice sprinting on the straightaway over distances of 120 to 140 yards. Repeat 3 or 4 times. Emphasize both running form and relaxation.
4. Spend 15 to 30 minutes on weight-training and/or tension exercises (see pp. 8 and 11).

Tuesday

1. Run 6 to 8 sectors of 220 yards each at a rate of 32 to 35 seconds. Include a 2-minute interval of jogging between each running sector.
2. Practice the visual method of baton passing 4 to 6 times (see Relay racing, Chapter 7).
3. Execute an optional number of sprints at distances ranging from 100 to 150 yards.

Wednesday

1. Make use of interval running. Run 6 to 8 sectors of 440 yards (72 to 75 seconds each) interspersed with 3 to 4 minutes of jogging.
2. Sprint 100 to 150 yards. Repeat 3 or 4 times.
3. Participate in weight-training and/or tension exercises for a period of 15 to 30 minutes.

Thursday

1. Run 880 yards in 2 minutes, 30 seconds.

2. Jog for a period of 5 to 7 minutes.
3. Run 660 yards within a time range of 1 minute, 45 seconds to 1 minute, 50 seconds.
4. Run 440 yards at $\frac{7}{8}$ effort.
5. If further practice is found desirable, run a distance of 220 yards in 30 to 32 seconds and repeat 3 to 5 times.
6. Sprint 50 to 60 yards and repeat twice.

Friday

Friday's practice should not be extremely fatiguing because Saturday's practice will be strenuous.

1. The quarter-milers will run 330 yards as follows: run the first, third, and fifth 55 yards at $\frac{7}{8}$ effort and the second, fourth, and sixth 55 yards at $\frac{3}{4}$ effort.
2. The half-milers will run 660 yards as follows: run the first, third, and fifth 110 yards at $\frac{7}{8}$ effort and the second, fourth, and sixth 110 yards at $\frac{3}{4}$ effort.

These practices are designed to develop the knack of alternations in pace. During this practice note the degree of knee lift (Fig. 5-1, A) and the height of the heel at the moment it passes under the body (Fig. 4-4).

Saturday

Note the conditions under which you will be required to compete: (1) the starting alignment (abreast or staggered), (2) the lane position drawn or assigned, (3) the direction and velocity of the wind, and (4) the racing habits of opponents. For an acceptable method of distributing energy, the athlete is referred to Table 5-2 for the 440-yard run and Table 5-3 for the 880-yard run.

1. Warm up with the quantity and type of exercises that will fit you for competitive racing conditions. This rests with the individual, and he learns by experience. A suggested warm-up procedure before competition is as follows:
   a. Jog 800 yards.

b. Walk 100 yards.
   c. Run 100 yards at $\frac{3}{4}$ effort.
   d. Spend 5 to 8 minutes on varied exercises, exerting only moderate effort. These may include stretching, bounding, bending, skipping, and similar mild forms of calisthenics.
   e. Stride 300 yards, the first 100 yards, at $\frac{1}{2}$ effort, the second 100 yards, at $\frac{3}{4}$ effort, and the last 100 yards at $\frac{9}{10}$ effort.
   f. Set the starting blocks and run 30 yards at top speed. Repeat once.
   g. Conclude this section of the warm-up 15 to 20 minutes in advance of the race, stay off the feet, and retain body warmth.
   h. Five to 8 minutes before the race is called, reassure yourself of the correct starting procedure and stride out 50 yards at top speed.
   i. Practice deep breathing immediately before assuming the starters ready position.
2. Plan to distribute your effort wisely. Take the mark, observing the same technique recommended for a sprinter. The baton may be carried so as to become accustomed to it.
3. Quarter-milers run 330 yards, emphasizing pace judgment. Half-milers run 660 yards, emphasizing pace judgment.
4. Relax for a period of 20 to 30 minutes but keep moving.
5. Quarter-milers run 220 yards at a pace comparable to the first 220 yards of the 440-yard race and emphasize relaxation and running form. Half-milers run 440 yards at a pace comparable to the first 440 yards of the 880-yard race and likewise emphasize relaxation and running form.
6. Walk and jog for a period of 10 to 15 minutes.
7. After an adequate warm-up, the half-milers will run 440 yards at $\frac{9}{10}$ effort, and the quarter-milers 220 yards at $\frac{9}{10}$ effort.

8. Conclude the day's practice with 10 to 15 minutes of jogging.

Midseason. The middle distance runner, as well as other track and field athletes, is benefitted by retaining a fair degree of condition by regular workouts throughout the year. Hasty and strenuous preparation at the last minute is less desirable than a gradual and moderate building-up period. Practice during the fall, winter, and early spring on distances beyond those required in his races will provide the athlete with stamina and endurance. Experimentation on changes in running form, such as the degree of trunk lean or the length of the stride, should be made in the off season or else during the periods of preliminary and early season practices. The majority of coaches are aware of individual differences existing in candidates for a given event and therefore adjust the practice schedules accordingly.

Therefore, when midseason arrives and meets are scheduled on each week end, the contestant who has systematically prepared himself through workouts of progressive intensity may well concentrate on the more advanced phases of racing. Speed and judgment of pace are stressed, although endurance is not to be ignored.

Midseason heavy duty workouts customarily are scheduled early in the week. They are designed either to select the personnel of the team or to provide a dress rehearsal for competition. Whenever a meet is scheduled for Friday, these strenuous workouts usually are conducted not later than Wednesday. Many coaches prefer to conclude vigorous practices on Thursday when the contest is not held until Saturday.

There are numerous plans for conducting heavy duty workouts in the middle distance runs (for example, on Tuesday), and the following are five suggested alternatives:

1. Engage in interval running, which consists of speedy sectors of 110, 220, 330, or 440 yards interspersed with jogging. As the athlete improves, he can decrease the length of time allotted to jogging. Repeat as many times as the condition of the athlete requires.

2. Run less than the racing distance at overspeed (330 or 660 yards). Rest 10 minutes. Run either 110 or 220 yards at full effort.

3. Run more than the racing distance at $9/10$ effort (660 yards or $3/4$ mile). Rest 5 to 10 minutes. Sprint 100 yards.

4. Run 50 percent of the racing distance at full effort. Walk, jog slowly, or rest for 15 to 20 minutes. Repeat once. Walk or jog for 5 to 10 minutes. Conclude with a sprint of 220 yards.

5. Run the distance of the race at full effort (440 or 880 yards). Walk or jog slowly for 15 to 20 minutes. Finish the practice with either 110 or 220 yards at full effort.

Experimentation is necessary before one can decide the most effective type of workout. It should be evident to the novice that these plans are not rigid and may be varied to suit his requirements.

Plan 1 may be utilized for the purpose of developing endurance, coupled with speed, by means of repetitive activities. The athlete learns to drive a tiring body and at the same time to retain acceptable running form during the late stages of the race. Furthermore, this type of practice provides variety and thus reduces the chance of boredom. The inclusion of alternative distances (110, 220, 330, and 440 yards) requires that the athlete learn variations in effort, cadence, and racing tactics. Stop watch readings may be announced if they aid either the athlete or the coach.

Plan 2 emphasizes speed and at the same time aims to teach conservation of energy. The term "overspeed" indicates that the cadence is more rapid than that employed when running the exact racing distance. Numerous coaches advocate this plan because they believe it enhances speed, judgment of pace, and ability to repeat. Should the athlete require additional drill on endurance, he may, after walking or jogging for 15 minutes, swing through a third sector of vigorous practice by sprinting 220 yards.

Plan 3 is designed for the athlete who wishes to emphasize endurance, such as the sprinter who is desirous of competing in the middle distance runs. The fractional designation of $\frac{9}{10}$ effort means that the competitor runs in practice exerting but $\frac{9}{10}$ the normal effort employed while running in competition the distance selected.

Plan 4 lays stress on developing ability to carry a pace faster than that required for a particular middle distance event. After experiencing the superspeed method in practice, during the race the athlete should be able to carry the normal pace apparently with less effort. Following a rest period of about 20 minutes, he may not have recovered fully and may feel some degree of fatigue. The second and third vigorous sectors of the workout assume that some fatigue is evident and are designed to prove to the athlete that he can execute a creditable performance even though he is somewhat tired. Furthermore, this type of workout gives further proof of the need for an adequate warm-up in advance of the first contest of the day.

Plan 5 is suggested for the athlete requiring drill on the precise method of running the full racing distance, and during this practice stop watch readings may be announced at its successive stages. The exact distance of the race is run in practice whenever the coach is obliged to make a team position choice between evenly matched athletes. This plan has a potential disadvantage in that some athletes who run all out in practice early in the week may not be able to recover sufficiently by the time of week-end competition.

Monday

1. Utilize the type of warm-up that has proved to be the most effective.
2. Engage in the Fartlek system of exercises for a period of 20 to 30 minutes.

3. Quarter-milers run 660 yards at a pace ranging from $\frac{7}{8}$ to $\frac{9}{10}$ effort. Half-milers run $\frac{3}{4}$ mile at a pace ranging from $\frac{7}{8}$ to $\frac{9}{10}$ effort.
4. Walk and jog for a period of 10 minutes.
5. Establish a fixed interval for rest periods between sectors, and then run 220 yards 4 times at $\frac{3}{4}$ to $\frac{7}{8}$ your racing pace.
6. Sprint ($\frac{9}{10}$ effort) distances ranging from 100 to 150 yards. Repeat 3 or 4 times. Learn to run when you are partially fatigued.
7. Conclude the practice with weight-training exercises and tension exercises in case they have proved helpful.

Tuesday

1. After warming up, take 3 or 4 sprint starts (without use of the pistol) and 4 starts with the pistol.
2. Engage in one of the suggested plans indicated on p. 73. If Plan 1 is selected, run either 220, 330, or 440 yards slightly slower than your racing pace. Repeat 6 to 10 times. Emphasize the gradual reduction of the length of the intervals of jogging.
3. Sprint 100 to 140 yards. Repeat 4 or 5 times, and then conclude the practice by jogging several laps, gradually slowing down the pace.

Wednesday

1. Devote 10 minutes to baton handling, which includes accuracy in striking the target, optimum speed, and baton receiving and passing. (Refer to Relay racing, Chapter 7.)
2. Sprint 75 to 100 yards 4 or 5 times.
3. Quarter-milers will run 330 yards at their racing pace. Half-milers will run 660 yards at their racing pace. Jog for a period of 10 minutes and repeat once.

4. Alternately jog and walk for a period of 15 minutes.
5. Quarter-milers will run 220 yards, 4 to 6 times, slightly slower than their racing pace. Half-milers will run 440 yards, 3 to 4 times, slightly slower than their racing pace.

Thursday

In case competition is held on Friday, substitute for Thursday the Friday schedule below.

1. Start the day with the regular warm-up.
2. Run 50 percent of the racing distance at racing pace. Walk and jog for 10 minutes. Repeat once.
3. Take 3 to 5 baton passes under conditions simulating competition.
4. Walk and jog for 10 minutes, and finish with a sprint of 50 yards.

Friday

When competition is held on Saturday, practice on Friday is either omitted or reduced to easy jogging with a few short sprints interspersed, preferably on the turf.

Saturday

Competition.

Late season. During late season the competition is more intense, frequently requiring trial heats on Friday. The tendency is to concentrate on one event, which for some middle distance runners may be the 1-mile relay. Practice runs may be shorter in length but speedier than during midseason. Frequently, interval or repeat sections of sprinting are recommended.

In some types of high school competition the athlete is restricted to one middle distance run and one relay. Obviously these regulations should be anticipated well in advance of the contest. However, with or without restrictions, the careful competitor and his coach will stay well within the limits of the ability of the athlete.

Monday

1. Warm up in the customary manner.
2. Quarter-milers run 660 yards at a relaxed pace, at about ⅞ effort. Half-milers run ¾ mile, emphasizing relaxation, at about ⅞ effort.
3. Engage in baton handling, which may include intrasquad competition over shortened distances.
4. Quarter-milers run 330 yards at ⅞ effort. Half-milers run 440 yards at ⅞ effort. Jog and walk alternately for 10 minutes.
5. End the practice with 5 minutes of calisthenics.

Tuesday

1. Warm up as usual.
2. If speed is to be stressed, run both the 440-yard and 880-yard relays on intrasquad teams that are about equal in ability. Rest 20 minutes.
3. Repeat the relay.
4. Spend 5 to 10 minutes on baton handling, executing the transfers as in competition. Walk and jog for 10 minutes.

Wednesday

1. Follow the daily warm-up plan.
2. Quarter-milers run a series of 220-yard sprints with a jog between each. Three of the 220-yard sectors should be covered at a rate slightly faster than the racing pace. Half-milers increase the distance of each sector to 330 or 440 yards and adopt the plan for quarter-milers.
3. Take 3 to 5 baton passes under competitive conditions. Rest 5 minutes.
4. Run 220 yards at top effort.
5. Finish the day's work with 10 minutes of walking and jogging.

Thursday

If a meet is scheduled for Friday, the athlete either may take light jogging on Thursday or stay away from the athletic field.

If competition is held on Saturday, proceed as follows:

1. Begin with your regular warm-up.
2. Run 50 percent of the distance of the race at racing pace. Jog for 5 minutes.
3. Run a series of 50-yard sprints, and place emphasis on relaxation between each. Walk for 2 to 3 minutes.
4. Spend 5 to 10 minutes on baton handling.

Friday

If the Saturday contest is away from home, inspect the track and either engage in easy jogging or refrain from dressing for a workout. On occasions when the list of entries is large, qualifying races are obliged to be run on Friday.

Saturday

1. The athlete who has successfully passed the qualifying round should have ample knowledge of the opponents he will meet in the final race. As on Friday, he should know the lane positions of his major opponents as well as his own.
2. He should be familiar with the time schedule so that he may warm up properly without undue haste.
3. Some coaches advise their athletes to forget their opponents and to "run against the watch." This means to distribute one's energy over the entire race to the best advantage, regardless of the strategy employed by the rivals. Frequently such an athlete sets as his objective a time performance which is $\frac{3}{10}$ or $\frac{4}{10}$ of a second faster than he has heretofore accomplished.
4. In some meets, by agreement, the chief timer calls out to the competitors the elapsed time at successive points in the race, so that all competitors are enabled to compare it with their predetermined plan of energy distribution.
5. At the conclusion of his first event the athlete, after jogging and walking, will rest until his second race is called and then warm up as for the first contest. Moderate body massage between races has been found beneficial to some athletes.
6. Following the last assignment, the middle distance runner tapers off by jogging.
7. He should record the body weight and analyze the fluctuations during each week in late season.

Chapter 6

The distance runs

For the purpose of this discussion the distance races are confined to the 1-mile and the 2- or 3-mile events, since these contests are the ones most frequently run in America. The metric distance comparable to the 1-mile is the 1,500-meter (1,640.4-yard) race. Although there is no metric distance included in the Olympic program that is comparable to the 2-mile event, the 3,000-meter (3,280.8-yard) steeplechase is included in the Olympic races.

The distance events are run both indoors and outdoors. It is worthy of note that 2-mile runners occasionally make better time indoors since by keeping close to the inner curb they gain distance on every lap and there are significantly more laps required on the indoor track. Races longer than 2 or 3 miles are referred to as long distance runs.

GENERAL CONSIDERATIONS

Types of competitors. Although there is a wide range in the size of distance runners, the heavy individual is the exception. The range in weight is from 120 pounds to 170 pounds, and the range in height is from 5 feet 8 inches to 6 feet 3 inches. The tall, rangy man of medium weight with long, rather than thick muscles seems to have the advantage in distance running.

Qualifications. Before an athlete decides to become a candidate for the distance events he should first determine if he has a sound, normally functioning body. It is important that the coach ascertain the health history of the prospective candidate. These facts are easily obtained by means of a routine physical examination. If the physical requirements have been met, the candidate must consider whether or not he is willing, through rigid training, to pay the price to acquire physical condition compatible with such strenuous exertion as that demanded by distance running.

The athlete should acquaint himself with the normal physiologic changes which will take place as his training continues and by following these changes should keep track of the success or progress of his training. There are some who contend that in many cases the increase in heart size, characteristic of the distance runner, is only apparent since most successful distance runners are endowed with large, strong hearts at the outset. At any rate, the runner, to compete in the longer events, either must possess a strong heart or be able to acquire it through training.

In past years distance running was referred to as the "older athlete's game" as contrasted to sprinting, which was referred to as the "young athlete's event." However, the foregoing statement would not hold true for distance runners of today. A survey of the ages of current champions indicates that many of them have established world records at ages ranging from 19 to 24 years. Some champions in the longer runs have turned in their best performances when they were between 25 and 30 years of age.

It is of interest to note that as the persistent distance runner advances in years (30 to 35) he tends to shift his competition to the longer events. He may choose the increased distance either because he has gained the additional endurance required for these contests or because he has lost some of the speed essential in the shorter races.

Adaptability is an essential requirement of the distance runner. He must be able to meet such situations as an increased cadence of rather long duration as well as to change back to an optimum pace when the conditions permit.

Champions recognize that rhythm is an essential qualification for successful distance running. They believe this so keenly that they spend considerable time and practice in developing fine rhythm adjustment. A rhythmic pace enables the runner to maintain his adopted speed in a manner more effortless than if the cadence is jerky and irregular.

Determination to spend oneself is a quality possessed by the consistent winner of distance events. Courage is required to command a tiring body to produce a burst of speed toward the finish yarn—a quality which cannot be developed solely in competitive races but which must be an objective during the practice sessions.

Comparative marks in competition. In Table 6-1 are found comparative times which may be of aid to the novice competitor in the 1-mile run. Since these are placing times (not winning times) for average performances, it is obvious that they will not apply to those areas where the quality of the 1-mile runners is either extremely high or extremely low. The performances of the distance runner's competitors in his particular area are of great importance and should be taken into account before a contest.

Equipment. The distance runner should exercise special care in the fitting of his

Table 6-1. Comparative marks in scholastic competition of distance runners

Meet	No. of places scored	1 mile (min.:sec.)
Dual high school	3	4:20-4:40
Qualifying—state	3	4:15-4:30
State or province	5	4:10-4:20

shoes. Added precaution is necessary in distance running because the length of the race requires that the shoe be worn for a much longer time in actual competition than in any other running event. For example, in a 2-mile race the feet make approximately 1,700 contacts with the track as compared with 50 or less in the 100-yard dash. An ill-fitting shoe with spikes that are incompatible with the texture of the track makes for blisters and irritations as well as shin-splints and muscle soreness. The distance runner is advised to include exercises for the feet in his training program, thus reducing the hazards of injuries to the arches. For protection of the heels, heel cups are recommended in some cases.

TECHNIQUE OF THE DISTANCE RUNS

One of the main points around which the technique of distance running is built is the conservation of energy. Since distance runners may start from a crouch position with the aid of starting blocks and sprint 20 to 30 yards so as to be assured of a favorable running position, the principles set forth

Fig. 6-1. The stride plan and body position in distance running.

for the sprint start apply to distance running. However, the majority of successful distance runners assume a standing position rather than a crouch at the start of a race. They contend that the standing position permits a greater degree of muscular relaxation so essential in distance running and believe that the sprinter's crouch causes unneeded muscular tension. The form employed by distance runners during both the starting and the transitional strides is also quite similar to that used by sprinters. For a discussion of these points, the reader is referred to pp. 44 and 45.

Full-speed strides. In executing the full-speed strides the runner is urged to learn to stride with a minimum output of energy. This is accomplished by stressing further the relaxation of muscles, the rhythm of striding, and the optimum breathing position. In contrast to middle distance running, the following points are further stressed.

Trunk. The angle of the trunk (from the vertical position) is less in distance running, being inclined from 5 to 9 degrees, as contrasted with approximately 15 degrees in middle distance running and about 25 degrees in sprinting (Fig. 5-1, *B*, and Fig. 6-1, *B*).

Arm action. The arm action is less vigorous and is performed in a more relaxed manner. The arms should be swung so as to necessitate a minimum amount of fixation of both the thorax and the shoulder girdle.

Hands. The hands are carried slightly cupped, thus promoting relaxation of the forearm (Fig. 5-1, *B*, and Fig. 6-1, *D*).

Arm action and trunk carriage. The arm action and trunk carriage should be such that the breathing movements are facilitated, never hindered.

Foot. The foot should touch the track so as to distribute the work evenly among the muscles of the leg. This is accomplished by executing a ball-heel landing. A few authorities recommend that the landing be made on the heel so that as the body comes forward a rock-over movement occurs from the heel to the toe. It is claimed that the heel landing relieves the driving muscles from the landing jar, requiring as their only assignment the propulsion of the body forward.

Strides. A conscious attempt should be made to execute smooth rhythmic strides of optimum length. Since the stride in distance races is shorter than that in races of lesser yardage, the runner should take advantage of this fact and make the anatomic and physiologic adjustments which are necessary for long-continued smooth striding action.

Heel lift. A relatively high heel lift at the conclusion of the stride serves to shorten the radius and thus increase the speed of the subsequent forward leg swing. The success of European long distance runners seems to be due to their ability to adjust the trunk, leg, and arm action so as to permit a full-speed stride in which there is a maximum of muscular relaxation. They are able not only to cover distance with a minimum expenditure of energy but also to facilitate the meeting of the oxygen requirement through body adjustments which are most favorable to the respiratory movements.

The distance runner, through practice and study, must cultivate the muscular relaxation and the body adjustments which are compatible with efficient striding.

Coast. The location of the coast in the distance races as shown in Fig. 6-2 is a suggestion for beginners only. As the distance runner becomes proficient in his event, he learns to employ a coast whenever he feels the necessity of a short period of rest. This may occur in any section of the race and may be repeated 2 or 3 times. He may accomplish this by lowering the arms, by concentrating on relaxation, by changing the length of stride, and by altering the rhythm of breathing momentarily.

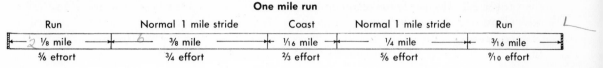

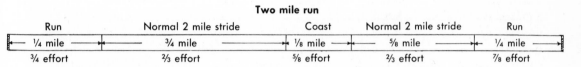

Fig. 6-2. An effort distribution chart for beginners in the 1-mile and 2-mile runs.

Finish. The finish of a distance run consists of exerting as much effort as is consistent with remaining energy during the last 25 to 20 percent of the race. At the same time the runner should make a supreme effort to maintain good form until the finish line has been crossed. It might be added that full-effort striding toward the end of a distance run is materially different from that in short races. The runner, through necessity, dare not run the last 25 to 20 percent of the distance race with the same degree of muscular fixation or tenseness as that employed in the 100-yard dash. Such an effort would, no doubt, result in tying up before the finish yarn was reached. The average distance runner who has exerted himself during a 2-mile race cannot be expected to cover more than 150 yards running on his toes as does the sprinter.

RACING FUNDAMENTALS

For the most part the racing fundamentals in the distance events are the same as those described for the middle distance runs. Where outstanding variations occur, they are discussed. The reader is referred to Chapter 5 for a discussion of knowledge of opponents, speed at the beginning of a race, passing an opponent, meeting a challenge, and maintaining the stride.

What has been termed the "danger line" holds true in distance events the same as in middle distance races. In the 1-mile race the athlete, if he expects to win, may permit an opponent of equal ability no more than a 25- to 30-yard lead. For the 2-mile race the distance is 40 to 50 yards. This recommended distance is quite flexible, yet a runner always must be conscious of the danger of permitting an opponent to gain too great a lead in any section of a race.

As has been stated previously, the longer the race, the more attention the runner must give to the distribution of his energy. A scheme of energy distribution for the novice is depicted in Fig. 6-2. As the athlete becomes more proficient, he will find that adjustments in his energy distribution are required.

James Ryun of the United States, in 1967, covered the 1-mile distance in 3 minutes, 51.1 seconds.

As a guide for those who aspire to creditable performances in running either the 1-mile or 2-mile race, Tables 6-2 and 6-3 show suggested elapsed times at specified points in the race, depending on the athlete's objective total time.

In 1965, Michel Jazy of France ran 2 miles in 8 minutes, 22.6 seconds.

PHYSIOLOGIC EFFECTS OF DISTANCE RUNNING

There are those who tend to discourage young men from entering the distance events because they believe that the ef-

Table 6-2. The 1-mile run showing the elapsed time at specified division points of the race*

| At ¼ mile | | At ½ mile | | At ¾ mile | | |
Proportional time (sec.)	Elapsed time (sec.)	Proportional time (min.:sec.)	Elapsed time (min.:sec.)	Proportional time (min.:sec.)	Elapsed time (min.:sec.)	Total time (min.:sec.)
77	73	2:34	2:30	3:51	3:48	5:08
75	71	2:30	2:26	3:45	3:42	5:00
74	70	2:28	2:24	3:42	3:39	4:56
73	69	2:26	2:22	3:39	3:36	4:52
72	68	2:24	2:20	3:36	3:34	4:48
71	67	2:22	2:18	3:33	3:32	4:44
70	66	2:20	2:16	3:30	3:29	4:40
69	65.5	2:18	2:14	3:27	3:26	4:36
68	65	2:16	2:13	3:24	3:23	4:32
67	64	2:14	2:12	3:21	3:20	4:28
66	63	2:12	2:10	3:18	3:17	4:24
65	62	2:10	2:08	3:15	3:14	4:20
64	61	2:08	2:06	3:12	3:11.5	4:16
63	60	2:06	2:04	3:09	3.08.5	4:12
62	59.5	2:04	2:03	3:06	3:05.5	4:08
61	59	2:02	2:01	3:03	3:02.5	4:04
60	58	2:00	1:59	3:00	2:59.5	4:00
59	57.5	1:58	1:57.6	2:57	2:56.5	3:56
58	57.2	1:56	1:56.7	2:54	2:55.7	3:52

*The competitor's objective speed is shown in the last column. (For an interpretation of this table, see footnote to Table 5-2.)

fects of prolonged strenuous exercise are harmful.

In view of our own experience and the investigations of others, we believe that distance running is not harmful to young men provided that they are normal in the beginning, that they carefully observe the prescribed process of training and practice, and that they taper off at the conclusion of the season with exercises which are progressively less intense.

The questions raised concerning the effects of distance running are: (1) Is it detrimental to health? (2) Does it shorten the span of life of the participants?

The most extensive and trustworthy investigations of these questions give negative answers. Jones and Best,[1] at the University of Wisconsin, report that over a period of 52 years 185 individuals have been awarded major letters in cross-country running. Of this number of athletes, two have died from accidental causes and seven from unspecified causes. As compared with similar groups, the athletes participating in endurance events seem to have a better record of longevity than those who do not take part in such exercise.

Karvonen[2] in Finland compared the longevity records of cross-country skiers to the records of a comparable group of non-athletes. He reported that the active group lived, on the average, 7 years longer than the inactive group. Although this study has obvious limitations, it does suggest that participation in endurance events may contribute to a lengthened life span.

Currens and White[3] reported these clinical, physiologic, and autopsy findings on distance runner Clarence DeMar.

Table 6-3. The 2-mile run showing the elapsed time at specified division points of the race*

At ¼ mile		At ½ mile		At 1 mile		At 1½ miles		
Proportional time (sec.)	Elapsed time (sec.)	Proportional time (min.: sec.)	Elapsed time (min.: sec.)	Proportional time (min.: sec.)	Elapsed time (min.: sec.)	Proportional time (min.: sec.)	Elapsed time (min.: sec.)	Total time (min.: sec.)
90	84	3:00	2:54	6:00	5:54	9:00	8:55	12:00
85	79	2:50	2:44	5:40	5:34	8:30	8:25	11:20
81	77	2:42	2:36	5:24	5:18	8:06	8:01	10:48
79	73	2:38	2:32	5:16	5:10	7:54	7:50	10:32
77	71	2:34	2:28	5:08	5:02	7:42	7:38	10:16
75	70	2:30	2:24	5:00	4:54	7:30	7:26	10:00
74	69	2:28	2:23	4:56	4:50	7:24	7:20	9:52
73	68	2:26	2:21	4:52	4:47	7:18	7:14	9:44
72	67	2:24	2:19	4:48	4:43	7:12	7:09	9:36
71	66.5	2:22	2:17	4:44	4:39	7:06	7:04	9:28
70	66	2:20	2:15	4:40	4:36	7:00	6:58	9:20
69	65.5	2:18	2:13	4:36	4:33	6:54	6:52	9:12
68	65	2:16	2:12	4:32	4:30	6:48	6:47	9:04
67	64.5	2:14	2:11	4:28	4:25	6:42	6:41	8:56
66	64	2:12	2:10	4:24	4:22	6:36	6:35	8:48
65	63.5	2:10	2:09	4:20	4:19	6:30	6:29	8:40
64.5	63	2:09	2:08	4:18	4:17	6:27	6:27	8:36
64	62.5	2:08	2:07	4:16	4:15	6:24	6:24	8:32
63.5	62	2:07	2:06	4:14	4:14	6:21	6:22	8:28
63	61.6	2:06	2:05	4:12	4:13	6:18	6:19	8:24

*The competitor's objective speed is shown in the last column. (For an interpretation of this table, see footnote to Table 5-2.)

In 1909 at the age of twenty-one, Clarence DeMar placed fourth in a long-distance, cross-country run at the University of Vermont, where he was later awarded a letter in athletics. His last race was run in 1957 when, at the age of sixty-nine, he ran a 15-kilometer "marathon" in Bath, Maine. The intervening forty-nine years is a saga of marathon running unequaled in the annals of marathoning in this country. During this time he entered 34 and won 7 of the 25-26 mile marathons from Hopkinton (formerly started at Ashland) to Boston sponsored by the Boston Athletic Association. On 15 occasions he finished among the first 10 in the field. In 1954, at the age of sixty-six, he ran his last such marathon, finishing 78th in a field of 133. In all, "Mr. Marathon" had participated in over 1000 long-distance races, including 100 true marathons of 25 miles or more.

DeMar was also the subject of considerable medical investigation and figured prominently in the studies of A. V. Bock and his associates, who published their "Studies in Muscular Activity" in the *Journal of Physiology* in 1928. It was during these studies that the efficiency of "Mr. Marathon" was demonstrated, in that during heavy exertion lactic acid did not accumulate in the blood as it did in other males of his age who were not in training.

Our own studies were carried out in 1953 to determine the presence or absence of heart disease, since "Mr. Marathon" had been told many years before that he had a "weak heart." The question of a murmur had been raised the year he won the first marathon and was one of the reasons given for his not competing in the marathon during the next eight years.

The striking anatomic finding in the heart at autopsy was the relative size of the coronary arteries, which were estimated to be two or three times the normal diameter. A quantitative estimation of the size of the lumen of these arteries was considered to be unrewarding since there is much variation in the size of coronary arteries in this age group, which would make any comparison of this one case with the normal range very difficult.

Gross and microscopic examination showed that there was some atherosclerosis of the coronary arteries and of the aorta, but there was no serious obstruction of the lumen of either. No evidence of previous coronary occlusion could be found, but it was impossible to inject the coronary-artery system.

The question regarding the athlete's heart is old and one that has been discussed at considerable length without much in the way of anatomic data. The fear of straining or injuring the heart from excessive physical effort has not been substantiated; strenuous physical effort, so far as is known, does not adversely affect the heart. Few athletes have had such a long period of physical effort during their lifetime as DeMar, who carried on an active practice of running during his adult life; it is for this reason that we have recorded the clinical and autopsy findings in this case.

Nothing was found in the examination of the heart to indicate that the long-continued physical exercise had adversely affected it.

The coronary arteries of the heart were found to be larger than one would expect for his age. Atherosclerosis of the coronary arteries was present but was relatively mild in degree.[3]

That strenuous exercise brings about definite chronic changes in the physiologic condition of the athlete is evident from the following.

Heart rate. The pulse rate of the trained athlete is as much as 15 percent below that of the untrained individual.

Heart volume and weight. Strenuous exercise causes a definite increase in the volume and weight of the heart. This increase is due to muscular changes and not to a dilation of the chambers of the heart.

Hemoglobin. It is well recognized that the blood of trained distance runners has a higher oxygen-carrying capacity than nontrained individuals.

Systolic blood pressure. Contrary to earlier reports, it appears that highly trained individuals have lower resting systolic blood pressure measures than nontrained or inactive individuals.

Red blood corpuscles. There is a definite increase in the number of the red blood corpuscles in those who train strenuously.

Vital volume.* Exercises of endurance increase the vital volume as much as 20 percent.

The consensus of those who have investigated the chronic physiologic effects of distance running is that the extent of the changes brought about by it is dependent on the severity and duration of training and exercise. Furthermore, it is quite generally accepted that there is a retroversion to the normal condition after the cessation of strenuous exercise.

SIDE ACHE[4]

Side ache is experienced by many athletes, especially runners. Activity too soon after meals, after an inadequate warm-up, and in cold weather causes it to occur more frequently. Although there have been several explanations of side ache offered, the most likely cause is anoxemia of diaphragmatic muscles.

SCHEDULES OF PRACTICE FOR DISTANCE RUNS

Previously it was recommended that athletes aspiring to success in distance running distribute their practice over a considerable period of time. Some athletes are capable of devising their own workouts. Others may not profit to the fullest extent by adopting the optional practice plan. For example, many 1-milers and 2-milers have been benefited by practicing and competing in cross-country running during the fall season. In the winter months the runners may dress warmly and run outdoors on the road or sidewalk if an indoor track is not available. In some institutions an outdoor board track provides satisfactory training facilities for the distance runner.

It should be evident to the novice that the distance run requires a longer preparatory period of training than possibly any

---

*Vital volume is the amount of air that can be expelled by the most forceful expiration following the most forceful inspiration.

other track or field event. During the so-called off season, practice runs on 2 or 3 days a week will not only maintain but also build up distance running condition.

Basic exercises were indicated in Chapter 1 under preliminary season and should have provided a foundation for the next stage of development, the early season workouts. The athlete's objectives are endurance, speed, judgment of pace, relaxation, and rhythm. They differ from those of the middle distance run chiefly in the fact that the longer races require less speed but more endurance.

Early season. This schedule follows the preliminary season schedule, p. 7.

Monday

1. Record the stripped body weight daily, both before practice and after the bath, when thoroughly dry. See p. 23 for a discussion of weight fluctuations as observed on the daily weight sheet.
2. Protect the feet against blisters and abrasions (see p. 29). Running shoes provided with both short spikes and sponge rubber heels reduce the strain on the front muscles of the leg and help eliminate the hazard of shin-splints.
3. Engage in the Fartlek system of exercises for a period of 20 to 30 minutes and/or interval running as follows: run 440 yards in 75 seconds, jog for a period of 4 minutes, and repeat 5 to 7 times.
4. Sprint 100 to 150 yards on the straightaway at ¾ effort. Repeat 2 or 3 times.
5. Participate in weight-training and/or tension exercises for a period of 10 to 20 minutes. (For an explanation of these exercises, see pp. 8 and 11.)

Tuesday

1. After the customary warm-up, practice interval running in the following manner:

   a. Run 220 yards in 33 to 36 seconds.
   b. Jog for a period of 3 to 4 minutes.
   c. Repeat 4 to 9 times.
2. Sprint 100 to 150 yards at ¾ effort and emphasize relaxation and running form. Repeat 2 to 3 times.
3. Conclude the practice with tapering off jogging.

Wednesday

1. Proceed as follows:

   a. Run 330 yards in 46 to 48 seconds.
   b. Jog for a period of 3 to 4 minutes.
   c. Repeat 4 to 9 times.
2. Sprint 100 to 150 yards at ⅞ effort; repeat twice.
3. Conclude the practice with 10 to 20 minutes of weight-training and tension exercises.

Thursday

1. Engage in interval running at increased and decreased distances as follows:

   a. Run 220 yards at ¾ effort and jog for a period of 3 to 4 minutes.
   b. Run 440 yards at ¾ effort and jog for a period of 3 to 4 minutes.
   c. Run 660 yards at ¾ effort and jog for a period of 3 to 4 minutes.
   d. Run 880 yards at ¾ effort and jog for a period of 3 to 4 minutes.
   e. Run 660 yards, jog for a period of 3 to 4 minutes, and repeat the decreased distances (440 yards and 220 yards) to an extent determined by your physical condition.

Friday

In view of the fact that in Saturday's trials the candidate for the 1-mile run will be expected to cover ¾ of a mile and the candidate for the 2-mile or 3-mile run will be expected to cover 1½ miles, Friday's practice should be arranged so that energy is conserved.

1. Jog 220 yards on the grass, walk 100 yards, and then stride 440 yards at ¾ effort.

2. Skip rope for 2 to 3 minutes.
3. Stride through ¾ mile at an optional pace and bear in mind that you should be in readiness for a trial the following day.

Saturday

1. Make the body adjustments for the time trial in the same manner you would in preparing for competition. The warm-up should be completed so as to permit 15 to 20 minutes of rest before the start of your race. Since the type and quantity of warm-up varies with different individuals, the competitor should analyze his activities carefully and determine definitely his exact requirements for a good race. A suggested warm-up, which may be altered to suit individual needs, is presented.
   a. Jog 440 yards, walk 100 yards, and run 220 yards, starting at ½ effort and ending at $\frac{9}{10}$ effort.
   b. Execute 4 to 5 minutes of varied exercises which are moderate in intensity, such as bending, stretching, high kicking, squatting, and skipping rope.
   c. Jog 220 yards, walk 25 yards, and run 220 yards at ¾ effort.
   d. Put on additional clothing and retain the body warmth. Ten minutes before your race is called, start easy jogging and walking for 2 to 3 minutes.
   e. Break from the mark, running 50 yards at $\frac{9}{10}$ effort. Repeat twice. Ventilate the body with deep-breathing exercises.
2. Run a time trial over ¾ your regulation competition distance (¾ mile for the 1-miler, 1½ miles for the 2-miler, and 2¼ miles for the 3-miler) and distribute your energy according to a prearranged plan. The novice is referred to Fig. 6-2, and the experienced runner is referred to Table 6-2

for the 1-mile run and Table 6-3 for the 2-mile run. Have your elapsed time recorded at the end of each ¼ mile.
3. Relax for a period of 25 to 30 minutes but keep moving.
4. Warm up a second time and stride ½ mile at ⅞ effort.
5. Walk and jog for a period of 10 minutes.
6. End the workout with a few minutes of calisthenics followed by a jog. Record the body weight and study the weight fluctuations for the week.

Midseason. By midseason the distance runner is presumed to have become grounded in the basic phases, such as strength, endurance, speed, coordination, and judgment of pace. The novice will understand that these fundamentals are not to be discontinued. However, he should be ready for the more advanced stages of training. Schedules of practice are arranged for competition on Saturday. Whenever the meet falls on Friday, the schedule is moved forward one day. The high school athlete may, after running 1 mile early in the program, run 880 yards or in the 1-mile relay toward the end of the day. The especially able college runner may compete in the 1-mile run and later in the day in the 2-mile or 3-mile run. Some scholastic associations limit the high school runner to only one race when the distance involved is 880 yards or more. In college and other amateur contests for older athletes, the tendency is to concentrate on only one distance race in a major meet.

The suggested practice schedules are presented for the athlete competing in but one event, either the 1-mile, the 2-mile, or the 3-mile run.

Individual differences require adjustments in the schedule of practice, chiefly if time trials are run. In this book they are recommended on Tuesday, thereby permitting more time for recuperation required for Saturday's competition than if the trials are conducted on Wednesday.

Similar to the middle distance events, there are four basic plans for holding the major practice of the week, the time trial. It should be evident to the novice that these plans may be altered or combined so that his objectives may be reached. The athlete may run the time trial according to one of the following optional plans:

1. Run at full effort over the exact distance (1 mile, 2 miles, or 3 miles).
2. Run underdistance at overspeed ($\frac{3}{4}$ mile, $1\frac{1}{2}$ miles, or $2\frac{1}{4}$ miles).
3. Run overdistance at $\frac{9}{10}$ effort ($1\frac{1}{4}$ miles, $2\frac{1}{4}$ miles, or $3\frac{1}{4}$ miles).
4. Run 50 percent of the racing distance **at full effort.** Rest 10 to 15 minutes ($\frac{1}{2}$ mile, rest, $\frac{1}{2}$ mile; or 1 mile, rest, 1 mile; or $1\frac{1}{2}$ miles, rest, $1\frac{1}{2}$ miles). Repeat once.

The reasons for presenting each plan are similar to those given for the middle distance runs (see Chapter 5).

Monday

1. Participate in the Fartlek system of exercises, the 1-milers for a period of 20 to 30 minutes and the 2-milers and 3-milers for a period of 30 to 40 minutes.
2. Proceed as follows:
   a. Run 220 yards in 28 to 30 seconds.
   b. Jog an optional distance or period of time but aim to reduce the successive jogging intervals gradually.
   c. Repeat 5 to 7 times.
3. Sprint 100 to 150 yards at $\frac{9}{10}$ effort. Repeat 3 or 4 times.
4. Jog and run at an optional pace for a period of 5 minutes.
5. If weight-training and tension exercises have proved beneficial, continue them.

Tuesday

1. After the customary warm-up, engage in interval running as indicated:
   a. Run 440 yards at racing pace.

b. Jog for a period of 3 to 4 minutes after the initial sector of running, but therafter reduce either the time or distance of the intervals of jogging.
   c. Repeat 9 to 14 times.
2. Sprint 100 to 150 yards at $\frac{9}{10}$ effort. Repeat 3 or 4 times.
3. Follow the customary tapering-off activity by jogging an optional distance.

Wednesday

1. Perform the following activities:
   a. 1-milers run 440 yards at racing pace and then jog for 5 to 10 minutes. Repeat 4 to 6 times.
   b. 2-milers and 3-milers run 880 yards at racing pace and then jog for 5 to 10 minutes. Repeat 4 to 6 times.
2. Continue as follows:
   a. 1-milers run 220 yards at a rate slightly faster than racing pace and then jog either a reduced distance or for a shorter interval. Repeat 1 to 3 times.
   b. 2-milers and 3-milers run 440 yards at racing pace and then jog either a reduced distance or for a shorter interval. Repeat 6 to 8 times.
3. Sprint 75 to 100 yards at $\frac{9}{10}$ effort. Repeat twice.
4. Provided weight-training exercises have improved running performances, continue them.

Thursday

In case competition is scheduled for Friday, Thursday becomes a day of easing off. If competition is held on Saturday, follow these suggestions.

1. Warm up according to your customary plan.
2. Take 2 or 3 starts, sprinting 30 yards and then gradually swinging into your regular stride, keeping muscular tension at a minimum.

3. Run one half of the distance of your race at racing speed.
4. Walk and jog for 10 minutes.

Friday

Whenever competition is held on Saturday, Friday becomes a day of reduced activity, which consists of jogging at optional distances.

Saturday

Competition. On the day of competition, the athlete must inspect his personal equipment and consider the starting time of his race, condition of the track, direction and velocity of the wind, and caliber of his opponents.

1. Take sufficient warm-up, starting 1 hour before the race, jogging 1½ miles, followed by calisthenics.
2. Sprint distances of 50 to 100 yards 3 or 4 times.
3. Rest for 20 to 30 minutes.
4. Retain body tonus by continuous jogging 5 to 10 minutes prior to the race.

Late season. Toward the end of the track season, when the quality of the competition is the highest, the distance runner who has run more than one race in meets ordinarily confines his activity to only one contest. As a general rule, in late season the amount of practice is reduced. The more intensive workouts are completed by Tuesday, or Wednesday, so that three full days of toning up are permitted before Saturday's meet.

Distance runners of international prominence have thrived on workouts extremely divergent in character. For example, some athletes have profited by omitting strenuous practice, including time trials, during midweek, and have conserved their effort for the week-end race. Other equally proficient runners have engaged in vigorous distance trials from Monday to Thursday inclusive, resting on Friday only.

The important sections of the late season training program of Bannister, shortly before he was awarded his medical degree, are worthy of note. The demands on his time were such that it was necessary for him to adopt an individualistic plan in preparing for the 1-mile run. Although the plan selected by Bannister met his needs adequately, he makes no claim that his procedures will revolutionize existing methods.

Shortly after running 1 mile in 3 minutes, 59.4 seconds, Bannister's late season schedule was reported by the United States press to have been as follows: During the last 3 weeks before the meet he punished himself unmercifully with a set program of workouts on a small track near the hospital during the moments he could spare from his duties. Following are the highlights of Bannister's training schedule leading up to the record attempt.

April 12,	1954	Consecutive half-miles at an average of 2:10 (resting about 5 minutes between each)
April 14,		¾ mile (61, 61, and 60 seconds) in 3:02
April 15,		½ mile solo in 1:53
April 16-18,		Holiday away from London, hiking and climbing
April 22,		10 consecutive quarter-miles at an average of 58.9 seconds (presumably resting a few minutes between each quarter-mile)
April 24,		¾ mile paced in 3:00
April 26,		¾ mile in 3:14; rest 10 minutes; ¾ mile in 3:08.6
April 28,		¾ mile solo in 2:59.9
April 30,		½ mile solo in 1:54 (ceased practice until May 6)
May 6,		Competition; 1 mile in 3:59.4; successive quarter-mile times (in seconds): 57.5, 60.7, 62.3, and 58.9.

Monday

1. Review the race of the previous week end. What can be done to improve the performance? What was learned from the recent meet?
2. Proceed with your usual warm-up which should include 5 minutes of calisthenics.

3. Spend 15 to 25 minutes on Fartlek system exercises (p. 7).
4. Run 330 yards at top effort 2 or 3 times, resting about 5 minutes between each sector.
5. Conclude the day's work with alternate jogging and walking.

Tuesday

1. Warm up as usual.
2. Run alternate 220 and 440 yards at ⅞ effort, jogging 1 lap between each. Reduce the number of sectors run during midseason but set a faster pace, striving for a fast finish over the final 50 to 75 yards.
3. Jog and walk for 5 minutes. Then conclude the practice with 5 minutes of flexibility exercises.

Wednesday

1. Spend 30 minutes on Fartlek system.
2. Participate in one 440-yard relay (intrasquad) and one 880-yard relay on teams of equal ability.
3. Run 50 percent of the distance of the race at racing pace.
4. Walk and jog for 10 minutes.
5. Run 440 yards at ⅞ effort.
6. Walk and jog alternately. Then conclude with 5 minutes of calisthenics.

Thursday

Should the schedule call for competition on Friday, substitute either light flexibility exercises or no practice on Thursday.

1. Take a long slow warm-up on the turf.
2. Sprint distances of 75 to 100 yards 2 or 3 times.
3. Jog and walk for 10 minutes, and complete the practice with 3 to 4 minutes of calisthenics.

Friday

The athlete may either engage in light jogging or remain away from the athletic environment.

Saturday

Competition (see suggestions made for Saturday in midseason).

CROSS-COUNTRY RUNNING

The distance covered in cross-country running varies from 1 mile to 6 miles, depending on the age of the contestants. A customary race for the high school or preparatory school boy is over a course about 2 miles long. The college races are conducted over hill and dale, on paths or roads, at distances set by mutual agreement at either 3, 4, 5, or 6 miles. The National Amateur Athletic Union championships are contested on courses measuring 10,000 meters (6 miles, 376.1 yards); the N.C.A.A. championships, over 6-mile courses.

If cross-country courses are not available, the team race of either 1 or 2 miles provides a substitute for hill and dale contests in the fall of the year. In such a race the places are scored similar to cross-country: first place scores 1 point; second place, 2 points; and fiftieth place, 50 points. The team, which may consist of any number of contestants previously agreed upon, scoring the lowest number of points is declared the winner.

A course may be laid out on turf, through parks, around the border of golf courses, on bridle paths, or on unsurfaced roads, It is not unusual to find courses routed through city streets.

While cross-country racing has many of the characteristics of distance running on the track, there are several points of difference. The rough type of footing necessitates the use of a more substantial shoe with a padded heel. The unevenness of the ground demands that the athlete pay attention to the spot where he sets his foot. Uphill running requires form alterations, such as a shortening of the stride, a more vigorous pumping action of the arms, and a more pronounced forward trunk lean. When running downhill, the athlete must cultivate the art of relaxing, maintaining ample speed, and avoiding a severe jar when landing on the heel. The latter is a fault that is similar to applying the brakes. In addition, the trunk is more nearly upright when racing downhill. As in track races, whenever the distance is increased, the requirements of an even spread of exertion are likewise more pronounced.

There is a lack of uniformity of opinion among American coaches regarding both the amount and intensity of practice schedules for cross-country running. The differences are noticeable especially in the prescription of the distances to be run and the running speed. There is also a lack of uniformity of opinion concerning the designated intervals at which stop watch readings are to be announced.

The majority believe that relatively strenuous practice should be held on at least 1 or 2 days each week, with the inclusion of drills which stress judgment of pace. Whenever competition occurs on Friday or Saturday, the most vigorous workout may well be prescribed for Monday or Tuesday, thus allowing 2 or more days of less exacting practice.

For example, on the heavy work day (say Tuesday), one of the following alternative plans may be adopted:

1. Run a distance equal to the competitive race at slightly less than racing speed, but at its conclusion continue for ½ mile at full effort.
2. Run ¾ the distance of the competitive race at full effort. Walk and jog for 15 minutes. Repeat once.
3. Run ½ the distance of the competitive race at full effort. Walk and jog for 5 to 10 minutes. Repeat once.
4. Run the exact distance of the competitive race at racing speed. This plan is prescribed less frequently than any of the others.

Schedules of practice. As a further guide to the cross-country runner, the following schedule of practice for 1 week, in midseason, is suggested:

Monday

1. Warm up with jogging and alternate walking and sprinting 25 yards for a period of 3 to 5 minutes.
2. Make use of progressive resistance exercises (weight-training exercises) preferably after obtaining advice from a qualified individual who may supervise the practice.
3. Run overdistance (50 percent to 75 percent beyond your competitive racing distance) at approximately ⅞ effort. As an alternative measure, follow the practice plan recommended in the Fartlek system (see p. 7).

Tuesday

1. Warm up according to the method you have found to be the most effective.
2. Run cross-country trials, selecting one of the four plans indicated on this page. Make use of the stop watch if it provides aid in distribution of your energy.
3. Walk and jog for 10 minutes.
4. Conclude the workout with 220 yards at full effort.

Wednesday

1. Take your customary warm-up.
2. Run ¼ the competitive distance, emphasizing speed. Walk and jog for 5 to 10 minutes. Repeat 3 or 4 times.
3. Spend 5 to 10 minutes running over hilly terrain. Run 200 yards uphill and then jog 2 minutes. Repeat once or twice.
4. Terminate the practice with 440 yards at ⁹⁄₁₀ effort.

Thursday

Whenever competition is scheduled for Friday, the workout on Thursday will be revised so as to consist of either light jogging or no practice.

1. Initiate your warm-up with jogging, calisthenics, or progressive resistance

exercises (weight-training exercises).

2. Emphasize pace judgment by running 880 yards and walking 3 minutes. Repeat an optional number of times.

3. Conclude with sprints of 50 yards, alternating with walking.

Friday

1. Confine the practice to light jogging or dispense with all physical activity.

Saturday

Competition.

Other methods of training for the long distance runs. There are persons who believe that schedules of practice such as those presented are too exacting. For athletes who wish to follow less formal plans, the following schedules are described.

A Swedish plan. By choice, in Sweden, much of the training for distance running takes place over the turf, mainly through the woods where the footing is softer than that on most running tracks. According to Holmer,[5] this type of footing reduces the chances of suffering from tired muscles, thus eliminating resort to massage and hot baths as relief from hard muscles. Swedish distance runners are advised by their coaches to limit training on the cinder track to preparing the legs for track running and developing a knowledge of pace.

Athletes in Sweden no longer train by following set schedules based on periods of time, where the athlete runs precise distances at established degrees of effort or speed.

In case a running course over the turf or in the woods is unavailable, use is made of tracks or paths covered with sawdust.

Holmer holds that the runner must learn to analyze himself so that he can decide on his own training routine from day to day. When this idea is in vogue, no group plan is established for all runners. This type of training coincides with that described as the Fartlek (speed play) system. Although

the Fartlek plan was discussed on p. 7, an additional example of a day's workout, to be done on the turf, is as follows:

1. Warm up with 5 to 10 minutes of easy running.

2. Run at a steady pace for ¾ to 1½ miles.

3. Slow down to a fast walk for about 5 minutes.

4. Then run at an easy pace, bursting into sprints occasionally for distances of 50 to 60 yards. Repeat to the point of mild fatigue.

5. Continue easy running with the distance strides broken now and then by 3 or 4 sprint strides. The trunk is tilted forward to balance the body while accelerating, as though to stave off a challenge or to make a final effort.

6. Sprint uphill for 170 to 200 yards (this is recommended for 2 days per week, perhaps twice on Monday and once on Thursday).

7. Run fast for 1 minute.

8. Finish with a number of laps on a cinder track, the number depending on the distance for which you are training. The objective of the track running is to gain knowledge of pace.

The Swedish distance runners who follow the Fartlek system of training stress both speed and endurance on each training day. This is more work than is usually prescribed by American and British coaches. In addition, 1 day out of 10 is devoted to really hard training by Swedish runners. Both physical and mental relaxation is advocated. This is accomplished by walking through the woods or other restful environments. On days when there is no running scheduled, a 2- to 4-hour walk is suggested.

Dyson[6] believes that constant training on a cinder track may become extremely boring and therefore harmful. He recommends the inclusion of some of the Fartlek system in the week's work even though it requires more time and is actually a much harder form of training than most distance men in Britain employ.

A Czechoslovakian plan. Another method of training for distance running, differing from those of the Swedish, British, and American plans, is that of Zatopek, as described by Kerssenbrock.[7] Zatopek's system of training consisted in running daily throughout the year, wherever he might be. The schedule called for interval running, that is, running specific stretches at a fast pace, with intervals of slow running interspersed, together with variation of speed running. The amount of training in which this great runner indulged depended on the weather, the competition for which he was preparing, and his evaluation of his condition, commensurate with prospective demands. Usually the daily training schedule was as follows: run 200 meters 5 times, 400 meters 20 times, and then 200 meters 5 times. These runs were not continuous but were spurts which were interspersed by about 200 meters of easy running. In case speed seemed lacking, more of the 200-meter sections were included; however, if endurance seemed lacking, the number of 400-meter sections was increased. This schedule often was adhered to up to the day of competition.

Zatopek engaged in no gymnastic exercises and did not include a separate warm-up before daily practice. However, on competition days a warm-up was included which consisted of the following.

1. Running about 1,500 meters, sprinting 4 or 5 times, followed by stretching exercises.
2. Resting 20 to 30 minutes.
3. Jogging for 10 minutes preceding the race.

As a matter of strategy Zatopek sought to break down the opposition with numerous sprints interspersed at irregular intervals during the race. This runner was still able to add an amazing burst of speed at the finish.

Zatopek believed that success in distance running is acquired best by "running and more running." It appears that the effectiveness of this system depends chiefly on the ability of the athlete to pass judgment on his condition at any given stage of training, and therefore it is best suited to the finished performer.

A Russian plan.[8] Vladimir Kuts' training schedules serve as samples of those utilized in the Soviet Union. Kuts, with his coach, Nikiforov, has built up his training system from the experience and preceptorship of Emil Zatopek of Czechoslovakia. In contrast to the latter, Kuts has not confined himself solely to interval running of 200 and 400 meters; in addition he has taken 800-, 1,200-, 1,600-, and 2,000-meter runs. The tempo at which the double Olympic champion runs the short distances is somewhat faster than his racing tempo, but his longer-timed runs in training are several seconds slower than his racing tempo. His training schedule follows.

Spring training:
Monday

Practice in a park or forest. Warm up by jogging and performing gymnastics for 25 minutes. Perform 25 minutes of accelerated running. Perform 6 trials of 120 to 150 meters. Run through the country for $1\frac{1}{4}$ hours, engaging in 10 accelerated runs of 600 to 800 meters each. Spend 15 minutes in running, springing from the balls of the feet.

Tuesday

Again, practice in a park or forest. Warm up for 30 minutes. Perform 8 trials of accelerated running, consisting of 100 meters each. Next perform special gymnastics. Run 200 meters 20 times, each at a rate of 28 or 29 seconds, followed by 5 trials of 400 meters (68 seconds). Spend 15 minutes springing from the balls of the feet.

Wednesday

Perform 90 minutes of cross-country running either in the country or through the forest, interspersing them with 10 accelerated runs of 1,000 meters each, at about 2 minutes, 50 seconds.

Thursday

Active rest. Warm up for 1 hour in the morning.

Friday

Practice in a stadium or forest. Spend the first 30 minutes warming up. Then perform 5 runs of 120 to 150 meters at maximum speed. Follow this with gymnastics. Execute five 200-meter runs, consuming 28 to 29 seconds for each. Then run 400 meters 20 times at a rate of 67 to 69 seconds. Run 200 meters 5 times at a rate of 28 to 29 seconds. Follow this with 15 minutes of springy running. Finish with prescribed exercises.

Saturday

Practice in the fields. Run cross country for 105 minutes, including in the run 12 bursts of 600 or 800 meters each, consuming 1 minute, 32 seconds to 1 minute, 35 seconds for 600 meters and 2 minutes, 8 seconds to 2 minutes, 10 seconds for 800 meters. Perform special gymnastics. Finish with light gymnastics.

Sunday

Active rest. One hour of warming up optional.

Summer training, normal week:
Monday

Practice on a running track. In the morning perform slow running and gymnastics for 40 minutes. In the afternoon warm up for 35 minutes. Perform 80 to 100 meters 5 times at an accelerated pace. Run at a changing tempo 200 meters 3 times, consuming 27 to 28 seconds for each. Next, run 400 meters 15 times—the first 11 at a rate of 64 to 65 seconds, then 3 runs at 67 to 68 seconds, and the last at 63 seconds, with 100 meters of jogging between each of the fast runs. Spend 15 minutes in springy running. Finish with some type of exercise.

Tuesday

Practice in the forest, in the morning only. Run 40 minutes with a changing tempo.

Wednesday

Practice on a running track. In the morning warm up for 45 minutes. In the afternoon warm up for 35 minutes. Then engage in accelerated running over the distance of 150 meters. Perform 400 meters 5 times, each trial consuming 61 to 66 seconds; 1,200 meters twice, each trial consuming 3 minutes, 15 seconds to 3 minutes, 16 seconds, and 400 meters 3 times at a rate of 65 to 66 seconds. Spend 10 minutes in springy, balls-of-the-feet running.

Thursday

Practice in the forest. Run 90 minutes with a changing tempo, interspersing steady running with accelerated zestful bursts of 100 to 600 meters. Spend 15 minutes on special gymnastics.

Friday

Practice in the forest and on the running track. In the morning engage in slow running in the forest followed by gymnastics. In the afternoon work on the running track as follows: Warm up for 25 minutes. Execute 200 meters of accelerated running 3 times. Run 100 meters fast, 6 times. After each run, cover 600 meters slowly (2 minutes, 42 seconds to 2 minutes, 46 seconds). Finish with 15 minutes of springy running.

Saturday

Active rest.

Sunday

Work in the forest. Perform 30 minutes of special gymnastics in the morning. In the afternoon warm up with special gymnastics for 35 minutes. Follow this by accelerated running of 150 meters 5 times. Run at a changing tempo as follows: 1,600 meters 3 times (4 minutes, 40 seconds to 4 minutes, 47 seconds) and 400 meters 6 times (65 to 67 seconds). Between each fast run, jog 100 meters. Finish with 10 minutes of springy running. Observe a cooling-off period.

Before competition:
Monday

Warm up for 40 minutes in the forest. Active rest.

Tuesday

Practice in the stadium. In the morning warm up for 35 minutes. In the afternoon warm up for 30 minutes. Perform accelerated running. Run a distance of 120 to 150 meters 5 times. Run at a changing tempo as follows: 400 meters (61 to 65 seconds) 5 times with 100 meters of jogging in between; 1,600 meters once (4 minutes, 23 seconds), followed by an 800-meter jog; 1,200 meters once (3 minutes, 20 seconds), followed by a slow 600-meter run; and a 400-meter run 3 times (65 to 66 seconds). Perform 10 minutes of springy running. Finish with gymnastics.

Wednesday

Practice in the forest. Run across the forest for 50 minutes. Do accelerated running as follows: 400 meters 10 times (63 to 65 seconds) and 200 meters 5 times (28 to 29 seconds). Finish with 10 minutes of springy, balls-of-the-feet running.

Thursday

Practice on a track. Warm up for 30 minutes. Perform accelerated running as follows: 200 meters 4 times; 2,000 meters once (5 minutes, 33 seconds), with a 600- to 800-meter jog in between. Follow these with 10 minutes of springy running. Finish with gymnastics.

Friday

Practice in the park in the morning. Perform 40 minutes of slow running, followed by gymnastics.

Saturday

Warm up in the evening for 35 minutes.

Sunday

Competition.

• • •

In all of the training plans described, the distance runner will recognize that stress is placed on running form, body carriage, development of endurance, speed, pace judgment, relaxation, and mental attitude. Practice schedules should be planned so as to conform to the amount of time allotted, the types of running paths available, and the length of the race selected.

STEEPLECHASE—2 MILES OR 3,000 METERS

Description. The steeplechase is an event requiring the endurance of the distance runner and some of the qualifications of the hurdler and the broad jumper.

In the United States the 2-mile steeplechase first was placed on the program in 1889 (winner, A. B. George, in 11 minutes 17.4 seconds), and after intermittent years of omission, it held a permanent position after 1919. In 1932, presumably to conform to international standards, the distance was established at 3,000 meters.

The rules state that there shall be five jumps (obstacles), including a water jump (obstacle), in each ¼ mile. The water jump (obstacle) shall be 12 feet (3.66 meters) in width and length and the water 2 feet 6 inches (76 centimeters) in depth at the hurdle end, sloping to the level of the field at the farther end.

The hurdles shall be 914 millimeters (3 feet) high. The hurdles at the water jump shall be fixed firmly. It is recommended that the hurdles be approximately 3.66 meters (12 feet) wide and heavy enough so that they cannot be overturned easily.

Each competitor shall go over or through the water, and any one who steps to one side or the other of the jump (obstacle) shall be disqualified. The competitor must clear each jump (obstacle).

Qualifications. The steeplechase is an event that calls for endurance, speed, distance perception, judgment of pace, and a fair degree of agility in clearing the five obstacles.

A candidate for the steeplechase usually is one who has had experience in running distances ranging from 1 mile to 5 miles.

Experience in distance running contributes to meeting the requirement of endurance. However, the distance runner is obliged, in both early and midseasons, to drill on both hurdle clearance and the water jump. He must be able to adjust the strides (when approaching an obstacle) so that there is no hesitancy when accepting the "striding" or jumping challenges. He strides over the four hurdle obstacles. He jumps over the water by placing the foot of the leading leg on the top of the bar of the water obstacle and permits the body to lean approximately 25 degrees before he completes the spring from the bar. Such a technique means that the steeplechase runner applies jumping force to the water obstacle by utilizing the foot opposite the customary take-off foot. For this reason, some steeplechase competitors rightfully develop the ability to take off from either foot.

Long jumping exercises and drills on distance perception (when running toward the five obstacles) are included in the training routine.

Schedules of practice for steeplechase running. From the previous discussion, the athlete recognizes the need for a long period of endurance-building exercises, coupled with drills in hurdling and jumping.

A schedule of practice for 1 week in midseason for Charles N. ("Deacon") Jones,

University of Iowa, is cited as a representative schedule of practice for an experienced competitor.

In 1957 he established an American record of 9 minutes, 49.6 seconds for the 2-mile steeplechase, which is approximately 240 yards more than 3,000 meters.

In one of the 3,000-meter steeplechase heats in the 1960 Olympic games, Jones was credited with the time of 8 minutes, 47.4 seconds.

One of the authors, who served as Jones' coach during his collegiate career, supervised the following plan for his midseason activities.

Monday

1. Warm up in the customary manner.
2. Spend 40 to 50 minutes on the Fartlek system of exercises.
3. Sprint 120 to 150 yards at a pace approaching full effort. Jog for a period of 2 or 3 minutes. Repeat 4 to 6 times.
4. Weight-training exercises, customarily included on Monday, are omitted. (Weight-training exercises were a part of both the preliminary and early season schedules.)

Tuesday

1. Follow the usual warm-up pattern.
2. Engage in interval running as follows:
   a. Run 880 yards at racing pace. Reduce the customary interval of jogging to 440 yards in 2 minutes, 30 seconds. Repeat twice.
   b. Run 440 yards, slightly faster than racing pace. Reduce the customary interval of jogging to 440 yards in 2 minutes, 30 seconds. Repeat twice.
3. Practice on the clearance of both the hurdles and the water jump for a period of 30 minutes.
   a. Develop the knack of becoming proficient at taking off from either foot. (It is more desirable to take

off from the same foot at each obstacle unless stride alterations do
not make it feasible).

b. Attempt to maintain a normal running stride as the obstacles are approached and thus avoid loss of
momentum either by floating or by
step shortening. The athlete attempt to drive into each obstacle.

c. Make an effort to develop hurdling
mechanics similar to top-flight 400-
meter hurdlers. (See Hurdles,
Chapter 8.)

d. When the foot is atop the water-
obstacle bar, permit the torso and
leg to rock over on the foot in
order to execute a spring that pro-
pels the center of body weight forward and upward. (Some steeplechase runners spring too soon and
thus emphasize upward rather
than forward momentum.)

e. Conclude the day's activities by
running approximately 2 miles on
turf at an optional pace.

Wednesday

1. Start the day with the usual warm-up.
2. Set five hurdles (3 feet high) in approximately the position of the five
obstacles used in a race.
   a. Run (over the hurdles) 440 yards
   in 65 or 66 seconds.
   b. Jog 440 yards in 2 minutes, 30 seconds.
   c. Repeat 9 times.
3. Run 440 yards (without the hurdles)
in 66 seconds. Jog 440 yards in 2 minutes, 30 seconds.
4. Run 440 yards (without the hurdles)
at full effort.
5. At this stage of the steeplechase runner's development, weight-training
exercises may be reduced in quantity
or omitted.

Thursday

1. Begin practice with the customary
warm-up.
2. Participate in interval running.
   a. Run 220 yards in 30 or 31 seconds.
   b. Jog 110 yards.
   c. Repeat 9 times, and gradually increase the speed of each succeeding sector until the last sector is
   run in 26 seconds.
3. Spend 15 to 20 minutes in perfecting
the techniques of obstacle clearance
(both the hurdles and the water
jump).

Friday

Remain away from an athletics environment.

Saturday
Competition.

REFERENCES

1. Jones, T. E., and Best, R.: Personal communication.
2. Karvonen, M. J.: Effects of vigorous exercise
on the heart, In Rosenbaum, F. F., and Belk-
nap, E. L., editors: Work and the heart, New
York, 1959, Hoeber Medical Division (Harper
& Row).
3. Currens, J. H., and White, P. D.: Half a century of running, New England J. Med. **265**:988,
1961.
4. Capps, R. B.: Cause of the so-called side ache
in normal persons, Arch. Int. Med. **68**:94, 1941.
5. Holmer, G. (Chief Coach, Swedish Olympic
Track Team): A training program, Track &
Field News, 1949, Los Altos, Calif.
6. Dyson, G. H. G. (Chief National Coach, Track,
Great Britain): Comments reported by Cordner
Nelson in Track & Field News, 1950, Los Altos,
Calif.
7. Kerssenbrock, K.: In Leichtathletik, Prague, reported in Track & Field News, 1953, Los Altos,
Calif.
8. Fowler, N.: A Russian plan, Track & Field
News, 1958, Los Altos, Calif.

Relay racing

A relay race is an event in which two or more men run a specified distance, one relieving the other at some designated point within a fixed zone.

The large number of relay carnivals held each year is an indication of the general favor that this event has met with all over the world. This popularity is deserved since a relay race offers spirited team competition and provides places for a large number of athletes. The grouping of distances run also provides competition for almost every type of athlete from the sprinter to the distance runner.

Under former rules, before a relief runner could begin his sector of a relay, he was required to touch the hand of the oncoming contestant in a zone of transfer. However, this method presented the difficulty of judging whether there was an actual hand-to-hand contact. In order to overcome this objection, the baton was introduced, and now the oncoming man must hand the baton to the relief runner. Baton transfer furnishes a hazard to the relay race, thus making it an exciting and spectacular event. In order to reduce baton-passing hazards to a minimum, rather definite techniques of transfer have been worked out.

Since relay racing requirements and techniques have so many things in common with sprinting, middle distance running, and distance running, the chief points which need special consideration in presenting this event are the technique and finesse of carrying and passing the baton.

GENERAL CONSIDERATIONS

Types of relay races. By agreement, the total length of the race, the length of each sector of the race, and the number of athletes participating may be set at the pleasure of the games committee. At present the length of relay races varies from 220 yards to any number of miles. However, on the basis of total distance, the relay races which appear most frequently on the track and field program are as follows:

High school

1. 440 yards (4 × 110)
2. 880 yards (4 × 220)
3. 1 mile (4 × 440)

4. 2 miles (4 × 880)
5. Medley, 1 mile (440, 220, 220, and 880)
6. Shuttle hurdle, 480 yards (4 × 120)

College

1. 440 yards (4 × 110)
2. 880 yards (4 × 220)
3. 1 mile (4 × 440)
4. 2 miles (4 × 880)
5. 4 miles (4 × 1 mile)
6. Medley, sprint, 1 mile, 440, 220, 220, and 880)
7. Medley, distance, 2½ miles (¼, ½, ¾, and 1 mile)
8. Shuttle hurdle, 480 yards (4 × 120)

International

1. 400 meter (4 × 100)
2. 1,600 meters (4 × 400)
3. 3,200 meters (4 × 800)
4. Medley, 1, 000 meters (100, 200, 300, and 400)

Miscellaneous

1. Shuttle (flat) 220 yards (4 × 55)
2. Shuttle (flat) 440 yards (4 × 110)
3. Intercity (running the distance between cities)

Equipment. The only equipment peculiar to relay racing is the baton. Its form and weight are governed by rules which specify that it shall weigh not less than 50 grams (1.766 ounces), shall be not more than 30 centimeters (11.81 inches) long, and shall have a circumference of 12 centimeters (4.724 inches).

Comparative marks in competition. As a guide to the members of scholastic relay teams, Table 7-1 shows the estimated placing times (not winning times) for customary relay races. Since these times represent average performances, they will not apply to those sections of the country where the relay talent is either very good or very poor. Therefore, as in other track and field events, the relay runner should acquaint himself with the abilities of his rivals.

TECHNIQUE OF BATON PASSING

The introduction of the baton into the relay race has stimulated considerable investigation as to the best method of transfer, and as a result, a number of techniques have been suggested. Some of these methods and their application to various types of races are discussed.

Definition of the baton pass. For all relay races the baton is transferred within a 20-meter passing zone, formed by lines drawn 10 meters on each side of and parallel to the start-and-finish line (Fig. 7-1). Within this 20-meter zone each runner must pass the baton to the relief runner, the teammate succeeding him in the next sector of the race. No member of a relay team, in order to relieve his teammate, may run outside of such zone. However, in the 440-yard and the 880-yard relays, the runner who is to receive the baton may utilize the

Table 7-1. Comparative marks in competition in scholastic relay racing

Type of relay	No. of places scored	Meet	
		Qualifying (state) (min.:sec.)	State (min.:sec.)
440-yard (4 x 110)	5	43.0- 45.0	41.5- 43.0
880-yard (4 x 220)	5	1:30.0-1:34.0	1:28.0-1:32.0
1-mile medley (440, 220, 220, 880)	5	3:35.0-3:40.0	3:30.0-3:35.0
1-mile (4 x 440)	5	3:20.0-3:28.0	3:15.0-3:22.0
2-mile (4 x 880)	5	8:05.0-8:10.0	7:50.0-8:05.0

additional 10-meter zone (Fig. 7-1) in which to accelerate his run but must receive the baton within the 20-meter passing zone. The baton actually must be passed, not thrown or dropped by the contestant and picked up by the runner succeeding him. Failure to pass the baton shall disqualify the team from competition in the event in which is has occurred. After passing the baton, the passer should jog straight ahead unless he be in either the inside or outside lane, in which case he should step off the track as quickly as possible.

Methods of transfer. On the basis of the position of the head and eyes, there are two commonly accepted methods of passing the baton. In one, the awaiting receiver keeps the eyes focused on the baton in the hand of the passer until the transfer is made. This is designated as the visual pass. In the other method, the awaiting receiver keeps the eyes focused on the passer until the latter reaches a designated spot or target on the track about 6½ yards (approximately 6 meters) away (Fig. 7-1). Instantaneously the receiver turns his head and eyes to the front and starts running. This is described as the nonvisual pass.

The visual method of passing is suitable to all relay races but is more commonly employed in the longer distances where the degree of fatigue of the oncoming runner must be gauged accurately. Therefore, in contests in which an athlete runs a sector of the relay which is 300 yards or more in length, the receiver watches the passer, evaluates his speed, and keeps the baton in his vision until it is within his grasp. Meanwhile the receiver gets in motion so that he is under way when the transfer occurs. The visual method is consid-

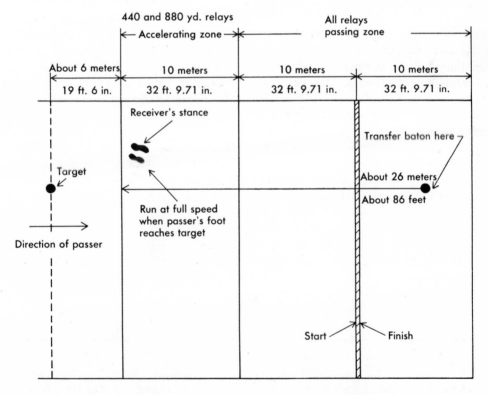

Fig. 7-1. A scheme of baton pass (nonvisual method) adaptable to the sprint relay.

ered by some authorities to be safer than the nonvisual because both the runner and the baton are in the receiver's line of vision until, and during, the critical moment of the transfer. This method does not permit the speedy transfer offered by the nonvisual method, because the receiver cannot gain optimum speed when his head, eyes, and trunk are turned sideward and backward.

The nonvisual method is universally used in all sprint relays (220 to 880 yards) and in those sections of medley relays in which the passer runs a distance of 300 yards or less. It has already been inferred that there is a greater degree of risk in making the transfer while the baton is out of the range of vision. Insurance against an inaccurate pass must give way to speed in the shorter relay, a factor which adds thrill and uncertainty to the sport and makes relay racing interesting to contestant and spectator alike.

Styles of arm-hand position. There are several commonly used styles of arm-hand position in baton transfer (Fig. 7-2). In all styles the receiver assumes a stance near the back line of the passing zone as shown in Fig. 7-1. The passer executes the transfer with the left hand, and the receiver in running stride accepts it with the right hand and shifts it to his left hand as soon as possible.

1. (Fig. 7-2, *A*) The receiver extends his right arm back and slightly below the height of his shoulder. The elbow as well as the palm is up, and the thumb is pointed toward the body (to the left). The passer extends his left arm and aims to synchronize its downward swing with the forward stride of his right leg when making the transfer. The arrow indicates the direction of moving the baton.

2. (Fig. 7-2, *B*) The receiver extends his right arm back and slightly to the right at a height 4 or 5 inches above the plane of his hips. The palm is up

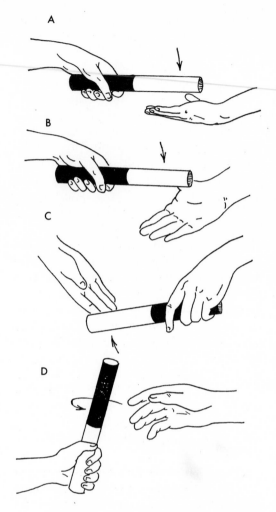

Fig. 7-2. Styles of hand positions during the baton pass.

and the thumb is pointed toward the rear. The elbow is down. The arm action of the passer is quite similar to that described for form *A*.

3. (Fig. 7-2, *C*) The receiver extends his right arm back so that the hand is at a height approximating the plane of his hips. Some good competitors prefer to hold it below the level of the hips. The palm is to the rear, with the thumb pointing downward. The passer extends his left arm forward, contacting his teammate's hand

on the upward rather than on the downward movement described for styles *A* and *B*.

4. (Fig. 7-2, *D*) the passer holds the baton upright in his left hand while he extends his left arm. The receiver then graps the exposed postion of the baton.

Types of baton grasp. Frequently little attention is given to the problem of holding the baton by relay runner No. 1 when in position on the mark. True enough, relay races have been won and will continue to be won by teams whose lead-off competitor gives little heed to the hand grasp. However, teams have suffered disappointment because their No. 1 man either left the mark minus the baton or had it knocked from his hand because of either an incorrect carriage or an insecure grasp. The latter hazard is more common to the lead-off athlete than to his three succeeding teammates, especially in races in which the start is not staggered. When the starting runner of each team is not placed in a staggered or echelon form, all lead-off men come to the mark shoulder to shoulder on a line across the track.

At the start of the race, the No. 1 runner grasps the baton in a manner to his liking. Five commonly used types of grasp are shown in Fig. 7-3. It will be noted that the baton is carried in the left hand as a matter of convenience but not of necessity. One reason for the left-hand hold lies in the fact that the receiver usually takes a stance partially turned toward the outside of the track. In such a stance the backward reach is facilitated by employing the right hand rather than the left hand. Therefore, to eliminate the necessity of shifting the baton to the left hand, the initial runner carries it in his left hand while on the mark.

During the main part of a race the baton may be held in any manner that feels comfortable to the competitor. If the passer allows a considerable amount of exposed surface at the forward end of the baton, he

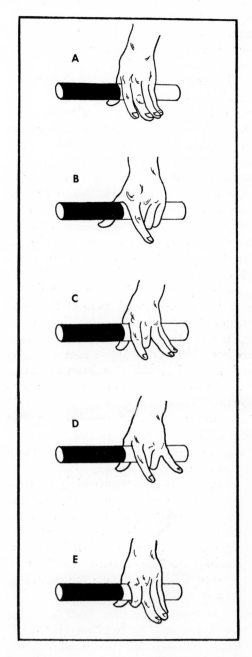

Fig. 7-3. Types of grasp of the baton at the start of a race.

will facilitate passing. To phrase it another way, he gives his teammate "the big end of the stick."

In the type of pass shown in Fig. 7-2, *A*, the receiver should grasp close to the passer's hand so that when (during the first stride) he shifts the baton from the right hand to the left hand he will have ample space for the left-hand grasp. In other words, the left hand will grasp the unshaded half and leave free the shaded portion for the next transfer.

The type of pass shown in Fig. 7-2, *B*, requires that when the receiver executes the shift to the left hand the shaded portion of the baton be swung outward and forward. At one stage in its movement, while in a plane parallel to the ground, a line drawn through the extremities of the baton forms a right angle to the body. Thus the baton protrudes to the right side. When competitors are closely bunched, there is a possibility of having the baton knocked from the grasp.

In the types depicted in Fig. 7-2, *C* and *D*, the receiver may grasp the fore part of the baton and shift it so that the left hand grasps it at the rear half, again providing ample space for the next receiver's hand hold.

No matter which type of grasp is employed, the objectives are economy of movement and the exposure of ample baton surface to permit a substantial grasp by the succeeding teammate. It appears reasonable to assume that time is lost if the athlete, once having possession of the baton, is required to press it against his thigh and slide the hand inward for the purpose of providing a grasping surface for his teammate.

Again, the shift from the right hand to the left hand should be accomplished with the minimum detraction from sprinting form. To this end, the shift usually is made when it causes the least interference, namely, in the first stride after the baton is taken. Occasionally a fatigued distance

relay runner makes the mistake of executing a right-hand cross-body shift of the baton to the left hand within the last few strides, at a time when his body control is least efficient.

Relation of arm-hand position to visual and nonvisual passes. The type depicted in Fig. 7-2, *D*, is utilized in the visual method of transfer. The positions shown in Fig. 7-2, *A*, *B*, and *C*, may be employed with both the nonvisual and visual methods of baton passing.

It was pointed out previously that the nonvisual method was used in races in which the passer covered 300 yards or less in his sector of the relay. Obviously its use is recommended in both the 440- and 880-yard relays. Furthermore, it can be used effectively in medley relays whenever the passer runs less than 300 yards, even though the receiver runs 880 yards. On the other hand, a competitor running a sprint sector of a medley relay race should employ the visual method when accepting the baton from a teammate who has negotiated more than 300 yards.

Factors to consider when adopting a baton passing style. When selecting the proper style of baton passing, the coach and competitors make their choice on the following bases:

1. The distance of the relay race. (In sprint relays the nonvisual method is adopted, and in longer races the visual method is used.)

2. The mechanical efficiency of the arm-hand styles.

3. The adaptability of the style to the athletes.

4. The degree of certainty that a particular style provides.

5. The amount of free distance gained by the forward reach of the passer and the backward reach of the receiver.

6. The style providing optimum speed for both the receiver and the passer at the instant of transfer.

7. The distance of the receiver's target from the back line of the passing zone (Fig. 7-1) if the nonvisual method is selected. The placement of the target may vary rightfully from the suggested 6½ yards to fit the passer and receiver. If the passer is exceptionally fast, the target may be set at 7 to 10 yards. The point of transfer may range from 15 to 18 yards from the back line of the passing zone.

Variations in the nonvisual method of baton transfer. A common procedure in executing the transfer in the sprint relays is as follows: The receiver extends his right arm and, when his teammate reaches the target, turns his head and eyes to the front and darts away. The right hand is kept well extended backward from the onset of the receiver's getaway until the baton is within his grasp. Obviously the right arm, because of its constrained position, has not provided its share of compensating reaction to the movement of the legs. Therefore, some relay runners vary the procedure as follows: The receiver assumes the customary stance and, when the passer reaches the target, runs at top speed. However, he uses both arms as in sprinting until he reaches the last 5 to 6 yards of the passing zone, at which time he swings the right arm back into a receiving position until the baton is in his grasp. The latter method offers more opportunity for a speedy transfer because it is more conducive to acceleration. A disadvantage of this method rests in the fact that the receiver frequently misjudges the timing, or the direction, or the height of the backward hand swing. The first method described (continuous arm extension) has the advantage of proffering a target (the receiver's hand) throughout the passing zone.

Variations in baton handling. The usual admonition of the coach is, "Receive with the right hand, pass with the left hand." It was pointed out earlier that when the baton is taken in the right hand by the receiver, he is facing the outside of the track, a position that readily permits him to extend his right arm in the direction of the passer.

However, numerous coaches have adopted a plan whereby the relay runners are not obliged to shift the baton from one hand to the other. This technique is used frequently in indoor relay races where the running oval is smaller than the customary outdoor track. Furthermore, this type is employed frequently outdoors in sprint relays whenever the receivers are obliged to accept the baton while stationed on a curved portion of the track. Under this plan each athlete carries the baton through his sector of the relay in the same hand in which it was placed at the onset. The second and fourth runners receive the baton in the left hand while facing the inside of the track. The third runner assumes a stance facing the outside of the track and takes the baton in the right hand. Obviously, if runner No. 1 carries the baton in the right hand, none of the runners is obliged to shift the baton from one hand to the other. The advantage claimed for the no-shift method is the elimination of cross-body arm motions by each of the last three team members. The disadvantages cited are as follows: The second and fourth runners are obliged to assume a stance which may be variant from the other competitors, and furthermore, the carrying of the baton in the right hand may expose it to interference.

ARRANGEMENT OF A RELAY TEAM

The four members of a relay team usually manifest a range in characteristics and ability. On numerous occasions athletes have performed better while a member of the relay team than in either a time trial or in their chosen event in open competition. Seldom are they equal in both ability and knowledge of racing tactics. The competitor may be assigned his order of running either at random or after a careful analysis of his strength and weakness. The intelligent instructor balances the factors and decides on the most efficient baton-passing and running combination. The points to be considered are as follows:

1. The length of the race. This determines whether the visual or nonvisual method of transfer will be employed.
2. Which athlete runs best when behind?
3. Which athlete runs best when in the lead?
4. Who is the fastest starter?
5. Is the fastest starter cool headed so that he will provide team stability should he be selected as No. 1 man?
6. Who are the two best baton handlers? (Obviously the second and the third runners each have two movements to execute, while the first and the fourth runners each perform only one movement.)
7. What lane position has the team drawn?
8. Is the competition outdoors with ample room to get around opponents, or is it indoors where the acquisition of the lead position is very advantageous?
9. In what order of relative strength is the opposing team lined up?
10. What passing-receiving pairs work most effectively together? Adjustments are frequently required when men of varying heights and arm lengths are to be fitted into a smooth passing combination.

If the four members of a relay team are listed in the order of their ability to cover their respective distances in the shortest interval of time, they may be designated as 1, 2, 3, and 4.

The most commonly accepted arrangement of a team based on the running skill is 2, 4, 3, 1. In such a plan the most efficient team member is placed in the anchor position or, in other words, the fourth sector of the race. This arrangement assumes his ability either to retain the lead given him or to retrieve any loss in distance that he might have inherited. The second fastest team member is assigned the lead-off position in the hope that he will run on even terms with his competitors or possibly hand over a lead to his teammate. That team member having the least ability is assigned to run the second sector so that, should he suffer a loss of distance, there remain two men of fair ability to make up the yardage.

Another order of running calls for placing the men 4, 3, 2, and 1 (in the reverse order of their ability). When all members of the team are adept at running a race from behind, this sequence is satisfactory. It has a disadvantage in that frequently the first runner, pitted against relatively faster opponents, suffers a yardage deficiency, which keeps the three remaining teammates in difficulty.

Occasionally, in indoor relay competition the acquisition of the lead is quite important, especially when it is difficult to run around opponents on a track which is either short or narrow. To meet this condition, the members of the team are sent to the mark in the order of 1, 2, 3, 4.

A further deviation consists in placing the runners in the order of 2, 3, 4, 1. Here the slowest runner is assigned the third sector in the hope that the first two teammates may turn over a distance advantage to him. In case he should not retain this lead, the heavy-duty work will be assumed by the relay team's best performer, who will anchor the race.

A sound procedure consists of analyzing carefully the four runners, determining the most effective order of carrying the baton, emphasizing judgment of pace so that each will run his respective sector at his optimum pace, and then retaining this order throughout the season. The confidence and composure of a team are frequently disturbed by a last-minute change in its running order. Needless worry over the possible outcome of the contest is the result.

SPECIFIC ASSIGNMENTS OF THE PASSER AND THE RECEIVER

To be successful, a transfer of the baton requires certain definite characteristics of both the passer and the receiver. An effective pass is defined as one in which the baton is transferred when the two team members involved are running at an equal rate of speed, this rate being the optimum for each. The requirements vary only slightly when the athlete is required to change from the visual to the nonvisual method. The duties are discussed under the responsibilities of the passer, the responsibilities of the receiver using the visual method, and the responsibilities of the receiver using the nonvisual method.

Responsibilities of the passer. The tasks imposed on the passer are discussed in the order in which they are to be completed.

1. He must judge and distribute his strength and effort so as to reach his teammate in the shortest period of time. For example, in the longer races (beyond 220 yards), excess speed at the start may cause him to tie up at the finish.

2. The passer must pick out definitely the teammate to whom he expects to pass the baton so that he may steer his path in the correct direction. Furthermore, he should direct his path so that the baton is in alignment with the receiver's hand.

3. He should have a knowledge of where his opponents are going to make the transfer. For example, he should know whether the team wearing blue jerseys, whose runner is just ahead of him, intends to cut to the inside or to the outside of the track.

4. The arm should be extended at the proper time, neither too early nor too late. If it is extended too soon, valuable arm synchronization is lost. The error of an overdelayed extension is obvious. In sprint relays the most effective passes occur 15 to 18 yards from the back line of the passing zone (Fig. 7-1). In longer races the pass should occur 5 to 12 yards from this line.

5. When the arm is extended, it should synchronize with the legs.

6. A sufficient amount of the exposed baton should be provided for the receiver. Give him the big end of the stick.

7. Provided that the receiver holds his hand at the correct height, the passer is responsible for the correct height of the transfer.

8. The passer is responsible for applying the correct amount of pressure to the baton in the transfer. He must retain his grasp of the baton until he is sure that his teammate has a secure hold of it. The baton, laid in the teammate's hand with a moderate amount of pressure, brings about an automatic grasping of the baton by the receiver.

9. The passer should continue in his own lane until he is "uncovered." He should slow down gradually until the opposing teams have passed the baton, at which time he has a clear path to retire from the track.

10. The passer must not slow up when he approaches his teammate, nor should he anticipate the pass. Instead he should run close to his receiver and carry through for several yards beyond the ideal spot of transfer.

Responsibilities of the receiver (visual method). The following tasks are imposed on the receiver using the visual method of transfer.

1. He must be certain that he is in the

correct lane. This is especially true when there are six or more teams competing.

2. He must have a correct stance in his lane, namely, one that will permit a fast getaway and give the passer room to run.
3. He must judge the speed of the incoming runner. Since he is required to watch the teammate coming down the track, he needs drill on running in a straight, forward direction with the head and eyes to the rear. As a safety measure he may glance quickly in the direction of his run, an instant before starting his getaway, so that he may be sure the forward path is clear.
4. Closely associated with speed and and judgment, the receiver must gauge the degree of fatigue of the passer. This holds true in sectors of more than 220 yards.
5. He must time his getaway correctly, starting neither too soon nor too late.
6. To facilitate an effective transfer of the baton, there are certain definite positions of the hand and arm which are necessary:
   a. A wide spread of the fingers, thus providing a sizeable target.
   b. A correct degree of height of the hand depending on the style of arm-hand position agreed upon.
   c. The most desirable lateral position of the arm and hand so that they are neither too far to the left nor to the right.
   d. Steadiness of the hand is important. It must move in an even plane with the ground.
   e. The response to the touch of the baton must be automatic (in other words, reflex).
7. The shift of the baton from the right hand to the left hand should be made at a time when it least affects the running stride. Some athletes make the

shift on the back stretch when the field of runners is not closely bunched and others toward the end of their run. The majority execute the shift during the first running stride.

Responsibilities of the receiver (nonvisual method). In addition to the tasks enumerated for the receiver using the visual method, the athlete has some further duties to perform when he receives the baton when the head and eyes are to the front.

1. In addition to knowing that he is in the correct lane, he must be sure that he knows the exact location of both the back and the front lines of the passing zones. This applies especially when the entire race is run in lanes.
2. The application of foot drive should be the same as in a start with a pistol, provided it is a sprint relay.
3. He must use his own judgment as to the correct moment of initiating the getaway. This means that he should not rely on the verbal signals "go" or "wait."
4. He should accustom himself to running for a period of 3 to 4 seconds before expecting the baton to touch his outstretched hand. An otherwise excellent transfer has been ruined because the receiver became worried needlessly and reduced his speed, fearing that he was running away from his teammate, even though both were well within the passing zone.

SHUTTLE RELAY (ON THE FLAT)

The shuttle relay derives its name from the similarity of the back-and-forth course of the runners to the movement of the shuttle in weaving. This contest may be held either on the cinder straightaway or on the flat enclosure within the oval track. Quite frequently one-half the team takes a position on one goal line of a football gridiron and the other half on the opposite goal line.

This race is popular with youthful competitors since the distance assigned to each athlete may be reduced to 50 yards or less. Again, the number of runners in each team is unlimited, being determined by agreement.

The odd-numbered runners (1 and 3) take their positions at one end of the course and the even-numbered runners (2 and 4) at the opposite end. If the number of men is even, both the start and finish are at the same end of the course.

Ordinarily the baton is not utilized in these races because the runners are going in opposite directions, making it difficult to execute the transfer and also to determine where the pass actually occurred. As a substitute for the baton, the relief runner starts when the incoming athlete touches his outstretched hand. As a further aid to the judges in determining a legal touch-off (one in which the relief man remains behind the scratch line until touched), restraining posts for each team are planted on the scratch lines. Therefore, for a given team, the odd-numbered runners, except the first, will use one restraining post and the even-numbered runners the other restraining post at the opposite end of the course. Restraining posts may be either fixed or movable. In meets where portable or movable posts are used, the rules frequently require that they be left standing after the touch-off. The lead-off man starts from the crouch position, and all relief runners start from a standing position, in which the right arm is extended forward at shoulder height and to the right of the restraining post. At the instant of hand contact, the relief runner quickly draws back his right arm and strides out with the right foot. Obviously his body passes to the left of the restraining post and the incoming runner passes on the opposite side.

The practice schedule, the placement of runners, and the responsibilities of the team members quite closely resemble those of the sprint relay previously described.

SHUTTLE HURDLE RELAY

The shuttle hurdle relay is the same as the shuttle relay except hurdles are placed at the regulation distances. The height of the hurdles, as well as the distance between them, is determined by the games committee. In collegiate or A.A.U. competition, the obstacles are customarily 42 inches high, spaced according to the rules for the high hurdles. This usually permits 15 yards from the start to the first hurdle and 15 yards from the last hurdle to the finish line. For scholastic meets the hurdles may be either 39 inches high (10 yards apart) or 30 inches high (20 yards apart).

It is a common practice to provide two lanes of hurdles for each team. When only one lane is available for each team, a displaced hurdle must be reset immediately. This causes considerable confusion, and consequently, double lanes for each team are strongly recommended. When two lanes are provided, the athletes should run in the lane to the left.

Neither the restraining post nor the baton is employed in the shuttle hurdle relay. The rules suggest (but do not demand) that an inspector be assigned each runner.

The responsibilities of both the oncoming hurdler and the relief hurdler correspond, in general, to those discussed under relay races when the baton is utilized. The oncoming hurdler should finish his race on the correct side of the lane.

The relief hurdler is responsible for completing adjustments which include getting on the mark. This should be done shortly after the oncoming hurdler starts his sector of the race. The set position should be taken as soon as his teammate clears the last hurdle. The set position must be held until the oncoming hurdler crosses the restraining line.

In addition to the suggestions made for the order of running in the relays already discussed, the coach takes into consideration such points as the ability of the competitor to run when behind, the ability of the competitor to run when ahead, and the direction and velocity of the wind. Athletes who perform well, even when behind, are usually placed third and fourth, and those who run better when ahead are ordinarily placed first and second. It is customary to assign the fastest man to run the anchor position.

Generally, the 175-pound hurdler is less affected by a head wind than his 150-pound teammate. The more rugged and taller athletes are frequently assigned the sections that require facing the wind.

In general, the practice schedule for the shuttle hurdle relay is the same as for hurdles. However, in addition to hurdling drills, practice in coordinating the starts for the second, third, and fourth legs of the race should be engaged in 2 or 3 days each week. These drills may be taken over one hurdle (15 yards from the start, 15 yards to the finish). Three or four coordinated starts at full effort should suffice for 1 day's workout.

Adjustments in both the height of the hurdle and the length of the race provide opportunity for participation by grade school youths as well as mature athletes.

Chapter 8

The hurdles

Hurdling is an interesting and spectacular contest because it consists not only of sprinting but also of clearing obstacles of various heights placed in the path of the runner. The range in distance in hurdle races is from 40 yards to 440 yards. The outdoor distances are of standard length, whereas the indoor course is limited by the size of the quarters utilized for the track and field meet. Although steeplechase running presents many of the characteristics of hurdling, in common parlance it is not spoken of as a hurdling event.

Hurdle races are sometimes classified according to the height of the obstacle cleared and frequently on the basis of distance run. On the basis of the height of the obstacle placed in the course of the runner, the heights are as follows:

1. The low hurdles (high school and indoor college meets), 30 inches
2. The intermediate hurdles (college, Amateur Athletic Union, and Olympic games), 36 inches
3. The interscholastic high hurdles (high school and academy), 39 inches
4. The intercollegiate and international standard high hurdles, 42 inches

When classified according to distance, the most common hurdle races are as follows:

1. 120-yard high hurdles (high school and college)
2. 180-yard low hurdles (high school)
3. 440-yard (400-meter) intermediate hurdles (college)

In 1934 the National Federation of State High School Athletic Associations recommended that the height of the interscholastic high hurdle be reduced to 39 inches with the idea of encouraging younger competitors. They are still required to negotiate 10 barriers over a distance of 120 yards. Like the rules for the low hurdles, the regulations for the high hurdles have been approved generally by the various state high school athletic associations and were finally placed in the rules in 1936.

The standard high hurdle utilized in college, A.A.U., international, and Olympic competition is 42 inches in height. The distance between hurdles (10 yards) and the approach to the first hurdle (15 yards) are the same for both the 120-yard and 110-meter events.

When the course is marked in metric distances, the 120-yard high hurdle race is measured as 110 meters (120.3 yards); the 440-yard course is measured as 400 meters (437.4 yards). It should be noted that only metric distances are run in the Olympic games.

A survey of hurdling competition shows that the 120-yard high hurdle race was first included in major competitions in America when George Hitchock of the New York Athletic Club won the national A.A.U. championship in 1876 with a time of 19 seconds. Eleven years later, in 1887, A. F. Copeland of the Manhattan Athletic Club was named the first national champion in the low hurdles, his time being 27 seconds. The intermediate hurdles of 440 yards, or 400 meters in all countries except the United States and the British Empire, were popular on the Continent years before W. H. Meanix of Boston Athletic Association captured the 1914 national championship in 57.2 seconds.

GENERAL CONSIDERATIONS

Comparative marks in competition. The schoolboy hurdler who desires to know how fast he will have to run in order to place at the various levels of competition is referred to Table 8-1. The times listed therein represent placing and not winning performances. Since these times are those of average performers, they will not apply to athletes in those areas in which the quality of the hurdlers is either very high or very low. The athlete is advised to become familiar with the performances of his opponents.

At the present time data are not available dealing with placement marks for the 440-yard hurdles in academy and high school competition because of the infrequent inclusion of this race on the interscholastic program.

Equipment. The majority of hurdlers prefer ordinary sprinting shoes with heel cups inserted in the shoes.

The ankle and the knee of the take-off leg should, from the start of the season, be protected by sponge rubber or some similar substance which is shock proof and light in weight. A courageous and fearless attitude toward the spring and the hurdle clearance is generated by such protective devices. Furthermore, the event is made more pleasurable if there is some insurance against bruises and lacerations. Injury is conducive to timidity, which, in turn, detracts from form. As the athlete gains proficiency in the event, the knee and ankle protectors may be omitted.

Qualifications. The most successful hurdlers have long legs. They may or may not be tall. In general, the tall man has the advantage in low as well as in high hurdling.

Table 8-1. Comparative marks in scholastic competition in hurdle races

Meet	No. of places scored	120-yard high hurdles 39 in. (sec.)	180-yard low hurdles 30 in. (sec.)
Dual high school	3	15.0-16.0	20.0-21.0
Qualifying—state	3	14.6-15.6	19.5-20.5
State—province	5	14.2-14.8	19.2-20.0

Hurdlers are usually of the long muscled type rather than the thick-muscled type. Good competitors range in weight from 145 pounds to 170 pounds. Since 440-yard hurdling is a combination of quarter-mile racing and obstacle clearing, the type of competitor varies. In this race, endurance is at a much higher premium than in either the high or low hurdles.

An ideal hurdler has speed, spring, courage, and endurance. The latter qualification is especially important for the low and the 440-yard hurdler.

Coordination and rhythm are of paramount importance in the timing of the lift and the hurdle clearance. This may be described as ability to regain sprinting form rapidly after the obstacle has been cleared.

Up to the present time hurdlers have been found among the younger age group of athletes, a situation that does not prevail in distance running. Thus far there have been few champions over the age of 26 years. There are no apparent ana-tomic reasons why the youngster should not compete in hurdle competition.

Judgment of distance and good vision are important assets to anyone who aspires to proficiency in running the hurdles.

TECHNIQUE OF THE HURDLES

Although there is considerable similarity in the mechanical execution of the various hurdle races, there are enough important differences to warrant a separate discussion of each hurdle event.

120-yard high hurdles. It has been pointed out that prior to 1934 high school and college men alike competed over hurdles 42 inches high. Although it has been recommended by the rules committee that the height of the hurdle be reduced to 39 inches, not all high schools have adopted this height. Because of this fact it is necessary to give attention to both the 42-inch and the 39-inch hurdles. In all descriptions it is assumed that the hurdler drives off the ground from the left foot.

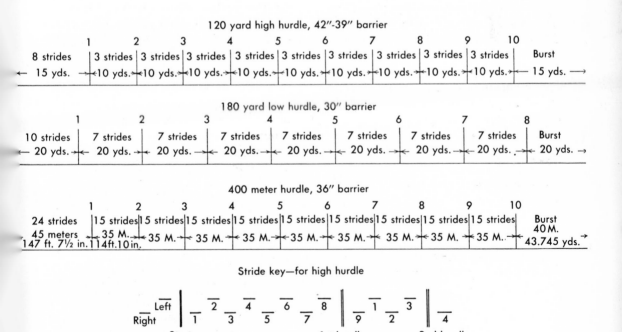

Fig. 8-1. Stride plans for hurdle races.

Start. The start of a hurdle race is as important as the start of a sprint. The items of foot spacing, body tension, weight distribution, and reaction time should be given the same consideration by the hurdler as by the sprinter. These coaching points are discussed in detail in Chapter 4.

A hurdler may be required to vary his normal sprint start by reversing the position of the feet (placing of the right foot forward) when coming to the mark so as to get the correct number of strides to the first hurdle and to reach the take-off spot with the left foot. The start is the same regardless of the height of the hurdles.

Strides to the first high hurdle. The stride plan for the entire 120-yard high hurdle race is shown in Fig. 8-1 and is the same for both the 42-inch and 39-inch barriers. In the diagram the number of strides from the start to the first hurdle is shown as 8. The majority of hurdlers adopt this approach, although there are some hurdlers who cover the 15-yard distance in 7 strides. These individuals reverse the position of the feet in the starting position.

The strides are gradually increased in length as the hurdler leaves the starting mark, and a proficient man tries to react as rapidly in his approach as he would when competing in the 50-yard dash. Exercises designed to develop speed and strength should reduce the need for the novice to stretch the fifth, sixth, and seventh strides in the approach.

The trunk lean during the first 7 strides is quite similar to that assumed in sprinting. On the eighth stride the body is inclined forward in anticipation of the spring and the trunk bend (Fig. 8-3, *A*). A word of caution is in place here. The athlete must not execute the trunk lean too soon. A premature bend detracts from the effectiveness of the spring.

There is little choice between the 7-stride and the 8-stride approach if both are properly executed. The shorter and the average-sized hurdlers apparently gain momentum better by employing the 8-stride method. To be sure, the hurdler selecting the 8-stride plan must maintain a cadence 14 percent faster than his 7-stride rival. On the other hand, the competitor using the 7-stride approach is required to lengthen his steps on the average of 14 percent and must necessarily run at a reduced cadence. The extremely long-legged man can execute the 7-stride approach better than his shorter opponent. This discussion applies equally well to both the 42-inch and the 39-inch hurdles.

Clearance of the first high hurdle. As the hurdler reaches the end of the eighth stride, he makes preparation for clearing the first

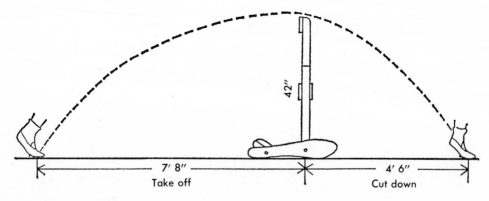

Fig. 8-2. The method used for determining the distance of the take-off and the cut-down in hurdle clearance.

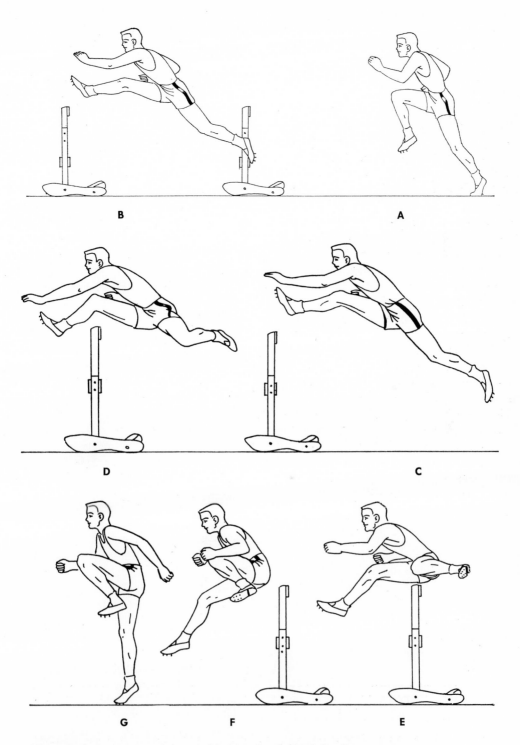

Fig. 8-3, A-G. A series of acceptable form for the high hurdles.

barrier. The average distance from the front spike mark of the left shoe to the center of the first hurdle is 7 feet 3 inches, and the average distance from the front spike mark of the right shoe (cut down, Fig. 8-2) to the center of the hurdle is 4 feet 11 inches. The stride key (Fig. 8-1) for the 120-yard high hurdles shows the distribution of the strides in the approach, the clearance of the first hurdle, the 3 strides between the first and the second hurdles, and the clearance of the second hurdle.

At the completion of the eighth stride (Fig. 8-3, *A*), the hurdler lifts the right knee and straightens the left leg so that the shoulder, knee, and foot are in the same plane. Concurrently with this movement, a rock-up on the toes and a double arm thrust are executed (Fig. 8-3, *B*). It should be noted that the left arm movement is synchronized with that of the right leg and is extended vigorously forward and parallel to it. The right arm bent at the elbow is only partially swung backward. The degree of this backward swing depends on the hurdler. It is less in the case of tall hurdlers with light legs and heavy arms and more for short men with heavy legs and light arms. The arm movement is more emphasized and forceful than in the normal running stride. As forward progress is made, the left leg is extended (Fig. 8-3, *C*), and the trunk is bent sharply forward. A few champion high hurdlers drop the head downward momentarily when at the crest of hurdle clearance. They claim that this action aids both in the body balance and in the cut-down. This is simply a high exaggerated step over the obstacle. At the same time the snapping up of the left leg is begun. Motion pictures of well-trained hurdlers show that the plane of the head remains nearly constant during the race. This indicates that simultaneously with the execution of the leg lift the trunk is bent forward.

When the right foot is within 12 inches

of the hurdle, a vicious cut-down of the right leg is started. This is simply the movement of bringing the foot down rapidly on the far side of the barrier (Fig. 8-3, *C*). By starting this movement sufficiently early, the hurdler assures himself of a quick landing. This action is to be desired in view of the fact that propulsion cannot be resumed until one foot is on the ground. As the leg is brought downward, the trunk straightens up to a running position.

As soon as the right leg clears the hurdle (Fig. 8-3, *D*), it is quickly and partially bent and brought downward and backward with a kind of pawing-the-ground movement, which ensures that the foot will alight on the ground running, or moving backward at the same pace the runner is moving forward; otherwise the stride would be checked, and the hurdler probably would stumble. The foot alights, and the spikes engage the track just under or very slightly behind the center of weight. The right toe is pointed forward, and the foot is in line with the run. The snap forward of the left leg, begun as shown in Fig. 8-3, *C*, is continued as shown in Fig. 8-3, *D*, and completed as illustrated in Fig. 8-3, *E*. When the take-off leg is snapped up properly, two right angles are formed, one by the foot and leg and the other by the leg and thigh. Soaring over the hurdle is checked abruptly, partly by rapidly cutting down the right leg and partly by the straightening of the trunk.

The take-off leg is whipped rapidly across the barrier as shown in Fig. 8-3, *F*, so that it may, in turn, be snapped down into a rapid running stride. As the trunk is straightened, the left arm is brought back for the purpose of maintaining balance, and the right arm swings forward with the forward swing of the left leg.

The landing position shown in Fig. 8-3, *G*, is one in which the hurdler temporarily changes to a sprinter for the next 3 full

Table 8-2. Showing the distribution of the distance covered in the take-off and cut-down for the various hurdle races*

Type of hurdle	Take-off	Cut-down
The first hurdle		
42-inch high hurdle	7 ft. 3 in.	4 ft. 11 in.
39-inch high hurdle	7 ft. 5 in.	4 ft. 9 in.
30-inch 180-yard low hurdle	7 ft. 9 in.	4 ft. 3 in.
36-inch 400-meter and 440-yard intermediate hurdle	7 ft. 6 in.	4 ft. 7 in.
The second and succeeding hurdles		
42-inch high hurdle	7 ft. 8 in.	4 ft. 6 in.
39-inch high hurdle	7 ft. 7 in.	4 ft. 7 in.
30-inch 180-yard low hurdle	8 ft. 1 in.	3 ft. 11 in.
36-inch 400-meter and 440-yard intermediate hurdle	7 ft. 9 in.	4 ft. 4 in.

*In each case measurements were taken on a ground line from the mark made by the front spike to a spot directly under the center of the hurdle (see Fig. 8-2). These represent the average measurements obtained from a large number of hurdlers.

strides. This means that he utilizes the trunk lean and the arm work of a sprinter. The left foot strikes the ground at the end of the third stride in preparation for clearing the second hurdle.

The only adjustment necessary in applying the technique just described to the 39-inch hurdle is the distribution of distance covered in clearing the barrier. With the 39-inch hurdle the take-off may be moved 2 or 3 inches farther back and the landing 2 or 3 inches closer to the hurdle (Table 8-2). This means that the total distance covered is practically the same, namely, 12 feet 2 inches.

Strides between the high hurdles. The same number of strides (3) between the obstacles applies to both the 39-inch and the 42-inch high hurdles. It will be noted that if the distance negotiated in the hurdle clearance, 12 feet 2 inches, is deducted from 30 feet, the distance between the barriers, there remains 17 feet 10 inches to be covered in 3 full strides. The average length of each stride is slightly less than 6 feet, but the first full step between hurdles is shorter (about 5 feet 5 inches) and the third full step longer (approximately 6 feet 5 inches). A smoother body action is

obtained when the 3 strides between the barriers are of equal cadence. Naturally the clearance step consumes more time than any other stride. It should be evident to the novice that the stride interruption incurred by the clearance slightly reduces forward momentum. A shorter first stride is employed to gain momentum in the same manner that the sprinter uses shorter strides when driving off the starting blocks. The beginning hurdler should understand that an extremely short first full stride between hurdles is not recommended. If he covers only a short space of ground on this step, he throws an added burden on the second and third strides. Speed is sacrificed if the athlete is required to stretch these two steps.

From the previous discussion it should be evident to the novice that he should cover the ground between the barriers with the same form and cadence that the sprinter utilizes in running races on the flat. This is especially true of the trunk lean, the arm-and-leg synchronization, the rock-up on the toes, the tension of the body, and the rapidity of cadence. The focus of the eyes should be momentarily on the top of the hurdle until clearance has begun. Then the focus is directed to the top of the next hurdle.

The beginner is urged not only to keep his vision in his own lane but also to build up a defense against distractions to his right and his left which may cause him to shift his view to see what is going on around him. Many experienced hurdlers have crashed into their barriers because they changed their focus of vision either to learn the proximity of their opponents or because they heard the clatter of falling hurdles.

At the end of the third full stride the competitor makes preparation for the clearance of the second hurdle.

Clearance of the second high hurdle. The clearance of all hurdles from the second to, and including, the tenth offers a slightly different problem from that presented by the first hurdle. The difference lies in the following facts: (1) the runner may not be at top hurdling speed when the first barrier is cleared; (2) there is a tendency to play safe on the first obstacle, clearing it somewhat higher than is absolutely necessary; and (3) the distance between the hurdles must be covered in 3 strides.

Although all athletes hope to be running at top speed when the first hurdle is reached, it must be remembered that some individuals do not attain peak momentum until 15 yards or more have been run. Furthermore, since the first hurdle is 15 yards from the starting line, the athlete begins his clearance before he has covered 13 yards. Although the general body actions are the same, differences in speed require adjustments in timing.

Perhaps the ideal situation occurs when the hurdler merely skims the top of each obstacle at a uniform height. We find in practice that the high hurdler is somewhat cautious and attempts to clear the first barrier with a margin of safety. The added height requires a more vigorous spring. The time consumed in flight is increased because clearance of the first hurdle assumes some slight aspects of a jump action rather than a step action.

As an athlete approaches the first hurdle, he is free to adjust his strides both as to number and length. On the contrary, the 30 feet between hurdles must be negotiated in 3 full strides plus the hurdle step. This difference requires that the distance of the cut-down, the length of the first full stride, the length of the second full stride, and the spot of the take-off must be uniform for the last 9 hurdles. For the 42-inch obstacle the average take-off distance is 7 feet 8 inches and the cut-down is 4 feet 6 inches. For the 39-inch barrier, the average high school boy takes off 7 feet 7 inches away and cuts down at 4 feet 7 inches.

Finish. After clearing each barrier, including the last, the hurdler should consider himself a first-rate sprinter. He should comport himself as a champion dash man and observe all the laws of body mechanics pertaining to sprinting.

During indoor high hurdle competition the athlete frequently competes in races in which the distance from the last hurdle to the finish line is shortened to 5 yards. This shortened distance permits less time for the burst for the yarn.

The technique of running the finish of a hurdle race is very similar to running the finish of a sprint race. This point is discussed in Chapter 4, which deals with sprinting events.

Low hurdles. The committee which formulated the rules for schoolboy competition had in mind altering this event so that the difficulties of stride adjustment would be less burdensome to the more youthful hurdle aspirants. First, the distance between the hurdles was reduced from 20 to 18 yards so that high school competitors could cover the distance in 7 full strides. Next, the distance from the starting line to the first hurdle was reduced from 20 to 18 yards so that the less mature athlete could reach the first barrier in 10 strides. The distance from the last hurdle to the finish line was retained at 20 yards, and the height of the barrier was left unchanged at 30 inches. As a result of experimentation under competitive conditions by a number of state high school athletic associations, the Rules Committee of the N.F.S.H.S.A.A. recommended in 1950 that the official low hurdle race be 180 yards with the barriers spaced 20 yards apart.

Start. The discussion of the start in the high hurdles and the suggestions in the chapter dealing with the start of the sprints apply equally well to the low hurdle events. In fact, many coaches expect the low hurdler to be as proficient in the getaway as

the sprinter. In many instances he is also the leading point winner in the 100- and 220-yard dashes.

Strides to the first low hurdle. A plan of strides for the 180-yard event is shown in Fig. 8-1. From the starting line to the first obstacle the number shown is 10 strides. Deviations from this plan have been made by first-class hurdlers. For example, some hurdlers have added 1 stride to total 11, and others have subtracted 1 stride for a total of 9. In both of the variations the position of the feet was reversed when coming to the mark.

The most effective combination of ca-

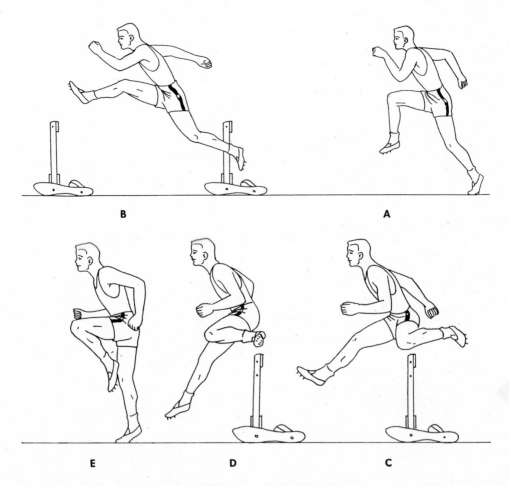

Fig. 8-4, A-E. A series of acceptable form for the low hurdles.

dence with stride length is the determining factor. Therefore, the novice is referred to the corresponding topic previously discussed for the 120-yard high hurdles.

Normally the approach to the low hurdle is faster than that to the high barrier for two reasons: (1) the space of 20 yards permits sufficient distance for the athlete to gain momentum, and (2) the low barrier does not require so much time in preparation for clearance as does the high obstacle. The ideal situation in both high and low hurdling occurs when neither the preparation for clearance nor the execution of the spring appreciably reduces forward momentum.

At the end of the tenth stride the left foot strikes the ground in the preparation for the take-off and the clearance of the first hurdle (Fig. 8-4, A).

Clearance of the first low hurdle. The take-off for the first low hurdle is farther away than it is for the 42-inch barrier, the average distance being 7 feet 9 inches in the 180-yard event (Table 8-2). The landing is closer, being about 4 feet 3 inches (Fig. 8-4, E).

The trunk is not inclined so far forward when clearing the low barrier as is the case in high hurdling (Figs. 8-3, B, and 8-4, B). The spring is likewise less pronounced, because there is a 12-inch reduction in the height to which the body must be elevated. It appears, then, that the 30-inch obstacle requires less springing effort and more stepping action than does the high hurdle.

The right knee lift is less pronounced in the low than in the high hurdles (Figs. 8-3, A, and 8-4, A). The lower barriers are less exacting in the precise carriage of the arms when clearing the obstacle. The novice, however, should not construe this deviation to mean that arm action is regarded lightly. More personal leeway is permitted the low hurdler in the use of his arms provided he violates no laws of body mechanics in using them for balance. When the

arms have completed their task of aiding body balance, they should be utilized instantaneously to the best sprinting advantage. For example, as shown in Fig. 8-4, B, the right arm must be thrust rapidly forward so that it can invite effectively the speedy forward striding action of the left leg (Fig. 8-4, E).

The left leg and thigh of the low hurdler need not form a right angle since the 12-inch reduction in height eliminates the necessity of a high left knee lift. However, the left toe should be raised sufficiently high for safe clearance (Fig. 8-4, C).

The left leg whips speedily across the the barrier as shown in Fig. 8-4, C and D, so that it is in readiness for the first full step in the 7-stride section between the hurdles (Fig. 8-4, E).

The low hurdler need not skim closely over the obstacle, as is recommended in high hurdling, if he is required to throw the trunk extremely forward to gain this form. If he throws the trunk forward, he would be required to elevate it again after the hurdle clearance, thus adding two unnecessary movements. For this reason, many capable authorities refrain from advising low hurdlers to clear the obstacles by a narrow margin provided the athletes have not developed the fault of spread-eagling or soaring over the barriers. The action desired is one of a speedy, synchronized step rather than a free-wheeling drift.

During the clearance, the low hurdler aims to relax as completely (yet briefly) as possible those muscles that are temporarily off duty. This momentary respite permits freer circulation and, in addition, is a partial guard against tying up in the later stages of the race.

When the right or leading foot is within 15 inches of the barrier, the runner initiates a sharp cut-down of the right foot as shown in Fig. 8-4, B, continued as in Fig. 8-4, C and D, and concluded in Fig. 8-4, E.

The landing is on the ball of the foot, and the relationship of the foot to the ground is the same as described for the high hurdles. Some athletes touch ground lightly with the heel, but this procedure is not generally recommended.

Strides between the low hurdles. Alteration of the stride plan (Fig. 8-1) for the scholastic low hurdles may be required by some short-striding contestants. One change consists of adding 2 strides for a total of 9, each being shorter in distance and taken at a more rapid cadence. Another variation is made by adding 1 step for a total of 8, thus requiring an alternation of the feet when taking off for each successive hurdle. This means that if on the first hurdle the take-off is executed on the left foot the spring for hurdles 3, 5, 7, and 9 is likewise made from the left foot. Under these conditions the take-off and spring is from the right foot for hurdles 2, 4, 6, 8, and 10. The latter stride plan requires that the competitor spend extra time practicing to equalize his ability to spring from either foot.

Even though the competitor has planned to run the race using 7 strides between the obstacles, he may encounter adverse conditions such as a strong head wind or a muddy track which make continuance of this stride plan impractical. For example, after the sixth or seventh barrier, he may accomplish better results by shifting to the 9-stride plane. The competitor and the coach, with the aid of the stop watch, will be able to determine the most effective number of strides between the low hurdles.

From the frequent comparison of hurdling with sprinting, the novice already should realize that the strides between the low hurdles are taken just as he strides when sprinting at top effort.

Clearance of the second low hurdle. The second hurdle and all the remaining 8 hurdles present a technique differing only slightly from that for the first hurdle. The chief difference lies in the clearance of the barrier necessitated by the fixed number of strides, 7, between the obstacles. For the 180-yard event, the average distance of the take-off spot is increased to 8 feet 1 inch and the cut-down decreased to 3 feet 11 inches. The objective in either contest is to clear the hurdle without undue spring and to return to the ground as rapidly as possible so that sprinting may be resumed (see Table 8-2 and Fig. 8-2).

Finish. After clearing the last hurdle, the athlete adopts his top-speed sprinting stride in the dash to the finish line. A good performer will not unduly anticipate the beginning of the sprint. Should he make this error, his body may touch the hurdle, and even though the contact be slight, he may be thrown off balance. Therefore, he should complete the hurdle clearance, including the cut-down, before assuming any of the actions of the sprinter. The finish of all low hurdle races calls for the same execution as in the sprint races.

400-meter intermediate hurdle (440-yard hurdles). In the United States this event has received special attention every fourth year because of intensive preparation for the Olympic games. It is now included in the collegiate progam but very rarely, if ever, in the interscholastic order of events.

The demands of this contest are considerable in view of the fact that to become a winner an individual must combine a number of qualifications such as the speed of the sprinter, the endurance of the half-miler, the form of the high hurdler, the relaxing ability of the distance runner, and the pace judgment of the quarter-miler.

The number of obstacles (10) and their height (36 inches) indicates certain similarities to both the 120-yard high and 180-yard low hurdle events. There is a similarity of clearance form perhaps midway between that for the high hurdles and that for the low hurdles. The ability to start rapidly is a requirement common to the three races. Endurance, which is an asset in high hurdling and which is required in low hurdling, is demanded in the 400-meter hurdles. In both the high and the low hurdle events stride adjustment was fixed and definite for a given individual. To the contrary, in the intermediate hurdles, the stride plan in a given case may be fixed in advance but permissibly may be altered at the onset of fatigue. An ideal 400-meter hurdler is perhaps one who can cover the entire course using a fixed number of strides, say 15 between hurdles. The similar and dissimilar phases of the three types of hurdle races are covered in detail in the discussion which follows.

Start. What has been said for the start of the two shorter hurdle races, in addition to that for the 440-yard run, can well apply to the intermediate hurdle event.

Strides to the first intermediate hurdle. The stride plan for the intermediate hurdles (Fig. 8-1) is based on metric measurements for the hurdle spacing of the 400-meter hurdle event because this distance is scheduled not only in the majority of foreign nations but also in the United States. For the 440-yard hurdles, both the height (36 inches) and the placement of the 10 hurdles are the same as those for the 400-meter hurdles. The rules of both the National Collegiate Athletic Association (United States) and the Amateur Athletic Union (United States) conform to the international regulations governing hurdle placement in the intermediate hurdle event. The increased distance required in the 440-yard hurdle contest (2.555 yards) is obtained by increasing the number of yards between the tenth hurdle and the finish line. In both of the intermediate hurdle events, the distance to the first barrier is 45 meters (147 feet 7½ inches), and the space between each 2 hurdles is 35 meters (114 feet 10 inches). For the average athlete, 24 strides are required in the approach to the first intermediate hurdle.

The speed requirement in approaching the first obstacle is the same for both events

and is comparable to that for the first 40 yards of the quarter-mile. The first 40 yards are run at approximately $\frac{9}{10}$ effort as contrasted with full effort in the two shorter hurdle contests. Obviously when approaching the first intermediate hurdle, the competitor is more relaxed than when he strides to the first high or low barrier.

A contestant running the 400-meter hurdles is permitted greater freedom in selecting the number of steps to the first hurdle than when he approaches the first high or low hurdle. The reason for this leeway has been pointed out previously; namely, the longer race coupled with a longer approach makes individual adjustments necessary in judgment of pace.

Some successful competitors add 1 stride and others subtract 1 stride in the plan just described. Whenever an odd number of strides is used, the position of the feet at the start is reversed in the same manner as described for the low and the high hurdles.

As the 400-meter hurdler completes the twenty-fourth stride, he is in readiness for stepping the first obstacle.

Clearance of the first intermediate hurdle. The method of negotiating the first obstacle is depicted in Fig. 8-5. The degree of force expended in the spring is about midway between that utilized in the high and in the low events, since the height of body elevation required is halfway between the two.

The take-off spot is farther away from the first intermediate hurdle than is the case in the 120-yard event and closer than that required in the 180-yard contest. For the first intermediate hurdle this distance is approximately 7 feet 6 inches. The distance of cut-down is midway between those for the high and the low barriers, with an average distance of 4 feet 7 inches (Table 8-2).

When driving off for the first barrier, the intermediate hurdler carries the left arm upward and forward in the manner shown in Fig. 8-5, A. The right knee is lifted to a

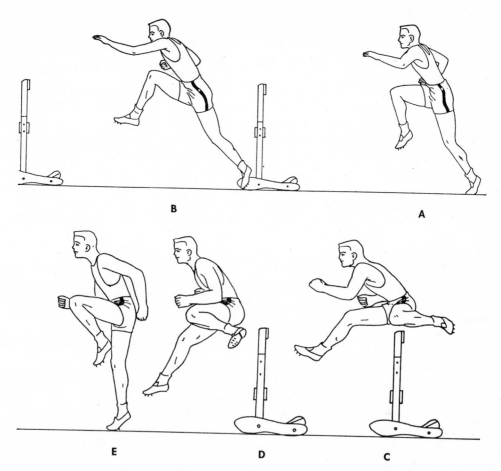

Fig. 8-5, A-E. A series of acceptable form for the intermediate hurdles.

height slightly above that for the low hurdle (Fig. 8-4, A) and lower than that for the high hurdle (Fig. 8-3, A). When the right foot is about 14 inches from the barrier, the cut-down with the right leg is started.

The degree of trunk lean corresponds more nearly to that executed in low hurdling. In other words, the carriage is more erect than in the approach to the high hurdle. The intermediate hurdle height requires an intermediate degree of trunk bend as shown in Fig. 8-5, B.

When the body is atop the obstacle, the arms function similar to their action in high hurdling (Fig. 8-5, C and D). How-

ever, many coaches do not insist on a specific plan of arm carriage in this event on the theory that the longer race requires that more attention be paid to pace judgment and the distribution of energy. They believe that arm work should be relegated to the background of the athlete's mind whenever the relative values of the two techniques are involved. Relaxation, when the hurdler is over the barrier, must be quite complete yet very brief.

The degree of forward leg bend (Fig. 8-5, B) approximates that for the high hurdle event (Fig. 8-3, C). The left leg is whipped rapidly across the obstacle (Fig. 8-5, C and D), but the left knee is not lifted (Fig. 8-5, *D*) to the same height as in the high hurdles (Fig. 8-3, *F*). As the cut-down is completed (Fig. 8-5, *E*) the intermediate hurdler is in a position to stride out between the obstacles.

Strides between the intermediate hurdles. The steps bewteen the 40-meter hurdles (Fig. 8-1) are indicated as 15. The currently accepted technique consists of continuing with 15 strides the full distance. However, some runners become sufficiently fatigued by the time they reach the seventh hurdle that it is expedient for them to shift to 17 strides between each of the remaining hurdles.

An additional alternative consists of employing 15 strides between hurdles from the first to the fourth, 17 strides between hurdles from the fourth to the eighth, and 19 strides between hurdles from the eighth to the tenth.

This plan may be considered a temporary expedient for the novice hurdler. Whenever he has progressed sufficiently in his practice routine, he may chose to alter the 19-stride sector to 17 strides and ultimately to execute the commonly accepted 15-stride technique between all of the hurdles.

It should be evident that the speed of the competitor between obstacles is somewhat less than when he runs the same distance with the hurdles removed from the track. He must hold something in reserve for the spring from the ground.

The body tension, trunk lean, and arm carriage are quite similar to the form employed when the athlete runs 440 yards on the flat.

It must be remembered, however, that the 440-yard flat is not always run in lanes the entire distance. Here the competitor may be required to alter the evenness of his effort by increasing or reducing the speed to meet the tactical maneuvers of his opponents. Since the 400-meter hurdles are run in lanes, there is no hazard of an opponent cutting into his path. There-

fore, in any race run in lanes, the athlete is assured a clear course from the start to the finish line, but he cannot help but take slight cognizance of the position of his opponents during the race.

The knowledge of the position of rivals while a race is in progress must not be gained at the risk of stride miscues. The eyes must be focused ahead on the hurdler's own lane, and any information relative to rivals must come through the ears or through peripheral vision.

As the fifteenth stride is taken, the athlete prepares to take off for the second obstacle which, in the 400-meter hurdle event, is 114 feet 10 inches from obstacle 1.

Clearance of the second intermediate hurdle. The second and all succeeding barriers in the 400-meter hurdles are taken with the same form. At least this is the ideal method, but circumstances, such as fatigue, may alter it. The average take-off is 7 feet 9 inches, and the average cut-down is 4 feet 4 inches from the barrier. These measurements also apply to the 440-yard hurdle race.

Minor departures from the clearance technique described for the first barrier are necessary because the strides between hurdles are fixed in number. Frequently the competitor drives off less vigorously over the second and succeeding obstacles. The period of relaxation, like that for the first hurdle, must be rapid and complete.

The 10 short intervals of muscle rest take the place of the period of coasting commonly employed in the 440-yard dash.

Arm carriage during the clearance is depicted in Fig. 8-5, *C*, *D*, and *E*, but in actual practice many good hurdlers deviate from this style by employing a sideward swing of the right arm (to the right at shoulder height) for the purpose of maintaining balance. This alteration is generally acceptable, provided that the right shoulder is not drawn backward, an action which detracts from straight forward body momentum. Again, the right arm, if swung sideward, must be brought forward speedily and partially flexed so that it will assist in the instantaneous striding out of the left leg (Fig. 8-5, *E*).

When the last hurdle has been cleared, the athlete is free from the constraint of a definite number of strides and directs his attention on running form to the finish yarn. The same caution against undue haste in hurdle clearance given for the low hurdles applies to both the 400-meter and the 440-yard hurdle races.

Finish. The finish pattern set for the intermediate hurdler is the same as that for the quarter-miler, but one must bear in mind that the addition of 10 obstacles requiring a 12-foot stride in clearance makes its fulfillment a man-size task.

COMMON ERRORS IN THE HURDLES

The novice may recognize some phases of hurdling in which errors are likely to occur, but for his guidance those most frequently encountered are pointed out.

In the start. Briefly, any divergence from accepted good form in sprint starting is an error. The possible causes of incorrect starting discussed in the chapter dealing with sprinting apply to all hurdle races.

In the strides to the first hurdle. Evidently, if the first few strides are too short, the athlete will be required to overstride the succeeding steps so that he may still reach the barrier with the predetermined number. Stepping out with an overlong stride detracts from good performance because the cadence is too slow.

Since the first 13 or 18 yards of either the high or the low hurdle race closely resemble sprinting form during the corresponding section of sprint races, it can be assumed that the potential errors are quite similar. It is obvious that running in a direction which is not straight toward the hurdle detracts from efficiency. If the approach has been properly run, all spike marks made by the right foot will form a line which is straight and parallel to those

made by the left. Difficulties in the length of strides are often eliminated by reversing the position of the feet at the start, adding one step if the take-off is too far away, or subtracting one step if the take-off is too close to the barrier. If the heel-toe direction of the left foot at the instant of take-off is other than straight forward, the effectiveness of the spring is diminished.

In hurdle clearance. A ball-heel contact of the left foot is permissible at the instant of take-off, although good hurdlers believe they need not touch ground with the heel, especially when negotiating the last 9 hurdles.

The short-legged hurdler requires a more vigorous spring than the long-legged athlete and may have a greater tendency toward committing errors in the execution of the take-off.

Failure to straighten the take-off leg completely and to follow immediately with the rock-up on the toes is an obvious fault.

Especially in high hurdling, the premature forward bend of the trunk restricts the upward body lift and frequently leads to displacement of the hurdle because of insufficient elevation of the body. To the contrary, if the trunk is carried in an erect position, the competitor experiences difficulty in raising the rear knee sufficiently high when clearance is made. Again, if an erect trunk carriage is maintained to the cut-down stage, the landing is likely to be jarring or abrupt. Even in the low hurdles in which trunk lean form is the least exacting, a moderate forward bend is desirable. However, a full buck, or chest-to-knee thrust, is decidedly a fault in low hurdling and frequently is detrimental to the high hurdler. Another fault is a failure to take advantage of the action-reaction in the buck and clearance.

Occasionally hurdlers spread both arms to the side and soar or sail over the obstacles. Valuable time is lost both because the clearance is too high and because the malposition of the arms makes impossible their use in aiding forward leg action.

In high hurdling the double arm thrust has not been universally accepted because some hurdlers believe that this style did not harmonize with their sense of balance. They contend that a sideward and backward sweep of the right arm helps them retain body pose. Further they point out that, if the right arm is to synchronize with the left leg (which has been back), likewise the right arm should be back. In any hurdling style the arm movement is faulty if it does not aid body balance in addition to providing a stimulus to the legs.

Since the eyes are important in guiding the athlete in his course, any deflection of the vision from straight ahead may detract from good hurdling. The exception to this is that some excellent hurdlers tilt the head downward sharply when at the crest of clearance and then quickly bring it upright. They claim that the downward tilt aids them in both body balance and the execution of the cut-down.

If the athlete gets no relaxation when above the barriers, his running and hurdling form may become stilted. Furthermore, undue tenseness throughout the early phase of the race may result in his tying up during the later stages of the contest.

Imbalance is clearly a fault and may be caused by improper sideward action of either or both arms or by an out-of-line swing of the leading leg.

If the high hurdler fails to execute the two right angles with the left leg, thigh, and foot, the barrier may be either touched or displaced. The downward trailing of the left toe necessitates spending energy to lift the entire body higher than otherwise is necessary.

In case the high hurdler fails to whip the left knee and ankle across the obstacle a sufficient distance before lowering the foot, he may bruise the ankle on the barrier. Again he may err in whipping the left knee too far forward before straightening

the leg. This error causes either a turning of the body from the direction of the run or an uncoordinated stepping movement.

Some capable low hurdlers vary the left leg technique by trailing the knee until the torso has cleared the hurdle and then instantaneously snapping it across and forward. Therefore, the delayed whipping across of the take-off leg is not a fault in all cases.

It has been pointed out that the cut-down should be anticipated by starting the downward movement of the leading foot some distance before it reaches the barrier. Undue delay in the cut-down causes a prolonged flight in the air, thus detracting from sprinting opportunity. The close cut-down is an obvious but infrequent error.

In the strides between the hurdles. The athlete may mar an otherwise creditable performance by faulty stride work between the barriers. Here again, any radical departures from good sprinting form tend to reduce efficiency. Frequently, after the hurdle has been cleared, the athlete plants the left foot too rapidly without gaining the distance needed in the first full stride. If the first full stride (after the landing foot has touched the ground) is too short, the athlete is required to overstretch the succeeding steps in order to strike the next take-off spot correctly. A pause or a break in the continuity of movement just as the first stride is started is a fault that occurs frequently. It has been pointed out previously that unevenness of cadence is a fault.

The eyes must be kept to the front even when running between the hurdles.

The corresponding strides between the obstacles should be equal in length.

In the finish. Improper body balance after clearing the last hurdle is a frequently occurring fault in the finish of hurdle races. Overanxiety to reach the line, causing inaccuracy in timing, is mainly responsible for imbalance.

Misjudging distance from the last hurdle to the finish line has been costly to many hurdlers. This is particuly true in indoor competition, in which lack of space prevents the full finish distance.

In summary, then, a race free from errors is one in which the competitor darts from his mark like a 50-yard dash champion, clears each obstacle with rhythmic, flawless, mechanical precision, instantaneously returns to his sprinter's form, and vigorously dashes to the finish line.

SCHEDULES OF PRACTICE

Typical schedules of practice are presented for 1 week each in early season, midseason, and late season with the objective of meeting hurdlers requirements, such as speed, endurance, and form. Plans are made for athletes who compete in both the high and the low barriers, and variations in procedure are appended for those preparing for the intermediate hurdles. Some hurdlers apparently are benefited by well-supervised and well-planned progressive resistance exercises. These exercises may be included in the schedules at the discretion of the coach.

Early season. This schedule follows the preliminary season schedule, pp. 7 to 13.

The beginner is advised to start his drills on the turf so that cinder burns may be avoided. He is strongly urged to pad his heels with sponge rubber and likewise to protect the knee and ankle of the take-off leg. A padded top bar or a loosely hinged hurdle reduces the chances for abrasions and bumps.

Monday

1. Start with jogging, running, and walking alternately for 25 yards of each exercise.
2. Spend 2 or 3 minutes on exercises, chiefly stretching.
3. Set the starting blocks and take 3 or 4 starts without the pistol, running 40 yards.
4. Set two 30-inch hurdles 15 yards from the starting line. Space the two hur-

dles 4 or 5 feet apart, and on their top edge lay a piece of lath so that it is in the same lane as the starting blocks. The more youthful hurdler may substitute a 24-inch barrier.

5. Assume your regular starting position and at full speed courageously sprint toward the obstacle. At the end of the eighth stride, raise and extend the right leg in a stepping fashion while pushing off with the left foot. The right leg should not be extended rigidly; instead it should be carried partially bent. When the right foot is 12 inches from the top bar, execute a sharp groundward movement of the forward foot. Simultaneously the left knee and foot are drawn up rapidly and across the hurdle (Fig. 8-4, C) in readiness for the first full stride (Fig. 8-4, E). Repeat 3 or 4 times.
6. Set a second barrier (lath or crossbar) 30 inches high 10 yards beyond the first obstacle. Run from the start, clear the first obstacle, and take 3 full strides to the second barrier, stepping over it in a manner similar to that described for the first. Repeat 2 or 3 times.
7. Continue the use of a readily displaced lath instead of the regulation hurdle until correct form is achieved. Bruises can be eliminated and confidence in oneself gained by this procedure. Add a third barrier 30 inches high, placed 10 yards beyond the second obstacle. Run at top speed, taking 8 strides to the first barrier as before and 3 strides between the succeeding obstacles.
8. Take part in weight-training and/or tension exercises for a period of 15 to 30 minutes. For a description, see pp. 8 and 11.

Tuesday

1. Begin the work with 2 or 3 minutes of stationary running, 200 yards of

jogging, and 25 yards of running at $\frac{7}{8}$ effort.

2. Execute 3 to 5 minutes of stretching exercises such as the trunk bend, touching the fingers to the ground while keeping the knees rigid, swinging the legs forward and backward, and kicking high with alternate legs.

3. Set 3 obstacles 36 inches high at 15 yards, 25 yards, and 35 yards, respectively, from the starting line. Again use lath or crossbars as substitutes for hurdles. Employ the technique previously described and at top speed step over the 3 barriers. Follow the description of hurdling technique previously presented and aim to execute perfect form. Repeat 2 or 3 times, always at top speed. The younger hurdler may advance from the 24-inch to the 30-inch barrier.

4. Add 2 or more barriers as proficiency is attained, until a total of 10 are set in the 120-yard course. Run the entire distance 2 or 3 times.

5. Join the jumpers and take 3 or 4 trials each of the standing long jump and the long jump.

6. End the day's practice with 2 minutes of stretching exercises and a 300-yard jog.

Wednesday

1. Start with 2 or 3 minutes of bounding, jogging, and running.

2. Execute 20 seconds of inverted hurdling. This exercise is performed as follows: lie on the back and extend the legs, thighs, and trunk upward until the weight of the body rests on the shoulders. Steadiness in this upright position is maintained by placing the hands on the hips and resting the elbows on the ground. Inverted running is accomplished by moving the legs as in bicycle pedaling. The novice will readily understand that he may simulate the entire hurdle

race by performing inverted hurdling. He will note that the 20 seconds' effort represents more than 120 yards of high hurdling and more than 150 yards of low hurdling.

3. Join the jumpers and take 3 or 4 trials of the running high jump.

4. Place three or four 39-inch (42-inch for college) hurdles at the regulation distance from the starting line (Fig. 8-1) and run through at full effort. Repeat 2 or 3 times.

5. Set 4 or 5 hurdles for either the 180-yard lows or the 440-yard intermediates (Fig. 8-1) and hurdle them at full speed. Repeat once or twice.

6. Spend 15 to 30 minutes on weight-training and/or tension exercises.

Thursday

1. Begin the workout by jogging 300 yards, walking 100 yards, bounding 50 yards, and sprinting 25 yards. Spend 2 or 3 minutes performing pull-ups on the high bar and dips on the parallel bars.

2. Sit on the ground in a position similar to that assumed when clearing a high hurdle (Fig. 8-3, E). Vigorously throw the trunk forward so that the chest touches the thigh. Simultaneously swing the left arm well forward, and partially thrust the right arm to the front. At the same time raise the left toe upward. Next swing the trunk upward and repeat the exercise 4 or 5 times so that the movements described are coordinated speedily. Be cautious of undue strain when practicing this feat the first time.

3. Set 6 high hurdles and step them at full effort, walk or rest for 10 minutes, and repeat. The 440-meter intermediate hurdlers will substitute six 36-inch barriers and rest 10 minutes before repeating.

4. Assume the same sitting position as

described in item 2. Call on another hurdler to sit in a similar manner directly in front, so that the right foot of each athlete touches the left knee of his teammate. Extend and clasp left hands. Seesaw back and forth (pull and be pulled) to stretch the muscles of the trunk and thigh. Simultaneously with each forward bend of the trunk raise the left toe. Caution is advised so that exceptional strain is avoided. Take only 3 or 4 trials, rest a few minutes, and repeat 2 or 3 times. Even though the action seems unnatural, reverse the position of the feet (left leg forward) and repeat the exercises for the purpose of symmetrical body development. In later discussions this exercise will be referred to as mat hurdling because this practice is frequently taken on gymnasium mats.

5. Place 6 low hurdles in their proper position and run them at top speed. Rest 10 minutes. Repeat once.

6. Conclude the day's work with 2 minutes of hopping and bounding followed by running 330 yards at 7/8 effort.

Friday

1. Prepare for practice with rope skipping, bounding, and jogging.

2. Join the sprinters and take 2 starts, without the pistol, and then 3 starts with the pistol, running 30 yards in each case.

3. Set 1 high hurdle 15 yards from the starting line and place the finish yarn 15 yards beyond the hurdle. Take 2 starts with the pistol, and at full effort clear the barrier and sprint for the yarn. Bear in mind the faults incident to this phase of the race, namely, undue haste in the cut-down, imbalance, and improper carriage of the head and eyes. Note the number of full strides taken between the last

hurdle and the finish line. Substitute the 36-inch or 30-inch hurdle for the high barrier, place them at the official distance (Fig. 8-1), and repeat the procedure.

4. Place 2 or 3 high hurdles at regulation distances. On the top bar of each hurdle set two 1-inch blocks of wood, each 3 inches from the end of the bar. Take a start with the pistol and clear all the obstacles at full effort. Repeat 3 or 4 times. Some high hurdlers believe that their clearance height is correct if the blocks are displaced by the thigh or the running pants and the top bar is not touched. The novice will bear in mind that a slightly higher clearance is a permissible deviation for beginners. The beginning hurdler will recall that the intermediate and the low hurdles are not closely skimmed in the same manner as are the higher obstacles.

5. Prepare for trials the following day (Saturday) over the full distance in your chosen events. End the practice with 2 or 3 minutes of stretching exercises followed by a jog of 440 yards.

Saturday

1. Warm up in a manner designed to put you in physical and mental readiness for competition. A typical warm-up includes (a) a jog of 350 yards, (b) a walk of 100 yards, (c) 1 or 2 minutes of leg- and trunk-stretching exercises on the hurdle, (d) 1 or 2 minutes of push-ups and dips, (e) 2 sprints of 30 yards at gradually increasing speed, (f) 2 top-speed trials over 1 hurdle, and (g) 2 top-speed trials over 3 to 5 hurdles.

2. Reassure yourself of heel, ankle, and knee protection so that you can take the obstacles fearlessly.

3. In case your hurdling teammates provide insufficient competition for you, station in the adjoining lane a mod-

erately proficient runner who will sprint the distance without stepping the barriers.

4. Set the starting blocks and make adjustments for the 120-yard high hurdles. Run a time trial the complete distance at full effort. Keep moving after the trial and retain body warmth. Rest 20 minutes.

5. Set a full lane of low hurdles and run a time trial. Sometimes an athlete is aided by giving a teammate a 5-yard handicap. The 400-meter intermediate hurdlers may run only 1 trial over the full distance and omit the high and the low obstacles.

6. End this week in early season with 2 or 3 minutes of calisthenics, a jog of 350 yards, a shower, and a massage.

Pre

~~Midseason.~~ Practice workouts are outlined on the assumption that the athlete is competing in two hurdle events. In case he is engaged in high school competition, the events are the 120-yard high hurdles and the 180-yard low hurdles. For the collegiate athlete the races planned for are the 120-yard high hurdles and the 440-yard intermediate hurdles. Further alterations may be required should the athlete participate in events in addition to the hurdles.

Monday

1. Begin the day with a jog of 300 yards, a walk of 50 yards, a run of 100 yards, and a sprint of 25 yards.

2. Spend 4 or 5 minutes on stretching exercises such as (a) laying the front (right) leg on the top of the hurdle and bending the trunk forward and backward; (b) placing the rear (left) knee atop the hurdle, forming two right angles as in hurdle clearance, and dipping the trunk forward until the hands touch the ground; and (c) assuming position b and extending the arms through the lower crossbars of the obstacle until the hands touch the ground.

3. Stand at the side of the hurdle with the weight resting on the right foot. Lift the left leg to form two right angles and practice whipping the leg across the barrier. Simultaneously rise up on the ball of the right foot to obtain sufficient clearance. Repeat 12 to 15 times.

4. Review the correct and incorrect execution of the various phases of hurdle racing as exemplified in the last contest. Set about eliminating faults in form.

5. Take 4 trials over 5 high hurdles at top speed, using a pistol at the start and a finish line 15 yards from the last hurdle. Note carefully the distance and speed of the approach, the form in hurdle clearance, the evenness of stride between obstacles, and the transformation from hurdling to sprinting in the last 15 yards of the race. Any speed other than full effort alters the timing of hurdle execution. Therefore, whenever less strenuous work is desired, reduce the number of hurdles cleared or the number of trials taken.

6. Hold yourself in readiness for a time trial over 10 high, 8 low, or 10 intermediate hurdles on the following day (Tuesday).

7. Run over 5 low hurdles at top speed or 5 intermediate hurdles at top speed 4 times.

8. Take 3 or 4 trials of the running high jump.

9. Engage in weight-training exercises provided they have proved beneficial to hurdling.

Tuesday

1. Warm up as you would for important competition, keeping your routine definite and fixed once you have determined the type most effective for your races. (See Hurdles, Early season, Saturday.) Extremely strenuous

stretching exercises are not recommended on days of either time trials or competition.

2. Run a time trial over 10 high hurdles. Compare with the times previously recorded for like distance. Better progress is made by concentrating both mentally and physically on one good practice race rather than by running indifferently throughout 2 or 3 trials.

3. Rest 30 minutes (note the competition-day time schedule for the interval between races) and run a time trial over 8 low hurdles or 10 intermediate hurdles. If on Saturday low hurdles are contested around a curve, hurdles should be placed similarly in Tuesday's trial. Note carefully the type of warm-up which best suits you for the second race. Ordinarily if body warmth has been retained after running the high hurdles, easy jogging, light calisthenics, and 2 trials over 2 or 3 hurdles should suffice.

4. Avoid cooling off too quickly by walking and jogging.

5. Dry off perspiration and, the weather permitting, expose the body to the sun for 10 minutes.

6. In case the competitor is preparing for the 400-meter intermediate hurdles, substitute 1 time trial over the full 400-meter distance for the 2 time trials over the shorter distance. Hurdling drills with both the 42-inch and and the 30-inch obstacles are beneficial to the athlete competing in the 400-meter hurdle race. Have a stop watch held so that time can be read at the 200-meter mark, which is half the distance. The 400-meter hurdle chart shown in Fig. 8-1 depicts a method of running the distance wherein the competitor takes 24 strides to the first barrier, 15 strides between obstacles. Some good athletes reduce the number of approach strides to 23, and a few taller competitors take but 22. Whenever a competitor utilizes the greater number of approach strides, he is able to run at a faster cadence. In addition, he conserves that type of muscular exertion required between barriers, namely, the reaching or long-striding type of leg action. Should the novice encounter difficulty in maintaining 15 strides, he may rightfully shift to 17 strides. Above all, the running should be even and rhythmic. On the other hand, he may carry 15 strides beyond the seventh obstacle, ultimately gaining ability to carry the 15 strides between all 10 hurdles.

7. Finish this, the most strenuous practice day in midseason, with 2 or 3 minutes of trunk exercises and a jog of 440 yards. It should be noted, however, that some authorities believe that full-distance time trials are too strenuous. They vary the procedure just described by running trials over only 7 hurdles on Tuesday.

Wednesday

1. Begin the practice with a warm-up consisting in jogging, rope skipping, squatting, stretching, and running.

2. Join the sprinters and take 2 or 3 starts with the pistol, going 35 to 40 yards.

3. Perform 20 seconds of inverted hurdling. Repeat twice.

4. Select a teammate, assume the mat-hurdling position on the grass, and execute 30 seconds of crosshand bending forward and backward.

5. Vary the procedure by setting the hurdles on the grass but spacing them at the regulation distance. Take 4 or 5 trials over 4 high hurdles. Rest 5 minutes. Take 4 or 5 trials over 4 low hurdles. For the 400-meter hurdles, substitute 4 trials over 4 hurdles.

6. In case the low hurdles are to be con-

tested around a curve and on a straightaway rather than completely on the straightaway, that portion of the low hurdle schedule in item 5 may well be transferred to the curved portion of the track. Many authorities claim that when running low hurdles counterclockwise around a curve the competitor who takes off from the right foot (extends the left foot forward) is able to execute a more efficient clearance. It is conceivable that this smoother technique permits shorter running time around the curve.

7. Continue exercises in weight training to the extent that you have found desirable.

Thursday

The schedule for Thursday is formulated on the assumption that there is no competition until Saturday. If the calendar calls for competition or trials on Friday, only moderate limbering work should be taken on Thursday. Furthermore, the practice presented for Wednesday should be reduced in both amount and intensity.

Many coaches look upon Thursday's practice in midseason and late season as an optional workout day. The athlete is given leeway in selecting both the type and quantity of physical activity. Coaches frequently judge the morale and spirit of their track men by the zest and enthusiasm exhibited in Thursday's practice. To be sure, excess activity or engaging in hazardous stunts is out of order on this midseason day.

1. Start the workout with jogging, running, and short distance sprinting.
2. Perform 5 to 10 minutes of exercises optional to the competitor, such as high kicking, trunk bending and twisting, and tumbling.
3. Take a sun bath for 10 minutes if the weather permits.
4. End the workout by a jog of 440 yards, followed by a shower and massage.
5. It should be noted that the Thursday schedule is based on the assumption that there are no trial heats run Friday. Obviously Thursday's practice should be reduced to limbering up or should be eliminated entirely in case trial heats are required on Friday.

Friday

1. Take inventory of your personal equipment to make sure that all is in readiness for Saturday's competition.
2. Consult the coach regarding Friday's routine, which may call for complete absence from athletics or may require suiting up and taking light exercise.
3. Without undue fretting or worrying, outline a plan of attack for use in case the weather becomes rainy or windy. A rain-soaked track may require adjustments of spike lengths. A strong wind may necessitate alteration of striding effort, depending on whether the breeze is from the front, the side, or the back.
4. If your Friday plan calls for dressing in athletic garments, limber up and inspect the track layout.
5. Forget the coming contest and divert the attention from athletics by studying, reading, or attending an entertainment selected with the objective of relaxation.

Saturday

1. Warm up with a definite type and amount of exercise, knowledge of which has been gained from previous competition. Refer to hurdles, early season, Saturday, for warm-up suggestions. Time the warm-up so that the peak of your finer physical and mental adjustments coincides with the start of your event. This requires a knowledge of the time schedule as well as the number of your

heat and lane. Since ordinarily the high hurdles are contested before the low hurdles, the first consideration is preparation for the former event. In case trial heats are necessary, make no mistake in careless form or loafing habits merely because it is not a final race.

2. Steel yourself for a supreme effort, and with confidence and determination run the high hurdles.

3. Regain composure while walking or jogging for a few minutes. Retain body tonus by putting on additional clothing. Rest and relax while awaiting your next competition.

4. Warm up for the low hurdles, or intermediate hurdles, bearing in mind that a short but speedy warm-up is required rather than a slow one of long duration, unless the weather is cold.

5. End this competition day with a jog of 440 yards. Analyze the week's fluctuations in the body weight.

Late season. In late season the most important contests of the year are scheduled, and ordinarily the large number of competitors necessitates trial heats on Friday. In midseason, competition usually requires only 1 day (Saturday), but occasionally 2 days are needed. With this in view, the hurdler must be prepared to compete 2 days in succession. He may be satisfied with merely qualifying on Friday for the final race, but he will remember that easing up or "running under wraps" in hurdle races is quite different from coasting through a preliminary heat in the sprints. Reduction in speed or effort by the hurdler alters the finer adjustments of spring, clearance, and cut-down. These alterations may result in either striking an obstacle or striding unevenly.

In the preliminary heats in the 120-yard high hurdles very little effort is conserved by taking things easy. Therefore the novice is urged to run the trial heat at full effort.

In the low hurdles the competitor may hold something in reserve by covering the approach and the space between barriers at his best effort, but he may rightfully prolong the short interval of relaxation when atop each low hurdle. Again, he may carry through from the last hurdle to the finish line without tapping bottom, or summoning all his sprinting ability.

The 400-meter intermediate hurdler who is called upon to run a trial heat on Friday has a more difficult problem in conserving strength than does the high or low hurdler. In case he takes things easy during his approach to barrier No. 1, his rivals may gain an advantage which will be difficult to overcome. Since this contest is run in lanes from a staggered start, he frequently is not aware of his position among the competitors until the head of the straightaway is reached. Therefore he cannot take chances of conserving too much effort. In trial heats the competitor may hold something in reserve even though he runs the approach and the distance between hurdles with optimum effort. He may prolong the period of rest or relaxation over each obstacle, similar to the moment of relaxation over the low hurdles.

Some intermediate hurdlers in their trial heats substitute 17 strides for the customary 15 strides between obstacles on the theory that the shortened stride plan is less fatiguing. In the final race they resume the stride action previously found most effective. The novice is advised to retain his customary stride plan in both the preliminary and final races. This is done on the theory that considerable drill is necessary to gain the ability to make stride adjustments quickly. Between the last obstacle and the finish line (a distance of 40 meters) the intermediate hurdler may adjust his expenditure of energy to meet the conditions of the trial heat.

With the Friday and Saturday competition in mind, the most strenuous workouts are scheduled for Tuesday to allow a 2-day period of toning up for the week end.

In the schedule presented, the Tuesday time trials at full effort call for the use of only 7 barriers for the high, the low, and the intermediate hurdles. Seven was decided upon because the distance is sufficiently long to call for a test of both form and endurance. The last 3 of the 10 hurdles are omitted to conserve energy and to help retain a competition edge.

A further variation in the practice indicated for Tuesday in late season calls for reducing the number of hurdles to 5 in each the high, the low, and the intermediate events. This schedule fits the individual who thrives on short, explosive time trials and who competes better by omitting during late season those workouts necessitating tests of hurdling endurance.

On the other extreme are those who perform better by running time trials over the entire 10-hurdle course. However, these are the exceptional rather than the ordinary athletes.

Earlier in the discussion the novice was advised to experiment with a reversed position of the feet at the start of the race so that he would be in readiness either to add 1 stride or to subtract 1 stride in the approach. After midseason and some late season experience he may find that a change in the number of approach strides is desirable. This suggestion is an exception to customary late season advice, wherein the athlete is urged to refrain from shopping around in search of new styles of hurdle execution. The change in form is justified if the athlete has not arrived, so to speak, until late season.

The competitor was urged to reverse the position of the feet at the start rather than to reverse the position of the feet when taking off for the hurdle, because less inconvenience is experienced by making only one adjustment at the start rather than ten adjustments over the hurdles.

Monday

1. Initiate the practice with the customary jogging, walking, running, and sprinting activities.
2. Perform 4 or 5 trials of the running high jump at gradually increasing heights.
3. Join the sprinters in executing 2 or 3 transfers of the baton.
4. Set the sixth to the tenth high hurdles, inclusive, in their regular stations. Assume your position at the starting line and, starting with a pistol, sprint at full effort the 65 yards to the first obstacle, clearing it and the remaining 4 barriers. Repeat once or twice. This drill has been found effective when emphasizing maintenance of form over the last 4 or 5 barriers.
5. Set the fourth to the eighth low hurdles, or the sixth to the tenth intermediate hurdles, inclusive, in their regular stations. Sprint at $\frac{9}{10}$ effort to the first obstacle, clearing it and the remaining 4 barriers. Similar to item 3, this exercise is pointed toward form drill in the face of oncoming fatigue. One trial only may be sufficient for Monday's endurance work because of time trials Tuesday.
6. Make use of weight-training and/or tension exercises.

Tuesday

1. Begin the day's practice with jogging, bounding, and running exercises.
2. Spend 3 or 4 minutes on stretching exercises such as high kicking, running hitch kicking, and mat-hurdling stunts. A trainer of wide experience claims that hurdlers are not so susceptible to pulled leg muscles as are sprinters. He believes that the stretching exercises taken by the hurdler condition the hamstring muscle group for strenuous effort.
3. Prepare for a time trial by com-

pleting your usual precompetition warm-up routine.

4. Set 7 high hurdles at regulation distance, brush the track so that the spike marks are visible, and run the 90 yards at full effort.

5. While recuperating, study the distance covered on each stride in the approach, the cut-down, and the finish.

6. After a 15-minute rest, set 5 low hurdles in proper position, brush the track again, and run this reduced course at top speed.

7. Study the stride pattern as shown by the visible spike marks, and make the adjustments that appear necessary.

8. Set 7 intermediate hurdles and run a time trial over a 300-meter distance. Study the length of stride as shown by the spike marks.

9. Variations in the distance for each time trial have been pointed out previously. There are individuals who compete better by running the full 10 hurdles in each race, whereas others prepare to better advantage by covering only 5 barriers in each the high, the low, and the intermediate hurdles.

10. End Tuesday's workout, the most strenuous in late season, by a run of 300 yards to 440 yards at $9/10$ effort, designed to develop endurance. If speed is to be stressed, substitute 220 yards at full effort.

Wednesday

1. Begin the day's work with 3 or 4 minutes of easy jogging.

2. Expose the body to the sun for a period of 10 to 15 minutes.

3. Join the sprinters and set 1 high hurdle in your lane 15 yards from the starting line. Take 2 or 3 starts with the pistol, clearing the obstacle but paying no attention to the sprinters to the left and to the right. Add 2

or 3 hurdles and continue the drill so that you will maintain habitually the focus of the eyes on your own lane.

4. Participate for 5 to 10 minutes in some other track and field event which can have no detrimental effect on your hurdling efficiency.

5. The low hurdler or intermediate hurdler may substitute the 30-inch or 36-inch obstacle in taking the drill described in item 3.

6. In midseason the low hurdler or intermediate hurdler may have been called upon to run 440 yards in the 1-mile relay, but the advent of a higher caliber competition during late season may require that he discontinue this. However, the endurance gained from the quarter-mile running should be highly valuable in running both the low and the intermediate hurdles.

7. Either include or omit weight-training exercises in the light of your past experiences.

Thursday

This day's practice is arranged on the assumption that there are to be preliminary heats on Friday. In case there are no preliminary heats, the hurdler may follow the schedule outlined for Thursday in midseason.

1. Limber up lightly, inspect the track layout, and plan your activities for the remainder of the week.

2. Spend 5 minutes on exercises of your own choice, which are light in intensity.

3. Terminate the practice with a jog of 880 yards.

Friday

1. In case you are competing in preliminary heats, begin the practice gradually and warm up so that the peak of your physical and mental condi-

tion coincides with the time of the start of your first race.

2. If you are sufficiently sure of your hurdle clearance and have been wearing knee and ankle pads, remove them if you are conscious of their attachment.

3. Adjust yourself for your trial heat in the high hurdles and run at full effort with your attention fully fixed on your own race.

4. Retain your body tonus while walking or jogging to regain composure. Dry off perspiration and keep free from extremes of heat or cold.

5. Warm up for the low hurdles or intermediate hurdles. Run the trial heat in the hurdles, depending upon your rating in the field of competitors. In case you are confident that you do not need to "tap bottom," methods have been described in the midseason schedule of practice for conserving effort. However, the alert athlete does not permit himself to be surprised by opponents of unknown ability.

6. End the day for qualifying heats by an easy jog on the grass.

Saturday

1. Prepare for the most important day of competition by following your well-defined procedure.

2. Adjust yourself mentally for the start of the high hurdles. Think of your opponents simply as aids or stimuli in establishing your best competitive

mark. By this time the admonition regarding the fixation of both the attention and the vision should not be needed since proper habits will have taken care of it automatically.

3. Take your position at the starting mark and, with a clear-cut pattern of what you expect to do, run the high hurdles at full speed.

4. Keep moving until partially recovered, dry your body, and stay off your feet until the time to start your warm-up for the low or intermediate hurdles. Calisthenics and stretching exercises at this time are not recommended.

5. Again obtain the most effective physical and mental poise and run the low or intermediate hurdles at optimum effort.

6. When the intermediate hurdles are run, proceed with the customary warm-up and adjustments for the start of the race. Run the 400-meter hurdles, keeping in mind that these differ from the high and the low hurdles in that more strength must be kept in reserve during the early stages of the contest. Judgment of pace is highly important, and you must know how fast you are traveling the first half of the race. Better yet, you should know the elapsed time at the 100-meter marks and the 300-meter marks.

7. Conclude the day's activities with a 5- to 10-minute jog.

Chapter 9

The long jump

The long jump as an event on the track and field program can be traced to ancient times. No doubt, its appearance in early competition can be attributed to its use by man in his search and pursuit of food and in escape from his enemies, both man and beast. In the development of the warrior the long jump took its place along with spear throwing, running, weight casting, and wrestling. The reason for the inclusion of the long jump as a military exercise for the combatant is clear when we recall the need for jumping ability where trenches and barbed wire fences were employed as agencies of defense.

History tells us that the long jump was one of the first events in the ancient Olympic games. It probably had its inception in the track and field programs of America in 1868, the year of the founding of the New York Athletic Club. The first performance recorded by the Amateur Athletic Union as an American championship was in 1876, when I. Frazer of the Yonkers, New York, Lyceum won first place with a leap of 17 feet 4 inches.

The date of the introduction of the long jump into the preparatory schools is somewhat uncertain. However, after the organization of the annual Interscholastic Track and Field Meet by the University of Chicago in 1901, it became a standard preparatory school event. The University of Pennsylvania, through the Penn Relays, which were organized in 1895, afforded preparatory and high school relay competition.

When the record of I. Frazer is compared with performances by John Bennett of Marquette University, Ernie Shelby of Kansas University, Greg Bell of Indiana University, Jesse Owens of Ohio State University, Darrell Horn of Oregon State University, and many others, it is apparent that there are underlying factors responsible for the increases in distances jumped. Ralph Boston of the United States was credited with a jump of 27 feet 4¾ inches in 1965. Is the present-day equipment chiefly responsible for greater distances, or is it the inspiration of our times and the desire to emulate?

A comparison of the present-day athlete with his predecessor is time worn but even now is capable of precipitating debate. No single item can account for the improved performance in the long jump; rather, a combination of a number of factors is responsible for it. There is much doubt that the present-day athlete has more native ability than the competitor of years gone by. Increased interest in the long jump has caused the entrance of more contestants, thereby inspiring greater efforts. The desire for improved performance has led the athlete to a more thorough study of the event and a more complete analysis of his own strong and weak points. The inspiration of the times and the enthusiasm for the long jump have spurred us on to improved technique and instruction. Paralleling the advances in technique and instruction, more equipment, which makes present performances possible, has been developed. When all these things are added together, the answer to the question, "What is responsible for the steady improvement of performance in the long jump?" is at once apparent.

GENERAL CONSIDERATIONS

Comparative marks in competition. For the high school long jumper who desires to determine the distance he will be required to jump if he is to score points at the various levels of competition, Table 9-1 is presented. Similar to the tables provided previously in this text for other track and field events, Table 9-1 lists the placing and not the winning distances of the long jump. Since these distances represent average performances, they will not apply to those areas where the quality of the long jumpers is either extremely good or extremely poor.

With a knowledge of the distances that are likely to place in the various classes of competition, the next thing to which the long jumper should give his attention is equipment.

Equipment. Every jumper should know the type of equipment conducive to his best performance. It should be realized, however, that the quality and the type of equipment are not entirely under the control of the jumper, and circumstances may arise where he will have to adjust himself to conditions as he finds them. In spite of this, the responsibility for certain items in in the equpiment falls chiefly upon the contestant. In this discussion the most acceptable equipment is described. Such elements as money, space, and labor may prohibit the establishment of an ideal layout. Under these conditions the resourcefulness of the competitor is called upon to make adjustments to meet the situation.

Shoes. The ordinary sprinting shoe without a counter and without heel pads is the lightest footgear available. A sprinting shoe without inner heel pads may not afford sufficient protection against bruises. It is also important to remember that the addition of thick heel pads to the ordinary

Table 9-1. Comparative marks in scholastic competition for the long jump

Meet	No. of places scored	Distance
Dual high school	3	19 ft.-21 ft.
Qualifying—state	3	21 ft.-22 ft. 6 in.
State—province	5	22 ft.-23 ft. 6 in.

sprinter's shoe makes the counter too shallow, and because of this shallowness the athlete may cast the shoe during the event.

The shoe which is recommended is similar to the ordinary sprinting shoe except that it has a counter sufficiently high to permit the insertion of pads or heel cups and at the same time to ensure a snugly fitting heel.

Protective heel pads. The heel of the take-off foot of every jumper from the first day of the season should be protected from injury because it is subject to a considerable amount of force at the moment of take-off.

A heel cup, made to measure after obtaining a plaster-of-Paris cast of the heel, is constructed of layers of fiber glass bonded with resin. A description of the heel cup is found in Chapter 3 under Heel protection.

Pads of either felt or rubber can be used. The rubber pads may be made of coiled rubber tubing, solid rubber, bath sponge rubber, or flat sponge rubber. The jumper is advised to experiment with these protective devices and determine their effectiveness. The prevention of bruised heels obviously is simpler than their treatment.

Qualifications. The points to be considered in discussing the physical qualifications of a long jumper are age, height, endurance, spring, neuromuscular coordination and rhythm, and speed.

Age. There is no physiologic reason, so far as is known, why boys should not participate in the long jump at an early age. An examination of the record holders in the long jump shows that they became champions between the ages of 22 and 28 years. However, learning the long jump is like learning to play the piano. Both diligence and patience are needed to bring about perfection of movement.

Height. The question of height has been mentioned previously. Although short men have attained proficiency in the long jump,

the tall man has an advantage. Experience teaches us that, as a rule, the tall man is able to lift his body and legs higher in his transit across the landing area and to reach farther with his feet on landing. By so doing, he is able to utilize to the maximum his forward leap and to permit a full extension of the legs an instant prior to landing, thus attaining greater distance. A short man may compensate for his lack of stature by attaining greater speed and by developing a more powerful spring.

Endurance. The average person considers the long jump to be an event that does not require endurance. The contestant should be fortified, however, with sufficient reserve to meet the demands of the most strenuous competition, which include several practice runs without jumping, several practice jumps, and seven competitive jumps. The amount of effort expended in other events before the jump also must be considered.

Spring. In order to acquire distance in the long jump, momentum must be combined with height. Momentum is gained by the speed of the run, while height is obtained by the spring from the take-off board. The force of the spring depends on the strength of the foot, leg, and thigh muscles and their ability to respond efficiently and quickly.

Neuromuscular coordination and rhythm. One may be an excellent sprinter possessing a powerful spring and yet fail to gain distance in the long jump. This, no doubt, is due to a lack of neuromuscular coordination. In executing the long jump, a fast sprinter may attempt to employ a rate of speed that is too great to permit him to gather or collect just prior to the instant of the foot plant on the take-off board. This lack of coordination results in a jump of insufficient height. As opposed to this, an excellent high jumper who undertakes to execute a long jump may attempt a spring with such emphasis that he attains a height out of proportion to his speed, thus incorrectly making a high jump of the event rather than a long jump. In order to attain maximum distance, the movements of the arms and legs must be synchronized properly for forward and upward movement during and at the end of the flight.

The execution of the long jump requires proper coordination and rhythm, which are evident in the following phases of the jump: the bend of the knee, the leg extension and thrust, the rock-up on the toes coordinated with the run, the timing of the upward swing of the forward leg with the spring from the take-off board, the timing of the first movement in the stride-in-air, and the timing of the extension of both feet forward at the instant of landing, coupled with the forward thrust of the arms.

Speed. The importance of speed in the long jump is obvious. The additional distance gained in this event over the standing long jump is due to the speed of the run. A long jumper should strive to acquire speed comparable to that of the best 100-yard sprinter in his competitive class.

Experiments by Sills and Carter[1] indicated that the varsity sprinters serving as subjects attained maximum velocities at distances ranging from 45 to 90 feet.

Since the top-flight sprinter who competes in the long jump does not utilize 100 percent of his potential velocity in the approach, it may seem logical to conclude that he can attain his desired long jump approach velocity with a run shorter than 90 feet.

However, the difference can be attributed to the fact that in the long jump, the jumper rightfully accelerates smoothly and gradually, whereas in a sprint race he starts explosively. The approach should be characterized by poise, confidence, and an absence of undue tension. The reader should not construe the degrees of effort indicated in Fig. 9-1 for checkmarks 3, 2, and 1 as being gearshifting signals. In the attainment of adequate velocity, some muscular tension is necessary. The long jumper, like the sprinter, must determine the optimum degree of tension and thus avoid tying up.

Objectives. During a conference with Coach Gordon Fisher of Indiana University (now retired), he suggested that the three main objectives of the long jumper are as follows:

1. The greatest possible (controllable) speed at the instant of contacting the take-off board should be attained.
2. Adequate height should be gained so as to permit the jumper to execute the moves he wishes to make in the air and to delay the landing as long as possible.
3. The trunk and arms should be utilized so that the jumper is able to attain a full extension of the legs and, in addition, to control his movements when landing.

TECHNIQUE OF THE LONG JUMP

After 1 or 2 weeks of weight training, tension exercises, jogging, running, and calisthenics, which are explained in detail in the typical schedules of practice, the candidate for the long jump is ready to receive instruction in the technique of the event. This is discussed under four divisions in the sequence of their execution: the approach, the take-off, the flight, and the landing.

Approach. The approach is discussed as follows: stride plans, comparison of plans, method of adjusting checkmarks, and speed between checkmarks.

This event possibly could be conducted without the restriction that limits the take-off board to a width of 8 inches. A larger board could be installed so that the jumper would be free to plant the foot on any portion of it. Measurements would be taken from the point of body contact with the landing area to the mark on the board made by the jumper's foot.

However, the current rules applicable to the long jump actually require a two-part test of skill. The first part deals with the approach (including the foot plant) and the second part involves the leap in the air.

In conformity with present-day long jump rules, proficiency in the approach is an essential.

After an adequate amount of sprinting practice, the jumper undertakes the task of determining his individualistic checkmarks. These adjustment techniques should not be considered as added chores that can be omitted at will. Accuracy in the run toward the take-off board should permit the jumper, who gains optimum momentum, freedom to concentrate on the major objectives—height and distance. It is recognized that with increased proficiency the

athlete rightfully may reduce the number of checkmarks from 3 to 2, and in exceptional cases he may utilize only one checkmark.

After the long jumper has determined the measurements of his checkmarks, he must develop the knack of readjusting them whenever he encounters such variables as wind, weather, and runway conditions.

Elsewhere in the text it was pointed out that there is a limited number of individuals who have jumped 27 feet. However, there is no limit to the number that can achieve perfection in striking the take-off board with accuracy.

Stride plans. The type of approach

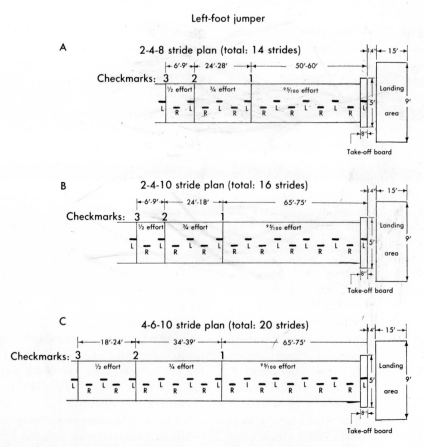

Fig. 9-1. Three commonly accepted plans of approach for the long jump.

taught the beginner depends on whether momentum is gained slowly, fairly fast, or extremely fast. There are three plans for stride adjustment and a number of variations from them. For the sake of simplicity, these plans are discussed as the 2-4-8 stride plan, the 2-4-10 stride plan, and the 4-6-10 stride plan. For clarity of discussion, a diagram of the various plans is shown in Fig. 9-1. It should be noted that the diagrams are made for a jumper who drives off the board from his left foot.

2-4-8 stride plan: In this stride plan the jumper marks off on the runway 3 spots (Fig. 9-1, *A*), which he aims to strike with the toe of his left shoe (take-off foot) and which are 2, 4, and 8 strides apart. With the jumper starting with the left foot on checkmark 3, checkmark 2 is placed 2 running strides toward the take-off board, and checkmark 1 is placed 4 running strides from checkmark 2. There remain 8 running strides from checkmark 1 to the front edge of the take-off board. The total number of strides in this plan is 14.

2-4-10 stride plan: In this stride plan (Fig. 9-1, *B*) it is seen that, when the athlete starts with the toe of the left shoe on checkmark 3, checkmark 2 is placed 2 running strides toward the take-off board, and checkmark 1 is placed 4 running strides from checkmark 2. There remain 10 running strides between checkmark 1 and the front edge of the take-off board. The total number of strides is 16.

4-6-10 stride plan: In this stride plan (Fig. 9-1, *C*) it is seen that when the jumper starts with the toe of the left shoe on checkmark 3, checkmark 2 is placed 4 running strides toward the take-off board, and checkmark 1 is placed 6 running strides from checkmark 2. There remain 10 running strides between checkmark 1 and the front edge of the take-off board. Here, the total number of strides is 20.

Comparison of plans. The first question that naturally arises is, "What stride plan shall I use?" The answer to this question

depends on the ability of the jumper to gain proper momentum before striking the take-off board.

The individual who gathers speed slowly usually requires a greater number of strides to reach his optimum speed when striking the take-off board. For this type of jumper, the 4-6-10 stride plan may be chosen. The individual who gathers speed quickly requires the least number of strides to gain his optimum speed at the take-off board. The 2-4-8 stride plan may suit him best. The majority of jumpers gather speed at a rate that falls between the relatively slow and the extremely speedy jumpers, and they may select the 2-4-10 stride plan.

It must be remembered that the fewer strides a jumper takes, the easier it is to keep the checkmark adjustments accurate. For accuracy and for conserving effort, a jumper should use the lowest possible number of strides that will permit him to gain optimum speed at the take-off board.

Method of adjusting checkmarks. The long jumper must participate in sprinting practice before he attempts to determine his checkmarks, since uniformity in striding activities is a prerequisite. Repeated sprinting routines prepare the long jumper for the standardization of the stride. Painstaking care in the adjustment of checkmarks amply rewards the long jumper. If the approach (checkmark adjustment) is incorrect, the jumper will do one of two things: either plant his foot over the front edge of the take-off board, resulting in a foul which nullifies the performance, or plant his foot back of the board, depriving himself of the full measure of his leaping effort, since measurement is made from the front edge of the take-off board to the nearest break in the ground. For sake of illustration, adjustments for the 2-4-8 stride plan are described.

The method of adjusting checkmarks is as follows: On a runway that has been brushed so that the spike marks from the shoes of the jumper are visible, measure exactly 50 feet up the runway from the front edge of the take-off board.* Place checkmark 1 here temporarily. Always place the checkmarks on the side of the runway next to the take-off foot. Scratch a line across the runway from the checkmark at the side. Temporarily place checkmark 3 approximately 35 feet up the runway from checkmark 1 and likewise scratch a line across the runway. Stand with the front spike of the take-off shoe on checkmark 3, run down the runway, strike checkmark 1 with the front spike of the take-off shoe, run through the landing area, and pay no attention to the take-off board. The run should be accelerated gradually so that when the take-off board is reached the jumper will be at 95 percent of his best effort for 100 yards. An observer locates the position of the take-off foot at the end of the eighth stride from checkmark 1 and measures its distance from the front edge of the take-off board. These instructions should be repeated until there is uniformity in the position of the front spike of the take-off shoe at the end of the eighth running stride. This procedure is termed "standardizing the stride." Next, move checkmark 1 so that the front spike of the take-off shoe will be 5 or 6 inches beyond the front edge of the take-off board at the end of the eighth stride from checkmark 1. This overstride is the allowance that should be made for the cut-down before the beginning of the spring. After these adjustments have been made, checkmark 1 is marked and measured. This completes the standardizing of the 8-stride section. The jumper now is ready to locate checkmark 2 for the 4-stride section.

In order to locate checkmark 2, the jumper runs through the course again, being sure that the front spike of the take-off shoe strikes checkmark 1. An observer then marks the spot 4 strides back of checkmark 1. This is temporarily marked as checkmark 2. With the runway brushed, the jumper repeats his trials, running through the path, over the board, and through the landing area. In order to prove checkmark 2, the jumper runs through the course a number of times, being sure that the front spike of the take-off shoe strikes checkmark 2, checkmark 1, and a point 5 or 6 inches beyond the front edge of the take-off board. The next step is the adjustment of checkmark 3 for the 2-stride section.

With the runway brushed, the jumper starts his run with the front spike of the take-off shoe on temporary checkmark 3 and runs through the path as before. The correctness of checkmarks 2 and 1 should be retested in each trial run. The observer marks the spot where the front spike of the take-off shoe strikes 2 strides back of checkmark 2 and marks this spot checkmark 3. This checkmark, together with the other two, is proved by repeated trials. Accuracy is paramount in every case. This procedure completes the checkmark adjustment.

The checkmark adjustments for the 2-4-10 stride plan and for the 4-6-10 stride plan and for their variations are made in a similar manner.

Speed between checkmarks. It has been pointed out previously that the speed of the jumper smoothly accelerates from the initial stance to the take-off board. Between checkmarks 3 and 2 the jumper should exert about $\frac{1}{2}$ effort, between checkmarks 2 and 1 he should exert about $\frac{3}{4}$ effort, and between checkmark 1 and the take-off board a speed should be gathered that represents about $\frac{95}{100}$ effort.

The question immediately arises, "Why should a jumper not be running at 100 percent of his speed for 100 yards?" When the individual sprints 100 yards and later competes in the long jump, he has different ob-

---

*As a substitute measure, the long jumper's path can be laid out on the running track. A limed rectangle 4 feet by 8 inches can be used to simulate the take-off board.

jectives. In the sprint the objective is to stride the cinders in the shortest possible time. In the long jump, in addition to speed, attention must be given to striking the checkmarks, striking the take-off board, and gathering for the leap. Speed must be reduced slightly during the last 2 or 3 strides for the sake of accuracy and spring. If the speed of the run is too great, the jumper will suffer in the effectiveness of his spring. (See pp. 39 to 40 on velocity.)

Some excellent long jumpers favor toeing out on the next to last step, claiming that it shifts the body weight over the jumping foot as it strikes the board. This adjustment is an important point to be considered.

The take-off. The first phase of the take-off is the planting of the foot on the take-off board, pointing in a direction straight ahead. Motion picture studies of this activity indicate that the majority of the skilled performers make the first contact with the ground with the heel.

Center of body weight. The center of body weight (with respect to the take-off foot) when the jumper is striking and leaving the take-off board rightfully is subject to change. At the instant of the first contact with the take-off board, the center of the body weight is above a point on the ground that is *back* of the take-off foot. Shortly before the midpoint in the body lift, the center of the body weight is directly *above* the take-off foot. At the completion of the leg thrust, the leg extension, and the rock-up on the toes (prior to breaking contact with the take-off board), the center of the body weight is above a point on the ground that is *ahead* of the take-off foot.

The take-off leg is nearly straight at the instant the heel of the take-off foot strikes the take-off spot *ahead* of a point on the ground that is directly below the center of body weight. This action causes the center of body weight to be lowered slightly (Fig. 9-2, A). The right leg is flexed at the

knee, and the right heel is swung high, thus shortening the radius in preparation for the subsequent forward swing. The arms are swung in opposition to the legs; that is, the right arm is swung forward (and partially across the body) while the left arm is swung backward. The head is up, and the eyes are focused at a point forward and above the horizon (Fig. 9-2, A).

The take-off foot is in contact (flat-footed) with the take-off board (Fig. 9-2, B). The direction of the momentum of the center of body weight is being changed to an upward direction by the vaulting action of the extended take-off leg.

The take-off leg is then flexed slightly at the knee and absorbs a portion of the shock of the vaulting action while it assumes a position to prepare for the upward spring. The center of body weight is shifted to the left toward a point directly above the take-off foot (Fig. 9-2, B).

The flight. The flight through the air is defined as that phase of the jump that begins when the contact with the take-off board is broken and ends at the instant the heels touch the landing area. There are several acceptable types of flight through the air, the most commonly employed being the stride-in-air and knee-tuck types. Variations from these types have been employed successfully by numerous athletes. The mechanics utilized in the stride-in-air type are applicable, in some measure, to the other types.

Stride-in-air flight. The take-off leg is extended vigorously (the spring) at the knee so as to assist in changing, to an upward direction, the momentum of the center of body weight (Fig. 9-2, C). The free leg is swung upward vigorously, thus aiding in lifting the center of body weight by the transfer of momentum from the leg to the body. There is a slight backward lean of the torso. The arms are swung vigorously in opposition to the leg movements (as the right leg swings forward, the right arm swings backward) (Fig. 9-2, C).

shift of the center of body weight over and then beyond the feet, aided by a leg-thigh folding movement. These actions result in a smooth, well-balanced recovery.

Knee-tuck flight. In this type of jump, as illustrated in Fig. 9-3, the knees are drawn up in a sitting position. Although this jump lacks some of the advantages of the stride-in-air type, it is easier to execute.

The majority of jumpers using the knee-tuck style leave the take-off board when the trunk and legs are inclined at an angle of 60 to 70 degrees (Fig. 9-2, *B*). The body is inclined farther forward than in the stride-in-air style of flight. The free leg swing in the knee-tuck style is slightly more pronounced than in the stride-in-air type for the reason that the free leg is not called upon in the initiation of a backward-downward drive. The thigh of the take-off leg is brought parallel to that of the free leg, and the knees are drawn up in front and the trunk is bent slightly forward (Fig. 9-2, *C* and *D*). It is obvious that there is no treading action in the transit over the landing area. The knees are kept in a tuck position until the loss of altitude begins, at which time the first preparation for the landing is made.

At this phase of the jump, some excellent athletes make use of a delayed leg swing, which is sometimes called the drag. While the legs are extended, slightly bent at the knees, the trunk is approaching an upright position. As the body traverses the landing area, there appears to be a momentary hesitation in the forward swing of both legs prior to landing. Although some competent authorities are critical of this type of leg action during the flight, there are a number of jumpers who have achieved their best performances when employing it.

The preparation for the landing for any type of jump consists of the extension of the legs, the forward inclination of the trunk, and the backward swing of both arms.

The landing. There are only few funda-

mental differences in landing between the stride-in-air and the knee-tuck types of flight. The objective in either case is to touch the ground with the legs extended as far forward as possible and at the same time maintain balance. In a proper landing the surface is touched with the heels in line but far enough apart to maintain lateral balance. In addition, the center of body weight should be in such relationship to the feet when they strike the landing area that the jumper will not fall backward. For instance, the center of body weight should not be so far forward that it impedes the forward leg reach, thus causing the jumper to lose well-earned distance (Fig. 9-2, *I* and *K*, and Fig. 9-3, *F*). The body weight may be brought forward by a vigorous trunk lean and a forceful forward swing of the arms (Fig. 9-2, *J*, *K*, *L*, and *M*, and Fig. 9-3, *G* and *H*). This completes the technique of the execution of the event.

COMMON ERRORS IN THE LONG JUMP

For purposes of ease in following the discussion, common errors are pointed out in chronologic order: in the warm-up, in the run, in the take-off, in the flight, and in the landing.

In the warm-up. Many jumpers make the mistake of entering competition without sufficient warm-up, especially of the active type; this means sufficient bodily exercise such as jogging, running, and sprinting. A passive warm-up, consisting either of massage or heat from wet towels or a lamp, may be insufficient. Once the warm-up has been completed, the body tonus should be maintained by wearing adequate clothing.

In the run. A common error in the run is the improper acceleration in approaching the take-off board. Some jumpers reach their maximum speed too far up the runway and have inadequate speed when the take-off board is reached. The opposite error of too little speed in the beginning is obvious.

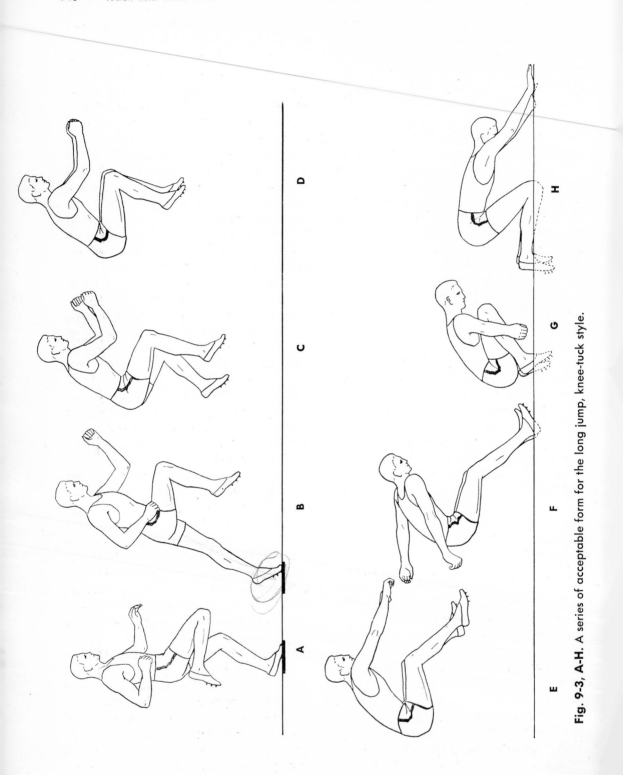

Fig. 9-3, A-H. A series of acceptable form for the long jump, knee-tuck style.

Inaccuracies in striking the checkmarks are also common and result in uneven strides. The uneven strides cause improper striking of the take-off board, the results of which have been stated previously. If the successive checkmarks are carefully hit, the jumper is relieved of doubt concerning the striking of the take-off board. Therefore, he is able to concentrate on the most important phases of the event, momentum and lift.

The semicoast is defined as the reduction of effort during the last 2 or 3 strides. In this phase of the event it is desirable to maintain as much momentum as possible with a reduced application of sprinting effort. This adjustment permits the jumper to shift the emphasis from speed to lift. The omission of the semicoast detracts from the efficiency of the spring, while an overaccentuated coast results in a loss of momentum. Excessive speed prohibits a jumper from properly shortening the last stride.

In the take-off. Some jumpers do not attain their best performances because they fail to strike the take-off board properly. The jump may be hindered by erroneously setting the foot in a direction that is not straight down the path. The head and eyes should not be directed at the landing area; they should be directed forward and upward.

Another common error in the take-off is the failure to straighten the leg and thigh, depriving the jumper of some of the available force. Likewise, an incomplete rock-up on the toes and failure to utilize fully the potential of the free leg swing will detract from maximum performance. The chief fault in body carriage occurs when the center of body weight is not ahead of the take-off foot at the moment of leaving the board. This results from carrying the trunk too erect at the take-off.

In the flight. It has been pointed out previously that the essential differences between the stride-in-air and the knee-tuck types occur in the flight. The common errors are discussed for each type of jump.

Stride-in-air flight. One of the common faults is the extreme outward throw of the forward leg. This causes a turning of the body out of line with the jump and a subsequent loss of distance. The body should always be kept facing in the direction of the jump. Some jumpers make the error of describing a sideward swinging motion of the take-off leg when bringing it forward, thus throwing the body out of alignment. There is a natural tendency toward a more forceful pawing with the take-off leg than with the free leg. This is a source of imbalance at the very beginning of the flight.

It is a common error for beginning jumpers to start the treading motion almost immediately upon leaving the board, causing a boomerang effect because forward progress is retarded. Furthermore, there is a tendency for many jumpers to continue the stride in air too far through the flight. The causes of this failure are that the jumper either executes the treading motion too slowly or attempts to add an extra step, both of which prevent a proper preparation for the landing.

The natural arm action is reflex and parallels the action of the legs. For example, when the left knee comes forward, the right arm comes forward, this movement being similar to actual walking.

The most common error in the body carriage is a pronounced forward lean in the early stages of the flight. When this occurs, the proper amount of knee elevation is hindered. However, the extreme forward lean is very essential in the preparation for the landing in order to keep the center of body weight forward.

Knee-tuck flight. There are some errors that are common to both the stride-in-air and the knee-tuck types of flight. (Obviously, the treading action errors do not occur in the latter form.) A pronounced mistake in the knee-tuck style is a lateral spreading of the knees. The knees should be held fairly close together. A moderate lateral spread is permissible as an aid in landing, but it is obviously an error in technique to fail to draw the knees sufficiently upward and forward as a preparation for the forward thrust of the feet in landing. If the trunk is carried too erect, the jumper will be unable to obtain the maximum reach forward with both heels and at the same time maintain his balance. Theoretically, the arm action is synchronized with the legs as in the stride-in-air type of flight, but many times the arms are extended sideward in a winglike manner for the purpose of correcting an unbalanced condition arising at the take-off.

If the jumper who employs the delayed leg swing is too late in bringing the legs forward, a reduction in the distance jumped may be the consequence.

In the landing. A common error in landing is an overemphasized extension of the legs which results in sitting back in the landing area at the completion of the jump. However, if the feet are not carried far enough ahead, valuable distance is lost. In order that the legs may be carried well forward, the trunk should lean at an angle as shown in Fig. 9-2, *J, K,* and *L,* and Fig. 9-3, *E, F,* and *G.*

Many jumpers fail to get maximum forward distance because they do not execute a backward swing of the arms just before the heels touch the landing area. The tendency to sit back in the landing area may be overcome by swinging the arms sideward and forward when landing (Fig. 9-2, *K, L,* and *M,* and Fig. 9-3, *G* and *H*).

DAILY SCHEDULES OF PRACTICE

In this discussion schedules of practice are presented for early season, midseason, and late season. They are intended to develop skill in the long jump and to maintain as well as to improve the physical condition of the jumper. Emphasis is placed on exercises that develop the legs and trunk. The use of the bath and massage has been discussed elsewhere. The long jumper should place the same emphasis on body weight changes as other track and field athletes do.

Progressive resistance exercises (weight-training exercises) have proved highly beneficial to a number of athletes, including some international champions in the long jump. The athlete is advised to consult with an individual who has specific knowledge of the application of weight-training exercises. A given exercise may not benefit all athletes. Tension exercises (static-type muscle contractions) have been employed with favorable results in both Europe and America. A detailed description of both progressive resistance and tension exercises is presented in Chapter 1.

Early season. This schedule follows the preliminary season schedule, pp. 7 to 13.

Monday

1. Start the practice by jogging 50 yards and running 50 yards; repeat twice. Perform 2 or 3 minutes of body-building exercises, such as upward springs from the deep knee-bend position and high kicking both forward and backward.
2. Run through the approach 6 or 7 times for checkmark adjustments.
3. Take 4 or 5 trials of the standing long jump chiefly for form, emphasizing the arm swing and the leg drive.
4. Run through 30 yards at ⅞ speed, jumping over a finish yarn 2 feet 6 inches above the landing area at a distance of 12 feet from the take-off board. Be sure to execute long jumping and not high jumping form. Repeat 4 or 5 times, stressing height and not distance.
5. Execute weight-training and tension exercises for a period of 15 to 20 minutes.

Tuesday

1. Begin the day by jogging 25 yards and sprinting 25 yards; repeat once.

Spend 3 or 4 minutes on strength exercises, such as deep knee-bending of alternate legs and single and double leg raising while lying on the back.

2. Set the starting blocks and work on sprint starting. Take 3 or 4 starts with the pistol, and run 35 yards at $9/10$ effort.

3. Take 4 or 5 trials, using a short approach, at $3/4$ speed, emphasizing height and landing form.

4. Finish the work with a run of 250 yards at $7/8$ effort.

Wednesday

1. Warm up by jogging and running from 150 yards to 200 yards.

2. Perform 5 minutes of exercises for strengthening the trunk and abdomen. Sample exercises are raising the trunk from a position flat on the back and single leg and foot extension against the pull of the arms from a sitting position.

3. Execute 20 seconds of inverted running.

4. Take 3 or 4 trials to adjust checkmarks.

5. If checkmarks are correct, take 6 jumps with the run, emphasizing the approach.

6. Spend 10 to 15 minutes on weight-training and tension exercises, preferably under supervision.

Thursday

1. Begin practice by running 150 yards and by hopping and bounding 30 yards. Spend 2 or 3 minutes on vigorous trunk twisting and bending exercises.

2. Take 3 trials on the approach without jumping.

3. Set the starting blocks and work with the sprinters. Take 2 or 3 starts with the pistol, sprinting 50 yards at full effort.

4. Use a short fast run and take 4 to 6 long jumps, emphasizing height rather than distance.

5. Run through the approach either 4 or 5 times for checkmark adjustments.

6. Finish the workout by running 200 yards at $7/8$ effort.

Friday

1. Take easy work today in preparation for a hard day tomorrow.

2. Perform 5 to 10 minutes of varied exercises, such as chinning, push-ups from the front leaning rest position, squatting, swinging, and stretching.

3. Run 440 yards at $2/3$ effort.

Saturday

1. Warm up thoroughly, starting with 100 yards of jogging, 50 yards of running at $7/8$ effort, and 25 yards of running at full effort.

2. Perform 2 or 3 minutes of mild calisthenics with the objective of speed and coordination.

3. Verify checkmarks by running through the approach 2 or 3 times.

4. Set a target adjacent to the landing area a few inches beyond your best previous jump. Jump 6 times today. Emphasize speed and spring. Jump for distance. Put forth maximum effort.

5. Taper off by running 440 yards at $3/4$ effort.

Midseason. The following schedules of practice are suggested for midseason:

Monday

1. Begin with 150 yards of jogging and 225 yards of running, finishing with 25 yards at $9/10$ effort. Skip rope for 2 or 3 minutes.

2. Take 3 trials through the approach (without jumping) to reaffirm checkmark adjustments.

3. Take 4 or 5 trials, using a short approach, at $3/4$ speed.

4. Using a short approach, take 2 or 3 jumps, emphasizing height.

5. If you are satisfied with their effectiveness, engage in 15 to 30 minutes of weight-training exercises.

Tuesday

1. Jog 100 yards at an easy pace and then run 3 sprints of 25 yards each, with gradually increasing speed.
2. Run 4 or 5 dashes of 30 yards each at full effort with the sprinters. Study the spike marks for standardization of the strides.
3. Complete the workout with an easy jog of 400 yards. Remember that maximum effort is to be put forth on Wednesday.

Wednesday

1. Warm up and get mentally set as in competition by jogging 150 yards, sprinting 25 yards, walking 25 yards, sprinting 25 yards, and performing varied exercises for 2 minutes.
2. Run through 3 or 4 times for checkmark adjustments.
3. Execute 1 or 2 practice jumps for distance.
4. Take 3 or 4 jumps as in competition. Exert maximum effort in each of these jumps. Study the adjustment of the landing area target. Analyze the warm-up and either retain or adjust the procedure for quantity and type in the light of the performance in these jumps.
5. Execute 5 or 6 trials of the high jump, the last two being at a height either equal to or better than the best previous performance.
6. Taper off with a jog of optional speed and distance.

Thursday

1. Start the practice by running 150 yards at gradually increasing speed. Repeat once.
2. Perform 3 minutes of optional exercises which may involve inverted running, tumbling (cartwheels, handsprings, somersaults), and skeleton dancing.
3. Take 4 or 5 runs through the approach without jumping, reaffirming checkmark accuracy.
4. Remove sweat clothing, dry off perspiration, and take a 5- to 10-minute sunbath, exposing as much of the body as possible.
5. Pass the baton 4 or 5 times with the sprint relay candidates for the purpose of discovering latent ability in the relay.
6. Execute 3 to 6 long jumps for height, using a ¾ speed run.

Friday

1. Either rest completely or limber up lightly with exercises such as jogging and calisthenics. Some athletes prefer not to suit up at all. This gives the jumper a chance to take inventory of the physical equipment and prepare it for the day of competition which is to follow.

Saturday

This is competition day. The warm-up procedure depends on the order and number of events participated in by the jumper preceding the long jump. The suggested schedule for this day is made on the assumption that the athlete is participating only in the long jump. There are two objectives in the warm-up; the attainment of the proper body tonus and the correct mental poise.

1. Jog 150 yards, sprint 25 yards, walk 25 yards, and sprint 25 yards. Perform optional calisthenics for a period of 2 or 3 minutes. Avoid too much sunlight if the day is hot. Reassure yourself of proper heel protection.
2. Run through the approach 3 or 4 times for checkmark adjustments.
3. Take 1 or 2 practice jumps, empha-

sizing height and using a ¾ speed run.

4. Competition. Concentrate the best efforts on the early jumps.

5. Taper off by jogging an easy 440 yards, unless called upon to participate in other events.

Late season. Because of the nature of competition in late season, schedules of practice necessarily differ from those presented for mid-season.

Monday

1. Start the workout by jogging 100 yards, sprinting 25 yards, and walking 10 yards.

2. Perform 2 or 3 minutes of optional exercises such as flexing the thighs while hanging from the horizontal bar and mat hurdling stunts with a teammate (pp. 126 to 127).

3. Employ a short approach and jump 8 to 10 times, emphasizing both the speed of the rock-up and height.

4. Set the starting blocks and take 2 starts with the pistol, covering 30 yards at full effort. Study and measure the strides between the 15-yard and the 30-yard marks. Apply the knowledge gained to the last section of the long jump approach.

5. Take 3 or 4 trials of the standing long jump.

6. Jog 220 yards.

7. Continue weight-training exercises in late season provided they have proved beneficial to you.

Tuesday

1. Vary the procedure by starting with 2 or 3 minutes of optional calisthenics.

2. Set the starting blocks and break from the mark 2 or 3 times.

3. Run 50 yards at full effort with the sprinters.

4. Verify the checkmarks by 3 or 4 runs

down the approach and through the landing area without jumping.

5. Place the target adjacent to the landing area and jump 3 times for distance. Exert maximum effort.

6. Complete the practice by jogging 200 to 300 yards.

Wednesday

The type and quantity of work on this day are optional with the contestant. The following list of activities will serve as a guide for the choice:

1. Take a sun bath lasting from 5 to 10 minutes.

2. Run down the approach 2 or 3 times if it has been found necessary to practice checkmark accuracy daily.

3. Shorten the length of run, speed it up, and jump 4 to 6 times, stressing the lift, flight, and landing.

4. Accustom yourself to the feel of the javelin or the shot for the purpose of variety in the workout, as well as to uncover potential weight-throwing ability.

Thursday

1. Begin the day's practice by performing 2 or 3 minutes of inverted running, starting slowly but gradually increasing in speed. Jog 150 yards.

2. Run through the approach 5 or 6 times without jumping to further verify the checkmark adjustments.

3. Conclude the practice with a group game that calls for only mild exertion. Take no chances on a game that might result in injury or in reduction of efficiency in the competition-day jumps.

Friday

1. Either rest completely or limber up with light exercises. Study your fluctuations in body weight. Refer to Fig. 2-1 for an interpretation of weight changes.

2. Check the physical equipment and put it into proper condition for competition.

Saturday

This is competition day.

1. Warm up by jogging 150 yards, sprinting 20 yards, walking 20 yards, and running 30 yards, ending with a 10-yard sprint at full effort.
2. Reassure yourself of proper heel protection.
3. Execute 2 or 3 minutes of mild calisthenics which you have found will put you in trim for competition jumping.
4. Run 2 or 3 times for checkmark adjustments without jumping.
5. Run through twice for checkmark adjustments and jump, exerting only moderate effort.
6. Competition. Concentrate the best effort on the early jumps. Know how many preliminary jumps and final jumps are allowed in the competition.
7. Taper off with optional jogging. Analyze the fluctuation in body weight for the week.

REFERENCE

1. Sills, F. D., and Carter, J. E. L.: Measurement of velocity for sprint starts, Proc. Seventy-Fourth Annual Convention, Am. A. Health, Phys. Ed. & Rec., Research Section, 1959.

Chapter 10

The running high jump

The running high jump, like the long jump, dates back to antiquity. It was probably introduced as a competitive event in the American track and field program in 1868, the year of the founding of the New York Athletic Club. It was placed on the Amateur Athletic Union program in 1876, when H. E. Ficken of the New York Athletic Club took first place with a height of 5 feet 5 inches.

Among the contributors to the development of form in the running high jump was Michael F. Sweeney, who set the world record of 6 feet $4\frac{1}{2}$ inches in 1892. Three years later he bettered his own performance by jumping 6 feet $5\frac{5}{8}$ inches. His record stood for 18 years. The style of jump employed by Sweeney is referred to by many authorities as the Sweeney form.

In 1912 George Horine of Stanford University broke Sweeney's record when he cleared the bar at 6 feet 7 inches. This is of historic interest since it was the first time that an athlete using what is now designated the western form became the record holder. It should be recalled that a contemporary of Horine's, a fellow Californian, Edward Beeson, surpassed Horine's mark, also using the western form, with a jump of 6 feet $7\frac{5}{16}$ inches.

In 1957 Yuri Stepanov of Russia cleared a height of 2.16 meters (7 feet $1\frac{1}{8}$ inches) employing a modification of the straddle form of high jumping. Certain writers have described his form as the dive straddle.

In 1960 John Thomas of Boston University, utilizing a form that was basically the straddle (with individual alterations), cleared the crossbar at 7 feet $3\frac{3}{4}$ inches.

Valery Brumel of Russia, in 1963, cleared the crossbar (outdoors) at a height of 7 feet $5\frac{3}{4}$ inches and jumped (indoors) 7 feet 4 inches.

The marked improvement in performance is worthy of analysis. It can be accounted for partly by a change in form from the old-fashioned scissors, in which the jumper cleared the bar in a sitting position, to the forms in which the body layout is employed when crossing the bar. Improvement in the type of footing from which the take-off is made is another factor contributing to better performance. Such refinements as improved jumping shoes and shock-proof landing areas add to the efficiency of the jumper.

As time goes on, more and more athletes become interested in the running high jump. The widespread scheduling of the event on both the indoor and outdoor programs, ranging from the sand lots to the Olympic Stadium, has served as an incentive for increased participation. In addition, it should be mentioned that instruction in the running high jump is now more intensive, and advantage is taken of knowledge of body mechanics, physiologic responsiveness, and psychologic reactions.

Obviously, point winners in various grades of competition must acquire height, depending on the class of the field of opponents. The height required to place is given for the high or preparatory school aspirant.

GENERAL CONSIDERATIONS

Comparative marks in competition. In Table 10-1 are shown the heights which the schoolboy high jumper may be expected to clear in order to place in the various meets on his schedule. They will not apply to those sections of the country where the high jumpers are extremely good or very mediocre.

Whenever the opportunity arises, the high jumper should keep informed of the capabilities of his future opponents.

Equipment. The personal equipment required for the running high jump differs only slightly from that used in other events in that special attention is given shoe selection. The shoes may be adapted to jumping and hurdling by the addition of a high counter of soft leather, thus permitting the insertion of either a fiber glass heel cup or a rubber cushion (see Chapter 3 under Heel protection).

The use of a high jump shoe fitted with a specially built thick sole apparently has benefited certain athletes who claim an improvement of as much as 4 inches. The interpretation of high jump rules determines the extent to which jumpers adopt the wedge or built-up shoe sole, since it is believed this type of shoe permits application of force against the ground for a longer period of time, and in a direction nearer to the vertical than the conventional shoe (see rule book).

Types of competitors. A study of successful competitors in the running high jump leads us to the conclusion that they do not conform to any set type. In general, they are rather tall with well-developed lower extremities.

Qualifications. Many of the qualifications of the running high jumper are so similar to those of the long jumper that further discussion would be repetition. There are, however, a few differences worthy of note.

Table 10-1. Comparative marks in scholastic competition in the running high jump

Meet	No. of places scored	Height
Dual high school	3	5 ft. 6 in.-5 ft. 8 in.
Qualifying—state	3	5 ft. 10 in.-6 ft. 2 in.
State—province	5	6 ft. 0 in.-6 ft. 4 in.

In the running high jump, for obvious reasons, the taller individual has an advantage, provided he possesses the requisite native ability. Since the objective of the running high jump is to gain maximum height, leg spring is of supreme importance. Because the participant in this event is called upon to execute body position changes while in the air and in the face of a hazard, the crossbar, neuromuscular coordination and rhythm are extremely important. The degree of speed necessary for the various forms of jump must be considered and thus presents a problem for the competitor. This phase of the jump is discussed later. Before attempting to adjust the checkmarks used in the approach, the running high jumper should have com-

pleted a considerable amount of sprinting practice. Accuracy of determining checkmarks is hastened by the jumper who has standardized the stride by means of repeated sprints at varying speeds.

Relaxation is of utmost importance not only at the beginning but also during the run. There is a similarity between the degrees of relaxation expected of the running high jumper, the long jumper, and the pole vaulter during the approach. The start of the approach in each of these events is not expected to be explosive, as is the case when a sprinter responds to the sound of the pistol. Instead, the run should be accelerated smoothly. In Fig. 10-1 the designation of the checkmarks, associated with the degrees of effort expended, should not be

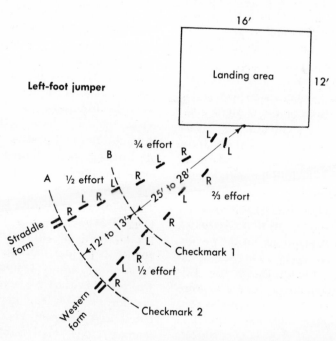

Fig. 10-1. Stride plans for the western and straddle forms of the running high jump. A satisfactory landing area may be made on top of the ground by the use of wood shavings, sawdust, or a combination of these materials. Bags of wood shavings piled to a height of 24 inches form the four walls of the landing area. Foam rubber (blocks or rectangles) has replaced shavings and sawdust in most recently built landing areas and is highly recommended.

construed to be gearshifting signals. There should be no abrupt changes in the amount of effort expended during the approach.

TECHNIQUE OF THE RUNNING HIGH JUMP

The running high jump is an event in which the objective is to attain a maximum height through a process of transferring the body from a vertical to a horizontal position. In order to accomplish this, there must be a synchronization of successive events which follow a running approach from which sufficient momentum is acquired to ensure crossbar clearance.

In discussing the techniques in the running high jump, the event is divided into its component parts. Each part is discussed separately so far as the nature of the event permits. An attempt is made to show the relationship of these various parts to the whole procedure. The order in which the component parts are taught is not necessarily the order in which the physical activities of the event are performed.

Those athletes who have attained the most noteworthy heights made use of either the straddle form or the western form of jump. The reader's attention is called to the fact that acceptable variations from the techniques described in this book have been employed successfully by certain athletes whenever these variations were suited to their individual talents.

Western form. The western form of jump probably had its origin on the Pacific Coast and received world-wide recognition about 1912, when George Horine and Edward Beeson, exponents of this form, were successful in excelling the accepted world mark in the running high jump. In 1953 Walter Davis cleared 6 feet 11½ inches while employing the western form of high jump.

Approach. The stride plan of the approach of the western form of jump is shown in Fig. 10-1. The angle of approach is approximately 45 degrees. The number of strides employed varies with different competitors, 8 strides being the average. The total distance from the initial stance to the crossbar ranges from 37 to 41 feet.

To ensure accuracy in the approach, two checkmarks are commonly used, 4 strides and 8 strides, respectively, from the point of take-off. The point of take-off is determined by addressing the bar at an angle of approximately 45 degrees and finding a spot from which the right foot, when it is swung forward and upward, barely misses the bar. The distance for the average jumper is approximately 3 feet 4 inches.

Checkmark 1 is found by measuring off a distance of approximately 25 feet (4 running strides at ⅔ speed) from a point directly under the crossbar. With this spot marked as temporary checkmark 1, set temporary checkmark 2 approximately 12 feet (4 strides at ⅓ speed) directly back of temporary checkmark 1. Brush the approach so that spike marks are visible. Stand with the feet together on temporary checkmark 2, stride off easily with the right foot, and strike temporary checkmark 1 with the front spike of the left shoe. Increase the speed from ⅓ to ⅔ effort, continue the run with elastic strides of moderate length, and run through without jumping. Now observe the relationship between the spike marks of the left shoe at the eighth stride and the previously determined take-off spot. Repeat the run a number of times until the relationship of the eighth stride and the take-off spot is constant. Next, adjust temporary checkmark 1 so that it is exactly 4 running strides from the take-off spot. This new mark is designated as permanent checkmark 1. Move temporary checkmark 2 so that it is exactly 4 running strides back of permanent checkmark 1. This becomes permanent checkmark 2. This procedure is known as standardizing the stride. It is worthy of the attention of the competitor that as he develops his technique the checkmarks may have to be adjusted further. It should also be borne in mind that the component materials used in constructing the runway may require additional checkmark adjustments. More specifically, a competitor who has made his original plan on a cinder approach may be required to compete on one consisting of an all-weather surface, turf, clay, or loam. It is not uncommon to compete on a gymnasium or armory floor.

A further consideration of approach adjustments is the direction and velocity of

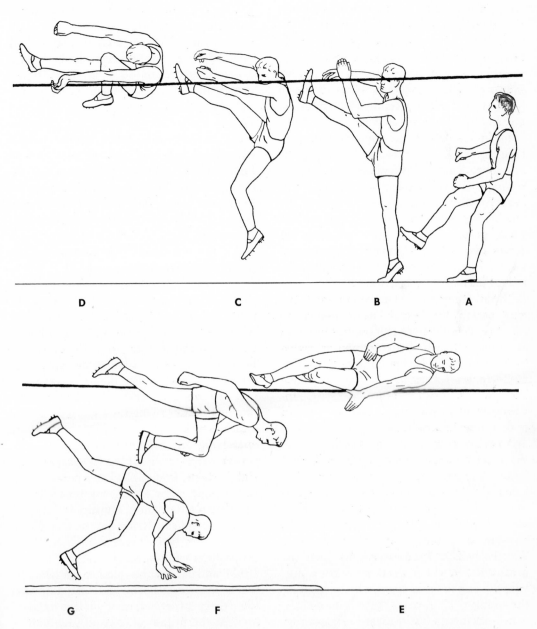

Fig. 10-2, A-G. A series of acceptable form for the western style of the running high jump.

the wind. If the wind is at the back, the length of the approach must be increased, and conversely, the approach is shortened if the contestant is called upon to run against it. It should be remembered that whether 7, 8, or 9 strides are used the number should remain fixed, but the length of the strides must be varied to meet the conditions of competition.

Although it is difficult to prescribe definitely a rate of speed between checkmarks, a competitor will not go far wrong in running at ½ his maximum effort between checkmark 2 and checkmark 1 and at an increasing speed up to ⅔ his maximum effort between checkmark 1 and the point of take-off. After all, it is necessary for the jumper to learn by experience the most effective speed relationships during the various parts of the approach.

Addressing the bar. As the jumper approaches the take-off spot, he gathers or settles down in preparation for an explosive spring. The shortening of the last stride, accompanying a backward lean of the trunk, tends to bring the center of the body weight above and back of the take-off foot. The jumper strikes the ground with the left heel. He executes almost simultaneously a flat-footed landing (Fig. 10-2, *A*), a vigorous swing of the right leg upward and forward (Fig. 10-2, *B*), upward swing of the arms, and a forceful rock-up on the toes as he springs from the ground. At the time the spring is executed, the body weight is directly above the left (take-off) foot.

Speed in the execution of the spring is of considerable importance. Lance and Tuttle[1] (see also Chapter 15 under Relationship between time spent in the spring and the height of a jump) found that the greater the height jumped by a given athlete, the less time he spent while executing the spring.

In executing the forward leg swing, some jumpers throw the right leg forward in a straightened manner, whereas others

perform this activity with the right knee slightly bent. Those athletes who use a forceful straight leg action assume a position in which the left knee is bent only slightly (at the start of the spring), while those who place less emphasis on the right leg swing assume a position in which the left knee exhibits a greater degree of flexion (at the start of the spring).

These, however, are characteristics of individual jumpers; the individual, through experimentation, must determine the degree of left knee bend that is most effective for him.

Near the end of the right leg swing, and closely coordinated with it, the jumper straightens the left knee vigorously and forcefully completes the rock-up on the toes (Fig. 10-2, *B*). After this phase of the jump, the center of the body weight is transferred to a point above (and forward) the take-off foot.

A study of a series of action photographs of champions using the western form of jump reveals the fact that some of them delay the rock-up on the toes until the right foot is swung as high as the crossbar, whereas other equally good jumpers execute the rock-up on the toes when the right foot is at a height several inches below the crossbar. These action pictures also show that jumpers using the delayed rock-up on the toes usually swing the right leg forward and upward nearly straight, while those employing an earlier rock-up on the toes usually swing the right leg forward and upward with considerable knee flexion.

The body angle necessarily varies during the course of the jump. During the run, the jumper assumes a body position in which the trunk is bent forward, approximating his position while sprinting. During the last stride and while the jumper gathers, he bends the trunk backward, thus throwing the center of gravity behind the take-off foot. At the instant of take-off, the body is erect, with the center of gravity directly over the take-off foot. Although during the run, the gather, and the take-off the front-back body angle necessarily changes, it is important to note that the lean should be neither to the left nor to the right.

At the end of the rock-up on the toes and the leg swing, the jumper leaves the ground. As he does so, he begins to flex the left leg and thigh (Fig. 10-2, C) so that when he reaches a point equal to the height of the bar these members of the body are in an extremely flexed position (Fig. 10-2, D). During the course of the flexion of the left leg, the right leg remains straight (with the toes pointing upward) and is kept high. The main objective in this phase of the jump is to lift the left leg as high as possible, just touching the right. The arms are still extended in front of the body.

Crossbar clearance. The force of the right leg swing is the impetus for the body turn. The jumper must acquire a position in which a line drawn through the shoulders is nearly perpendicular to the crossbar, while the toe of the left shoe, the left knee, and the left hip are in the same plane (Fig. 10-2, D and E). This is commonly called the layout. When the jumper reaches a position in which his right leg is straight and as high as possible and his left leg bent at a right angle, the body should be at the highest point in the jump. The left leg is brought up close to the right. The clearance is initiated by sweeping the right foot across the bar, followed or accompanied by the left arm and left shoulder clearance. As a result of the preceding movements, the hips are raised, aided by the reaction of the dropping of the left shoulder, thus completing the roll across the bar. The jumper is then in a position for crossbar clearance. Since the left hip is the lowest point of the body and the greatest hazard to clearance, a more nearly perfect clearance is attained by simultaneously snapping the left arm backward and downward and the head backward to the left in a conscious attempt to lift the left hip higher

(Fig. 10-2, E). If there has been proper synchronization of the events preceding the layout, the momentum of the run will carry the body across the bar.

A properly timed execution of the various phases of the jump will bring the body in a side layout at the crest of the leap (Fig. 10-2, E).

As the body reaches its greatest height, the execution of the following simultaneous movements (Fig. 10-2, E and F) completes the transit across the bar:

1. The left knee is snapped across the bar.
2. The left arm, which has cleared the bar, is thrust downward.
3. The right arm is swung to the right.
4. The extended right leg is swept across the bar to provide impetus for the roll.

The result of these movements is that the body is brought into a position in which the jumper is facing the landing area. The landing is made on the left foot and hands.

Landing. Although the landing is an aftermath of the jump proper, self-preservation still remains an important phase of the event. The ability to relax and to maintain body balance are the factors which make for easy landing (Fig. 10-2, F and G). A properly constructed and well-conditioned landing area materially reduces the hazards in falling.

The novice frequently experiences a sprained wrist at the instant of landing in the western form of the jump. This can be avoided by relaxation and a properly constructed landing area.

Head and eyes. The sequence of visual concentration is an important phase in all forms of the running high jump. For the experienced jumper, the general procedure is as follows:

1. Assume a position a short distance back of checkmark 2, spending some time gaining poise and confidence for the jump, with your eyes in the

general direction of the bar, yet not sharply focused on it.

2. As you step off lightly, look at checkmark 2 to strike it accurately with your left foot.

3. Give similar attention to checkmark 1.

4. From checkmark 1, sharply focus the eyes on the bar until it is cleared.

5. After the crossbar has been cleared, focus your eyes on the landing area.

Jumpers who are novices at the western form frequently make the mistake of consistently taking off too far away from the crossbar. For them it is sometimes recommended that the ideal take-off spot be marked and that vision be focused on this spot until the foot is planted. The vision must then be shifted quickly to the crossbar. This is a practice upon which authorities are not agreed.

Straddle form. The straddle form of high jump is sometimes described as the belly-roll or the dive-straddle form. Clearance of the crossbar and its accompanying layout is made facing downward and straddling the bar. In the western form, clearance is accomplished with the left side toward the crossbar.

Approach. The stride plan for the straddle jump is similar to that for the western form except that the angle of approach is approximately 30 degrees (Fig. 10-1). In fact, some excellent performers warm up with the western style and utilize it for the first heights of competitive jumping. Then as the crossbar is raised to greater heights, they use the straddle form.

The length of run is frequently as much as 12 to 14 strides. Two checkmarks at 8 strides and 4 strides, respectively, from the take-off spot are recommended and are obtained in a manner similar to that described for the western form. When some jumpers reach a point about 5 or 6 strides from the crossbar, they are able to deter-

C   B   A

Fig. 10-3, A-I. A series of acceptable form for the straddle style of running high jump.

F   E   D

I   H   G

Fig. 10-3, cont'd. For legend see opposite page.

mine whether or not they will strike the correct take-off spot. If necessary, they hop-step and switch strides just enough to obtain accuracy.

Although the angle of approach is usually 30 degrees, some excellent high jumpers change the angle to approximately 40 degrees.

The speed of the run is gradually increased so that the jumper is progressing faster, ½ effort at checkmark 2 to ¾ effort at the take-off. Here again, the rate of speed is an individual matter.

Addressing the bar. One objective of the jumper when addressing the bar is the maintenance of rhythm. As a rule the jumper requires just enough speed to carry the body over the crossbar. He usually coasts in just before the explosive lift from the ground. However, there are champions who speed up the last 3 strides on the theory that forward momentum may be transferred to upward motion by a forceful drive or lift and rock-up on the toes (Fig. 10-3, *A, B*, and *C*). The last stride is shortened. The heel-ball landing is made with the take-off foot (Fig. 10-3, *B* and *C*). The right knee is bent, but not to a degree sufficient to detract from the timing of the leg swing-up.

Numerous jumpers state that they utilize the extended take-off leg as a vaulting pole (Fig. 10-3, *B* and *C*).

As the jumper continues his execution (Fig. 10-3, *C*), he strikes the ground with the take-off foot to obtain rebound or lift. The right leg is swung high and toward the bar. It is not fully straightened but is carried slightly bent. Both arms are thrown upward, and the emphasis is on the forceful movement of the left arm which harmonizes with the right leg swing-up. The center of gravity is over the left foot, and the bend is gone from the left knee. From checkmark 1 (Fig. 10-3) the jumper's eyes have been focused on the crossbar, not the take-off spot. He still eyes the crossbar.

Upon the completion of the rock-up on

the toes and the right leg swing-up, the jumper has left the ground (Fig. 10-3, *D*). The right knee is slightly bent on the upswing, but the prime objective is to get the right foot well above the head. The left arm is being drawn to a position such that it will not strike the crossbar. The body is partially turned after the lift, not before.

Crossbar clearance. The force of the right leg swing, as in the western form, is the impetus for the body turn. Provided the right foot has been swung up properly, the chief concern of the jumper is to get the left leg over the bar (Fig. 10-3, *E*). He must use care to refrain from touching the bar with the left arm. Note how the left arm is carried across the bar. One variation in arm style is to hold the left arm close to the side.

Some jumpers strive to bring the left leg upward and then straighten it in one smooth rhythmic motion, whereas others execute a sharp spasmodic kick when atop the bar. This phase of the jump requires split-second precision and timing in order to avoid displacing the bar with the inside of the left leg (Fig. 10-3, *E*).

The jumper has progressed to the straddle stage (Fig. 10-3, *F*). The left arm is shot forward beside the head and away from the crossbar. The right leg has been straightened. The left leg continues its upward movement and is still being extended. This straightening is fully accomplished as shown in Fig. 10-3, *G*. Since the left arm is free of the bar, it can be dropped safely, together with the right arm and right leg.

There are jumpers who vary the technique by turning the head and eyes toward the left shoulder and extending the right arm toward the landing area. They claim that this adjustment aids the turn of the body, thus preventing the left leg from touching the bar as it is extended up and over the crossbar.

Landing. The landing is shown in Fig. 10-3, *H* and *I*. Here the shock of landing is absorbed by both arms and the right leg. Any style of landing is acceptable that reduces the jar and minimizes the danger of injury.

Comparison of styles of jump. Some coaches have fixed opinions on the effectiveness of the various forms of high jumping, and their pupils are usually schooled in only one particular form.

For the average beginner, the western form is recommended because it is quite efficient, since it requires less expenditure of energy in body lift and readily permits a well-defined layout. After mastering the western form, the straddle form may be adopted.

RELATION OF THE TIME SPENT IN EXECUTING THE SPRING TO THE HEIGHT OF THE JUMP

The importance of the relationship between the time spent on the ground in executing the spring and the height of the running high jump has been recognized for a long time. There were no experimental data available concerning this question until Lance and Tuttle[1] conducted a controlled experiment in an attempt to answer it.

The procedure used in collecting the data consisted of measuring the time spent in executing the spring and comparing this time with the height to which the athlete was attempting to jump. The results were quite conclusive. An examination of all the trained running high jumpers available showed that the higher the jump attempted, the shorter the period of time spent on the ground in executing the spring. In fact, the data seemed to fit into the formula for inanimate elastic objects, such as the bouncing of a rubber ball.

One of the important contributions made by Lance and Tuttle's investigation was that untrained jumpers exhibited the same characteristics as the trained jumpers. The high jumper should be taught to place emphasis on speed in completing the spring once the jumping foot strikes the ground.

COMMON ERRORS IN THE RUNNING HIGH JUMP

When a jumper fails to clear a height, his attempt should be analyzed in order to detect his shortcomings. There are certain faults common to the execution of the various parts of the jump which are pointed out and discussed.

In the approach. An obvious error in this part of the jump is a run that is either too long or too short. A run that is too long calls for a needless expenditure of energy. One that is too short fails to permit the acquisition of sufficient momentum for crossbar clearance. If excess speed is generated, insufficient time is permitted for the execution of the gather, the foot plant, the rock-up on the toes, and the leg swing. In general, only a moderate amount of speed is required for this event.

Any wide variation from the angles of approach as previously described should be avoided. The technique prescribed in any style of jump requires a rather close adherence to the proper angle of approach.

Errors in checkmark adjustments are reflected in a misplaced take-off spot. Even though the checkmarks are correct, a misjudged last stride may lead to the same error. The novice will understand that if the take-off spot is too close the crossbar may be displaced on the upward flight; and conversely, if it is too far back, the maximum height will be attained in advance, and the crossbar may be displaced on the downward flight.

To avoid vagueness, definite figures and measurements have been given for the length of run, the number of checkmarks, the speed of the run, and the distance of the take-off spot from the crossbar. It must be borne in mind that these figures are only a starting point from which to work. The experience of the individual and also the advice of the coach or observer will lead the jumper to the most effective approach adjustments. In order to determine their individual distances of take-off from the crossbar, some athletes stand with the side toward the crossbar, extend the arm until the finger tips touch it, and note the position of the take-off foot. This position of the take-off foot is accepted as the spot from which to take off.

In addressing the bar. Although the gather is executed during the last two strides, it is considered here as a part of addressing the bar. Some jumpers fail to gain height because they have not settled down during the last two strides and have not permitted themselves semirelaxation prior to the explosive sprint action. In other words, they are too tense.

Even though the take-off spot is struck accurately, if the last stride is too long, a loss of height results because the center of body weight is too far forward at the time of the beginning of the spring. Conversely, if the last stride is too short, the center of body weight is too far back, thus detracting from both the free leg swing and the upward propulsion of the body.

If the foot plant is executed at an angle other than that prescribed for a particular form of jump, the direction of the flight is impaired correspondingly. Obviously, a partially completed or half-heartedly executed spring is an error.

Many jumpers make errors in the degree of knee bend which they employ. In our previous discussion it has been pointed out that different forms of jumping call for varying degrees of knee bend. Errors in the amount of knee bend are fatal to good performance, yet the proper amount for the individual cannot be described accurately.

Some jumpers, while addressing the bar, make a mistake by leaning to the left or to the right. In the western form of jump, for example, a lean to the left tends to throw the left shoulder into the bar. The lean to the right in the western form hampers the layout because the left shoulder is too far away from the bar. Furthermore, the jumper is not in the most desirable position to execute the undercut of the left leg.

The following errors are to be guarded against in the forward leg swing: (1) incorrect direction, (2) insufficient height, (3) incorrect degree of knee bend, and (4) lack of vigor in the swing.

There are jumpers who detract from their effort by failing to achieve a complete rock-up on the toes. Closely associated with this point is the forward leg swing. These actions must be so timed that their combination gives maximum lift to the body. Inaccurate timing is a serious error.

The vigorous use of the arms is an aid to the forceful use of the legs, and it is obvious that dangling arms are merely appendages rather than effective working parts of the body.

In addressing the bar, the chief faults are insufficient spring and lack of vigor in the leg swing and the arm action.

In crossbar clearance. After addressing the bar, the jumper begins his flight upward, climaxing his efforts in the layout and the clearance and terminating in the landing. In the order of execution, the first possible error is a failure to rapidly snap up the take-off leg. If this movement is delayed, the forward flight has brought the jumper to the crossbar before the leg is elevated.

Any motion that keeps the body from attaining a bowed position (the layout) just prior to crossbar clearance is an error. An observer standing near the bar is in a position to note the parts of the body that are lowest. In the western form the left hip presents more difficulty than any other part of the body. A low left hip may be raised by snapping the head backward and to the left.

In the straddle form, many jumpers fail to elevate and straighten the take-off leg when above the crossbar. Displacement of the bar is usually caused by contact with the inside of the left leg.

Whenever there is a movement to execute, there is a possibility of error. The jumper must make use of his knowledge of body mechanics and physiologic principles in perfecting the form which is especially fitted to him.

DAILY SCHEDULES OF PRACTICE

In presenting the daily schedule of practice for the running high jump, repetition is necessary to some extent. However, exercises and procedures are suggested which apply especially to this event. It may be found by experience that the intensity of the schedule must be varied to meet the needs of the individual and that progressive resistance exercises may prove to be beneficial.

Early season. The schedules of practice for early season should be preceded by the preliminary season schedule (pp. 7 and 12).

Monday

1. Start by jogging 250 yards, walking 25 yards, and sprinting 25 yards.
2. Execute 3 minutes of exercises, including half squats, forward leg swings, and high kicks.
3. Run 100 yards at ¾ effort.
4. Brush the approach so that spike marks are visible and jump 5 or 6 times, gradually increasing the height of the crossbar. Analyze the approach for direction (angle), number of strides, placement of checkmarks, and length of each stride.
5. With the crossbar set at a moderate height, jump 3 or 4 times, placing emphasis on correctly striking the checkmarks and the take-off spot.
6. For a period of 10 to 20 minutes, engage in weight-training or tension exercises, preferably under supervision. For an explanation of these exercises, see pp. 8 and 11.

Tuesday

1. Limber up with a jog of 200 yards, followed by 50 yards of hopping and bounding. Alternate the effort from the right foot to the left.
2. Join the sprinters and prepare for starting practice. Sprint 35 yards and rest 3 minutes; repeat once.
3. Sit on the ground with the legs extended forward, feet together. Execute forward and backward body bends for 1 to 2 minutes.
4. Brush the runway, set the crossbar at a height sufficient to call for ⅞ effort, and jump 5 or 6 times. Reassure yourself of the most desirable rate of speed, the length of your strides, and, above all, the distance of your take-off spot from the crossbar. An observer standing in line with the crossbar can tell you at what point you reached the greatest height.
5. Take 3 or 4 trials with the bar at the same height, with attention focused on springing vigorously.
6. Complete the workout by running 200 yards at ⅞ effort.

Wednesday

1. Begin with a jog of 250 yards, a walk of 25 yards, a run of 25 yards, a walk of 25 yards, and a sprint of 25 yards.
2. Skip rope for 2 or 3 minutes.
3. Execute 3 or 4 minutes of gymnastic stunts of a type designed to develop the arms and the shoulder girdle, such as chinning, walking on the hands, and tumbling.
4. Set the crossbar at a height slightly below your best performance and jump 6 or 7 times. Concentrate on forward leg technique, including the degree of knee bend, the direction of the leg swing, the force of the swing, and the timing of the leg swing with the rock-up on the toes. One should know the height of leg swing that best coordinates with the rock-up on the toes.
5. Set the bar at a height equal to your best performance and jump 3 or 4 times. Make a conscious effort to use the arms effectively. Refrain from

needless worry in case the crossbar is displaced. Obtain form precision first, because successful clearance will be a later reward.

6. Join the long jumpers and take 2 or 3 trials.

7. Engage in weight-training and tension exercises.

Thursday

1. Initiate the workout with a jog of 150 yards, a walk of 50 yards, and a sprint of 50 yards.

2. Execute 7 or 8 trials of the standing long jump to develop spring.

3. Set the crossbar at a height just below your best effort, and emphasize the hip lift while in the layout position a fraction of a second prior to the crossbar clearance. In the western form the part played by the left arm and the head is illustrated by the following exercise: Stand erect with arms at the sides. Swing the left arm forward with moderate effort until the hand is head high and then jerk it immediately sideward and backward with considerable vigor. Simultaneously thrust the hips upward and forcefully tilt the head backward to the left. Jump 7 or 8 times, practicing these movements.

4. Perform 3 minutes of hopping and bounding exercises off the left leg and then the right leg. Vary the practice by standing erect and bending the trunk forward to touch the toes without bending the knees. The intensity of this exercise should be moderate at first, and then gradually increased.

5. Finish the practice by a jog of 250 yards.

Friday

1. Start with a jog of 200 yards, followed by 5 minutes of body-building exercises, such as trunk twists, push-

ups from the front leaning rest position, and high kicks.

2. Refrain from tiring practice today because of jumping for height tomorrow. Reassure yourself of the length, direction, and speed of the approach.

Saturday

1. Warm up with exercises of the type and intensity that experience has proved most suitable for your requirement. By this time the amount and quality of the warm-up should become standardized and should be used on those days when you are called upon to extend yourself, whether in team trials or in competition. A typical precompetition warm-up includes the following:

   a. A jog of 250 yards.
   b. A walk of 50 yards.
   c. A sprint of 25 yards.
   d. Two minutes of leg exercises, such as high kicking, hopping, and bounding.
   e. Two minutes of arm- and trunk-developing exercises, such as handstands, walking on the hands, front leaning rest and push-ups, and tumbling.
   f. Two or three high jump trials to prove correctness of the details of the approach.
   g. Two or three high jump trials to reassure yourself of accurate timing of the forward leg swing, the spring, the body turn, and the layout. The crossbar in these trials should be raised to a height barely sufficient to require moderate jumping effort. If the crossbar is too low, the task imposed is insufficient to require a fully executed spring and layout. If the crossbar is too high, energy is expended unnecessarily.

2. Set a limit of 9 or 10 trials. Develop the knack of complete relaxation be-

tween jumps. Raise the crossbar to successive heights just as in competition. The catch phrase, "one height, one jump" applies equally well to the high jump and the pole vault. An observer or an instructor should witness each trial to aid in correcting form.

3. Raise the crossbar 1 inch beyond your best previous effort and take 2 trials. Get accustomed to steeling yourself for top performance. In aeronautical terms, set a high ceiling.

4. Complete the day's workout with a jog of 150 yards, followed by a run of 100 yards at ⅞ effort. Record body weight, and study your weekly weight fluctuations. Refer to Fig. 2-1.

Midseason. A characteristic of this season of practice is a reduction of drill on such exercises as pertain to the arms and shoulders and the elimination of fatiguing calisthenics. The emphasis is placed on the acquisition of skill in crossbar clearance. In general, the athlete will jump at full effort on only 2 days a week, usually on Wednesday in practice and Saturday in competition. For the jumper who requires 3 days of rest, strenuous jumping can be changed to Tuesday.

Monday

1. Limber up with a jog of 150 yards, a walk of 25 yards, and a run of 25 yards, followed by a sprint of 25 yards.
2. Spend 2 or 3 minutes in exercises such as rope skipping, leg swinging, hitch kicking, and squatting.
3. Lie in the landing area in a position approximating the layout, and practice the leg movements used in crossbar clearance. Adapt the exercise to the form of jump used.
4. Review the faults of Saturday's competition and work on their correction.
5. Join the sprinters and take two 35-yard dashes.
6. Spend 5 or 10 minutes on both the

speed and the angle of approach. Checkmarks should be corrected at the same time. The jumper must bear in mind that spring must not be sacrificed to attain speed.

7. Spend 15 to 30 minutes on weight-training or tension exercises.

Tuesday

1. Jog 150 yards, walk 50 yards, and stride 100 yards at ¾ effort.
2. Perform 2 minutes of inverted running.
3. Practice stretching exercises, including the hitch kick, for 3 or 4 minutes.
4. Join the long jumpers and jump for distance twice. If the foot plant in the long jump interferes with the efficiency of the high jump spring, another event may be substituted at the discretion of the coach.
5. Expose the body to the sun for 5 to 10 minutes.
6. Tuesday's work is varied in nature, yet sufficiently light to permit the building up of body tone. Get set both mentally and physically to jump for height on Wednesday.
7. Conclude the day's work with light jogging.

Wednesday

1. Warm up as on a day of competition. See Saturday's schedule, early season.
2. Set the crossbar at the same height at which the competition will start in the next meet. Set a limit of 8 or 9 jumps. Gradually raise the crossbar so that the last height is 1 inch above your record jump.
3. Conclude the practice with 15 to 30 minutes of weight-training exercises.

Thursday

1. Take an optional amount of jogging, walking, sprinting, and calisthenics.
2. Spend 2 or 3 minutes verifying the different phases of the approach.

3. Join the field event competitors and participate in their workout for 10 minutes.
4. Taper off by jogging an optional distance. Then analyze your weekly body weight changes.

Friday

1. Jog 220 yards easily.
2. Make a study of the consistency of the approach and landing area. Adjust the shoes and length of spikes to meet the conditions.
3. Refrain from jumping but take light exercises of a varied nature which you have learned are best suited to your present needs.
4. Omit sun baths as well as sprinting. Keep off the feet until competition.

Saturday

1. This is the day of competition. Remember that the event can be won only on the field. Therefore, go about your daily routine in the regular manner. Conserve both nervous and physical energy.
2. By now you know the type and amount of warm-up you require. You also know whether you should allow 20, 30, or 40 minutes to elapse between the warm-up and the starting of the event.
3. Always be ready for your competition. Check the order of jumping on the official roster.
4. Maintain body tonus between jumps. Take advantage of this time for physical and mental relaxation.

Late season. The late season schedule of practice is lighter in intensity and designed to perfect jumping form and point toward further improvement in body tonus.

Monday

1. Start the day's practice by jogging 220 yards, walking 10 yards, running 25 yards, and sprinting 25 yards.

2. Discuss both the correct and incorrect execution of form in the previous Saturday's meet. A competitor's enthusiasm for the event is increased by having his own exemplification of correct technique pointed out.
3. Jump 4 or 5 times at a moderate height to eliminate any errors that may have been discovered.
4. Take part in a game for 5 to 10 minutes. The competitor will not participate in any contest or event that may seriously jeopardize his high jumping accomplishments. The game should serve the purpose of variety and relaxation in the workout. Continue weight-training exercises provided they have proved beneficial.

Tuesday

1. Begin by jogging 100 yards and walking 10 yards. Repeat twice. Jogging precedes calisthenics as a protective measure, since injuries occur in executing vigorous movements when the athlete is unprepared, just as in jumping vigorously when one is unprepared.
2. Spend 3 to 5 minutes on exercises, completing the entire repertoire of gymnastic feats that have proved of value in perfecting jumping ability.
3. Work on another event such as the shot-put or the javelin throw.
4. Reassure yourself of the optimum speed, direction, and length of the run toward the bar.
5. Do not jump today.
6. Conclude the practice by jogging 100 yards, running 100 yards, and sprinting 50 yards. This means 250 yards of continuous effort, starting slowly and culminating with a burst of speed.

Wednesday

1. Limber up with a jog of 200 yards and a run of 50 yards at $\frac{3}{4}$ effort. Conclude with 25 yards at $\frac{9}{10}$ effort.

2. Try 3 or 4 standing long jumps.
3. Spend 5 to 8 minutes on light gymnastic feats of special benefit to the high jumper.
4. Jump for height not to exceed 8 times, but emphasize form.
5. Practice weight-training exercises, reducing both intensity and duration.

Thursday

1. Take a warm-up, optional both as to type and quantity.
2. Prepare for weight events and take 4 or 5 trials.
3. Execute 4 or 5 trials of the running hitch kick. Since this event taxes the energy of some jumpers, good judgment must be used in the degree of effort applied.
4. Spend 2 minutes in bounding and bending exercises. If the approach is composed of cinders or an all-weather surface, shift this workout to the turf. Variety aids in improving body tonus.
5. Taper off with a jog of 300 yards at an optional pace.

Friday

There are two schools of thought relative to Friday's practice. One prefers that the competitors dress in competition suits and, after light jogging, sponge the body with tepid water and call it a day. The other contends that complete absence from the practice field is more desirable. The latter group further believes that nervous and physical energy are best conserved by avoiding contact with the event or its environment.

Saturday

1. The suggestions presented for Saturday's competition during midseason are applicable to late season. Conservation of energy during the day, relaxation between jumps, and alertness at all times are factors with

which the competitor is already familiar. For warm-up suggestions, see Saturday's schedules, early season.

2. Aim at your best effort, and make a resolution to clear each height on the first jump.
3. End the day with a jog of 440 yards and a shower. Analyze the week's fluctuation in body weight.

A RUSSIAN PLAN[2]

It has been stated that Russian high jumpers participate in more strenuous training programs than most American high jumpers. A sample of a daily practice for Russia's Yuri Stepanov, who jumped 2.162 meters (7 feet 1⅛ inches), indicates that such may be the case. Although the practice session for him that is outlined below may not be typical, it is interesting.

1. One hour in the gymnasium exercising on the Swedish ladder (similar to exercises by a ballerina on the bar).
2. Executing jumps off the right foot so that he swung the left leg 400 times. His objective was to develop the kick (free leg swing).
3. Clearing the high jump crossbar (set at 6 feet 6¾ inches) 10 times. Next he jumped (3 times each) at crossbar heights of 6 feet 7½ inches, 6 feet 8¾ inches, and 6 feet 9½ inches.
4. Frequently included were weight-training exercises (in which the maximum bar bell weight lifted was 220 pounds) and exercises on both the flying rings and the horizontal bar.
5. The practice session was concluded with jogging around the track.

REFERENCES

1. Lance, J. R., and Tuttle, W. W.: An informative article on the relationship existing between the time spent in executing the spring and the height of the jump, The Athlete 1:41, 1937.
2. Galli, J. H.: The New Zealand Sportsman, Wellington, New Zealand 13:5, 1957.

Chapter 11

The pole vault

The pole vault, like the long jump, can be traced to the days of primitive man. No doubt it was employed by early man as a means of gaining distance in jumping obstacles which confronted him in his pursuit of food and in his combat with the enemy. By adding the lift provided by the pole to the long jump, barriers such as streams and gullies, which otherwise might have been unsurmountable obstacles, could be crossed quickly. Thus it is seen that in the beginning the pole vault was a feat of horizontal distance rather than height. In early competition this idea predominated, and pole vaulting was placed on the program as a horizontal vaulting event.

As time went on, the pole vault evolved into an event for height, and in 1877 it was added to the championship program in America. During the first 10 years of competition, American athletes reigned supreme in the event, until Tom Ray of Ulverstone, in the north of England, became champion. The new British performers were designated as pole climbers, since they employed a peculiar technique which is best described by Baxter:

For years the world's record-holders all came from one small town, Ulverstone, in the north of England. The game probably had its inception in the fen country. This country is bisected by numerous small dykes and canals, and it has been the custom from time immemorial for the inhabitants to use long poles, by means of which they negotiate these obstacles.

The method employed by the "climber" was as follows: He used a long and rather heavy pole, shod at the lower end with a tripod of iron, with a spread of two and one-half to three inches. The vaulter ran slowly down to the take-off with the pole grasped in the middle, and planted the tripod about three feet in front of the crossbar. He then let his body swing up and began to climb; the upper hand was raised a foot or so on the pole, and the lower hand brought up to it. This operation was repeated four or five times. By this time, the pole would be off balance and would begin to fall forward. The athlete would then raise his feet and go over the bar in a sitting position.*

The peculiar technique employed by the Ulverstone school precipitated much discussion which finally resulted in a standardization of the method used in vaulting over the bar. In 1890 the pole-climbing technique was barred by American rules and later by Olympic rules. Beginning about this time the pole vault began to take on its present form.

The evolution of equipment is worthy of mention. The ancients no doubt cut a virgin pole from the forest and sharpened the lower end of it. When pole vaulting took its place as an event of modern competition, a pole of spruce, ash, or hickory, fitted with a iron prong or tripod, was introduced. Next came the spiked bamboo pole. This was followed by the bamboo pole with a mushroom-shaped plug in place of the iron tip. Even the introduction of the bamboo pole precipitated discussion when A. C. Gilbert of Yale used it in 1908 at the Olympic games in London.

With the bamboo pole came the elimination of metal tips for ground gripping.

---

*From Baxter, H. H.: An historical contribution from an early champion, Pole Vaulting, Spalding's Athletic Library, No. 504S.

A hole dug in the ground was substituted for the metal tip as a means of holding the pole. In years that followed, there was a lack of uniformity in the size of the hole, which naturally varied with soil condition. These irregularities were the basis for many objections. Therefore, in the 1924 Olympic games the wooden trough for planting the pole was introduced. As a result of experience and a desire for better performance, a metal or plastic pole-planting trough and a metal or fiber glass pole are recognized as standard equipment in American competition.

In 1962 the International Amateur Athletic Federation indicated its acceptance of the fiber glass pole when it approved a record performance by a vaulter who used one.

The evolution of technique in pole vaulting quite naturally has been accompanied by better performances. The record of 9 feet 7 inches made by G. McNichol in 1877 has been surpassed repeatedly, and so it is not surprising to learn that many top-flight performers are setting their objective at well over 17 feet.

A distinction in records is made between vaulting competitions conducted indoors and those held outdoors. In 1967, Paul Wilson of the United States was credited with a performance (outdoors) of 17 feet 7¾ inches, and in 1967, Bob Seagren of the United States vaulted (indoors) 17 feet ¼ inch.

The improvements in both the vaulting pole and the pole-planting trough have aided in vaulting greater heights. The introduction of the black and white crossbar, first used in 1920, has proved helpful to the vaulter. In addition, advances have been made in developing excellent runways and landing areas. The use of foam rubber instead of shavings to reduce the shock of landing has been an important factor in improved performances.

As time passes, competition has become keener, and more scientific methods in the execution of the vault have been employed. The event has become more than a vault; in fact, it is looked upon as a spectacular gymnastic feat, calling on contestants to make use of any knowledge they may gain from such sciences as physics, kinesiology, and physiology. Certainly, progress in vaulting has been made possible by the adoption of the most suitable and effective aids to the mechanical ability of the contestant so that he may make better use of body mechanisms in overcoming the force of gravity.

GENERAL CONSIDERATIONS

Comparative marks in competition. As a guide to the vaulter in determining the heights he must clear if he expects to place at the various levels of competition, Table 11-1 is presented. Since the vaulting heights listed are interpreted to mean placing rather than winning performances and are based on national averages, it is recognized that they may not apply to competitive situations where the vaulting talent is either excellent or poor in quality. The vaulter is advised to investigate the ability of his opponents.

The next point that naturally follows the knowledge of placement marks for the various grades of competition is equipment.

Equipment. It is essential in the pole vault as well as in any event that the contestant be familiar with the most acceptable equipment so that he may facilitate his progress by selecting those items which experience has shown are best suited for the event.

Shoes. The majority of vaulters prefer sprinting shoes because they are light in weight. Heel protection is provided by several devices, such as pads or heel cups, that are described in Chapter 3 under Heel protection.

The next and the most important piece of equipment to be discussed is the pole.

Pole. The fiber glass pole currently is the first choice of the world's leading vaulters. The best performances recorded to date, both indoors and outdoors, have been accomplished when using this type.

Fiber glass poles can be purchased in lengths of 12 to 16 feet. Varied construction patterns permit a selection to suit the body weight of the vaulters within a range of 135 to 200 pounds. The 12-foot pole suitable for a 135-pound competitor weighs approximately 4 pounds, and the 16-foot pole designed for a 200-pound athlete weighs approximately $6\frac{1}{2}$ pounds.

Claims are made that the fiber glass pole is stronger because a high density process in manufacture provides faster recovery, greater flexion without breaking, and the quality of lightness. This pole is fitted with a cork plug at the upper end and a rubber plug at the lower end.

Among the qualities of any given fiber glass pole that should be investigated by the vaulter are: (1) the bend (elasticity), (2) the catapulting or recovery force (thrust), and (3) the return to its customary shape (resiliency).

The vaulter is cautioned, "Do not drop the pole." Care must be exercised both when the pole is in use and when it is being transported. Tubular carrying cases can be purchased. Whenever the surface of the

Table 11-1. Comparative marks in scholastic competition for the pole vault

Meet	No. of places scored	Height
Dual high school	3	11 ft. 0 in.–12 ft. 6 in.
Qualifying—state	3	12 ft. 6 in.–13 ft. 6 in.
State—province	5	13 ft. 6 in.–14 ft. 6 in.

fiber glass pole becomes scarred or roughened, the application of spar varnish is recommended by the manufacturers.

Swedish steel vaulting poles are obtainable in lengths ranging from 12 to 16 feet and are fabricated in both uniform diameter and twin tapered types. The twin tapered Swedish pole, 15 feet 9 inches in length, weighs approximately 6 pounds.

Aluminum alloy poles are manufactured in varying lengths upon special order. The type that has been most popular is 16 feet long and at the point of hand grasp is $1\frac{1}{2}$ inches in diameter. The heavy duty aluminum alloy pole weighs 6 pounds 4 ounces, and the lighter duty type weighs 6 pounds.

Poles of fiber glass, steel, and aluminum alloy customarily are wrapped with one layer of friction tape for a distance of 3 to 5 feet in order to provide a nonslip surface for the hand grasp.

It is obvious that each type of vaulting pole has its advantages as well as its disadvantages. The finances available and the personal preference of the vaulter, in the light of his experience, are the factors that determine the type of pole selected.

Types of competitors. Successful pole vaulters do not conform to any set physical classification. There have been champions who were short in stature with well-proportioned, well-developed arms and shoulders. Fine sprinting ability was utilized in perfecting an effective approach to the bar. Their natural coordination was above average as was evidenced by excellent timing of the pole thrust, the swing, the pull-up, the push-up, and the throw-away. These successive movements were not sharply divided but were fused, one to the other. These vaulters may be classified as the speed-coordinating type.

Other champions were tall in stature, weighing more than the average vaulter, with arm and shoulder development seemingly in advance of the rest of the body. They did not deem it advisable to use a speedy run during the approach but were exceptionally effective with a moderately high handhold which made possible an unusually vigorous pull-up. The run at moderate speed relieved them of the necessity of rushing through the execution of the pull-up. This gave the vault the appearance of nonchalance with a fairly well-defined sequence of movements. The deliberate run was designed to result in timing that permitted the body to assume the optimum position for the execution of the push-up and throw-away. The arm and shoulder development gave them a decided advantage in this phase of the vault. They serve as examples of the pull-up, push-away type.

Still others were medium in stature and average in weight. Their approach was moderately fast. The arm and shoulder development was similar to that of the average vaulter. Their sense of coordination, superior to that of the ordinary vaulter, gave them an advantage in timing and in the control of the body from the take-off to the landing. They represent the push-up–coordinating type of vaulter.

Heavyweight vaulters are the exception because of the demand made on their arms and because of the necessity of speedy, precise body movements while the vaulter is off the ground.

Qualifications. A discussion of the qualifications of the pole vaulter necessarily covers points common to other events, especially the long jump and the running high jump.

Age. There are no objections to boys participating in the pole vault at an early age. Self-study, practice, and diligence over a period of years will reward the youth who is interested in this event. The age range of world champions is from 20 to 30 years.

Endurance. The vaulter is frequently required to be in readiness for vaulting over a 3-hour period. This event differs from the long jump in which the jumper may steel himself for only one supreme effort, achieve his objective, and retire for the day. The vaulter, on the other hand, must remain with the event, clearing or passing heights until the crucial point is reached. A vaulter unprepared for a sustained expenditure of muscular and nervous energy may meet defeat, even though he excels in vaulting form. Endurance is an important factor in pole vaulting.

Height. A comparison of the physical characteristics of vaulting champions has been presented. Although competitors short in stature have set records in the pole vault, the tall athlete has the advantage, just as he does in long jumping and hurdling. He is able to utilize a higher grasp on the pole with no more effort than his medium-sized rival who must take a lower hold. At the instant of the push-up and throw-away, the taller man, having longer arms, should be able to push the center of gravity higher over the crossbar than a shorter competitor of equal arm strength.

Spring. The vaulter seeks to propel the pole, carrying his body, to an upright position in the pole-plant box. The take-off leg contributes to this achievement by the extension of the leg at the knee and the speedy rock-up on the toes. As in the long jump, strong leg and thigh muscles which are capable of delivering effective force quickly are important. The amount of force exerted in the spring varies among vaulters. However, a competent vaulter will exert the maximum amount of force that is compatible with his entire vaulting routine.

Coordination and rhythm. Success in the pole vault, as in any gymnastic feat, depends on neuromuscular coordination and rhythm. There are a number of actions in the execution of the vault which occur at the same time and which must be perfectly synchronized if good form and high attainment are to be achieved. Also, certain movements in the vault must be blended into the preceding ones if the jump is to be most effectively executed. A poorly timed pull-up after the swing leads to poor vaulting. If the push-up and throw-away are not properly coordinated, the vaulter may lose all

he has gained by the run, the swing, and the pull-up.

Speed. The relationship of sprinting velocities to starting times is discussed in Chapter 4 (pp. 39 and 40). Track and field instructors are not in complete agreement on the amount of speed necessary in the pole vault. Obviously, they recognize that some vaulters require less speed than others, but in considering a single vaulter, coaches differ on the ideal rate of speed and acceleration.

An extremely fast run inhibits poise and gather at the instant of executing the pole-thrust. Even though perfect planting of the pole has been attained, excess speed brings the vaulter too rapidly to the crossbar. Often he is rushed and incompletely executes his swing and pull-up.

That group of instructors favoring moderate speed in the approach assert that vaulters require only enough speed to help raise the pole to the upright position. Speed beyond that point necessitates undue haste in completing those leg and body actions designed to place the vaulter high over the bar, squarely facing the runway, feet high in the air, with the arms in a position to aid propulsion up and away from the crossbar. On the other hand, a speed deficiency results in a failure to attain an upright position of the pole in the plant box. When the pole has to be released in other than a perpendicular plane, the vaulter is without adequate support when pushing downward prior to the hand release.

Those instructors favoring a fast approach recognize that obstacles must be surmounted to accomplish smooth pole planting and taking off. They claim that even with high speed these actions can be consummated with grace and poise. This group further claims that a vaulter using a fast approach will be certain to generate momentum sufficient to bring the vaulting pole to an upright position. Such a vaulter may begin the pull-up shortly after the take-off (sooner than does the vaulter who runs at a moderate rate) without fear of checking the upward progress of the pole. When a vaulter executes the pull-up in advance of the swing, there is a tendency to retard the forward and upward progress of the pole. Naturally this includes the vaulter, since he is clinging close to it, often with the knees bent or drawn up. Those coaches advising a speedy run approve an early pull-up, claiming that the pole will reach a perpendicular position and that by starting the pull-up early the vaulter will have his body in readiness for the crossbar clearance even though the pole is pivoting upright at a speed above the average. Here again, the competitor will be guided by his own experimentation and by the advice of his observers and instructors, since exponents of each method are able to cite championship performances to substantiate their claims.

Arms and shoulder girdle. The pull-up of the body during the upward flight and the push-up of the body at the crest of the vault are prime fundamentals of technique. Their successful execution is dependent upon the efficiency of the musculature of the arms and shoulder girdle. Muscle mass is not the only criterion; its strength and its plasticity are also determining factors. Simple exercises performed daily, gradually increased in intensity, are recommended for the development of the arms and shoulder girdle.

Air-mindedness. The ability to relax immediately after the throw-away is an asset to the vaulter. The competitor striking the landing area with arm or leg muscles tense experiences greater shock than the one who alights in a limp condition. The vaulter who does not inherit the characteristic of self-protection should attempt to develop fearlessness by falling relaxed from gradually increasing heights. Successful vaulters either inherit or acquire air-mindedness. This is the ability to orient oneself while in the air, making use of all faculties regardless of the body position. This is especially true

of the correct use of vision, from the start of the approach to the push-away and landing. Proper air-mindedness is considered essential for correct rhythm and balance in executing the pole vault.

TECHNIQUE OF THE POLE VAULT

The pole vault is an event that requires the gaining of optimum speed, the addition of impetus by a properly synchronized spring, and the initiation of a pendulum-like swing upon which are superimposed a pull-up, body turn, push-up, and throw-away. The difficulty that one encounters in describing the pole vault adequately is accentuated by the various body shifts on the pendulum-like swing. *While the actions in the pole vault are described individually, it is pointed out that some of them occur simultaneously, and others overlap.* After one becomes familiar with the details of the various body movements, he is ready to blend them together into one continuous, coordinated act.

Because the fiber glass pole is much more flexible than the aluminum alloy or the steel pole, certain aspects of the technique for vaulting with a fiber glass pole differ markedly from those for vaulting with an aluminum alloy or steel pole (that is, the pole plant, the hand shift, the foot plant and spring, the swing-up, the pull-up, the body turn and leg scissors, and the push-up). Other aspects of the technique for vaulting with the two types of poles are bascially the same (that is, the handhold and pole carry, the approach, the crossbar clearance, and the landing). In the discussion that follows, those aspects of the technique of vaulting that differ markedly for the two types of poles are described for each type of pole: that is, the aluminum alloy or steel pole, and the fiber glass pole. Fig. 11-3 depicts a vaulter who is using an aluminum alloy or steel pole; Fig. 11-4, a vaulter who is using a fiber glass pole.

Handhold and pole carry. The proper technique for holding and carrying the alluminum alloy or steel pole is basically the same as the technique for holding and carrying the fiber glass pole; hence, the description that follows applies to both types of pole. The discussion is based on the premise that the vaulter is right-handed.

The height of the right handhold depends on the vaulter's ability to overcome the force of gravity when propelling the pole, carrying the body, to a vertical posi-tion. This means that a vaulter with power-ful arms and shoulders can be expected to employ a higher right handhold than his less fortunate opponent. This also applies to both the exceptionally tall and the speedy competitor.

Since the right handhold is established as a fixed point, the method of carrying the pole is determined by the position of the left hand. There is general agreement

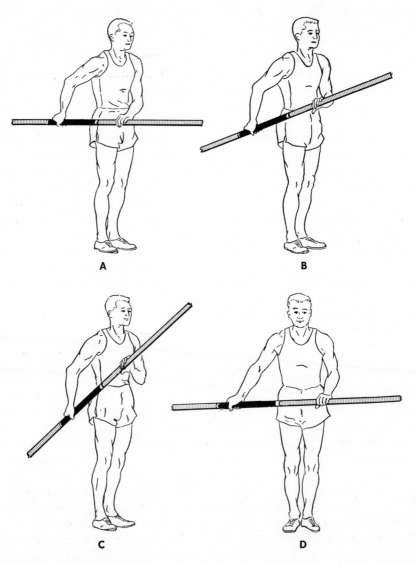

A

B

C

D

Fig. 11-1. Types of pole carry. **A,** Low point carry. **B,** Intermediate carry. **C,** High point carry. **D,** Cross-body carry.

among coaches that the experienced vaulter should not attempt to alter the height of the right hand grasp with each successive elevation of the crossbar. Prominent vaulters confine themselves to one established handhold regardless of the crossbar height. Measurement of the pole vault handhold is taken from the point of the vaulting pole. There are various methods of carrying the vaulting pole during the approach (four of which are shown in Fig. 11-1). In three of these the angle of the pole with respect to the ground accounts for the differences. In the high point carry the pole forms an angle of approximately 45 degrees with the ground, in the intermediate carry the angle is about 25 degrees, and for the low point carry the pole is approximately parallel with the ground. In the fourth type, known as the cross-body carry, the pole is not held in line with the approach. Instead it is held crosswise to the vaulter's trunk during the run so that it is approximately parallel with the ground.

The vaulter employing the low point carry (Fig. 11-1, A) at first may encounter difficulty in obtaining pole balance during the run, but he has a short distance to lower the pole point and thus has reduced chances for errors in the ensuing hand shift and alignment of the pole. Furthermore, this type is said to permit an efficient underhand thrust of the pole into the trough.

When using the intermediate carry (Fig. 11-1, B), the vaulter again may sacrifice ease in pole balance but may gain by the short distance he is obliged to lower the pole point. Numerous coaches and competitors contend that the intermediate carry permits the vaulter to attain greater speed during the approach than is possible with any of the other methods. They claim that the intermediate carry permits the body to assume a more effective running position.

With the high point carry (Fig. 11-1, C) the vaulter is permitted efficient pole leverage and balance during the approach, but he is obliged to lower the pole point through a greater distance in planting it in the trough. If he is slow in lowering the pole point, he may hinder the smoothness which is necessary for a proper thrust. Frequently the high point carry requires an overhand thrust, an action that is criticized by some authorities because it tends to induce errors in the alignment of the pole.

The cross-body pole carry (Fig. 11-1, D) allows for greater speed during the initial section of the approach. This method of carry is disadvantageous in that the pole must be aligned with the direction of the runway in the later part of the approach so as to ensure a proper pole plant.

The position of the hands on the pole is determined as follows: The vaulter grasps the pole with the right hand at a height that has been determined either through experience or coaching advice. He then takes the pole to the spot from which the approach is to be started. Facing the crossbar, with the right arm fairly well extended back and the pole at the right side, the vaulter grasps it with his left hand in a position so that the left arm is in contact with his body, the elbow forming a right angle. This gives a hand spread of approximately 2½ feet. This degree of spread is usually employed for the high point carry. From this position as a starting point, the other types of handholds and pole carries are established.

For a low point carry, the place of grasp of the left hand is found by sliding the hand the desired distance toward the planting point. The hand spread is usually greater than in the high point carry, the maximum being about 3 feet.

In describing the handhold, coaches usually say the right hand should be palm up and the left hand, palm down. However, this applies only when the pole is in front of the body and parallel with ground. The left hand grasp changes only slightly during the initiation of the approach. However, the right handhold depends somewhat on the method of pole carry.

After the spacing of the hands has been

determined, the pole should be grasped loosely enough so that the hands may turn and thus meet the demand set up by the position of the pole during the approach (Fig. 11-1).

Approach. The technique for the approach for the vaulter who is using an aluminum alloy or steel pole is basically the same as the technique for the approach for the vaulter who is using a fiber glass pole; hence, the discussion that follows is applicable to vaults for which either type of pole is used. The important points to be considered in approaching the crossbar are the plans of approach, a comparison of plans, the method of adjusting the check-marks, and the speed between the check-marks. The run is accelerated smoothly.

Definition of plans. The style of approach which a novice adopts will depend on his ability to gain momentum. There are plans of approach suitable for those who gain momentum slowly, moderately fast, and extremely fast. For the purpose of illustration, three plans are described: the 2-6-8 plan, the 4-6-8 plan, and the 2-8-10 plan. These plans are shown in Fig. 11-2. It is worthy of note that there are many variations of these three plans. In the discussion as well as in Fig. 11-2 it is assumed that the vaulter is a right-handed individual who drives off the ground from the left foot.

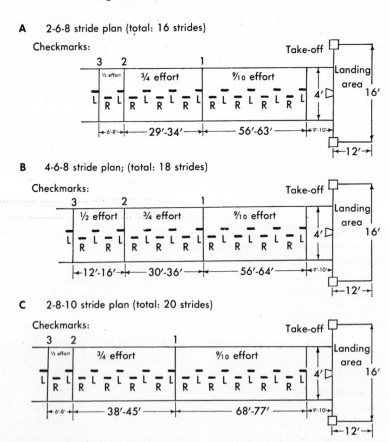

Right-hand vaulter - Left-foot take-off

A 2-6-8 stride plan (total: 16 strides)

B 4-6-8 stride plan; (total: 18 strides)

C 2-8-10 stride plan (total: 20 strides)

Fig. 11-2. Three commonly accepted plans of approach for the pole vault.

2-6-8 stride plan: The 2-6-8 stride plan (Fig. 11-2, *A*) means that starting with the toe of the left shoe on checkmark 3, checkmark 2 is placed 2 running strides toward the landing area. Checkmark 1 is located 6 running strides from checkmark 2. There remain 8 running strides between checkmark 1 and the point of take-off. The total number of strides is 16.

4-6-8 stride plan: If this plan is to be employed, the vaulter marks off on the runway 3 spots (Fig. 11-2) which he aims to strike with the toe of his left shoe (take-off foot). These marks are to be 8, 14, and 18 strides from the point of take-off. Starting with the left foot on checkmark 3 (Fig. 11-2, *B*), checkmark 2 is placed 4 running strides toward the landing area; checkmark 1 is placed 6 running strides from checkmark 2. There remain 8 running strides from checkmark 1 to the point of the take-off (front spike marks of the left shoe). The total number of strides is 18.

2-8-10 stride plan: This plan is shown in Fig. 11-2, *C*. Starting with the toe of the left shoe on checkmark 3, checkmark 2 is located 2 running strides toward the landing area. Checkmark 1 is placed 8 running strides from checkmark 2. There remain 10 running strides between checkmark 1 and the point of take-off. The total number of strides is 20.

Comparison of plans. The answer to the question, "What stride plan shall I use?" is similar to the answer given to a long jumper. Here, it depends on the ability of the vaulter, with the pole in hand, to gain optimum momentum when reaching the pole-planting and the take-off stages of the vault.

The vaulter who gathers speed slowly usually requires a greater number of strides between checkmark 1 and the take-off spot to gain his optimum speed when striking the take-off spot. The 2-8-10 stride plan is recommended for this type of competitor. The vaulter who gathers speed rapidly requires the least number of strides between checkmark 1 and the take-off spot to gain his optimum speed when striking the take-off spot. The 2-6-8 stride plan is recommended for him. As is the case in the long jump, the majority of contestants gather speed at a rate that falls between the relatively slow and the extremely speedy type. The 4-6-8 stride plan, therefore, is recommended for most vaulters.

In selecting a stride plan, the vaulter must remember that the approach, in addition to being a run, involves carrying a pole. However, a plan should be adopted that permits optimum speed at the take-off with the least number of strides. The addition of pole carrying to the approaching run may require a few more strides than in an ordinary sprint. The final adoption of a stride plan will be governed by the vaulter's experience and attainments.

Method of adjusting checkmarks. As is true of the long jump, patience and care in the adjustment of checkmarks will pay large dividends to the pole vaulter. Sprinting practice, both without and with the pole, is a prerequisite for the determination of one's checkmarks. The vaulter, with the pole in his hands, must standardize the stride if he expects to attain consistent accuracy in his approach. The fact that this event consists of the execution of a number of complicated movements, each depending on the one that precedes it, makes the importance of correctly adjusted checkmarks obvious.

For the sake of clarity, the adjustment of the checkmarks of the 2-6-8 stride plan is given. The details are as follows: On a runway that has been brushed so that spike marks will be well defined, measure off exactly 60 feet up the runway from the planting trough. Place checkmark 1 here temporarily. The vaulter who takes off from the left foot should place the checkmarks on the left side of the runway. Scratch a line across the runway from the checkmark. Temporarily place checkmark 3 approximately 35 feet up the runway from checkmark 1 and likewise scratch a line across the runway. Standing with the take-off foot on checkmark 3, carrying the pole, run down the approach and strike checkmark 1 with the front spike of the take-off shoe, continue down the runway, drop the pole into the planting trough, and run through the landing area. At this stage, temporarily ignore the pole thrust. The run should be accelerated gradually so that when the take-off spot is reached, the vaulter will be at $\frac{9}{10}$ his best effort. An observer locates the position of the take-off foot at the end of the eighth stride from checkmark 1 and measures its distance from the stopping board of the planting trough. These instructions should be repeated until there is uniformity in the position of the front spike of the take-off shoe at the end of the eighth running stride. This procedure is termed "standardizing the stride." Next, move checkmark 1 so that the front spike of the take-off shoe will strike 8 feet from the stopping board at the end of the eighth stride; 8 feet approximates the take-off spot for a vaulter grasping the pole with his right hand at a height of 10 feet. With this grasp, at the instant of take-off, the right hand will be 6 feet 10 inches directly above the toe of the left shoe. For a vaulter holding the pole with the right hand at the height of 12 feet 6 inches, the distance from the stopping board to the point of take-off will approximate 10 feet 3 inches. At the instant of take-off the right hand will be 7 feet directly above the toe of the right shoe. Therefore, it is clear that as the pole is grasped at greater heights, the point of take-off is moved farther away from the stopping board. Consequently all checkmarks should be moved a corresponding distance away from the board. This is especially true if the take-off spot is to be maintained on a plumb line with the right hand. After these adjustments have been made, checkmark 1 is marked and measured. This completes the standardization of the 8-stride section. The vaulter is now ready to locate checkmark 2, setting off the 6-stride section.

In order to locate checkmark 2, the vaulter carrying the pole runs through the course again, being sure that the front spike of the take-off shoe strikes checkmark 1. An observer marks the spot 6 strides back of checkmark 1. This is temporarily marked as checkmark 2. With the runway brushed, the vaulter repeats his trials, running down the approach, dropping the pole in the planting trough and continuing through the landing area. In order to prove checkmark 2, the vaulter runs through the course a number of times with the pole, being sure that the front spike of the take-off shoe strikes checkmark 2, checkmark 1, and a point 8 feet from the stopping board. He should forget about planting the pole, simply dropping the pole before the run through the landing area. The next step is the adjustment of checkmark 3, setting off the 2-stride section.

With the runway brushed, the vaulter with pole in hand starts with the front spike of the take-off shoe on temporary checkmark 3 and runs through the path as before. The correctness of checkmarks 2 and 1 again should be verified. The observer marks the spot where the front spike of the take-off shoe strikes 2 strides back of checkmark 2 and marks this spot checkmark 3. This checkmark, together with the other two, is proved by repeated trials. Accuracy is paramount in every case. When actually competing, the vaulter starts the run 1 or 2 strides back of checkmark 3.

The adjustments for the 4-6-8 stride plan and for the 2-8-10 stride plan and their variations are made in a similar manner.

Speed between checkmarks. It has been pointed out previously that the speed of the vaulter is gradually accelerated from the initial stance to the take-off spot. Between checkmarks 3 and 2, the vaulter should exert about $\frac{1}{2}$ effort; between checkmarks 2 and 1, about $\frac{3}{4}$ effort; and between checkmark 1 and the take-off spot, about $\frac{9}{10}$ effort (see pp. 39 and 40).

As in the long jump, the question again

arises, "Why should a vaulter not be running at 100 percent effort?" When an individual sprints 100 yards, subsequently competes in the long jump, and still later competes in the pole vault, he has different objectives. In the sprint the objective is to run the course in the shortest period of time. In the long jump, in addition to speed, the competitor must pay attention to striking checkmarks and the take-off board and to gathering for the leap. In the pole vault, the competitor must concern himself with carrying the pole, striking the checkmarks, striking the take-off spot, planting the pole, raising the hands, and gathering for the spring. The long jumper reduces speed for the sake of accuracy. The pole vaulter needs further to sacrifice speed for accuracy. During the run, the eyes should be focused successively on checkmarks 3, 2, and 1, and then on the pole-planting trough until the beginning of the swing-up. From this stage until the completion of the vault, the eyes should be focused on the crossbar.

Successive stages in the approach are shown in Fig. 11-3, *A* and *B*.

The vault: aluminum alloy or steel pole

The descriptions that follow apply only to the vaulter who is using an aluminum alloy or a steel pole.

Pole plant. The term "pole plant" is applied to that action whereby the vaulter, having attained optimum speed, lowers the point of the pole so that it drops on the V-shaped apron of the planting trough and slides forward to the stopping board at the rear of the trough. The target should be a point midway between the edges of the board. Excess shock may be reduced by placing a small quantity of sawdust or shavings in the trough.

There are two generally accepted types of pole planting: the underhand thrust and the overhand thrust. The latter is shown in Fig. 11-3, *B* and *C*. Although it is not a fixed

practice, the type of pole thrust selected by a competitor usually depends on the type of pole carriage he employs. The carry with the point high and the carry with the point low have been discussed previously. The low point carry is most frequently associated with the underhand thrust and the high point carry, with the overhand thrust.

A period of gather, coast, or freewheeling is common to all types of pole carry when the vaulter has decreased running effort and concentrates on his subsequent actions. Among the actions are the pole thrust, shifting the hands, and the foot plant. Vaulters usually gather during the last two strides, but some vaulters extend the gather over the last three strides. The gather in the pole vault is comparable to that in the long jump. In both events attention is transferred from speed to mechanical accuracy. The last stride rightfully may be shortened, thus permitting the center of body weight to be directly over the take-off foot at the instant of executing the spring from the ground.

The first activity in the gather is the pole thrust. As the point of the pole is lowered, the left hand is shifted either against or close to the right hand.

Those vaulters employing the underhand thrust underswing the right hand (which is grasping the pole) forward and close to the hip. Vaulters employing the overhand thrust bring the right hand upward and outward past the head before moving it forward. A number of coaches question the mechanical effectiveness of the overhand thrust, chiefly because of a possible lack of alignment of the hands and the pole shortly before the swing-up. Some vaulters employ what they term a "medium" thrust.

The next step, regardless of the method of thrusting, is the raising of the hands above the head and the flexing of the elbows at about right angles. The bend of the arms tends to reduce the effect of the shock caused by the impact of the vaulting pole against the pole planting trough.

The pole should be carried in such a

manner that the point of the pole, the tip of the pole, and the center of the stopping board are in the same plane. Momentum, as previously described, should be maintained. The dropping of the pole into the planting trough should be a smooth coordinated movement. The point of the pole should come to rest against the lower midpoint of the stopping board.

Hand shift. Shifting the hands and planting the pole are synchronized movements. The question immediately arises, "Why shift the hands?"

During the running approach to the pole-planting box, the hands are spread apart in order to support the weight of the pole (Fig. 11-3, *A* and *B*). If the hands were kept in a spread position at the beginning of the swing-up and pull-up, the right hand would be supporting practically all of the body weight. By sliding the left hand close

to the right hand (Fig. 11-3, *C* and *D*), the weight is more evenly distributed between the two arms. In addition, a smoother swing-up, a more powerful pull-up, and a higher push-up are possible.

All good vaulters keep the right hand at the same height from the start of the approach through the final push-up and throw-away. A majority of coaches favor a style in which the left hand is quite close to the right hand continuously from the shifting of the hands to the throw-away. However, there are some first-rate performers who execute the customary hand shift, swing-up, and pull-up, but at this point they vary the technique slightly. They lower the left handhold 6 to 8 inches as a means of aiding the body turn, keeping the hands in this position while performing the remaining movements in an orthodox manner. Only after studying repeated efforts can one

D   C   B   A

Fig. 11-3, A-K. A series of acceptable form for the pole vault (with a pole of moderate elasticity).

arrive at a technique that is most effective for a given individual.

Foot plant and spring. The foot plant and spring are evaluated differently by various coaches. Some believe that the spring obtainable in the pole vault should be comparable to that gained in the long jump and the high jump. On the other hand, there are those who tend to minimize the importance of the spring. They believe that the vaulter who places considerable emphasis on the spring will eventually lose in the swing and pull-up. Still others think that a moderately accentuated spring provides impetus for raising the body, but they recognize the fact that the subsequent immediate actions may be hampered by an extremely vigorous spring.

In evaluating the spring, one must enumerate the factors involved in bringing the

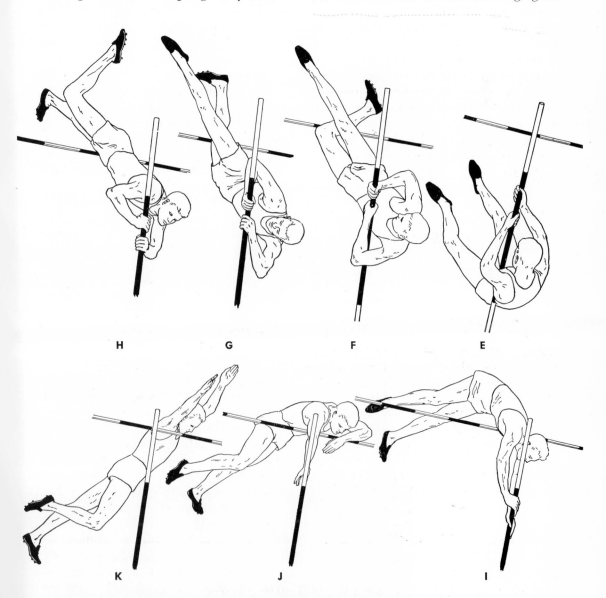

Fig. 11-3, cont'd. For legend see opposite page.

pole to an upright position. These are the momentum attained during the approach and the force obtained from the spring. A competitor executing an extremely vigorous spring may sacrifice momentum. A vaulter, having gained optimum momentum and failing to apply sufficient spring, may fail to bring the pole effectively to an upright position. As previously pointed out, the most effective height will be gained by a proper synchronization of momentum and spring. Through repeated trials the competitor will learn to apply the proper amount of force and will learn the extent of the rock-up on the toes and the optimum timing in relating to the right leg swing. In Fig. 11-3, C, the left heel is shown coming down at the conclusion of the foot plant. In Fig. 11-3, D, the left heel is shown being raised at the beginning of the spring.

A well-executed foot plant consists of striking the ground flat-footed with the knee slightly bent, immediately followed by a rock-up on the toes. Maximum spring is more readily attained if the heel and toes of the left foot are in line with the point of the vaulting pole. Furthermore, the foot must be aligned with the highest point of the upper hand which is grasping the pole. Vaulters vary slightly in this phase of the technique. There are those who place the foot so that the plumb line from the top edge of the upper hand touches the back of the heel. Perhaps the majority places the take-off foot so that the plumb line described comes to the ball of the foot.

During this period of the vault, the arms are flexed at right angles. Many excellent vaulters appear to thrust the hips forward and tilt the head backward. Because of the force applied in the spring, the heel should be well protected. The spring should be blended with the swing-up.

Swing-up. The swing-up is a movement initiated by a forward-upward knee lift of the right leg. Immediately thereafter the left leg is swung close to the right leg, and for a short period both legs are extended,

as close to the pole as possible. The arms, which were flexed at about right angles during the foot plant, now are bent only slightly, since the extension of the arms permits an effective pendulum-like swing. During the swing-up, many excellent vaulters drop the head slightly backward, claiming that the head tilt facilitates the elevation of the legs. The center of the pendulum swing is the shoulders and not the hands.

The hips should be flexed at about the moment they become even with the vaulting pole during the swing-up, thus shortening the radius and increasing the speed. At this stage the majority of vaulters flex the knees (bringing them toward the chest), which further shortens the radius and increases the speed. Other excellent performers place less emphasis on flexing the knees and claim that their technique enables them to extend the feet higher at the end of the swing-up. The majority of coaches believe that the swing-up should be substantially completed prior to pulling the body close to the hands and that the movement should be continuous between the swing-up and the pull-up (Fig. 11-3, E and F).

If a vaulter sets the take-off foot too far to the right or left of a center line, there is a tendency to swing sideward and upward rather than directly upward. According to physical principles, the swing is most effectively executed from a position in which the hands are directly over the head as previously described.

Pull-up. The time of the execution of the pull-up (Fig. 11-3, F) depends on the style of the vaulter. Vaulters who rely on speed and coordination rather than on arm strength will begin the pull-up earlier than other types. The pull-up and push-away type of vaulter, who depends on excepcional arm strength and a minimum of speed, will delay the pull-up longer than the others. The push-up–coordinating type running at average speed, with average shoulder strength but with excellent coordinating ability, may begin the pull-up at a point somewhere betwen the extremes previously described.

Toward the end of the swing, as the pole approaches a perpendicular position, the pull-up is executed by a strong flexion of the arms, thus raising the body. At the same time an attempt is made to maintain the forward-upward swing of the legs unimpeded. The pull-up should not be started until the hips reach the level of the shoulders. In fact there are some authorities who believe that the pull-up should not be started until the hips reach a level considerably higher than that of the shoulders. The vaulter is cautioned (if selecting the latter method) to avoid permitting the body to swing too far past the pole. During the pull-up the thighs and knees are flexed, but they are straightened just before crossbar clearance. The combination of arm pull and a free swing of the right leg is the initial factor in accomplishing the body turn which may be considered a continuation of the pull-up.

Body turn and leg scissors. Near the completion of the pull-up, the pole has reached a position approaching the vertical (Fig. 11-3, *E*). At this instant the body is pulled close to the pole by a flexion of the arms (Fig. 11-3, *F*). The forward and upward momentum of the legs continues. Since the vaulter is obliged to face the runway in order to be in the proper position for the push-up, it is necessary that he execute a body twist (half-turn). A combination of movements contributes to the turning of the body.

The left leg, bent at the knee, is forcefully straightened and swung forward and downward (Fig. 11-3, *F, G,* and *H*). The reaction to the left leg movements turns the left hip backward and upward. Simultaneously the extended right leg is swung backward and upward. The reaction to the right leg movements pushes the right hip forward and downward. The combination of the reactions of the scissorslike move-

ments rotates the hips, and the vaulter is in a position similar to a gymnastic handstand (Fig. 11-3, *H*). The pole is brought to a vertical position which is essential for an effective push-up.

Push-up. The push-up phase of the vault is executed most efficiently at the moment when the legs and hips are well above the crossbar and the elbows are slightly flexed (Fig. 11-3, *H*). At this stage, the vaulting pole is in a vertical position and close to the right shoulder. The legs may be permitted a moderate lateral spread but must be employed in order to maintain balance, thus centering the mass of the body directly above the hands. Many excellent vaulters retain a full extension of the left leg while flexing the right knee. Frequently the right foot of these vaulters is directly above the head at the instant of reaching the handstand position.

The push-up consists of a vigorous extension of both arms simultaneously, thus elevating the legs and trunk. There is no sharp line of distinction between the push-up and crossbar clearance since the force of the arms is being applied to the vaulting pole during the transit of the body over the crossbar.

The vault: fiber glass pole

With the advent of the fiber glass pole, the heights cleared by outstanding vaulters have increased significantly. These increases are made possible by the marked flexibility of the fiber glass pole which enables the vaulter to transform the kinetic energy developed in his approach and take-off into potential (or stored) energy in the bend of the pole. During the final stages of his vault, this potential energy is converted back into kinetic energy as the pole unbends, thereby raising the vaulter to an increased height. When an aluminum alloy or steel pole is used, no such storing of energy to be utilized during the final stages of the vault is possible.

Pole plant and hand shift. Because the

Fig. 11-4, A-L. A series of acceptable form for the pole vault (with a fiber glass pole).

horizontal velocity of the vaulter provides the principal contribution to the bending of the pole at take-off (and shortly thereafter),[1] the vaulter who utilizes a fiber glass pole strives for the maximum velocity at which he can effectively control the body movements required for an efficient take-off.

The technique for the pole plant with a fiber glass pole is basically the same as for the aluminum alloy or steel pole (p. 181) with one important exception. The vaulter who uses a fiber glass pole does not shift his left hand up the pole to a position near his right hand during the pole plant as is done with an aluminum alloy or steel pole. Instead, the left arm is kept fairly straight during the pole plant and the hands are kept 15 to 18 inches apart on the pole (Fig. 11-4, A). This wide hand spacing causes most of the force resulting from the vaulter's momentum to be thrown on the right (top) hand at take-off and, thereby, produces a maximum pole bend. The wide hand spacing also enables the vaulter to better control his body movements during the later stages of the vault than would be the case if his hands were close together.

Foot plant and spring. The techniques for the foot plant and spring with a fiber glass pole are fundamentally the same as for the aluminum alloy or steel pole (p. 183) except for the position of the take-off foot with reference to the hands. With the aluminum alloy or steel pole, the ball of the vaulter's take-off foot is planted on a spot that is directly below the point at which his right (top) hand grasps the pole (Fig. 11-3, *D*). With the fiber glass pole, the ball of the take-off foot is planted on a spot directly below a point on the pole that is about midway between the vaulter's hands (Fig. 11-3, *B*). This foot placement causes a major portion of the force generated by the vaulter's momentum to be exerted at take-off against his right (top) hand, thereby producing a maximum pole bend.

Swing-up. The swing-up is a movement initiated by swinging the right leg forward and upward and simultaneously extending the left (take-off) leg at the knee (Fig. 11-4, *B*). Immediately thereafter the left leg is swung upward until it is about in line with the right leg (Fig. 11-4, *C* and *D*) and, for a short period, both legs are extended. The right arm which, together with the left arm, was bent at about a right angle is now bent only slightly (Fig. 11-4, *C*), permitting an effective pendulum-like swing of the body and legs.

As the legs reach near alignment, the vaulter flexes them at the knees, and by bending at the hips and rotating his body upward around his shoulders, raises his feet to a point above his head (Fig. 11-4, *D* and *E*). He then extends both legs at the knee and, simultaneously, initiates the pull-up movement (Fig. 11-4, *F*).

Pull-up and body turn. As the pole rotates forward to a position nearly perpendicular with the ground, the vaulter brings his body and legs into alignment by extending his legs at the hips (Fig. 11-4, *G*). He then pulls vigorously by flexing both arms at the elbows, driving his body and legs upward. Simultaneous with this movement, he begins to rotate his body about its long axis in a direction toward the pole (Fig. 11-4, *H*) by pulling (with his left arm) his left shoulder toward the pole.

Push-up. In a motion that is continuous with the pull-up, the vaulter extends his arms at the elbow vigorously, pushing his body upward into a near-handstand position on the pole (Fig. 11-4, *I*). It is essential that there be no hesitation between the pull-up and the push-up movements. If the vaulter hesitates between these two movements, he will be unable to overcome the inertia of his body and, consequently, cannot continue the push-up portion of the movement.

To assist in rotating his body around its long axis, the vaulter swings his right leg upward (the reaction to which moves his right hip downward) and his left leg downward (the reaction to which moves his left hip upward). The two reactions combined serve to rotate the vaulter's body around its long axis to a position in which he is face down (Fig. 11-4, *J* and *K*)—a rotation of 180 degrees from his take-off position (Fig. 11-4, *C*).

Crossbar clearance. The clearance of the crossbar may be accomplished by the use of one of several methods. The vaulter, when at the crest of the vault, may raise the hips by dropping the feet (Fig. 11-3, *I*). In this case the feet are lowered to a point about equal to the height of the handhold, but meantime the hands continue the push-up action. In some instances, the vaulter clears the crossbar by executing the scissors, which completes his rotation about his long axis (Fig. 11-4, *K*), and immediately follows this movement by raising his arms and shoulders upward and away from the crossbar (Fig. 11-4, *L*).

Again it is pointed out that each vaulting

action must blend with the next, and frequently some of the techniques herein discussed individually are obliged to be executed simultaneously. For example, the throw-away is initiated while the body is clearing the crossbar.

Throw-away. The release of the pole may be accomplished by the use of either the double-hand release, which consists of releasing both hands simultaneously, or the single-hand method, in which the left hand releases its grasp of the pole while force is still being applied by the right hand. Finally the right hand is swung upward and backward, away from the crossbar. There are some successful vaulters who turn the body to the left as it drops to the landing area (Fig. 11-3, *K*). Other good vaulters land in a position facing the approach (Fig. 11-4, *K* and *L*). Provided that maximum force has been applied by both hands during the push-up, both styles of pole release can be effective. The vaulter selects the method of clearance that permits him to avoid displacement of the crossbar.

The vaulting pole is released by a flip of the hand (Fig. 11-3, *J* and *K*, and Fig. 11-4, *J* and *K*) so that it drops away from the landing area. The throw-away must be executed so that the falling pole does not strike either the crossbar or the vaulting standards.

Landing. As soon as the vaulter has completed the throw-away, his attention should be focused on the landing. Pieces of foam rubber piled above the ground and held in place by a covering net provide the safest landing area and relieve the vaulter of practically all concern about the manner in which he lands. If the vault has been properly executed, the vaulter, relaxed, will alight near the middle of the landing area. A landing area in which a cushion of either wood shavings, foam rubber, or sawdust 2 feet or more in depth is placed on top of the ground rather than in a pit is satisfactory. The shavings and sawdust are kept from scattering by means of burlap bags filled with sawdust which are stacked around the sides of the landing area. Another device for holding the shavings or sawdust is a landing box about 16 feet in width and 12 feet in length (conforming to the dimensions specified in the rule book), with side walls about 30 inches high. Those landing boxes that are constructed on skids are portable, and they may be used both indoors and outdoors. Many good vaulters touch the landing area with their feet and roll backward on the buttocks.

Position of standards or crossbar supports. Unlike the high jump, it is permissible in the pole vault to move the standards toward or away from the vaulter. The reason for this is that the fixed point in the pole vault is the pole planting trough, while in the high jump it is the crossbar. The vaulter moves the standards so that the crossbar is at the point where he attains his greatest height. As a rule, the lower the crossbar, the farther the standards are placed back of the pole planting trough. As the height of the crossbar is increased, the standards are moved toward the runway until, for the supreme effort, the crossbar is directly over the stopping board of the pole planting trough. In a few exceptional cases it may be in front of the stopping board.

The position of the standards is determined by placing the pole in a vertical position in the planting trough and estimating the desired distance between it and the crossbar. For example, a novice vaulting at 7 feet correctly may place the crossbar 9 inches away from the pole when it is in a vertical position. With the crossbar at 11 feet, the standards may be set correctly 6 inches from the vertical pole. At 13 feet 6 inches, the standards may be set wisely directly over the stop board. Although excellent vaulters utilize these distances, it must be undertsood that each vaulter through experience, aided by an observer, determines the optimum position for the various heights vaulted.

COMMON ERRORS IN THE POLE VAULT

Since the pole vault is a gymnastic feat involving a series of coordinated movements, errors in technique detract not only from the grace of the event but also from the height attained. In order that they may be avoided, some of the most common errors are pointed out.

In the handhold and pole carry. If the vaulter grasps the pole too high, he fails to generate sufficient momentum to bring the pole to an upright position. If he grasps the pole too low, he fails to gain optimum height even though he executes the event properly. The vaulter should, through experience, determine the maximum height at which he can grasp the pole and, from his approach run, generate sufficient momentum to carry the pole to an upright position. He should utilize the grasp at this height on the pole for all vaults, regardless of the height of the crossbar. Each change in the height of the handgrip on the pole requires a corresponding change in the checkmarks for the approach run; hence, such changes are not practical.

A vaulter may be inefficient in carrying the pole because he grasps it too tightly. Tenseness in the arms and shoulders is an error which prevents freedom of movement in the carry.

In the approach. Common errors in the approach are excess speed, insufficient speed, inaccurate checkmark adjustments, undue tension, and an erratic run. The correction of these errors is obvious from the discussion of the approach.

In the pole plant. The chief mistakes in planting the pole are lack of concentration of vision on the target, which is the center of the stopping board, failure to hit the apron of the trough properly, and inaccuracy in combining the run and the plant.

In the hand shift. If the vaulter uses a pole of moderate elasticity (aluminum alloy or steel), a failure to shift the left hand close to the right hand is the most noticeable error in this stage of the vault. As previously pointed out, this error prevents the most advantageous pull-up. If the vaulter uses a fiber glass pole, the above statement does not apply.

In the foot plant and spring. It has been previously stated that one of the imperfections to be guarded against in this part of the vault is an incorrect position of the foot. The possibilities are planting it too far to the right or to the left and too far back or in front of that spot previously determined as correct. It is obvious that a plant in which the heel and toe are not in a line with the pole and at right angles to the crossbar detracts from a straight forward lift.

In the swing-up. Extreme muscular tension of the arms tends to retard the swing-up, and a premature pull-up checks the forward-upward momentum. If the body swings too far away from the pole, the movement becomes sideward and upward rather than forward and upward. A lack of continuity of momentum detracts from the height of the vault.

If, during the swing-up, there is undue delay in flexing the thighs, the center of the body weight swings past the pole, a position that hampers an effective pull-up.

In the pull-up. Costly miscues befall the vaulter who delays his pull-up too long. The late pull-up does not permit the vaulter to assume a position from which to execute the body turn, since the pole has attained a vertical position too soon. On the other hand, a premature pull-up reduces the efficacy of the pole erection. A jerky pull-up contributes to imbalance and is to be avoided. An incomplete pull-up detracts from attaining height, which is the major objective in vaulting.

It is apparent that the maximum force of both arms is essential for a satisfactory pull-up and failure to bring the pole close to the right shoulder hinders the most effective use of the arms.

In the body turn and leg scissors. Some

vaulters fail to keep the feet high, even though they have sufficient speed and lift to do so. Still others fail because of an incomplete turn to get the body in position for the push-up and the throw-away. The chief method for correcting the latter defect consists of kicking the left leg vigorously forward and downward and the right leg backward and upward (Fig. 11-3, *F* and *G*, and Fig. 11-4, *J* and *K*).

In the push-up, crossbar clearance, and throw-away. In case the vaulter's arms have been partially straightened before the application of push-up force, proper leverage is not provided. If he reaches the push-up stage with the arms extremely flexed, he is in a position to exert ample force when straightening them, but the upward movement of the body is not effective. The time required to extend the arms from an extremely flexed position is sometimes so long that the forward-upward momentum of the body and legs has been spent, thus causing them to displace the crossbar. Frequently the effectiveness of the push-up is lost because it is incomplete or is executed with less than full effort.

Some vaulters have a tendency to hasten the push-up before the pole attains a vertical position. If the pole is in a position other than vertical, the direction of the force of the push-up is sideward rather than downward. Vaulters frequently permit the feet to drop too far below the level of the handhold before initiating the pole release. Thus they put themselves in a predicament that may be costly in two ways: (1) the force of the push-up is effective in lifting the shoulders only, rather than the whole body, and (2) this precarious position hinders the push-up and compels a hurried throw-away. An obvious fault is the failure to lift the hands sufficiently high to clear the crossbar. The deviations from accepted mechanical principles in the straight forward movement of the pole, the swing-up, the pull-up, and the body turn manifest themselves very definitely in a faulty push-up and throw-away.

The crossbar can best be avoided if the eyes are focused on it.

In the landing. If the previous steps in vaulting technique have been executed properly, there are only a few mistakes that can be made in the landing. No penalty can be assessed if the crossbar has been cleared. Self-protection through the art of relaxation ensures safety. A landing area constructed above ground, filled with foam rubber or wood shavings, rather than a pit reduces the distance of the vaulter's fall.

In conclusion, a properly executed vault consists of blending a number of movements, each depending on the movements that preceded it.

DAILY SCHEDULES OF PRACTICE

There is naturally some overlapping with the practice schedules for other events. It is deemed advisable to repeat those points which are common to other events rather than to refer to them. It should be noted also that for purposes of warming up and tapering off there is a variety of exercises that serve equally well. In view of this fact, no attempt is made to duplicate the schedules exactly where these points are under consideration. The same instructions regarding bath, massage, and body weight given in the schedules of practice for other events apply to the pole vaulter. A sizeable number of vaulters have included progressive resistance exercises and report favorable results. The vaulter is advised to undertake such exercises only after consulting competent authorities and preferably under adequate daily supervision.

The preliminary season schedule has already been discussed. The schedules presented here are devised for early season, midseason, and late season.

Early season. This schedule follows the preliminary season schedule on pp. 7 and 12.

Monday

1. Begin the day by jogging 50 yards and running 50 yards; repeat twice.

Perform 3 minutes of body-building exercises such as push-ups from the front-leaning rest position and deep knee bends.

2. Carry the pole and run through 6 or 7 times for checkmark adjustments.
3. Take 4 or 5 vaults at a low height chiefly for form, emphasizing the swing and pull-up.
4. Practice the push-up and pole throw-away without the crossbar.
5. Take two 40-yard sprints, stressing the leg drive; then rest 5 minutes.
6. Spend 15 to 30 minutes on weight-training and tension exercises under supervision. (For a description of these exercises, see pp. 8 and 11.)

Tuesday

1. Start the practice by jogging 100 yards and sprinting 50 yards. Spend 4 or 5 minutes kicking for height, bending and twisting the trunk, and climbing the rope.
2. Without the pole, lie on the left side in the landing area, with the right leg raised. Execute the scissors action 5 or 6 times by kicking the right leg backward and upward. Note the resulting body turn.
3. Set the blocks and work on sprint starting. Take 3 or 4 starts with the pistol, running 35 yards at $9/10$ effort.
4. Run through 4 or 5 times for checkmark adjustments.
5. Finish the practice with a run of 250 yards at $7/8$ effort.

Wednesday

1. Run and jog 150 to 200 yards.
2. Perform 3 minutes of calisthenics designed to strengthen the abdominal muscles. A sample exercise is alternate leg and trunk raising while lying on the back.
3. Spend 20 seconds doing inverted running.
4. Hold the pole in a vertical position with the hands close together, lie on

the back in the landing area, and simulate the body turn and scissors by kicking the right leg backward and upward in a vigorous manner. Repeat 8 or 9 times.

5. Take 3 or 4 trials for checkmark adjustments.
6. If checkmarks are correct, take 6 vaults, emphasizing the pole carry and the correct acceleration to suit the individual needs.
7. Engage in weight-training and tension exercises that have proved beneficial to pole vaulters.

Thursday

1. Initiate the workout by running 150 yards and by hopping and bounding 30 yards.
2. Perform 3 minutes of exercises, such as the underswing and push-away on the horizontal bar and the handstand and push-away on the low parallel bar.
3. Set the starting blocks and work with the sprinters. Take 2 or 3 starts with the pistol, sprintng 50 yards at full effort to develop speed and leg drive.
4. Execute 4 or 5 vaults, emphasizing form. Vault twice at a mark beyond your best previous height. Strive to maintain your form and mental composure by generating confidence in clearing this added height.
5. Carry the pole in the manner utilized in the approach and, on the running track, alternately sprint and walk distances of 35 yards. The total distance recommended is approximately 440 yards.

Friday

1. Take easy work today in preparation for a strenuous practice on Saturday.
2. Perform 5 to 10 minutes of gymnastic feats. Suggested exercises are forward rolls, walking on the hands, standing high jumps, and traveling on the rings.

3. Run 440 yards at ⅔ effort.

Saturday

1. Warm up with an easy 200-yard run.
2. Perform 3 minutes of varied rope skipping.
3. Verify checkmarks by running through the approach 2 or 3 times.
4. Vault 8 times at increasing heights. Take as your slogan, "One height, one vault." Emphasize the correct speed of the approach, the mechanical perfection of pole planting, and hand shifting.
5. Take 2 trials at a height 3 inches higher than your best performance.
6. Finish the workout by running 350 yards at ¾ effort.

Midseason. The following schedules of practice for the pole vaulter are submitted on the assumption that the athlete engages in important competition once each week during midseason. Frequently the pole vaulter possesses scoring ability in one or more additional track and field events and, in dual meets, competes in such events. For these athletes, the schedules of practice suggested herein may require alteration.

Monday

1. Jog 150 yards and perform 3 minutes of arm exercises which include handstands, walking on hands, and handstand-and-push-offs, the latter simulating the arm action when clearing the bar.
2. Carry the pole and take 2 runs for checkmark adjustments.
3. Execute 7 or 8 vaults for height. Take 2 trials with the bar set 2 inches beyond your best previous effort.
4. Spend 10 minutes on gymnastic feats, including rope climbing, and pulley-weight, stall bar, and high bar exercises.
5. In case you have found either or both weight-training exercises and tension

exercises beneficial, spend 10 to 20 minutes in executing them.

Tuesday

1. Warm up by jogging 100 yards, walking for 1 minute, and striding 150 yards at gradually increasing speed.
2. Perform 3 minutes of exercises designed to develop the arms and shoulder girdle, such as chinning, and throwing a heavy weight (20 to 25 pounds).
3. Join the sprinters and sprint 35 yards twice.
4. Run through 3 times (carrying the pole) for checkmark adjustments.
5. Vary the schedule by performing a few trials in other events, such as the running high jump, long jump, or the javelin throw. Consult the instructor before participating in other events.
6. Bear in mind that on Wednesday vaulting for height is a part of the training schedule. Thus, Tuesday's work should not detract from body tonus.
7. Finish the workout with an easy jog of optional distance.

Wednesday

1. Warm up as for competition. By now the vaulter should know his individual requirements as to type and duration of activity.
2. Inspect the vaulting pole (taping), the runway, the landing area, and the standards to be sure that all is in readiness.
3. Run through the approach twice for checkmark adjustments.
4. Take 2 easy vaults.
5. Begin trials as in competition, vaulting not to exceed 12 times. However, some vaulters are more successful in competition whenever they limit vaulting for height practice to 1 day per week rather than 2 days per week.

6. Take 2 additional trials with the bar at a height 3 inches higher than any previous attainment.
7. Engage in weight-training exercises of such intensity and duration as you have found to be effective.
8. Complete the workout with a run of 300 yards at ¾ effort.

Thursday

1. Start the day with 2 minutes of jogging, hopping, and bounding.
2. Spend 5 to 10 minutes exposed to the sun if the weather permits.
3. This is a tapering-off day, and any further work is at the option of the competitor.
4. It is suggested that the day's practice be finished with a jog of an optional distance and pace.

Friday

Some authorities prefer that there be no regular practice scheduled for Friday. For those who require that the team assemble, it is suggested that the competitors dress in competition suits and shoes.

1. Inspect the equipment, including the landing area and the runway. Make sure that your personal equipment is suitable for the competition conditions that you expect to find Saturday. Will the runway be slow or fast? Study prevailing winds.
2. Jog 200 yards. With the pole in the hands, sprint 40 yards 3 or 4 times.

Saturday

This is competition day. The warm-up procedure is chiefly in the hands of the contestant. By this time he should know by experience the most effective type of work to perform. Keep in mind that the warm-up includes not only physical fitness for competition but also the attainment of the proper mental poise. Assuming that the pole vault is the first event on the program, the following procedure is suggested:

1. Jog 200 yards, walk 25 yards, run 25 yards, and sprint 25 yards.
2. Perform optional calisthenics for a period of 4 or 5 minutes.
3. Run through 3 or 4 times for checkmark adjustments (carrying the pole).
4. Take 1 or 2 practice vaults with the crossbar at a moderate height. This should reassure the vaulter that the warm-up is adequate and that his form is correct. If the warm-up is insufficient, take a few additional trials.
5. Competition. Concentrate on each trial so that your slogan, "One height, one vault," becomes a reality.

Late season. Since the most important contests usually occur in late season, the pole vaulter who in midseason has scored points in additional events such as the sprints, the hurdles, and the jumps may be obliged to forego participation in some or all of his secondary events. Therefore, he may be required to confine his training activities exclusively to the pole vault.

Monday

1. Begin with a jog of 220 yards, walk 25 yards, run 25 yards, and sprint 25 yards.
2. Engage in 3 to 5 minutes of exercises on the gymnasium side horse, such as squat, straddle, and front vaults.
3. Join the sprinters and run 50 yards at top speed. Repeat once.
4. Familiarize yourself with checkmark adjustments on various types of footing, such as all-weather surface, fast cinders, slow cinders, or turf, both with and against the wind. Run (carrying the pole) through the approach 3 or 4 times.
5. In late season, since less physical effort is required to maintain condition and form, the intensity of practice is reduced.
6. Continue weight-training exercises to the extent that you find them helpful.

Tuesday

1. Alternately jog, walk, and run for a period of 2 or 3 minutes.
2. Perform 5 minutes of either free or gymnastic exercises designed to develop flexibility and agility.
3. Carry the pole and sprint 30 yards. Repeat several times. Run faster than when vaulting and try to correlate the relation of speed to the gather.
4. Run through 3 or 4 times for checkmark adjustments.
5. Set the bar at an intermediate height, keeping the handhold the same as for championship heights. Vault 4 to 6 times. Concentrate on the correlation of speed with the gather. Keep the feet high in the air. This day's objective is form. The objective for Wednesday is height.
6. Expose the body to the sun for a period of 8 to 10 minutes.
7. Finish the practice with a jog of 440 yards.

Wednesday

1. Warm up as in competition by jogging, sprinting, and performing light exercises.
2. Reassure yourself of checkmark adjustments and properly prove the spots by approaching 3 or 4 times.
3. Set the crossbar at the same height as that required for the first vault in the ensuing meet. Limit yourself to 8 vaults, gradually increasing the height of the bar until it is 3 inches above your best effort.
4. Throughout the vaulting, maintain the handhold that you will use in clearing your best height. A uniform hold minimizes changes in checkmark adjustments as the height is increased.
5. Terminate the day's work with 5 to 10 minutes of gymnastic feats vigorously performed. It is important to note that strenuous gymnastic exercises are not prescribed on the day immediately preceding vaulting for height. Furthermore, 2 days of moderate exercise are recommended for the period preceding competition. This procedure avoids fatigue hangover and allows for building body tonus.
6. Either continue or omit weight-training and tension exercises in the light of your past experiences.

Thursday

1. The type and quantity of practice on Thursday is at the option of the vaulter. If there is some phase of the event that needs attention, such as the body turn and the leg scissors, he may concentrate on it profitably.
2. The intensity of the practice is being gradually diminished as the week end approaches. Therefore, confirmation of checkmark adjustments and correlation of speed and pole planting complete the day's routine.

Friday

The competitor may either remain away from practice or dress in competition clothes and limber up lightly. If on a foreign field, he may inspect and check the runway for consistency and note the direction of prevailing winds. In short, he familiarizes himself with the general surroundings.

Saturday

Make the necessary physical and mental adjustments for competition. Refer to Saturday, midseason schedule, for detailed procedure.

REFERENCE

1. Hay, J. G.: Pole vaulting: a mechanical analysis of factors influencing pole-bend, Res. Quart., Am. A. Health, Phys. Ed. & Rec. **38**:40, 1967.

Chapter 12

The shot put

A record of putting contests is supplied by the historians who described an event called putting the stone which was subsequently popular as an athletic contest in Ireland and Scotland. The ancient stone weighed 14 pounds and was block shaped with round edges. Later the stone was adopted as a standard unit of weight.

In certain nations today, the contest is designated as putting the weight.

Competitors of early times were able to throw the 14-pound stone more than 60 feet. The rules governing the contest were less restricting than those of today, since the competitor could follow the throw as far as he liked as long as he released the stone before he crossed the toe line. The effective use of body speed gained during the running approach made possible puts that exceeded those made from a 7-foot circle.

Shot-putting was first placed on the championship program of the Amateur Athletic Union in 1876. The event was won by H. E. Buermeyer of the New York Athletic Club with a put of 32 feet 5 inches.

James R. Matson of the United States was officially credited with a distance of 71 feet 5½ inches in 1967.

The contest, as first practiced with the stone, has evolved into its present form through a modification of the missile and limitations placed on the run by a circle.

The increased distance acquired by putters of our day is evidently due to improved methods and an improved control of the body mechanics involved.

GENERAL CONSIDERATIONS

Comparative marks in competition. As a goal for the competitor who hopes to place at the various levels of competition using the 12-pound shot, Table 12-1 indicates the estimated distances required. Emphasis is given to the fact that the distances presented are not those of the winners of first place. In those areas where the quality of shot-putting is either very good or very poor, these figures will not apply. Similar to the suggestions made for the other track and field events, the shot-putter is advised to become familiar with the performances

Table 12-1. Comparative marks in scholastic competition in the shot put

Meet	No. of places scored	Distance
Dual high school	3	45–50 ft.
Qualifying—state	3	48–55 ft.
State—province	5	56–65 ft.

of the athletes against whom he will compete.

Equipment. The principal equipment peculiar to shot-putting is the shot itself. The rules prescribe that it shall be a metal sphere weighing 16 pounds for college, A.A.U., and Olympic competition, 12 pounds for high schools, and 8 pounds for grade schools.

At present one finds shots of cast iron and of brass shell with a lead center. Since the diameter of the missile depends on the density of the material out of which it is made, shots rank in size as previously named.

The factors involved in the selection of a shot are economy, size, and wearing qualities. The cast-iron shot is the cheapest but the largest in diameter, whereas the brass shell is the most expensive but the smallest in diameter.

The contestant is the judge of the implement most suitable for his grasp, and he usually chooses one on this basis.

Those athletes who are required to compete from circles made of concrete will, of necessity, be obliged to alter the type of shoe. (See rule book for the latest interpretations.)

Qualifications. The information concerning the physical qualification for discus throwers applies very well to shot-putters. Speed, strength, and coordination are essential. Although shot-putters are usually large in stature, good performers have been known who weigh only 160 pounds.

TECHNIQUE OF SHOT PUT

By official rules, in the shot put the missile is pushed rather than thrown. Impetus is added to the push of the shot by a body shift across the circle. From the beginning to the end of the put there are a number of distinctive body movements. Although these movements are discussed separately, it should be recognized that they blend with one another in the execution of a successful put. Furthermore, some techniques, which are described individually, may either overlap or occur simultaneously with other shot-putting techniques. The objective of the shot-putter is continuity of speedy coordinated movements, and these are discussed in the order in which they are executed: preparatory activities, handhold, initial movements in the circle, shift, delivery, release, and recovery.

Preparatory activities. An adequate period of warming-up exercises well in advance of the hour of competition is essential. These exercises are discussed under schedules of practice at the end of this chapter. The proper emotional and mental patterns must be established before entering the circle, but the method of attaining them varies with each individual. Some putters appear to be sullen, avoid conversation, and concentrate deeply on their plan of action. They resent disturbances and sometimes exhibit petulance upon hearing the clicks of nearby cameras or the calling of their names over the public address system when they are about to compete. Frequently the athlete requests that the officials and other competitors step away from the area surrounding the rear of the circle.

Good shot-putters generate a feeling of confidence just before putting, but it is believed that confidence must be built up not

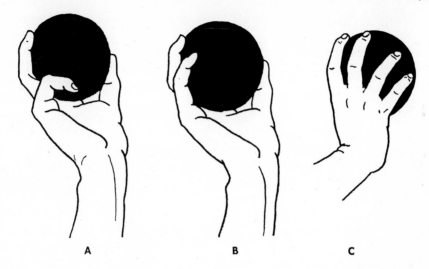

A   B   C

Fig. 12-1. Styles of handholds for the shot.

only at the time of competition but also in daily practice.

Equipment adjustments which are considered by the shot-putter may include the use of a towel on the hands, body, or shot; the use of powdered rosin, benzoin, or other legal nonslip aids; the tension of the trunk waistband; the tightening of the shoe laces; and the application of adhesive tape (while adhering to the rules) to the wrist or fingers.

Getting the feel of the shot is one of the activities performed by the athlete shortly before assuming his putting stance. Relaxation is an important aim of the shot-putter.

Handhold. There are several types of handholds based on the spread of the fingers, three of which are shown in Fig. 12-1. The shot-putter is assumed to be right dominant.

Fig. 12-1, *A*, represents the type in which the first, second, and third fingers are back of the shot. The little finger is bent and aids the thumb in maintaining lateral support. The handhold shown in Fig. 12-1, *B*, is more frequently used. The first, second, and third fingers, slightly spread, are likewise back of the shot, and again the thumb prevents sideward move-

ment of the missile. The hold shown in *B* differs from that shown in *A* in that the little finger not only aids in maintaining balance but also contributes force to forward and upward propulsion. The novice must remember that these are holds employed by experienced putters, and he will note that the shot is carried well up toward the finger tips. Beginners are advised to carry the shot lower down in the palm until the musculature of the hand is sufficiently developed to carry it higher. Finger development, it will be noted, is a highly important practice objective.

The type of handhold shown in Fig. 12-1, *C*, is that employed by men with smaller hands and shorter fingers. Here it is necessary to maintain a wider finger spread. The little finger is placed farther back of the shot so that it may be used for adding impetus to the put. The thumb is used to maintain lateral balance. With this type of hold the shot is ordinarily carried farther down in the palm of the hand.

Initial movements in the circle. The majority of shot-putters assume a relaxed standing position when stepping into the rear of the circle. The placement of the feet varies with the styles of putting selected. The body weight rests chiefly on the right foot. The distance between the feet range from 8 to 16 inches.

The shot may be held in the cradle formed by the neck and shoulders, on the neck close to the cheek, or directly above the shoulder at a distance ranging up to 8 inches from the right ear. Those athletes who adopt the away-from-the-ear plan claim that this method permits them to apply pushing force to the shot for a longer period of time during the delivery. Those who prefer to hold the shot against the neck contend that this technique aids them in obtaining adequate relaxation, a stable position during the shift, and intentional imbalance (balance is regained at the conclusion of the shift). They believe that intentional imbalance permits the gaining of the body momentum in the shift.

The degree of bend in the right leg at the initial stance is dependent upon the choice of the individual (for example, Fig. 12-2, *A* to *C*). The eyes are focused on a point 8 to 12 feet to the rear of the circle (Fig. 12-2, *A* to *E*). The trunk and shoulder are held at right angles to the direction of the put. The left arm may be either extended upward or bent at approximately a right angle.

In advance of the execution of the shift, the putter (Fig. 12-2, *B* to *D*) bends the trunk, extends the left arm forward to maintain balance, flexes the right knee slightly, and swings the left leg toward the stop board. The swing of the left leg calls for precision because, if the swing is too high, the trunk (including the shot) will be tilted too far downward. Next, the left leg is swung downward until the toe nearly touches the ground, and the left knee is flexed to approximately 90 degrees. Simultaneously the right knee is bent to about 70 degrees and the trunk is lowered until the back is nearly parallel with the ground (Fig. 12-2, *D*).

Shift. The objective of the shift is to gain momentum and to move the body into the most effective position for imparting force to the shot. This action is also known as the glide, sometimes inaccurately termed "the hop," which connotes an undesirable jump. There should be no hesitation between the shift and the delivery. Coaches differ in their opinions on the amount of speed the athlete should strive for in the initial movements in the shift. However, nearly all coaches recognize the merit in speed of body actions at the instant of delivery, provided the athlete is in a position to apply maximum force to the shot. Coordination should not be sacrificed for speed.

The athlete attempts to gain momentum through a state of imbalance, permitting the body to fall in the direction of the put. At the optimum point in the body fall, a vigorous push is applied by the right foot, and the right leg is extended fully from the toe to the hip. Simultaneously the left leg is kicked, straightened, or swung in a technique that may be termed "reaching for the stop board." This leg action is claimed by some coaches to be a factor contributing to body momentum. Immediately afterward, the right knee is flexed and the right foot is brought forward speedily and close to the ground. The right foot moves a distance ranging from 30 to 40 inches (measured from the toe to the inner edge of the circle), depending upon the build of the athlete. Measurements taken from the pattern of the athlete depicted in Fig. 12-2, *D* to *F*, indicate a clearance of 34 inches. The right foot, at the instant of concluding the shift, is pointed toward the rear of the circle at a spot directly below the shot.

When executing the shift, the center of gravity reaches a point above and beyond the center of the circle. This action is a phase of intentional imbalance and is designed to help move the weight of the body forward toward the stop board, a desirable position for the ensuing drive from the right leg and foot.

The head and eyes, with respect to the

Fig. 12-2, A-1. A series of acceptable form for executing the shot put.

body, have not changed position throughout the shift.

During the shift, the left arm, bent at the elbow, is swung to the left at shoulder height for the purpose of aiding body balance.

As the shift is concluded, the left foot is planted slightly to the left of the center of the stop board and usually flush against it. This placement affords a vaulting action by the left leg, subsequently employed in the delivery to aid in applying upward-forward momentum to the torso and the shot. Inexperienced shot-putters often plant the left foot 3 to 6 inches from the stop board in order to permit adequate distance for maneuvering the feet during the delivery, release, and recovery. Because this practice results in a loss of distance, it is not recommended.

The interval of time elapsing between the planting of the right foot and the left foot varies with the degree of speed generated in the shift. The athlete utilizing a high rate of speed in the shift usually plants the left foot a fraction of a second after planting the right foot. The athlete utilizing a slower rate of speed in the shift requires a longer period of time between the planting of the feet.

Shortly after the planting of both the right foot and the left foot, the shot-putter regains body balance which he relinquished intentionally at the beginning of the shift across the circle.

The degree of bend of the right knee at the conclusion of the shift depends upon the physical qualifications of the individual. Good shot-putters attempt to obtain as much bend in the right knee as their putting technique permits. Frequently the tall shot-putter employs the deep knee bend to less advantage than his shorter competitor.

Attention is called to Fig. 12-2, F. The athlete, in reality, has employed an acceptable spread between the left foot and the right foot; but because of the perspec-

tive, some individuals may conclude wrongfully that the feet are too close together.

The path of the shot during the shift varies with individuals. In Fig. 12-2, A to F, the shot (and the body) is lowered during the shift and then gradually elevated through the point of release. There should be no delay between the shift and the delivery.

Delivery. Simultaneously with the conclusion of the shift, the right knee is bent so that it is in a desirable position to contribute a vigorous upward-forward thrust when later it is straightened speedily (Fig. 12-2, F and G).

The hips are rotated swiftly to the left. The correct timing of the hip thrust is a very important phase; if the hip rotation is delayed, a reducion in leg force may result. At the other extreme, if the hips are rotated too soon, there may be a loss of force in the upward thrust.

At the completion of the shift, the right shoulder is lower than the left shoulder. The right elbow is in such a position that a straight line can be drawn from the elbow, up the forearm, and through the right shoulder to the left shoulder.

The shoulders are swiftly rotated toward the left, and emphasis is placed on a speedy, forceful lift of the right shoulder.

During the delivery, as the push from the right foot continues, it is pivoted so that it points approximately in the direction of the put. The right foot retains contact with the ground, thus providing support when pushing the shot upward and forward. Some shot-putters retain right foot contact with the ground until the shot has left the hand. However, photographs of putters of championship quality show that the right foot has been lifted from the ground while the shot is still in the athlete's grasp (Fig. 12-2, G). Provided that optimum use has been made of both the leg drive and the arm thrust, this foot-lifting action should not reduce the effectiveness of the put.

The left leg, which during the shift was

swung so that the left foot was flush against the stop board (or close to it), contributes a vaulting action that checks the momentum of the lower extremities and increases the momentum of the torso (including the shot). This pivoting action over the left leg, accompanied by the elevation and acceleration of the torso and right arm, is an objective of many proficient javelin throwers as well as shot-putters.

The position of the shot after the execution of the shift is either on the neck or close to the chin. In the delivery, while explosive force is applied in the arm push, leg straightening, and trunk rotation, the shot is propelled upward and forward in line with the right shoulder.

The head and eyes at the conclusion of the shift are inclined so that the focus is on the ground at a point 8 to 15 feet away. However, during the delivery the head is tilted backward so that vision is in the direction of the flight of the shot.

The left arm at the onset of delivery is moved from a flexed to an extended position while the trunk is rotated, thus contributing aid in maintaining balance. At the time when the shoulders are rotated to the front during the final effort, the left arm again is bent at approximately a right angle.

The path of the shot from the completion of the shift to the termination of the delivery is both forward and upward. Obviously, any body action that deflects the missile from a direction both upward and forward may reduce the distance of the put.

The top-ranking shot-putters seem to concentrate on speedy as well as forceful movements. During the delivery, the weight of the body, which previously rested chiefly on the right leg, is transferred to the left leg at approximately the instant of release.

Release. The shot is aligned with the right foot, hip, and shoulder during the release. Good form requires that the major force contact be maintained behind the center of the shot and in the line of flight. Impetus is added by means of a combina-tion of the wrist snap and finger flip. The final flip imparts a slight backward rotation to the shot.

While the release is executed, the head is tilted backward and the eyes are focused in the direction of the flight of the shot.

The angle of release of the shot, with respect to the ground, employed by numerous champions ranges from 37 to 42 degrees. Some authorities believe that 45 degrees is the optimum angle of release, provided that adequate velocity is attained.

Measurements taken on the performances of top-ranking shot-putters showed that the majority of their place-winning puts landed 3 to 8 inches to the right of a line bisecting the circle through the center of the stop board.

After completing the release, the shot-putter concerns himself with gaining body balance in the recovery phase of the put.

Recovery. Since the rules of the event permit the putter to touch the side of the stop board, he reverses the position of the feet so that the right foot is swung rapidly against the stop board. This is one of the techniques possible to help maintain balance. The left leg is swung backward to the right and upward to the level of the hips, thus helping the athlete stay within the circle. When he bends the right knee, he lowers the center of body weight—a further aid in solving the problem of balance (Fig. 12-2, *H* and *I*).

Either one or both arms may be extended to help the athlete remain within the circle and thus prevent fouling.

After a signal from the shot put official that the put has been marked, the competitor must retire from the circle by way of the rear half in order to avoid even the appearance of a foul.

COMMON ERRORS IN SHOT PUT

In the description of the shot put technique an attempt was made to show correct execution, and by inference some of the imperfections were pointed out. At the risk of repetition and for the purpose of emphasis, faults in execution are discussed.

In the preparatory activities. The shot-putter may lessen the distance of his puts if he neglects the following:

1. To determine the time (as accurately as the officials can advise him) he will be expected to begin competitive putting.
2. An adequate amount of practice putting or warm-up exercises in advance of official trials in the shot put.
3. The choice of shoes, which includes the type of spikes suitable to the condition of the ground on which the circle is marked. Obviously, a circle of concrete requires different shoes.
4. To establish the optimum emotional pattern, which means the avoidance of extremes of both frenzy and lethargy.

In the handhold. If the shot is grasped too low in the hand, the value of the finger propulsion is lost. If the hold is too far toward the finger tips, insufficient purchase on the shot may result in its slipping backward off the fingers. This miscue frequently causes pain and necessitates a brief period of rest before resuming hard putting exercises.

The faults of imbalance caused by inaccurate placement of the thumb and the little finger are obvious, in that the missile may fall ineffectively too far to the right or to the left. Deviation from a previously determined ideal finger spread decreases the possibility of exerting maximum force.

By carrying the shot in the left hand until ready for the initial stance the competitor averts possible fatigue of the putting hand. This may seem trivial to some athletes, but let them recall that in professional baseball, where fatigue costs in dollars and cents, the catcher, when making a return throw to the pitcher, relieves him of unnecessary effort by directing the ball to his gloved hand held shoulder high at the side.

In the initial stance. Shot-putters frequently make mistakes in the initial stance by attaining a position of extreme body tension instead of moderate relaxation. The placement of the feet both as to their direction and spread can contribute to low-grade performance if this placement differs to any great extent from the predetermined style. Imperfections in the knee bend may be corrected by the time the shift has been completed. Therefore, knee flexion variance at the initial stance may or may not be faulty.

In the shift. A shot-putter may have failed to gain creditable distance because his execution of the shift was harmed by any of the following:

1. Insufficient knee bend at the start of the shift.
2. Inclining the trunk too far forward or sideward.
3. Overdistance or underdistance.
4. Twisting the trunk to the left.
5. Failing to straighten the right leg effectively.
6. Aligning the feet improperly. The right foot should point toward the rear of the circle.
7. Failing to distribute the body weight correctly (mainly on the right foot).
8. Permitting the shot to get ahead of the body.

The method of correcting these faults, together with those mentioned later in the discussion, should be evident to the novice after he has studied the description of the shot-putting technique, the drawings illustrating form, and the schedules of practice.

In the delivery. Failure to attain maximum distance because of the technical defects during the period of delivery may be attributed to any of the following:

1. A lack of elbow height.
2. A failure to thrust the right hip upward and then forward.
3. The incorrect timing of the trunk twist with the arm push.
4. The improper coordination of the leg

drive with the trunk twist and arm push.

5. An insufficient or too deliberate straightening of the right leg.
6. The starting of an arm push which brings the shot to an improper angle (37 to 42 degrees is acceptable) when the release is executed.
7. A deficiency in the complete rock-up on the toes.
8. A carriage of the head and eyes in a position at variance with the direction of the body.
9. Failure to keep the hand directly in line with the elbow.

In the release. Lack of distance may be traced to the release if the tasks just preceding it have been completed satisfactorily. The arm movement determining the angle of release begins in the delivery but ends in the release. Obviously the lowering of the forearm decreases this angle and the raising of the forearm increases it.

Failure to complete a timely and vigorous wrist snap and finger flip will detract from performances otherwise technically sound. Distance is lost if there is an incomplete coordination of the sources of force just as the shot leaves the hand.

In the recovery. By the time the shot has broken contact with the fingers nothing more can be done to help or harm its flight. The sole concern of the athlete is the prevention of fouling. The rules prohibit him from touching both the circle and the top of the stop board with either his body or his clothing. Stepping over the circle or the stop board is likewise a foul. During the release, he has been losing balance by completing the follow-through. If he expects to have his put ruled fair, he must regain balance. The following are the main factors contributing to foul puts:

1. Failure to bring the right foot to the stop board immediately after the hand has ceased contact with the shot.
2. A lack of a speedy subsequent backward swing of the left leg.
3. An inadequate bend of the right knee, thus preventing a lowering of the center of body weight.
4. A careless attitude after the release, indicating a lack of determination to save the put. Careless practice habits while executing the recovery frequently are responsible for competition penalties.

SCHEDULES OF PRACTICE

Schedules of practice for the shot-putter during the preliminary season have been described previously. Suggested schedules are presented covering 1 week each in early season, midseason, and late season. Obviously, these schedules may have to be altered to suit the individual needs, to combine with events other than the shot, and to meet weather conditions.

There is little danger of arm or back injury from shot-putting. Therefore, the number of trials with full force is not limited as it is with the javelin. However, the shot-putter may not continue vigorous putting interminably. The novice's fingers and wrist are first affected, and he is strongly urged to prepare them by exercises begun weeks in advance of the competition season. Conscientious putters continue these exercises throughout the year. They are described in succeeding practice schedules.

A plot of the rate of improvement of shot-putters does not indicate a smooth, regular, upward curve, such as one finds when plotting a similar curve for runners. The line frequently flattens out for a period of 5 to 10 days, maintaining the same level, dropping slightly for 2 or 3 days, and then rapidly mounting to a plateau still higher than during the initial period. A staircase effect may be in evidence in a shot-putter's performance curve.

By knowing in advance that progress in the event may appear stationary for a number of consecutive days, a shot-putter will avoid being discouraged with his rate of improvement.

Early season. This schedule follows the preliminary season schedules, pp. 7 and 12.

Monday

1. Begin the practice by jogging 100 yards, walking 25 yards, and jogging 200 yards.
2. Master the technique of holding the shot. This will depend upon the size and the strength of your hand. Again, the handhold may vary with the type of shot used—iron or brass shell. Although implements weigh the same, they have varying degrees of specific gravity and thus vary in size. Three styles of holding the shot are depicted in Fig. 12-1.
3. Hold the shot in the palm of the hand in the early stages of practice, putting little or no stress on the fingers. As the fingers become stronger, the shot should be carried well up on them since added propulsion is gained by a finger flip. From the standing position, put the shot 20 to 30 times, concentrating on obtaining united forces from the leg, shoulder, arm, and wrist.
4. Hold the shot high in the air with the arm fully extended. Firmly grasp the forearm with the opposite hand. Snap the wrist while holding the forearm rigid, and note the potential aid obtainable from correct wrist action. Repeat 5 or 6 times. Measure the distance of each trial.
5. Join the high jumpers and take 6 or 7 trials at gradually increasing heights.
6. Spend 10 to 20 minutes on progressive resistance exercises (for a description, see p. 8).

Tuesday

1. Prepare for the day's workout with a jog of 100 yards, a walk of 50 yards, and a run of 50 yards at ¾ effort.
2. Skip rope for 2 or 3 minutes. Work on the shift across the circle without the shot, concentrating on foot and body position.
3. Perform 5 to 10 minutes of feats designed to develop muscles used in the shot put, such as the wood-chopping exercise, handstands, and throwing the 25-pound weight.
4. Join the sprinters, warm up thoroughly, and take 2 starts with the pistol and run 20 yards each time.
5. From the standing position, with the weight resting on the right foot and with the left foot close to the ground, put the shot 10 to 15 times, giving particular thought to the height of the elbow. Note the path of the shot.
6. Set the stop board at the edge of the circle and assume a standing position with the left foot against it and the right foot in the center of the circle. Using a moderate knee bend, put the shot 8 to 10 times.
7. Put the shot 10 to 12 times at moderate effort. The right foot must be brought forward to help maintain balance, thus preventing fouling. Call upon one or more observers, make use of the camera or, if facilities permit, have your movements recorded on motion picture film so that you may know how you are delivering. The term "reverse" is commonly applied to that action wherein, after the shot is released, the right foot is brought sharply to the toe board and the left foot is immediately shifted away from it. An improper concept of this phase of shot-putting is responsible for loss of distance among many schoolboy competitors. The shot-putter will be materially aided if he considers the reverse as an appendage to the put proper and as a device for maintaining balance.
8. Conclude the practice by jogging 100 yards, hopping and bounding 25 yards, and running 100 yards.

Wednesday

1. Start practice with a jog of 150 yards, a walk of 50 yards, and a sprint of 25 yards.
2. Grasp the shot so that its weight rests partially on the fingers. Temporarily curb your ambition to carry the shot far up toward the tips. In your earlier trials the palm provided the support awaiting the time when the fingers attained sufficient strength. Put the shot 15 to 20 times from the standing position and gradually increase the distance of the puts. Apply effectively your knowledge of the laws of body mechanics. Experiment with various angles of elevation of the shot when released and note the results. Physicists report that the optimum angle of trajectory of 45 degrees for artillery may not hold true in shot-putting unless exceptional velocity is attained. As pointed out previously, the customary angle for releasing the shot lies between 37 and 42 degrees, depending upon its velocity.
3. Assume the initial position at the back of the circle and put the shot 15 to 20 times with moderate effort, employing the shift. If the circle is of soft material, brush the surface of the circle and experiment on shifting varying distances. Note the footprints made after each trial.
4. Join the long jumpers and take 2 trials from the stand and 2 trials with a run.
5. Perform 15 to 20 minutes of progressive resistance exercises (for a detailed description, see p. 8).

Thursday

1. Begin the day's practice by jogging 200 yards, walking 25 yards, hopping and bounding 15 yards, and sprinting 25 yards.
2. Spend 2 minutes on stretching exercises, such as high kicking and trunk bending.
3. Prepare the fingers, wrist, arms, and trunk for moderate shot-putting trials.
4. Place the shot farther up toward the finger tips. Put it from 8 to 10 times, using the shift. The average putter stands with the right foot close to the rear of the 7-foot circle with the body weight resting chiefly on the right foot.
   a. After the shift is completed, in what position is the shot with respect to the right foot? Is the shot back of the right foot, directly over it, or ahead of it?
   b. Carry the right elbow at varying degrees and feel out the position that seems the smoothest and results in the longest puts. The moderately high elbow carriage is adopted by the majority of leading putters.
5. Review the activities of the day's practice and fix in your own mind a pattern of the most effective series of movements.
6. Join the long jumpers and take 2 trials of the standing long jump and 2 trials of the long jump.
7. Terminate the day's practice with 2 minutes of calisthenics, a jog of 200 yards, and a sprint of 20 yards.

Friday

1. Begin the day with a jog of 220 yards, rest 2 minutes, and run 50 yards at ¾ effort.
2. Skip rope for 2 minutes. Work on the shift across the circle without the shot.
3. Put the shot 5 or 6 times without the shift, concentrating your attention on getting force from the legs and trunk. As previously mentioned, the forward thrust of the right hip is an aid. Duplicate the height of elbow position that gave best results in your previous

workouts. Use the measuring tape when comparing one trial with another. Gradually increase the force applied to these puts, so that you will be ready for the next step—putting the shot with the shift.

4. Assume the customary stance at the back of the circle. Employ the shift and put the shot 8 to 10 times, applying gradually increasing effort. Concentrate on coordinating the shift with the onset of the delivery. Make certain your body is not extremely tense until the start of the final effort.

5. Use the shift and put the shot with full effort from 10 to 12 times. Use the measuring tape in these trials, thus eliminating guesswork when you are comparing various types of putting technique.

6. Engage in either tension exercises or weight-training exercises for a period of 15 to 30 minutes. Conclude the day's practice with 2 or 3 minutes of exercises designed to strengthen the fingers and wrist.

Saturday

1. Warm up with a jog of 250 yards, a walk of 25 yards, and a sprint of 20 yards. Prepare a record of your daily workouts so that you may intelligently set up a warm-up procedure that is best suited to your needs. This record may include a notation on weather conditions (such as the daily temperature), the amount of jogging, walking, running, sprinting, rope skipping, calisthenics, putting from a standing position, and putting with the shift.

2. Put the shot 15 to 20 times without using the shift. Concentrate on form and timing in the first few puts and then gradually add vigor to the succeeding puts. Station one or more observers who will report to you on specific actions in your putting.

3. Put 8 to 10 times with the shift, again gradually applying more force whenever the body becomes prepared for more vigorous effort.

4. Simulate conditions of competition by putting the shot with full effort while employing the entire repertoire of shot-putting technique. Limit your puts to four in the preliminary round and three in the final round. Draw your own conclusions as to the efficacy of your warm-up.

5. Complete Saturday's workout with a jog of 440 yards and a sprint of 25 yards.

It is imperative that the shot-putter make a creditable put during the preliminary trial in order to qualify for the semifinals and finals. If the distances of his successive puts are constantly increasing so that his best effort occurs on the fifth or sixth trial, he quite likely has had an insufficient amount of warm-up. If the distances of his puts in competition are less than in the warm-up and, furthermore, are gradually decreasing with each successive put, it is probable that the warm-up was excessive in either vigor or duration.

The object of the warm-up is to bring the athlete's physiologic mechanism to the peak at the time he enters competition. Booher[1] found that the majority of the best puts occur on the second trial. Next in order the best effort is obtained on the first put, and third in order comes the third trial. Even in meets where preliminaries are held on Friday and finals on Saturday, many of the winning performances occur in the preliminaries.

Therefore, the warm-up should be so timed and be of such intensity as to permit the shot-putter to achieve his best effort on the second, first, or third trial in the preliminaries.

The novice will note that 6 days of putting the shot during early season are prescribed on the presumption that no contest has been scheduled for Saturday.

Should a meet be scheduled for Saturday in early season, it is obvious that the vigor of Thursday's workout will be lessened, and on Friday little or no putting will be practiced.

During the early season, the beginner should be able to describe accurately the correct technique of putting the shot and to execute it with a fair degree of proficiency. If he goes through the routine without definite daily objectives, the benefits are largely nullified and his activity becomes aimless.

Midseason. During midseason the athlete is presumed to engage in competition each Saturday. The amount of actual putting the shot for distance is considerably reduced during this period of the season's schedule. There are two plans in general use for distributing the days of full effort. One plan calls for vigorous workouts on Monday and Tuesday, moderate practice Wednesday, light practice Thursday, and no putting Friday. The other plan prescribes vigorous workouts Monday and Wednesday, moderate practice Tuesday, light practice Thursday, and no putting Friday.

Those coaches who favor strenuous practice on 2 successive days, Monday and Tuesday, contend that such procedure prepares the athlete for competition in which preliminary trials are held one day and final trials the next. Since the shot put is not a fatiguing event, they believe 2 successive days in the early part of the week allows more time later in the week for emotional adjustments.

Those authorities who recommend strenuous practice Monday and Wednesday believe that better results are obtained by allowing 1 day of moderate workout (Tuesday) to intervene between the 2 days calling for extended effort. It is their belief that a vigorous workout on Wednesday still leaves a sufficient period of semirest before Saturday's competition.

By experimentation, together with the advice of his coach, the novice will determine the type of practice schedule he should adopt.

The schedule of practice which follows is based upon the plan calling for vigorous putting on Monday and Tuesday.

Monday

1. Prepare for distance putting by warming up with a jog of 250 yards, a walk of 15 yards, and a sprint of 25 yards. Repeat twice.
2. Skip rope vigorously for 2 or 3 minutes.
3. Sprint 15 yards at top speed. Rest for 2 minutes and repeat the sprint.
4. Become accustomed to handling a shot in rainy weather and to executing the shift and delivery from a circle that is muddy or slippery. Familiarize yourself with those competition aids whose use is legal. Do not overlook such seemingly minor items as longer shoe spikes, a dry towel, or rosin for the hands. Put the shot without using the shift 15 to 20 times and add force to each successive trial. Some athletes warm up by using a missile weighing 1 or 2 pounds more than the regulation sphere, so that when competition is called the shot seems light. Practice with the heavier weight has advantages, but occasionally its use alters the timing of both the shift and the delivery when the athlete resumes putting the official shot.
5. Take 5 to 7 puts at full effort, using the complete technique of shot-putting. Set several markers at 1-foot intervals to guide you in the distance and in the direction of your efforts. Increase or decrease the number of warm-up puts in the light of your previous experience. Your objective is the attainment of peak physical and mental condition for your best effort. Call on your teammates to observe

various phases of your putting and to report them accurately.

6. Put for distance 4 times. Allow an interval of time between each trial which corresponds to that encountered in your next competition. Measure each put and associate its success or failure with the body movements of that particular trial.

7. Rest 5 minutes. Put the shot with full effort 3 times, carefully analyzing each trial for the presence or absence of success. Take note of those movements that require drill at a later time, when you are not attempting to put for distance. Plot a curve showing the distance of each put in both the warm-up and the competition.

8. Perform 3 to 5 minutes of calisthenics. Spend 10 to 20 minutes on progressive resistance exercises.

Tuesday

1. Begin with a jog of 150 yards, a run of 50 yards at ¾ effort, and a sprint of 15 yards.

2. Perform 1 minute of wrist and finger exercises, such as the push-up on the hands, executed in a speedy manner.

3. Execute 3 to 4 minutes of body-building exercises, which should include leg swinging, arm swinging, tumbling, and running in place.

4. Join the sprinters, warm up thoroughly, take 4 or 5 starts with the pistol, and run 20 yards each time.

5. Add any item of warm-up technique which your past experience has proved beneficial.

6. Put the shot 6 to 8 times without the shift but emphasize snap and speed in the delivery.

7. Put the shot 4 to 6 times with the shift, concentrating on smooth coordination but adding force to each successive throw whenever good form is attained.

8. Prepare yourself as in actual competi-

tion. Brush the circle after each trial so that a record of your footwork is visible. Draw a line from the back edge of the circle through the center of the toe board and extend it 65 feet beyond. Note whether your best puts fall directly on this line, to the left, or to the right. Put the shot 7 times only. Plot a curve of Tuesday's performances and compare it with Monday's curve.

9. Conclude Tuesday's practice with a few trials of the long jump and the high jump, followed by a jog of 440 yards.

Wednesday

1. Start the day's practice by jogging 220 yards, walking 50 yards, hopping and bounding 15 yards, and running 50 yards.

2. Spend 5 to 10 minutes on an additional field event, such as throwing the discus, which combines well with the shot put.

3. Join the running high jumpers and jump 7 or 8 times at increasing heights.

4. Expose the body to the sun for 5 to 8 minutes.

5. Perform 5 minutes of general calisthenics.

6. Put the shot 5 or 6 times without the shift. Correct any faults noted in the vigorous putting of the 2 previous days. Set out a series of markers at 1-foot intervals so that you can gauge the distance of your puts. Call on your teammates for help in analyzing your form. Apply only moderate effort in these puts from the standing position, using the reverse after delivery.

7. Put the shot 5 to 6 times with moderate effort, using the complete form, including the shift, the delivery, and the reverse. Pay attention to coordination. Do not try for maximum distance but use the measuring tape so

that you may compare the distance attained with the force applied.

8. Spend 2 or 3 minutes on exercises designed to perfect the snap of the wrist simultaneously with the flip of the fingers. Hold the shot as far toward the finger tips as your stage of development permits. Wednesday's workout in midseason should be of moderate intensity but should be fruitful in providing form correction or improvement.

9. Engage in weight-training and/or tension exercises provided you have found them effective.

Thursday

1. Start with a jog of 200 yards, a walk of 25 yards, and a sprint of 25 yards.

2. Participate for 10 minutes in games or feats that are not strenuous in nature and that are free from the possibility of detracting from your shot-putting ability.

3. Take a sun bath for 5 to 8 minutes.

4. Execute 3 or 4 minutes of body-building exercises.

5. Put the shot 5 or 6 times without employing the shift. Select 1 or more items of form and point for perfection.

6. Take 10 to 15 puts, using full technique with only moderate effort. Note especially the body tension during the successive stages of the event.

7. Terminate the practice with calisthenics and a jog of 440 yards.

Friday

1. Check the equipment for which the competitor is responsible. If using your own shot, be sure that it meets specifications, especially that of minimum weight—8, 12, or 16 pounds.

2. Ascertain the type of circle from which you will put the shot Saturday so that suitable shoe spikes may be provided.

3. Omit handling the shot. Substitute

jogging, tumbling, and sprinting short distances.

4. End Friday's workout with 3 or 4 minutes of calisthenics and a jog of 300 yards.

Saturday

1. Make use of the experience gained from previous competition and putting trials. This means you should know the correct mental adjustments, the timely application of muscular tension and relaxation, and when you have reached the warm-up peak.

2. Prepare for competition by means of the proved formula for your warm-up, consisting of jogging, walking, calisthenics, and skipping rope.

3. Put the shot 4 or 5 times from the standing position. Reassure yourself of the correct placement of the feet and the proper carriage of the shot in the hand and fingers.

4. Employ the full technique and put the missile 6 to 10 times with gradually increasing effort.

5. Pause for a short period to get set both mentally and physically for a supreme performance.

6. Competition. Remember the satisfaction of being among the leaders during the first and second rounds.

7. Take 3 or 4 puts with full effort after the competition is over. Note whether they are better or worse than those made under tension and draw your own conclusions.

Late season. During the late season proceed as follows:

Monday

1. Prepare for the day's practice by completing a warm-up already proved suitable. What differences do you find in your warm-ups for practice days as compared to those for competition days?

2. Jump rope for 2 or 3 minutes.

3. Take 2 sprints of 15 yards each.
4. Take 3 or 4 trials for distance. Note how high the shot is carried on the fingers. How does this grasp compare with that used during early season? Midseason?
5. Draw a line from the center of the circle through the midpoint of the toe board, extending it a distance of 65 feet. If the circle is of soft material, brush the circle so that the spike marks will tell the story of your footwork. Put the shot 3 or 4 times for distance. After each trial note the spacing of the feet and the direction that they are pointing. How effective are those puts that fall directly on the center line? To the right? To the left?
6. Execute weight-training exercises that have been found beneficial to shot-putters (see explanation on p. 10).

Tuesday

1. Begin the day's activity with your customary jogging, calisthenics, and sprinting.
2. Brush the circle before each trial. Assume the foot position you normally take just before the final delivery. Put the shot 15 to 20 times. After each trial note the path of the feet. Were they too close or too far from the toe board? Was the direction of foot planting an effective one? Measure the distances of the last 2 puts and compare them with those executed later with the shift.
3. Put the shot with complete technique 10 to 15 times. How much do they exceed those executed without the shift? Coaches are not agreed on the distance gained by the shift, but a number of competent authorities claim that it should be 15 percent greater.
4. In case you have not practiced during inclement weather, provide artificially the impediments of a rainy day. Know

how to traverse a wet circle. Ascertain by practice how much aid you can get in controlling a muddy shot by the use of rosin, compound tincture of benzoin, or a dry towel. Take 5 to 8 trials under these man-made adverse weather conditions.
5. Conclude Tuesday's workout with a 5-minute drill on wrist and finger exercises. Their practice should become a routine daily matter even though they have not been specifically mentioned in each day's schedule of practice.

Wednesday

1. Start the day's practice with hopping, bounding, jogging, running, and sprinting.
2. Skip rope for 2 or 3 minutes.
3. Take a 5-minute sun bath if the weather is favorable.
4. Join the sprinters and run 20 yards twice at full effort.
5. Flip the shot in the air, catching it with the putting hand. Repeat a number of times sufficient to exercise the wrist and fingers thoroughly.
6. Obtain a shot 1 or 2 pounds heavier than legal specifications. Put this overweight missile 5 or 6 times, omitting the shift and a like number of trials employing the shift. Exert only $\frac{3}{4}$ effort.
7. Take 4 or 5 trials with the official shot. Has the practice on the heavier missile had a favorable or an unfavorable bearing on your form?
8. Spend 10 to 20 minutes on weight-training exercises if they have improved your shot-putting performances.

Thursday

Thursday in late season is frequently designated as one of optional practice, especially if preliminary or qualifying rounds are scheduled for Friday. The competitor is sometimes permitted to select his activities and to regulate the intensity of the exercise. The following suggestions apply when there are no preliminary trials for Friday.

1. Participate for 3 or 4 minutes each in the high jump, the long jump, or any other event that will not affect adversely your shot-putting ability.
2. Formulate your plans for competition day, checking such items as personal equipment, rest, diet, warm-up, and verification of the weight of the shot (in case you are using your own).
3. Take 8 to 12 moderate puts with the regulation shot, noting particularly the height and the angle of its flight. The optimum angle of release is dependent upon the velocity with which the shot leaves the hand.
4. Conclude the practice with calisthenics and jogging.

Friday

Two alternatives are presented for the conduct of the shot-putter for Friday in late season. One plan recommends complete absence from the atmosphere of athletics with the predominant idea of providing a recess, more mental than physical in its nature. The other alternative suggests suiting up, inspecting the field layout, and reviewing the plans for competition day. During this period of major contests, preliminary rounds of competition are required whenever a large number of athletes is involved. These qualifying trials frequently occur on Friday if the finals are scheduled for Saturday. Should preliminary competition start on Friday, it is obvious that the intensity of the practice suggested for Thursday would have to be reduced very materially. Preliminary trials are as vital as the finals. Therefore, a period of little or no exercise should precede these trials.

In case no trial puts are scheduled for Friday, a routine intended especially for contests away from the home field is recommended in the following paragraphs.

1. Dress in competition suit and shoes to reassure yourself that all personal apparel is in readiness and to become accustomed to an outfit other than that worn in practice.
2. Should you possess an assortment of detachable spikes, select the correct length to meet the conditions of the shot circle. Circles range in consistency from hard clay to loose cinders, and a corresponding range of spike lengths is desirable. For concrete circles, use spikeless shoes.
3. Omit putting the shot.
4. Jog and walk alternately for 2 or 3 minutes.

Saturday

The general admonition given athletes on the day of competition is to, "Keep off the feet." However, a certain amount of activity is an aid to the digestion of food and to the tonus of the body. There should be an amount of activity sufficient to stave off sluggishness. A number of excellent shot-putters have maintained their feeling of well-being by eating lightly, resting for 20 minutes after the meal, taking a walk for 15 minutes, and then resting in bed until called to the competition field.

1. Warm up in a precise manner, carefully noting the effect of each activity in your competition procedure.
2. Become accustomed to the shot that you are to use (in case it is one supplied by the local games committee).
3. At the earliest possible moment determine your putting order in the field of competitors. In the shot put, as in the discus throw, a large field of competitors is frequently divided into flights so that a group of 2, 3 or 4 athletes put before the next group begins. This knowledge of the exact hour of competition should be of value to you in timing the warm-up. Since the warm-up is a fluctuating

phenomenon, its timeliness is as important as its quality.

4. Put the shot from the standing position 5 to 10 times. Gradually increase the intensity in each succeeding put.
5. Put the shot 5 to 10 times, employ full putting technique, and emphasize form—not distance.
6. Competition. Strive to be among the leaders with your first put. Concentrate on getting distance without undue tension.

REFERENCE

1. Booher, H. D.: The relationship of warming-up to maximum performance in field events, M.A. thesis, 1938, State University of Iowa, Iowa City, Iowa.

Chapter 13

The discus throw

The early Greeks are credited with originating the discus throw, a contest which they later placed on the list of events of the ancient Olympic games.

The early competitors were required to throw the discus from a position on a pedestal, and this restriction reduced the opportunity for gaining angular velocity and momentum. Both the diameter and the weight of the ancient discus were greater than those for the implement in use today.

Because of the limitations imposed on the athletes of ancient Greece by the style of delivery and the weight and size of the missile, they were able to throw no farther than 100 feet. Down through the years the rules required that the discus be thrown after the Greek style until 1896, when the so-called free style was introduced. The free style permitted the competitor to throw from a 7-foot circle on the ground. In 1910 the International Amateur Athletic Federation adopted a circle measuring 2.5 meters (8 feet 2½ inches).

The discus throw became an event on the amateur Athletic Union program in 1897, when C. H. Hennemann of the Chicago Athletic Association won the championship with a throw of 118 feet 9 inches. In modern times, greater freedom in executing the preliminary swing, the turn, and the delivery has increased the possibilities of attaining greater distance. Ludvik Danek of Czechoslovakia was credited with a throw of 213 feet 11¾ inches in 1965.

GENERAL CONSIDERATIONS

Comparative marks in competition. The discus thrower using the implement weighing 3 pounds 9 ounces should be interested in the distance he will be required to throw the missile if he expects to score points. Estimated placing distances are presented in Table 13-1. The discus thrower should know that the performances listed are placing and not winning throws. He is further advised to keep informed on the capabilities of the rival discus throwers whom he will be obliged to face in future competition. It is recognized that these suggested plac-

213

Table 13-1. Comparative marks in scholastic competition in the discus throw

Meet	No. of places scored	Distance
Dual high school	3	135–145 ft.
Qualifying—state	3	145–155 ft.
State—province	5	155–165 ft.

ing distances will not apply to those areas where the class of discus throwers is either very good or very mediocre.

Equipment. Much of the equipment used in the discus throw is very similar to that used in other events. However, something should be said about the discus and the shoes.

Discus. The detailed specifications for the men's discus is adequately described in the rules of the National Collegiate Athletic Association, the National Federation of State High School Athletic Associations, and the Amateur Athletic Union of the United States. It might be added that the discus commonly used by women is described in the rules covering women's athletics published by the Amateur Athletic Union of the United States.

Briefly, the rules prescribe that the men's discus weigh not less than 2 kilograms (4 pounds 6.4 ounces). The diameter must be not less than 21.9 centimeters (8⅝ inches).

The discus designated as official for use in high school competition (United States) must weigh not less than 3 pounds 9 ounces. The diameter is 8¼ inches; the thickness ¼ inch from the rim, 0.48 inch; and the thickness at the center, 1⅝ inches.[1]

There is only one type of discus accepted in international competition, including the Olympic games. This discus is composed of a metal rim, permanently attached to a wooden body, with brass plates set flush into the sides of the wooden body. The games committee (for a United States college meet) is authorized to sanction the use of a discus with a wood or plastic body, permanently attached to a smooth metal rim. However, in the Na-

tional Collegiate Championships meet, a discus conforming to the specifications in the rules for the discus throw (N.C.A.A.) shall be the only one used by the competitors. The reader is advised to consult the most recent rule books published annually for the guidance of high school, college, or Amateur Athletic Union competitors. The discus constructed entirely of rubber is legal for high school competition if the discus meets specification for weight, size, and shape.

It is claimed by some that the rubber discus is more durable than the all-metal discus. It is not only resistant to both chipping and denting, but it is also less easily affected by dampness. Those favoring the rubber discus claim that it is safer since it inflicts less severe injury to anyone whom it might strike. This type of discus also lends itself to indoor use more readily than do the others.

Shoes. In circles of soft material field event shoes are commonly used in the discus throw. These are of oxford height with 6 spikes in each sole and 2 spikes in each heel. The shoe has a stiff counter to ensure firm support for the heel spikes. For championship contests of the National Collegiate Athletic Association (United States), concrete circles having a surface roughness of approximately 1/64 inch *shall be used* for the hammer throw, discus throw, and shot put. Furthermore, such circles are *recommended* for all track and field meets.

Obviously, the wearing of shoes fitted with spikes is impractical on hard-surfaced circles, and so the athlete is obliged to select footwear different from that just described, usually of the rubber-soled type.

This decision rests with the competitor and the coach. Careful consideration should be given the shoes to find those that give the best performance.

Qualifications. The qualifications for a discus thrower are quite similar to those of a good lineman in football. The better discus throwers are over 200 pounds in weight and 6 feet or more in height. In fact, they are found among the heavier and taller men in any class of competition.

Perhaps as important as height and weight are the size and strength of the hand, since a wide finger spread with abundant hand strength facilitates the grasp of the discus. The man with a long arm is at a decided advantage because, according to the laws of body mechanics, he is able to carry the discus through a greater arc, thus gaining the advantage of additional linear velocity. The competitor of lighter weight and shorter stature may compensate for his size by possessing a stronger arm appended to a better developed shoulder girdle.

The athlete with strong legs and thighs is at an advantage in throwing the discus since the final effort is a consummation of all sources of force.

In this event coordination and rhythm of movement are of prime importance. The synchronization of rotary movement with forward propulsion is an underlying factor which is necessary for success in throwing the discus.

TECHNIQUE OF THE DISCUS THROW

The attainment of maximum distance in throwing the discus requires a sequence of movements which involves forward momentum, initiated by intentional imbalance, and angular velocity, or the speed of body rotation. The final effort is a summation of all potential forces which includes those applied by body actions extending from the toes to the fingers.

There is only limited disagreement by coaches on the acceptable position of the body at the beginning of the delivery—the critical phase of discus throwing.

Variations in the opinions of the coaches are quite pronounced, however, on those techniques that lead up to the final throwing stance, especially the rotation of the body. This movement is also called the spin, pivot, or jump-turn.

There are competent authorities who determine the classification of a given style of discus throw by the extent of body rotation involved. These styles are termed the "$1\frac{1}{4}$ turns," the "$1\frac{1}{2}$ turns," and "$1\frac{3}{4}$ turns." It has been recognized for a long time that both forward momentum across the circle and speed of body rotation are prime objectives of the discus thrower. However, both of these fundamentals must be timed in order to permit the most effective throwing stance for a given athlete.

It has been demonstrated that the $1\frac{3}{4}$ turns permit the athlete to gain more speed of body rotation than does either the $1\frac{1}{2}$ turns or $1\frac{1}{4}$ turns. However, there are discus throwers who are unable to blend the added rotation speed with the delivery.

Those who select the $1\frac{3}{4}$ turns believe that they can utilize from 9 to 10 feet of the circle to gain momentum by traversing in a zigzag path rather than directly across the diameter of the 8 feet $2\frac{1}{2}$ inch circle.

On the other hand, the athlete selecting the $1\frac{1}{4}$ turns may claim that he is not unaware of the desirability of momentum but calls attention to his foot and body position at the delivery. He believes it to be more effective when he sacrifices a limited amount of speed gained by body rotation.

For the sake of clarity, the various stages of the discus throw are described individually, but it should be noted that there is seldom a well-defined pause between these stages. In reality some of them occur simultaneously and others overlap. Continuity of movement, as in the shot put, is required. This event is discussed under preparatory activities, handhold, initial movements in the circle, body rotation (gaining angular velocity), delivery, release, and recovery.

Preparatory activities. A series of warm-up exercises properly timed in advance of competition is a prerequisite for the discus thrower. As an aid to the novice, warm-up activities are presented in the schedules of practice.

Since the discus thrower is on his own, thus differing from the participant in a team contest, he alone is obliged to determine the emotional or mental adjustments necessary. He may include a keying-up process, a routine that is difficult to define with exactness. The athlete generates an optimistic attitude toward the forthcoming effort. He may not wish to chat with either athletes or officials immediately before stepping into the discus circle.

For a few minutes before each throw he calls on his powers of concentration, fixes his pattern of action, and repels outside stimuli of both sight and sound.

He builds up a state of self-assurance in his preparation to perform at peak ability. He may review his background of experience gained through both practice sessions and previous competition. He desires to assure himself that on this day he can equal or excel his past achievements. It should be evident, then, that the appropriate degree of confidence will not come as rapidly as a stroke of lightning. The build-up of his faith in himself is a season-long task, an item to be dealt with in daily practices as well as in the period shortly before competition. Many successful athletes channel their objective on the distance they strive to throw the discus and refrain from permitting the past records of opponents to influence their deliberations. They set up a defense against an inferiority complex.

A feeling of security may come after a number of equipment adjustments have been made, such as the use of the towel on the hands, body, or discus and the fitting of the type of shoe adequate for the terrain on which the discus circle is placed.

A short time before assuming the throwing stance, the thrower gets the feel of the discus. This may consist in adjusting the spread of the fingers and determining the desired position of the center of weight of the implement with respect to the hand. Perspiration or rain may lead him to select a nonslip aid (one which is not prohibited by the rules, such as powdered rosin or tincture of benzoin) in maintaining the grasp of the discus. Finally, he may apply adhesive tape wherever necessary, provided he does not violate the rules covering the use of such material.

Handhold. The method adopted for grasping the discus depends to a large extent on the size of the hand, including the length of the fingers. A hold suitable for the athlete possessing a hand sufficiently large is shown in Fig. 13-1, *A*. The discus is held flat against the palm with the first joint of each finger over the edge. The fingers are slightly and about evenly spread and grasp the edge firmly. The thumb is flat against the discus, extending in a line with the forearm. The grasp is such that the hand is either directly over the center of weight of the discus or slightly behind it. This method of handhold provides for balance and lends impetus to the spin as the discus leaves the hand.

Another acceptable hold for the athlete with a large hand is shown in Fig. 13-1, *B*. The difference between the two is in the spread of the fingers. In Fig. 13-1, *A*, the application of pressure is evenly divided among the fingers, while in Fig. 13-1, *B*, the pressure is applied chiefly by the first and second fingers.

A grasp commonly employed which varies from those just described is shown in Fig. 13-1, *C*. It is evident that the shorter fingers shown detract from a firm hold on the discus rim. In this method of grasping, the center of the palm is approximately over the center of the discus.

The talon grasp is shown in Fig. 13-1, *D* and *E*. This method of grasping the dis-

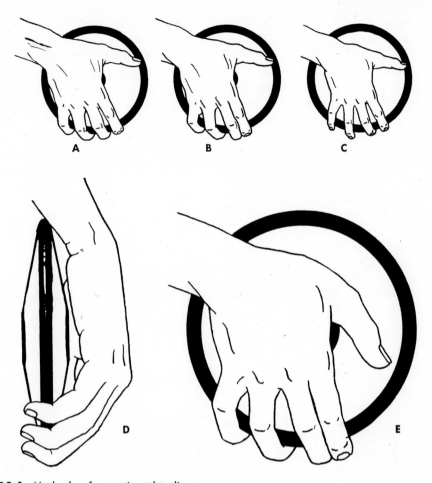

Fig. 13-1. Methods of grasping the discus.

cus is described by Hamilton, formerly of the University of California, as follows:

In grasping the discus the athlete's hand resembles somewhat the talon of the eagle. The hand is arched or cupped so that the lobes at the base of the fingers do not touch the discus, the back of the discus resting lightly on the wrist and the lobe of the thumb. With the exception of the fingers over the edge and the thumb resting lightly on the face of the discus close to the index finger, no other parts of the hand except those mentioned touch the discus. It is impossible to cup the hand properly for this style if the thumb is extended to the left as far as possible. It must be relaxed and carried reasonably close to the index finger. As the hand is set in the talon grip, the hand should be turned slightly to the right. This serves a double purpose—it allows for a little more wrist

snap at the conclusion of the throw and it will place the weight of the discus slightly in front of the fingers.[2]

Competent authorities claim that this method provides for greater hand flexion, more force, and less friction on the implement.

Initial movements in the circle. After the athlete steps into the circle, he assumes a semirelaxed position with the knees slightly bent. The weight of the body rests about equally on each foot.

The thrower (right-handed) at this stage is facing toward the rear of the circle. The direction of the feet during the initial stance is a matter of personal preference and the opinion of the coach. A critical phase of foot position occurs at the instant of initiating body rotation regardless of what the previous position has been.

Acceptable variations from the initial stance (facing the rear of the circle) consist of an added ¼ turn to the right or a ¼ turn to the left.

The use of one or more preliminary swings of the arm carrying the discus and the coordinated lifting and then planting of the left foot to maintain balance vary with different athletes. The left arm exerts only moderate effort and is either extended or partially flexed in a direction across the body from the discus. Its function is to serve as a counterweight in aiding balance.

The plane of the discus rightfully may change during the preliminary arm swings, but the position of the right arm and the

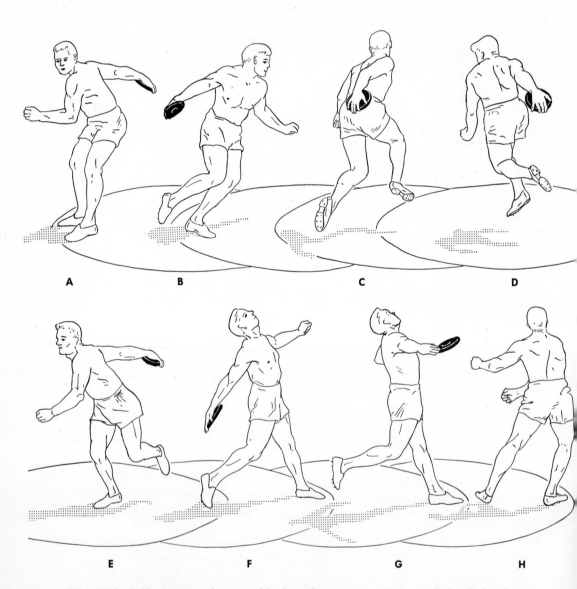

A   B   C   D

E   F   G   H

Fig. 13-2, A-H. A series of acceptable form for executing Style 1 of the discus throw.

plane of the discus at the end of the last swing are highly significant items. At this phase the discus and the arm must be in a position which is most effective in the ensuing rotation of the body. The trunk, during the preliminary swings, is rotated first backward and sideward to the right and then forward and sideward to the left. As indicated for the discus and the arm posi-

tion, the trunk position at the culmination of the last preliminary swing is likewise an important phase of discus throwing (Fig. 13-2, A, and Fig. 13-3, A).

The positions of the head and eyes, varying with the succeeding phases of discus throwing, are very essential elements of the event, because the eyes are employed to pilot the movements of the body.

A   B   C   D

E   F   G   H

Fig. 13-3, A-H. A series of acceptable form for executing Style 2 of the discus throw.

At the conclusion of the last preliminary swing, the head and eyes are turned to the right, thus permitting a longer arc for the back swing of the discus.

The termination of the last preliminary swing blends with the rotation of the body (pivoting on the left foot) and the acquisition of intentional imbalance, wherein the body is permitted to fall toward the front of the circle.

Body rotation (gaining angular velocity). The athlete, while pivoting speedily on the left foot, allows the body to fall in the direction of the throw. During the body spin, the head and eyes are turned toward the left shoulder for the purpose of both aiding the pivot and guiding the successive movements of the body. The accentuated body lean (the intentional imbalance action) is designed to contribute to forward momentum across the circle. The pivoting action permits the athlete to gain angular velocity (speed of body rotation).

At this stage the discus is held at approximately the height of the hips and well to the rear of the body, while the right arm is fully extended. Attention is called to a variation in the foregoing procedure that is executed by some excellent discus throwers. At about midway in the execution of the body turn, for a fraction of a second only, they lower the plane of the discus so that it is held relatively close to the body. These athletes claim that whenever the discus is held relatively close to the body they apply the physical principle of shortening the radius in order to increase the speed of rotation. Quickly thereafter, while body rotation continues, the discus is elevated either to the level of the hips or slightly above the level of the hips. The left arm, as previously described, continues to contribute a balancing action and may be either flexed or extended so as to fulfill its mission during the rotation of the body.

The right leg is bent slightly and is swung or thrust sharply in a counterclockwise direction.

The position of the head and eyes (relative to the body) is not changed materially in the early stages of the rotation of the body (Fig. 13-2, *B* to *E*, and Fig. 13-3, *B* to *E*).

At about the moment the athlete has pivoted so that he is facing the direction of the throw, he drives vigorously off the left foot, an action that provides impetus for both the rotation of the body and its propulsion across the circle. The emphasis on the left leg thrust is forward (and slightly upward), thus blending with the intentional imbalance movement. Refer to Style 1, Fig. 13-2, *B* to *D*, and Style 2, Fig. 13-3, *B* to *D*. For a short period of time both feet are off the ground as a result of the jumplike action.

The left leg, having broken contact with the ground, continues its movement in a counterclockwise direction. While the athlete is nearing the midpoint of the body turn, he refrains from permitting a wide spread of the legs. Contrarily, the thrower depicted in Style 1, Fig. 13-2, *D*, makes a conscious effort to keep the left leg flexed and close to the right leg.

At about the instant the thrower has completed one full turn of the body (and again is facing the rear of the circle), the right foot is brought rapidly to the ground at about midcircle. The pivoting action continues while the left leg begins to reach for the front of the circle (Fig. 13-2, *E*, and Fig. 13-3, *E*).

The pattern of footwork varies with different competitors. The athlete adopting Style 1 (Fig. 13-2, *B* to *D*) traverses the circle in a zigzag manner. He contends that such a pattern permits the maximum use of the distance within the circle, thus providing adequately for both forward momentum and angular velocity. However, the thrower who selected Style 2 (Fig. 13-3, *B* to *D*) executes his transit across the circle more nearly on a straight line. Exponents of Style 2 believe that the more direct path reduces the problems of timing, foot placement, and balance. All of these actions must be executed correctly before the thrower begins an all-important technique—the delivery.

In Style 1, Fig. 13-2, C and D, the athlete is portrayed as executing a jump-turn, which at first appears to lift the body higher than the thrower illustrated in Style 2, Fig. 13-3, C and D. However, the discus thrower shown in Style 1 bends both legs to a greater degree when lifting them from the ground. Hence, there exists little appreciable difference between Styles 1 and 2 in the height to which the body has been elevated.

Throughout the period of body rotation, the right shoulder, right arm, and discus are still dragging behind. This action represents a planned effort by the thrower and is considered acceptable technique. If the shoulder, arm, and discus (during the rotation of the body) were permitted to move otherwise, the potential distance over which force is applied when delivering the discus would be reduced. Whenever there is a reduction in the distance over which force is applied to the discus, there will follow a decrease in the distance it is thrown (Fig. 13-2, C to E, and Fig. 13-3, C and D).

The trunk leans in a direction away from the discus during the rotation of the body. One of the world's leading discus throwers who selected Style 1 stated that the head stays above the center of the circle and the body rotates around it.

The right foot (toward the end of the body turn) has been planted in a position pointing to the rear of the circle. The pivot is continued so that the right foot then points in the direction of the throw. No pause should be permitted between the termination of the body spin and the beginning of the delivery.

Delivery. During the first phase of the delivery, the athlete has both feet on the ground. He has regained the balance he intentionally relinquished in the early stages

of the rotation of the body, at which time the body was permitted to fall toward the front of the circle.

As soon as the rotation of the body has been completed so that the athlete is facing the direction of throw, the left foot is planted near the front edge of the circle. The left leg applies a vaulting action which checks the momentum of the lower extremities and increases the momentum of the upper extremities.

Some authorities claim that in the late phase of the delivery, the left leg (and left foot) contributes a lifting action and thus aids in discus propulsion. Other authorities (possibly the majority) compare the function of the left leg with that of the vaulting pole as it is lowered into the vaulting trough. When the pole is thrust against a solid object, momentum is checked, but the pivoting action (on the point of the vaulting pole) provides opportunity for increased upward-forward movement of the vaulter's body.

At the onset of the delivery, the right leg is vigorously straightened and maximum force is applied by the right foot (Fig. 13-2, E and F, and Fig. 13-3, E to G). Simultaneously the weight of the body shifts from the right leg to the left leg.

The pull on the discus is started from a position when it is well to the rear of the body and requires precision timing so that it is coordinated with the swift twist of the trunk to the left.

The left arm, as described in the earlier stages of the throw, contributes to body balance. The precise method of utilizing it is an individual matter, and considerable latitude is permissible in its bend or extension (Fig. 13-2, F and G, and Fig. 13-3, E to G).

During the delivery the head is tilted backward (a pronounced lift of the chin) so that the eyes are focused on a point considerably above the horizon (Fig. 13-2, F and G, and Fig. 13-3, F and G).

The shoulders and hips are rotated

swiftly to the front in movements that must be synchronized. If the shoulder is rotated prior to the optimum moment, complete advantage of the hip's contribution cannot be taken. If the rotation of the right hip is executed prior to the optimum moment, a reduction in the amount of forward-upward force may be expected.

While the discus is brought forward in the delivery, the trunk is straightened (Fig. 13-2, *F* and *G*, and Fig. 13-3, *F* and *G*). Now both feet are pointed toward the front of the circle.

An all-important effort is then expended in the throw of the discus. The flow of force extends from the right foot to the leg, hip, shoulder, arm, wrist, and hand.

Release. The angle of the discus (with respect to the ground) at the instant of the release ranges from 28 to 32 degrees. The athlete whose form is illustrated in Fig. 13-2, *G*, releases the missile at about the level of the shoulder and at an angle of approximately 30 degrees. The thrower depicted in Fig. 13-3, *G*, releases the discus at about the level of the chin and at an angle of approximately 28 degrees.

The release is made off the first finger which imparts a clockwise spin to the discus.

The final hand contact with the implement occurs at a point slightly ahead of an imaginary line drawn through both shoulders. While the release is being executed, the chest is carried upward and forward as one phase of the follow-through. Attention is directed to the belief that the follow-through is an aftermath of the throw and not an integral part of it. A favorable evaluation of the follow-through of a given throw usually means that the fundamental techniques of throwing have been well executed. If the follow-through is graded as unsatisfactory, it is quite likely that imperfections were detectable in the athlete's throwing pattern.

The head is tilted slightly backward dur-ing the release, and the eyes are focused on the flight of the discus.

The left arm is employed as a balancing member and is usually carried, rather than swung, vigorously to the left. In Fig. 13-3, *G*, the left arm is flexed at the elbow, but in Fig. 13-3, *H*, it is fairly well extended.

At this phase, the shoulders are turned to the front and are in such a position that a line drawn through them is about parallel with the ground.

The hips of the athlete illustrated in Fig. 13-2, *G*, are square to the front. This thrower employs a rapid reverse of the position of the feet. The right hip of the discus thrower shown in Fig. 13-3, *G*, is being rotated to the front position. This competitor differs from the one shown in Fig. 13-2, *G*, in that he employs a delayed reverse. In the same illustrations, the acceptable variations in the positions of the feet are indicated.

The continuation of the delivery drive for the athlete employing a rapid reverse requires the shifting of the body weight over the vaulting left leg (Fig. 13-2, *F* and *G*).

For the athlete employing a delayed reverse (Style 2), the continuation of the delivery drive transfers the body weight to the left leg, but it is slightly bent at the knee and so the vaulting and lifting actions are less pronounced in Style 2 (Fig. 13-3, *G* and *H*).

Recovery. The term "recovery" is applied to that stage of the discus throw in which the athlete strives to gain body balance and refrain from stepping either on or outside the circle. He was in a state of imbalance at the instant the discus was released. A recovery position in which the feet are reversed speedily is depicted for Style 1 in Fig. 13-2, *H*. The right foot is planted a few inches from the front edge of the circle, and simultaneously the left leg is swung groundward as an aid to balance. The body weight rests chiefly on the right leg.

For the athlete who selects Style 2 (Fig. 13-3, *H*) and who utilizes a delayed reverse, a variation in leg action is obligatory. The right leg is dragged rather than swung sharply to the front. A limited number of discus throwers who have adopted Style 2 alter the technique by refraining from a well-defined reverse in this, the recovery phase. The body weight of the athlete's choosing Style 2 is supported by both legs rather than the right leg alone.

The thrower customarily bends one or both knees, thus lowering the center of body weight, a device that serves to minimize the chances of fouling. The use of the arms in this balancing action is left to the discretion of the competitor.

After the discus has left the hand, the head remains tilted backward so that the eyes are focused in the direction of the flight of the implement. The novice discus thrower who wrongfully steps outside the circle in his eagerness to watch the flight of the discus may be obliged to deviate (temporarily) from this procedure. He may be able to eliminate fouling if, after the discus has left the hand, he focuses the eyes on the circle and thus sees where he is placing the feet. With more experience, he should be able to resume the use of the commonly accepted head-and-eyes technique in the recovery phase of the discus throw.

COMMON ERRORS IN THE DISCUS THROW

The description of the discus throw included the various techniques in the order in which they were executed. When establishing an order of teaching them on the athletic field, the coach rightfully may deviate from the sequence presented. For example, he may direct the athlete first to learn to handle the discus and throw from a standing position before attempting to traverse the circle. The suggested daily practice schedules presented at the end of this chapter are designed to help the coach establish a plan for teaching discus throwing techniques.

Numerous points of interest to the student of this event were omitted in order to avoid breaking the continuity of the successive body movements. Some of the discus thrower's imperfections were pointed out by inference. For the purpose of emphasis, and with the recognition of some repetition, faults in execution will be discussed.

In the preparatory activities. The performance of the athlete may suffer if he neglects the following:

1. A sufficient amount of warm-up exercises or throwing.
2. Determination of the direction and velocity of the wind. (See "release" under "Common errors in the discus throw.")
3. Selection of the proper footwear and spike length or other equipment.
4. Establishment of the most desirable state of keying up which includes confidence and concentration.

In the handhold. Errors possible in the grasp of the discus are as follows:

1. An inadequate placement of the hands with respect to the center of weight of the discus. Usually the hand is directly over the center of weight or slightly behind it.
2. A grasp which does not permit the end joints of the finger to extend over the edge.
3. A failure to have in readiness for rainy days the permissible aids in handling the implement.

In the initial movements in the circle. Discus throwers make mistakes because of the following:

1. The improper position of the head and eyes. The eyes are customarily focused at a point on or slightly above the horizon.
2. Failure to place the feet so as to take advantage of the entire circle.
3. An inadequate bend of the knees.

4. Unwarranted tenseness—failure to relax.

5. Failure to assume an initial stance that permits the optimum distance during body rotation for gaining momentum.

In body rotation—traversing the circle. The thrower may hamper his effort if he does as follows:

1. Fails to achieve intentional imbalance by permitting the body to fall toward the front of the circle.

2. Neglects to extend the right arm, holding the discus, fully to the rear. Both the plane of the discus and its height above the ground vary with different athletes (Fig. 13-2, A, and Fig. 13-3, A).

3. Obtains insufficient push from the left foot during and after the pivot.

4. Fails to keep the left leg both flexed and close to the right leg at the midpoint in the body rotation (Fig. 13-2, D, and Fig. 13-3, D.)

5. Permits the discus to catch up with the body during rotation. The body should lead the discus.

6. Covers either too much or too little distance in the placement of the right foot toward the end of body rotation. It should land about the center of the circle and point toward the rear.

7. Shifts the focus of eyes to a point other than the horizon.

8. Neglects to bend the right knee sufficiently.

9. Plants the left foot either too far to the left or too far to the right of a line bisecting the circle or plants the feet too close together. The objective is the midpoint of the front of the circle (or a few inches to its left).

10. Tilts the trunk either backward or forward to a degree that hinders body balance.

In the delivery. In the delivery stage of throwing, a reduction in distance may result if the athlete does as follows:

1. Hesitates between the body rotation and delivery.

2. Fails to initiate the final arm pull at a time when he can apply force to the discus over the longest arc and for the longest period of time.

3. Swings the left arm sharply to the left during the delivery. This action turns the right shoulder too rapidly to the front.

4. Brings the right hip forward too soon, thus losing potential force from a combined upward-forward thrust of the hip.

5. Fails to use the left leg as a brake to halt the forward movement of the lower extremities and thus aid the forward movement of the upper extremities.

6. Neglects to coordinate the rotation of the hips and shoulders.

7. Fails to straighten the trunk (Fig. 13-2, F, and Fig. 13-3, G).

8. Applies only moderate effort instead of an explosive action when straightening the right leg and rocking up on the toes.

9. Fails to apply a speedy vigorous whip of the arm and snap of the wrist when delivering the discus (Fig. 13-3, H).

10. Directs the sweep of the right arm in a manner resulting in throws which are either too high or too low.

11. Fails to coordinate the explosive burst of forces from the toes to the leg, hip, shoulder, arm, wrist, and hand.

In the release. The discus is released off the first finger, although numerous discus throwers report that at the beginning of the throw the second finger seems to exert the most pressure. Frequently errors in the release occur when the thrower fails to solve the problems of the direction and velocity of the wind. With little or no wind, the angle of release (with respect to the ground) and the plane of the discus should be about 30 degrees. The range is from 28 to 32 degrees. However, when the velocity of the wind is greater than 8 to 10 miles per hour, the problem of angles becomes difficult. Whenever there is a strong headwind, the thrower should elect a direction quartering into it and should release the discus at an angle of about 32 degrees. Whenever there is a strong following wind, the thrower should attempt to obtain an angle of release that is flatter than the average of 30 degrees, perhaps as low as 25 degrees.

Other possible errors are as follows:

1. Extremes of releases to the left or to the right.
2. Letting go of the discus before it reaches a point level with the shoulders and a few inches to the front.
3. Faulty arm and hand action that results in a wobbly flight of the discus.
4. Failure to straighten the trunk and bring the hips and shoulders squarely to the front.
5. Lack of continuation of the delivery drive which, when properly executed, shifts the body weight against the vaulting left leg (Fig. 13-2, *F* and *G*). This is frequently thought of as a part of the follow-through.

In the recovery. The main objective of the athlete during the recovery phase is the avoidance of fouling. Possible items of faulty execution are as follows:

1. Failure to bend the knees sufficiently. Individuals differ on the optimum degree.
2. Improperly raising and swinging the left leg as an aid in regaining balance.
3. Crowding the circle needlessly.
4. A careless attitude, such as shown by the athlete who does not make every effort to save the throw.

SCHEDULES OF PRACTICE

The amount of practice permissible in the discus throw is similar to that in the shot put. Many throws in daily practice may be taken without fear of injury. Like the shot-putter (and an athlete may well compete in both events), the discus thrower who understands the mechanics of the event and who diligently pursues daily exercises during the entire year will be in readiness for early season schedules of practice. In addition to developing the large muscle groups of the legs and trunk, he must develop strength in the fingers and wrist. Agility in footwork is as essential for him as for the boxer.

Progressive resistance exercises (weight-training exercises), described on p. 8, may be included in the plan of workouts at the discretion of the coach. Supervision at the time of executing these exercises is very desirable.

In early season, weight-training exercises may be listed on the workout plan on alternate days, 3 days per week; in midseason, 1 day per week; in late season, they may be omitted. However, there are some exceptional athletes who derive benefits from these exercises by continuing them during the entire competitive season.

By the time early season practices are called, the discus thrower is presumed to have completed the preliminary season workouts.

The attention of the discus thrower is called to the fact that he may not find his achievements progressing steadily onward and upward. There may be days when his advancement may be at a standstill or the distance of his throws reduced by several feet. He must try to solve the difficulties which may be only temporary faults in technique.

Schedules are presented for early season, midseason, and late season, based on a discus thrower competing in this event solely. If additional events are assigned the athlete, changes in the amount and character of the schedules will necessarily have to be made. The discus thrower may find certain coaching points in the shot put valuable and is referred to the schedules of practice for that event.

Early season. This schedule follows the preliminary season schedule, pp. 7 and 12.

Monday

1. Start the workout by jogging 200 yards, walking 25 yards, and jogging 150 yards.
2. Familiarize yourself with the various types of discuses: wood center, rubber, metal, and plastic. Experiment with the different styles of grasp (Fig. 13-1). Note that the grasps vary with the size of the hand and length of the fingers.
3. From the standing position, release the discus so that it describes a clockwise spin as it is pulled by the first finger. Adjust the wrist turn and the pressure applied by the fingers so that the missile spins, offering minimum resistance to the air. The angle of flight may vary slightly from 30 degrees. Repeat the efforts from 12 to 20 times or until the knack of sailing the discus has been mastered.
4. Throw from the standing position 10 to 15 times, emphasizing the force developed from the right leg and initiated by a forceful upward-forward movement of the right hip.
5. Jog 300 yards and sprint 20 yards.
6. Execute 6 to 8 minutes of exercises, such as handstands, squats, running in place, and vigorous bending. Spend 10 to 20 minutes on progressive resistance (weight-training) exercises (see p. 8).

Tuesday

1. Begin the day's work with a jog of 150 yards, a walk of 50 yards, a run of 25 yards, and a sprint of 25 yards.
2. Perform 6 to 8 minutes of body-building routines which may include exercises with the 25-pound weight, trunk or leg raising while lying on the back,

and vigorous high kicking, both forward and backward.

3. Throw the discus from the standing position 10 to 16 times. Study your effort for height, discus angle, angle of flight, and direction of throw, bearing in mind that throws falling outside the 60-degree sector are not recorded.
4. Skip rope for 2 minutes.
5. Join the sprinters and take 2 dashes of 25 yards.
6. Assume the initial stance that seems best fitted to you. Without the discus, go through the consecutive steps in traversing the circle. Repeat 8 to 10 times. An alternative exercise consists of using a discus to which has been attached a strap that fits snugly over the back of the hand. Obviously the strap helps the athlete maintain the grasp of the implement in those practice sessions that do not require him to release the discus. Therefore drills calling for pivoting or turning exercises can be held indoors as well as outdoors.
7. Grasp the missile in a manner to your liking. Experiment with the various methods of grasp even though you have found one that seems effective. Throw 4 or 5 times, using the turn and final delivery.
8. Complete the practice with a jog of 440 yards and a sprint of 20 yards.

Wednesday

1. Initiate the practice by jogging, running, and walking a total distance of 440 yards.
2. Throw the discus 15 to 20 times (using moderate effort) from a position near the front of the circle without employing the body turn or the foot reverse. On succeeding trials and before the final pull, vary the amount of knee bend employed. What degree of bend do you find produces the

greatest leg drive? What degree of bend produces a leg drive that can be imparted best to the discus?

3. Throw with moderate effort from the standing position 10 to 12 times, half of them with the implement held at arm's length high and to the back and the other half low and to the back. Note the success of the throws resulting from the extremes of arm elevation and draw your own conclusions.
4. Join the long jumpers and take 2 or 3 trials.
5. Jog 440 yards.
6. Perform progressive resistance exercises for a period of 15 to 20 minutes.

Thursday

1. Limber up with jogging, walking, and sprinting.
2. Execute 5 to 10 minutes of diversified exercises designed to develop the large muscle groups. Perform as many pull-up and chinning exercises as you feel capable of doing. Remember that the discus is an arm-pulling event.
3. Smooth out any faults in the release by delivering 15 to 20 times at ⅞ effort from the standing position.
4. Throw the discus 6 to 8 times with conscious effort placed on the right leg drive.
5. Join the high jumpers and take 5 or 6 trials.
6. End the practice by jogging 300 to 350 yards.

Friday

1. Start the day with jogging, hopping, and bounding.
2. If throwing from a soft-surface ring, brush the surface of the circle so that your spike marks are visible. With the discus in hand, traverse the circle, noting the distance covered in each foot movement. Again brush the cir-

cle and repeat throwing the discus 15 to 20 times until you are convinced that you have found the most efficient distribution of distance between the feet.
3. Experiment with various methods of traversing the circle, such as the 1¾ turns, 1½ turns, 1¼ turns, and their variations. Throw 4 or 5 times with each style. Aided by an observer, critically analyze your own application of these various forms. In early season, experimentation with different methods of crossing the circle is desirable. In the midst of the competitive season, shifting form is undesirable. Increase gradually the force behind each succeeding throw.
4. Vary the practice procedure by joining the long jumpers for 6 to 8 jumps.
5. Spend 10 to 20 minutes on progressive resistance exercises.

Saturday

In early season it is assumed that no contest has been scheduled for Saturday and that the athlete will have 6 days available for practice.

1. Warm up thoroughly, having in mind your individual requirements for efficient throwing. Jog 200 yards, walk 25 yards, hop and bound 10 yards, and sprint 25 yards.
2. Perform 5 to 8 minutes of moderate exercises, such as trunk bends, trunk twists, wood-chopping exercise, or complete body spins from the standing jump.
3. Skip rope for 2 minutes.
4. Throw 6 to 10 times, applying ¾ effort from the position at the front of the circle. Concentrate on coordination of force from foot to discus. Emphasize the follow-through and the whip of the arm across the chest. If the discus is sailing smoothly and at the correct angle, you are then ready for throws using the complete form,

including the progression across the circle. Place emphasis on intentional imbalance at the beginning of body rotation. In this movement the body is permitted to fall toward the front of the circle for the purpose of gaining momentum. Balance is regained as soon as both feet are planted. Note carefully the distance achieved in each successive throw so that you can judge the correct amount of warm-up.

5. Throw 6 or 7 times, employing the complete form. Analyze your turn or pivot to see whether optimum momentum is generated and whether the correct amount of distance is covered. Throw with increasing vigor until your last trial represents nearly full effort.

6. Rest momentarily and acquire physical and mental poise as though you were entering an important contest.

7. Throw with full effort 6 or 7 times, carefully observing the rules on fouling. An observer or coach will advise you after each throw on your correct and faulty executions.

8. End Saturday's practice with 3 minutes of vigorous exercises for the wrist and fingers, such as the wall push-away and wrist roll. Jog 250 yards. Analyze your weight chart for the week. Refer to the chapter on conditioning for its interpretation.

Midseason. Schedules for midseason are planned to meet a program calling for competition on Saturday. Like those for the shot put, midseason schedules in the discus event indicate reduction in throwing at full effort and provide for light activity on Thursday and Friday. The athlete should practice throwing the discus on rainy days and should experiment with recommended aids for the handhold, such as rosin and compound tincture of benzoin.

Many coaches agree that very little distance throwing should be prescribed after Wednesday. There is a division of opinion on the most desirable days for strenuous practice. One group favors throwing for distance on Monday and Tuesday, with tapering-off practices on Wednesday and Thursday. Another group advises throwing at full effort on Monday and Wednesday, using Tuesday as a light practice period. Again, there are some coaches who recommend strenuous throwing for distance during practices on Monday, Tuesday, and Wednesday and moderate throwing for form on Thursday.

Since excellent results have been obtained with the plans just mentioned, the competitor and coach will arrange this detail to fit individual needs. The first plan is described in the succeeding paragraphs.

Monday

1. Adjust yourself for a day of vigorous throwing by jogging, hopping, and sprinting.

2. Observe the direction and velocity of the wind and the temperature of the day. Then determine the type and quantity of warm-up you require.

3. Throw the discus 15 to 20 times, concentrating on form while traversing the circle.

4. Learn to relax between trials. Throw 4 times with full effort to conclude the strenuous section of Monday's practice.

5. Sprint 25 yards. Repeat 2 or 3 times.

6. Spend 10 to 15 minutes on progressive resistance exercises (see p. 8).

Tuesday

1. Begin the practice with a jog of 200 yards, a walk of 25 yards, a run of 100 yards, and a sprint of 50 yards.

2. Arrive at a definite procedure in your warm-up which will be adhered to whenever preparing for intensive throwing. Vary it only to meet exceptional weather conditions.

3. Skip rope for 2 minutes and then take 5 minutes of calisthenics.

4. Throw 15 to 20 times from the standing position and note the plane of the discus and the angle of its path shortly after the release; the drive of the legs, the trunk, and the arms; and the intensive wrist snap at the finish.

5. Throw 6 to 10 times, employing the turn, the release, and the recovery. Duplicate your predetermined ideal form on the distance of foot spread, the amount of knee bend, the speed of body rotation, the timing of the delivery, and the follow-through. Increase or diminish the number of preliminary throws so that you feel primed to give your best performance quite early in the next section of the workout. In other words, make certain that you have properly timed your warm-up.

6. Throw 4 times as in competition. Compare trial by trial your Tuesday efforts with those of Monday. With this background, adjust or retain your daily routine.

Wednesday

1. Start practice with jogging, sprinting, and calisthenics.

2. Spend 3 to 5 minutes on the footwork and turn, without carrying the discus.

3. Take 15 to 20 moderate throws from the standing position.

4. Spend 5 to 10 minutes throwing for form only and perfecting points of execution. Determine the degree of body fall (intentional imbalance) that is most effective for you. This action occurs at the beginning of body rotation. The number of trials and the amount of effort expended on each are left to the contestant.

5. Throw the discus 10 to 15 times at full effort.

6. Conclude the day's practice with weight-training exercises if they have proved beneficial to discus throwing.

Thursday

1. Warm up in your customary manner.

2. Make use of action photographs of yourself to visualize proper and faulty execution.

3. Spend 3 to 5 minutes on gymnastic feats such as handstands, walking on hands, and tumbling.

4. Deliver the discus 8 to 10 times with moderate effort. Emphasize handling it under various conditions of windage. Become accustomed to throwing from any type of footing—concrete, asphalt, clay, cinders, grass, or loam—dry or wet.

5. Conclude the strenuous section of this week's practice with 2 or 3 dashes of 50 yards. Note the change in your body weight.

Friday

There are two methods of dealing with Friday's activities, one calling for complete absence from the athletic environment and the other recommending light limbering up. If you choose to appear suited-up, investigate the type of circle you are to use Saturday, thus affording opportunity for adjusting length of spikes. Take cognizance of the prevailing winds as well as the weather forecast. Check on all personal equipment, especially the weight of the discus in case you are permitted to use your implement in competition.

1. Jog and walk alternately for 2 or 3 minutes.

2. Perform 3 or 4 minutes of light calisthenics.

Saturday

Since this is a day of competition, adjust your routine of rest, meals, study, or work so that you will be in readiness both mentally and physically for the contest. Arrange your preliminary exercises so that you allow 5 to 15 minutes between the end of the warm-up and the beginning of competition. If this rest period is unduly shortened, you will have insufficient time to acquire physical as well as mental poise. If the rest period is extremely long, you may lose the benefits already derived by a well-calculated warm-up.

1. Complete your warm-up, by this time a ritual on days of throwing at full effort.
2. Competition. If your practices have been fruitful so that your sequence of movement is automatic, you may concentrate on an explosive delivery.
3. Analyze your throws after the competition is over.
4. Throw 2 or 3 times after the competition is over when nothing is at stake. Carefully note the degree of body tension employed, together with the distance thrown. If these nonscoring throws are better than the scoring marks, you may well recheck your warm-up procedure.
5. End this week in midseason with 2 or 3 minutes of exercises for the fingers, wrists, and arms, followed by a jog of 440 yards. Study your fluctuation in body weight during the week.

Late season. When late season arrives, the athlete is presumed to have attained a proficiency in the fundamental skills of throwing the discus as well as a knowledge of how to comport himself in competition. Through experimentation he should have made a selection of the type of discus, the kind of shoe, the form of transit across the circle, the method of delivery, and the type of recovery.

While the athlete continually is seeking means of bettering his performance, he should hew to a line on the matter of form. He should avoid radical changes in his style unless, after continued mediocre performances and after counsel with a competent adviser, it appears that such a change will be of benefit.

Frequently one finds athletes who watch the mastery of the first-place winner carefully and blindly attempt to imitate his form. The desire to observe and to learn is a laudable one, and the novice is urged to keep both his eyes and ears open for new ideas. However, these newly discovered techniques should be analyzed to see if they will fit his qualifications. It is conceivable that a discus thrower who is 6 feet 3 inches tall, weighing 220 pounds, and desirous of speeding up his footwork might harm his progress by attempting to copy exactly the style of a competitor 5 feet 10 inches in height who weighs 175 pounds.

The athlete is urged to be patient, confining himself to a form that has been found effective through early season and midseason. Frequently an individual who seeks to make a radical change during late season has insufficient time to master the readjustment.

Late season practices differ from midseason in that the amount of physical work is reduced, there being fewer trials for distance prescribed. To use a term of the woodworker, this is the sanding and polishing stage.

Monday

1. Begin with the customary warm-up such as jogging, walking, sprinting, and calisthenics.
2. Throw the discus 6 to 10 times with moderate effort but do not vary the timing of the leg and arm work.
3. Take a sun bath for 10 minutes.
4. Practice on an event other than the discus for 10 minutes.
5. Draw a line through the middle of the 60-degree sector so that it extends from the center of the circle out 200 feet. Take 15 to 20 throws at moderate effort (since throwing for distance is scheduled for Tuesday), noting whether the discus falls to the left, to the right, or directly on this line. In which part of the sector do your best throws fall? What determines the direction of the flight? Were the throws affected by either the direction or velocity of the wind?
6. Complete the practice with weight-

training exercises if you have found them to be helpful.

Tuesday

1. Condition yourself for vigorous throwing by completing the routine of the precompetition warm-up.
2. Throw 8 to 10 times for form, applying only sufficient force to make good form possible. Observe the distance thrown even though you are not extending yourself.
3. If using a soft-surface circle, brush the circle before each trial so that your spike marks will provide a fixed record of footwork. Deliver the discus 7 times with full effort. Compare the foot measurements actually made with those of your ideal pattern and make whatever adjustments are necessary. Plot a curve of the 7 throws. Where does the peak of the curve fall? How does the first competitive throw compare with the last practice throw? The seventh competitive throw?
4. Take 2 additional trials for distance after a brief rest and compare them with your previous efforts.
5. If you employ the jump-turn style, has the left leg been drawn close to the right leg during the late stage of body rotation? Close proximity of the two legs is considered acceptable form. Throw 4 to 6 times for distance, emphasizing this phase of the technique.
6. Terminate the practice with 2 or 3 minutes of wrist and finger exercises (wall push-away, handstand, and swing on the rings), followed by a 300-yard jog.

Wednesday

1. After jogging, hopping, and bounding, join the sprinters for 3 dashes of 25 yards each.
2. Perform gymnastic feats for 3 to 4 minutes, including chinning on the high bar. Compare your chinning

ability now with that of early season or preliminary season.
3. Take 10 to 15 trials without the discus, emphasizing footwork technique in traversing the circle.
4. Throw the regulation discus 5 or 6 times with moderate force application immediately after trying the heavier implement. What adjustments do you require in the timing of the body turn?
5. Study action photographs (or motion pictures) of yourself taken immediately after completing the body turn. In this position you are preparing for the start of the delivery (Fig. 13-2, *F* and *G*, and Fig. 13-3, *F* and *G*). Note the carriage of the trunk. Is it inclined backward, forward, or sideward? In what position are the feet? The knees?
6. Throw the discus 3 to 6 times to improve any of these points of form. Because of the rapidity of action, a single observer may not be able to observe all of the movements. Therefore, select numerous observers, each with a single activity upon which to report.
7. End the day with tension and weight-training exercises provided they fit into your late season schedules of practice.

Thursday

1. Begin the workout with jogging and calisthenics for 3 or 4 minutes.
2. Weather permitting, take a sun bath for 10 minutes.
3. Join the long jumpers and take 3 or 4 trials.
4. Omit throwing today if preliminaries are held on Friday. Otherwise take 8 to 10 trials at less than full effort.
5. If your competition calls for Friday preliminaries in the discus throw, items 3 and 4 may be omitted. Conclude the day's activities with a 250-yard jog.

Friday

1. If your competition requires trial throws on Friday, your program will parallel that for Saturday in mid-season. Otherwise take only a light limbering-up workout.
2. Inform yourself of the correct time schedule of competition so that you may adjust your daily routine.
3. Check the field conditions as well as your own personal equipment.
4. Conclude your preparations by jogging 880 yards.

Saturday

With first-class competition such as one meets in late season, mental discipline is of great importance. The correct amount of confidence both before and during the contest is your objective. Learn your order on the official's roll call so that you may time your preparations intelligently even though you know the established hour for starting the event. Frequently, when the field of competitors is large, the athletes compete in flights of 2, 3, or 4 individuals. If you are listed in flight 4, your procedure obviously will be different from that required for flight 1.

1. Warm up thoroughly with the type and quantity of exercise that you have long since determined.
2. Throw from the standing position so as to become accustomed to your environment and the implement (in case the regulations limit you to that furnished by the games committee). Your own experience will determine the number and intensity of these throws.
3. Throw the discus 4 to 8 times for form. Increase or decrease the number to suit your needs.
4. Competition. Set an objective and apply your maximum effort. Build up a defense in case you should fall short of your goal. Try to maintain your warm-up even though considerable time elapses between your trials.
5. End the day with 2 sprints of 50 yards. What does the body weight chart indicate relative to your condition?

REFERENCES

1. Tuttle, W. W., Bresnahan, G. T., and Canine, H.: Designing the new high school discus, Scholastic Coach **7**:7, 1938. (U. S. A. Patent No. 2223091.)
2. Hamilton, B.: Discussion of discus throwing, Proc. Nat. Coll. Track Coaches A., Chicago, **2**:1, 1932.

Chapter 14

The javelin throw

The javelin throw has evolved into its present form from an ancient practice of throwing a spear for either distance or accuracy. When distance was the objective, the weapon was made with a blunt end equipped with a metal ring to give it weight. When it was thrown at a target, the end was sharp. Frequently, when accuracy was being practiced, the javelin was thrown from horseback at a target.

In the beginning the missile was provided with a leather strap, 12 to 18 inches long, known as a thong. This aid was bound around the shaft near the center of weight so that a loop was provided for the first and second fingers. The javelin was carried over the shoulder between the thumb and first finger. It was delivered by a terrific whip of the right arm, the force being applied to it through the leather strap. As the javelin left the hand, it not only was propelled forward with great force but it also was sent whirling through the air as a result of the unwinding of the leather strap. The forward propulsion and its whirling motion made it a deadly weapon.

The revival of javelin throwing at the Olympic games in 1906, when E. Lemming of Sweden threw the missle 175 feet 6 inches, was responsible for the introduction of this event in America. Javelin throwing first appeared on the National Amateur Athletic Union program in 1909, when Ralph Rose of the San Francisco Athletic Club won the championship with a throw of 141 feet $7/10$ inches.

At Oslo in 1964, T. Pedersen of Norway delivered a throw of 300 feet 11 inches that was officially recognized by the International Amateur Athletic Federation.

GENERAL CONSIDERATIONS

Comparative marks in competition. Since the javelin thrower is obliged to know the distance of the throws required to place at the various levels of scholastic competition, an estimation of such distances is given in Table 14-1. Attention is directed to the fact that the distances listed are placing, not winning, measurements. Because these distances represent either the average or the median performances, they will not apply to those areas where the quality of the javelin

Table 14-1. Comparative marks in scholastic competition for the javelin throw

Meet	No. of places scored	Distance
Dual high school	3	150–175 ft.
Qualifying—state	3	160–180 ft.
State—province	5	170–210 ft.

throwers is either very high or very low. The athlete is advised to become familiar with the caliber of the javelin throwers against whom he may compete at a later date.

Types of competitors and qualifications. Champion javelin throwers are found among all types of men—the slender, wiry, long-muscled individual, the short, stocky, well-muscled man, and the large, powerful type of competitor. All things being equal, the large, strong man has an advantage.

Although authorities differ on the importance of strength, we believe it to be an important asset to the javelin thrower. Since the javelin weighs less than 2 pounds, the weight of the competitor is not so important as in putting the shot and in throwing the discus.

For any type of competitor, coordination of movement is one of the most outstanding characteristics that contributes to success in casting the spear. In fact, many good javelin throwers have been skilled gymnastic performers.

Speed is of some import, but the ability to transfer speed into force against the javelin is far more important.

Equipment. The chief item in the equipment of the javelin thrower which needs special attention is the javelin itself. The international rules prescribe that the spear shall be of wood with a metal point. It must be constructed so that the space between the foremost point and the center of gravity is no greater than 110 centimeters (3.069 feet) or less than 90 centimeters (2.953 feet). A whipcord binding, 16 centimeters (6.3 inches) broad, around the center of gravity is required. No other throwing aid is permitted. The circumference at either edge of the binding must not exceed the circumference of the shaft by more than 25 millimeters (0.984 inches). The overall length of the shaft as thrown must be not less than 260 centimeters (8.53 feet) and its weight not less than 800 grams (1.765 pounds). (For diagrams of the javelin throwing lane and the restraining arc, see both the rule book and Fig. 17-1 in this book.)

The center of gravity of the javelin is very important to the competitor. Bud Held, a student of javelin construction, believes that the metal point of the javelin should be short. Furthermore, he contends that the center of gravity should be established at a spot on the javelin that lies very close to the limit permitted by the rules, which is 110 cm. (43.31 inches) from the sharpened extremity of the metal point.

The Amateur Athletic Union of the United States of America amended certain rules for the javelin throw to take effect in 1955. It stipulated that the shaft of the javelin should be either of metal or solid wood, "circular in section throughout." Therefore, the hollow wood javelin is not considered a legal instrument. Wind will no longer nullify a claim for a record throw of the javelin.

It should be added that a javelin of reduced size and weight is legal for use by women. A junior javelin has also been adopted for grade school competition.

Javelins are made of hickory, second-growth ash, or birch. It is of interest to note that manufacturers in Finland, Sweden, and Germany utilize birch. The objective is to produce a spear that is moderately rigid so as to maintain its shape at all times. If the shaft is too rigid, it may break when it hits the ground. If it is too limber or crooked, it will develop a tail spin which offers resistance to the wind and detracts from the distance of the throw.

The adjustment of the whipcord binding, either forward or backward on the shaft, moves the point of balance. It should be noted that the rules permit a whipcord adjustment of 20 centimeters, approximately 8 inches. Some competitors prefer a center of balance at a position farthest from the metal point, whereas others prefer it centered in the whipcord. Perhaps the majority prefer the center of gravity at a place in the whipcord as close to the metal point as the rules permit.

In selecting the javelin, a competitor should look for one with the following characteristics:

1. Straight shaft.
2. Clear, straight grain.
3. Correct degree of resiliency—neither too stiff nor too limber.
4. Size—a javelin of diameter that fits the hand. Some prefer the thick shaft and some the slender shaft.
5. Proper balance—one with the center of weight so placed that it will meet the desire of the competitor.
6. Type of point—provisions should be made so that the wood shaft may sway slightly once the point has been fixed in the ground at the end of the throw. An absolutely rigid union of the wood shaft and the metal point frequently causes the shaft to break at the junction. Cushioning devices of cord or rubber bands have been employed to keep the point firmly in place and to offer protection against breakage.
7. Specifications—the javelin must meet the rules requirements.

Experts on wood claim that the wooden javelin should be stored in a cool and moderately dry room. It should be suspended from the point. This is readily accomplished by slipping over the point of the javelin a leather washer about the size of a dollar with a $\frac{1}{2}$-inch hole in the center. It is then suspended from a rack provided with notches 2 inches deep and 1 inch wide.

Field event shoes are commonly a part of the equipment of the javelin thrower. Some athletes prefer those that lace moderately high; therefore, for dry weather they wear either a weight thrower's or a baseball player's shoe and for wet weather a football player's shoe.

TECHNIQUE OF THE JAVELIN THROW

Grasping the javelin. The type of handhold that an individual selects depends on the length and strength of his fingers, the size of the javelin shaft, and personal choice. Two ways of holding the javelin are shown in Fig. 14-1. The type shown in *A*, called the Finnish hold, consists of grasping the javelin at the rear of the binding so that the second finger encircles the shaft and barely touches the extended thumb. The first finger is approximately in line with the wrist and curls slightly around the shaft. The Finnish grasp finds ready acceptance among throwers since the shaft lies in the natural cradle of the palm of the hand, thus giving a feeling of security. The pull is exerted mainly by the second finger, which rests on the wood shaft and against the back of the binding.

In the hold shown in Fig. 14-1, *B*, called the American grasp, the spear is held with 3 fingers encircling the whipcord and the thumb resting lightly along the shaft. The chief difference between this type and the hold shown in Fig. 14-1, *A*, lies in the fact that the pull is exerted by the first finger. In the hold shown in Fig. 14-1, *B*, the javelin is held at a greater angle to the forearm.

In both grasps the amount of finger tension is essentially the same in that there is only a moderate degree of tension at the initial stance and during the approach but a high degree of tension at the start of the

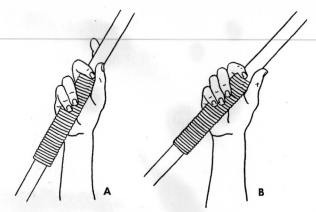

Fig. 14-1. Types of handhold for the javelin throw. **A,** Finnish grasp. **B,** American grasp.

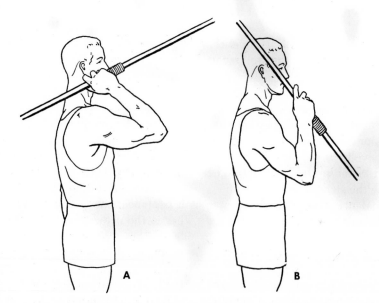

Fig. 14-2. Types of javelin carry. **A,** Overshoulder carry, point up. **B,** Front carry, point down.

delivery. There are, no doubt, deviations from these basic types of grasp which prove successful.

Carrying the javelin. Two methods of carrying the javelin during the approach are shown in Fig. 14-2.

The type of carry selected by a competitor depends on the ease with which he can fit it into the run, the drawing back of the arm, and the delivery. Usually the carry shown in Fig. 14-2, *B*, is associated with the Finnish form of throw and that shown in Fig. 14-2, *A*, is usually employed in the hop-step style.

Finnish form of throw. The outstanding success of javelin throwers from Finland has attracted the attention of all the world to the Finnish form. For the sake of clarity

Right-hand thrower

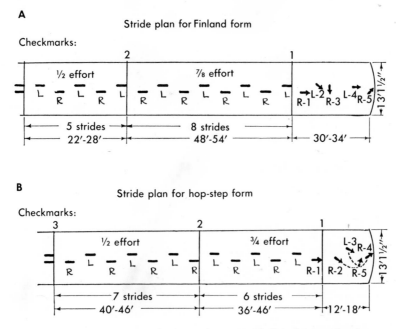

Fig. 14-3. Two commonly accepted plans of approach for the javelin throw.

in presenting this style, an action series for form, together with a stride plan of approach, is included.

Approach. The approach for the javelin throw is marked by two parallel lines 4 meters (13 feet 1½ inches) apart, and the throw is made from behind an arc of a circle drawn with a radius of 8 meters (26 feet 3 inches). Such an arc consists of a board made of wood or metal 7 centimeters (2¾ inches) in width, painted white and sunk flush with the ground. The javelin must be held at the grip (see diagram in rule book). The plan of approach is shown in Fig. 14-3, *A*. The competitor grasps the javelin as shown in Fig. 14-1, *A*, and assumes a front carry, point down, as illustrated in Fig. 14-2, *B*.

The run is started from a spot that is located a distance of 100 to 110 feet from the scratch line (arc). This spot is designated as checkmark 3. Checkmark 2 is set 5 strides toward the scratch line

(arc). Checkmark 1 is then set 8 strides from checkmark 2. The distance from checkmark 1 to the scratch line (arc) should receive the greatest attention because the delivery is completed during 4 of the last 5 strides. The fifth stride is the recovery step.

During the approach, the competitor strikes the checkmarks in the order of 3, 2, and 1, but in locating them the order is 1, 2, and 3. Detailed methods of adjusting checkmarks and standardizing strides have been discussed in detail in the chapters dealing with the pole vault and the long jump.

It should be noted that between checkmarks 3 and 2, which is the first section of the run, the athlete exerts only ½ effort. Between checkmarks 2 and 1 he gradually accelerates, so that by the time he reaches checkmark 1 he is running at ⅞ effort.

During the approach the javelin is carried to the front (Fig. 14-4, *A*). The thrower does not hold it in a stationary manner but moves it up and down, synchronizing the right arm action with the left leg action. Neither the body nor the hand grasp is extremely tense during the approach.

Delivery, release, and recovery. As the foot strikes checkmark 1, the competitor begins preparing for the throw. The movements involved are described first according to the foot position and then on the basis of the carriage of the javelin. Refer

to the actions portrayed in Figs. 14-3 and 14-4.

As described by Runar Ohls,[1] the Finnish competitors count 1, 2, 3, 4, and 5 for the five steps involved in the delivery and the recovery. The count is either silent or audible. At the count of 1 the right foot strikes the ground in the direction of the javelin restraining arc. At count 2 the left foot, pointed to the right, strikes the ground. At count 3 the right foot is swung

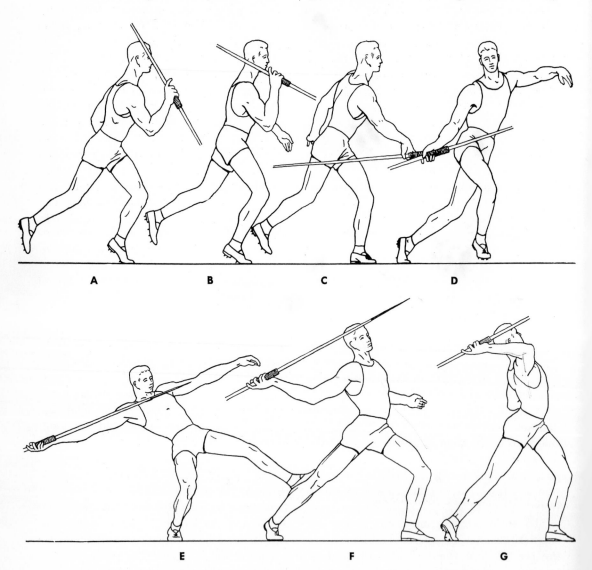

Fig. 14-4, A-J. A series of acceptable form for the Finnish style of javelin throw.

around and lands with the toe of the shoe pointed to the right. At count 4 an extremely long stride is taken, and the left foot lands in the direction of the throw. The throw is executed as shown in Fig. 14-4, G and H.

At the moment the right foot touches the ground on the step preceding the throw, the torso is inclined backward 35 to 40 degrees, and the center of body weight (at the level of the belt) is traveling forward at a rate of 15 to 25 feet per second. When the feet stop momentarily on the ground, the center of body weight continues forward, forcing the upper portion of the body to double (approximately) its forward momentum, thus materially aiding the whipping of the javelin arm forward. The positions of the feet during the throw and immediately after the javelin leaves the hand are shown in Fig. 14-4, H and I. At the count 5 the thrower brings the right foot close to the restraining arc for the purpose of halting body momentum (Fig. 14-3, A, R_5, and Fig. 14-4, J). In order to secure balance, the athlete may hop on the right foot simultaneously with an extension of the left leg to the side and the rear.

At the count 1 the javelin point is tilted upward. At count 2 the throwing arm is straightened and thrust forward, while the javelin is lowered and is approximately parallel to the ground. At this phase of the throw the javelin apparently stays in place while the torso catches up with and passes it as shown in Fig. 14-4, D. At the count 3 the throwing arm is drawn back completely, and at count 4 the initiation of the throw occurs. It should be noted in Fig. 14-4, G, that the elbow leads the hand. For those athletes whose form we analyzed, the javelin at the end of the release formed an angle with the ground that ranged from 35 to 40 degrees. Attention is called to the fact that some authorities recommend an angle of release that ranges from 46 to 50 degrees. Possibly the difference may be accounted for by the techniques of measurement. Furthermore, there are coaches who analyze the angle at which the javelin

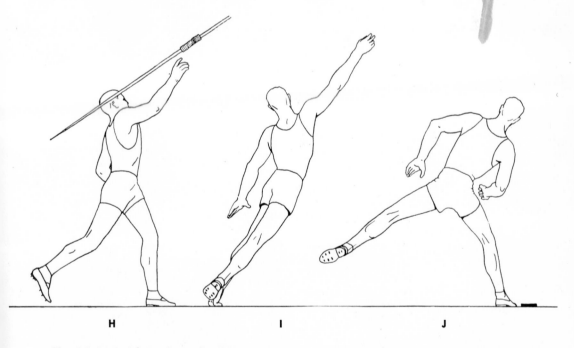

H   I   J

Fig. 14-4 cont'd. For legend see opposite page.

strikes the ground. They recommend that their athletes either increase or decrease the release angle, depending on the variance from the acceptable landing angle which they believe to be 45 degrees. The javelin thrower is advised to experiment and determine the angle of release that is most effective for him. The arm position immediately preceding and at the instant of the release is shown in Fig. 14-4, *G* and *H*. The javelin is released slightly above and in front of the right shoulder. In the recovery, the use of the arms in maintaining balance is an individual characteristic (Fig. 14-4, *J*).

Hop-step form of throw. The hop-step

Fig. 14-5, A-E. A series of acceptable form for the hop-step style of javelin throw.

form of throw has been utilized in numerous meets by high school and college performers. A series of form and a diagram of approach are presented.

Approach. A stride plan for the run in the hop-step style is shown in Fig. 14-3, *B*. The athlete grasps the javelin in a manner of his own selection, usually as shown in Fig. 14-1, *B*. He assumes either the over-shoulder carry (Fig. 14-2, *A*) or the front carry (Fig. 14-2, *B*).

The thrower begins his run at a distance ranging from 80 to 120 feet from the restraining arc. This point is designated as checkmark 3. From this point a 7-stride run is executed at ½ effort, the end of the seventh stride being marked as checkmark 2. From the checkmark 2 the speed is increased so that at the end of 6 additional strides ¾ of the best effort is being exerted. The end of the thirteenth running stride (6 strides from checkmark 2) is marked as checkmark 1. The distance from checkmark 1 to the restraining arc varies from 12 to 15 feet. It is during the third segment of the run that the all-important hop, gather, and throw are made. The position of the javelin during the approach is shown in Fig. 14-5, *A*. Here, as in all types of carry, the javelin need not be held rigidly. In the over-shoulder carry the javelin position tends to restrict the arm in aiding the run. During the run, only natural body tension is maintained, but the spear is grasped firmly at the instant of the first application of throwing force.

Delivery, release, and recovery. As the toe of the right shoe strikes checkmark 1, a hop, coupled with a quarter body turn, is executed (Fig. 14-5, *B*). The foot spread as shown in Fig. 14-5, *C* and *D*, is moderately wide. The position of the right foot at the end of the hop is depicted in Fig. 14-3, *B*, R_2, and the left foot is planted in a position as illustrated in Fig. 14-3, *B*, L_3, and Fig. 14-5, *C*. From this position the throw is made, utilizing the same style of body whip as that described for the Fin-

nish form. The footwork at the instant of release consists of swinging the right leg swiftly forward so that the right foot lands close to the restraining arc. The sudden planting of the right foot well forward serves as a brake to prevent fouling (Fig. 14-5, *E*). The right foot should be set as close to the restraining arc as possible, yet sufficient room should be allowed to permit the left foot (during the recovery) to touch the ground in fair territory (Fig. 14-3, *B*, R_4). Balance is gained by a backward swing of the left leg after the right foot has been planted close to the restraining arc (Fig. 14-5, *E*).

At the start of the hop, the initiation of the draw back of the throwing arm causes a quarter body turn (Fig. 14-5, *B*). As soon as the right foot is planted, the throwing arm is drawn well back (Fig. 14-5, *B* and *C*). Now, the weight is resting chiefly on the right foot but is transferred to the left foot as the javelin is carried forward (Fig. 14-5, *D*). The right elbow precedes the hand in its forward progress. The left arm is carried sharply backward. Good form in all styles of javelin throwing calls for a delivery in which the javelin path is close to the head. The action is an over-shoulder whip as contrasted to a sidearm swing. The release occurs just above and slightly in front of the right shoulder. As the javelin is released from the hand, it forms an angle with the ground ranging from 35 to 40 degrees.

The arm action in the recovery is solely for the purpose of gaining balance and depends on the method of foot action employed.

COMPARISON OF STYLES OF THROW

New developments are constantly being made in form so that the athlete may expect changes in javelin throwing. Many champions favor the hand grasp shown in Fig. 14-3, *A*, on the theory that the second finger provides more strength than the first.

In addition, this hold permits placing the javelin in the natural groove or cradle of the hand and gives the athlete a feeling of firmness of grasp.

The first finger, curved lightly around the shaft in the grasp shown in Fig. 14-3, B, provides lateral support during the overarm whip. There are athletes who claim that a clockwise spin, or rifling, of the javelin is imparted by a pull of the first finger at the instant of release. Other competitors believe that a premeditated attempt to spin the javelin may result in too much downward pull on the missile at the expense of forward propulsion. The type of hand grasp which a given thrower selects should be one that fits his type of carry and one that produces the greatest distance.

The chief consideration of the thrower in choosing the style of carry is the selection of one that will best permit him to cock the arm for the delivery and at the same time allow him to generate speed in the run. Those spearcasters using the front carry feel relieved of the responsibility of thinking about the javelin during the run. In addition, the pumping action of the right arm synchronizes with the left leg (as in the sprint) to a greater degree than in the other type.

The hop-step form of delivering the javelin comes quite natural to many throwers. Possibly it provides for ample potential throwing force once the competitor is set for the delivery, but there is bound to be an abrupt checking of running speed caused by the execution of the hop (Fig. 14-5, B). The sideward turn of the body may allow the use of the trunk-rotating muscles to provide force, but the turn frequently is accomplished with an ineffective utilization of force from the muscles that bend the trunk forward.

Because of its greater possibilities for transferring running speed to throwing momentum, the advantage seems to rest with the Finnish form. The javelin movement is synchronized with the footwork during the delivery to better advantage in the Finnish form than in the hop-step form discussed. The large muscles that flex the trunk function more readily in this form because the body is carried more nearly to the front. This technique of squaring off in the direction of the throw serves to prevent arm injury, because by promoting the overarm whip, the tendency toward the perilous side arm release is diminished. In addition, the overarm method prevents the loss of time (used in rotation) in getting the arm motion added to the body whip.

Because of the reasons previously cited and the proof given by championship records, many competent authorities favor the Finnish form of throwing the javelin.

COMMON ERRORS IN THE JAVELIN THROW

In the discussion of the techniques of javelin throwing, an attempt was made to present effective methods. It should be obvious to the beginner that any radical departure from the accepted forms will quite likely detract from the throw. There are, however, some errors which in our experience are encountered frequently.

In the handhold and carriage. In brief, any grasp of the javelin that fails to provide a firm hold at the instant of delivery and any carry that inhibits moderate speed in the approach or offers impediments to the draw back of the throwing arm obviously is bad form.

In the approach. Disproportionate amounts of speed during the various sections of the run are contributing factors to a poor throw. The beginner must bear in mind that varying rates of speed are recommended for different forms. This means that the speed generated should fit the form that the athlete adopts.

If the speed in the approach is too slow, force is detracted from the release. If the speed is too great, the thrower has insufficient time for blending the lift action of the legs with the forward movement of the trunk and arm.

It should be apparent to the beginner that if the checkmarks are too close to the restraining arc he will foul, and conversely, if the checkmarks are too far back, the distance from the point of recovery to the restraining arc is lost.

In the delivery, release, and recovery. Regardless of the style of delivery, there are mistakes that are common to all forms. Some of them are as follows:

1. An improper amount of hand tension when starting the delivery.
2. Unduly pausing when fusing the run into the delivery.
3. An arm draw back in which the javelin is out of alignment.
4. An incomplete arm draw back.
5. Delivering with a side arm swing rather than with an over-shoulder whip.
6. Imbalance during the delivery.
7. Releasing at an angle which is too high or too low.
8. Releasing before the full body force is applied to the spear.
9. Taking a short stride when getting set for the delivery.
10. Failing to have the right elbow lead the hand. This precaution helps to avoid injury to the throwing arm.
11. Failing to make use of the right hip thrust coupled with an instantaneous straightening of the right leg.

DAILY SCHEDULES OF PRACTICE

The schedules of practice for each day may be modified to meet either conditions of weather or special form requirements of the individual. An attempt is made to avoid needless repetition but at the same time to provide specific recommendations for the development of the javelin thrower.

It must be remembered that the javelin throw is one event requiring a minimum of trials at full effort because of the peculiar stress on the elbow. The utmost caution is recommended so that painful arm injuries may be prevented. Unusual care in the duration and type of warm-up as well as in the protection of the throwing arm between trials is urged. Just as on a hot day some baseball pitchers wear long woolen sleeves, so likewise do some javelin throwers. This practice is recommended especially on cold days.

The preliminary season conditioning of the javelin thrower has been discussed in an earlier chapter. In conformity with the plan for other events, weekly schedules are suggested for early season, midseason, and late season and may include progressive resistance exercises.

Early season. The following schedules of practice for early season are based on the assumption that no contest is planned for either Friday or Saturday. Therefore, after the preliminary season activities (see pp. 7 and 12) have been concluded, the javelin thrower should begin immediately a routine calling for 6 days of practice.

Monday

1. Begin the practice by jogging 250 yards, hopping and bounding 25 yards, and sprinting 25 yards.
2. Spend 5 to 10 minutes on exercises designed to develop the large muscle groups. Include push-ups from the front leaning rest position, half squats, trunk twists, handstands, handsprings, tumbling, and wood-chopping exercise. The latter feat is performed by jumping to a stride stand, clasping the hands with the arms fully extended above the head, and then vigorously swinging the arms downward while bending the body at the hips. The arms should be swung to the left, to the right, or between the legs with an abundance of energy.
3. Experiment with the various types depicted for grasping the javelin (Fig. 14-1).
4. From a standing position, deliver the

javelin 6 or 7 times into the vaulting or jumping landing areas from a distance of 15 feet. Your chief objective is to see that the throwing arm is well extended to the rear (not locked, however) and that the javelin point and tip when delivered are in a plane at a right angle to the javelin scratch line. The angle of elevation at the time of the release is ignored. A more desirable exercise which permits delivery at the correct angle consists of throwing into stacked bales of straw.

5. Assume the position of the javelin thrower but substitute for the spear a bag of sand weighing 2 or 3 pounds. Run through and deliver in the usual manner. This exercise develops strong throwing muscles.

6. Increase gradually the force applied to 8 or 9 jabs into the ground from a distance of 20 feet and add the following three items of form: (a) Keep the javelin joint close to the head and above the shoulder, (b) make an effort to have the right elbow lead the right hand as it passes the right shoulder, and (c) attempt to develop the wrist snap. By employing these actions, the thrower avoids a rotary or side arm movement. The possibility of elbow injury is appreciably reduced when the elbow leads the forearm. In addition, this procedure invites cooperative effort from the flexor muscles of the trunk. The novice will bear in mind that javelin throwing is an activity requiring infinitely more than mere arm action. A baseball pitcher depending on the arm alone cannot hope for success. He knows that the legs and the trunk must coordinate to produce effective pitching. For similar reasons the trunk and legs must become a part of successful javelin throwing form.

7. Jab the javelin 15 to 20 times into the ground from a distance of 25 feet, drilling particularly on a smooth release.

8. Engage in supervised weight-training and/or tension exercises for a period of 15 to 30 minutes. For an explanation of these exercises, see pp. 8 and 11.

Tuesday

1. Warm up effectively by whirling the arms vigorously, jogging 150 yards, walking 25 yards, and running 50 yards.

2. Jab the javelin 7 or 8 times into soft ground at a spot 25 feet distant. Note the change of tension of the grasp on the shaft during the period of delivery.

3. Spend 5 to 10 minutes on the approach and checkmark adjustments.

4. Deliver the javelin a distance of 40 to 50 feet, making a special effort to have the right hip lead the right arm at the onset of the delivery. Repeat 6 or 7 times.

5. Verify your checkmark adjustments by running through and releasing the javelin with about ½ your full effort. Make sure that you are perfecting the following:

   a. The full rear extension of the throwing arm.

   b. The straight forward alignment of the point of the spear during delivery.

   c. The javelin is brought forward, close to the head and directly above the shoulder.

   d. The right elbow comes forward in advance of the right hand (grasping the spear).

   e. The right hip is thrust forward and upward to initiate the propulsion of force from the legs and trunk in advance of the throwing arm.

   Since the above schedule calls for throwing at only ½ effort, the beginner may repeat 8 or 9 times.

6. Jog 250 yards, followed by a 10-yard sprint, thus ending the day's practice.

Wednesday

1. Limber up with jogging, walking, and sprinting. Experiment with the warm-up, so as to find one that best meets your personal requirements.
2. Perform 5 minutes of stretching exercises.
3. Join the sprinters and sprint 35 yards at top speed.
4. Jab the spear into soft ground 15 to 20 times, starting easily and gradually increasing the force applied. Stress the application of the laws of body mechanics on each trial.
5. Run through the approach (carrying the javelin) with the idea of adjusting speed between checkmarks. Repeat 6 or 7 times.
6. Release the javelin with about $\frac{2}{3}$ your best effort, making use of the knowledge gained in practice on the approach. Repeat 8 or 9 times.
7. Spend 15 to 30 minutes on weight-training and/or tension exercises.

Thursday

1. Jog 200 yards, walk 50 yards, and run 100 yards.
2. Join the high jumpers and take 5 or 6 trials at gradually increasing heights.
3. Prepare the arm for throwing by swinging it in a circle and jabbing the javelin into the ground without the run. The previous warm-up experience of the novice should guide him in the number of trials required and the amount of force applied to each succeeding trial. Usually 10 to 15 trials are sufficient.
4. Run through for checkmark adjustment 4 or 5 times, releasing the javelin with a minimum of effort. The objective is confined temporarily to speed and accuracy of the run rather than to the delivery of the spear.

5. Throw the javelin 6 or 7 times with the run, but deliver it at about $\frac{3}{4}$ your best effort. Concentrate on gaining force from the right leg. An observer or coach will be able to tell whether you are getting a proper extension of the body at an instant just before the release (Fig. 14-4, *G*). Action photographs of champions show a straight line from the toe of the right shoe through the right knee, right hip, right shoulder, and right elbow immediately after the release (Fig. 14-4, *I*).
6. Cease throwing just as soon as arm fatigue appears. When the arm begins to feel dead or begins to lose snap, substitute an activity other than throwing. Injuries occur more frequently after the onset of fatigue. When the thrower is tired, he tends to become careless in adjusting his throwing stance. Maladjustment of body mechanics in throwing leads to improper stress on the throwing arm, thus increasing the hazard of elbow strain.
7. End the day's routine with a jog of 200 yards and a sprint of 25 yards.

Friday

1. Begin with a jog of 150 yards, a walk of 25 yards, a run of 25 yards, and a sprint of 25 yards.
2. Refrain from hard throwing today because you are scheduled to throw Saturday (tomorrow) at $\frac{7}{8}$ your best effort.
3. Join the long jumpers and take 3 trials of the standing long jump and 3 trials of the long jump.
4. Verify the approach and checkmark adjustments by running through 5 or 6 times while carrying the javelin. You may release the javelin easily at the end of the run since it is difficult to execute the delivery strides without actually throwing.

5. Finish the day's practice with a jog of 300 yards.

Saturday

1. Initiate the practice with a jog of 200 yards, a walk of 50 yards, a run of 50 yards, and a sprint of 50 yards.
2. Analyze the length of time you require in the various phases of the warm-up as well as the amount of energy put into each phase. Execute 5 to 10 minutes of exercises, including arm swinging, trunk twisting, trunk bending, and bounding.
3. Jab the javelin into a landing area from a position 25 feet distant, taking one step with the left foot while delivering. Exert only a small amount of effort at the beginning and make each successive jab more vigorous until the last jab approximates the the amount of force applied to your best throws with the run. Draw your own conclusions as to the amount of jabbing required, since you will have to rely on this storehouse of experience at a later date. In early season, if the weather is cool, 15 to 20 trials of jabbing may be necessary. A woolen stocking pulled on the throwing arm and pinned to the shoulder loop of the jersey has proved effective as an aid in the warm-up and a protection from cool winds.
4. Run through the approach at a predetermined rate of speed (one that meets your personal needs) and at the same time have an observer note whether you strike the checkmarks correctly. Repeat twice.
5. Throw the javelin at ½ effort, then ⅔ effort, and then ¾ effort so that you are gradually increasing the vigor applied in preparation for harder throwing. A total of 6 to 8 trials should suffice.
6. Throw the javelin not to exceed 4 times at ⅞ your best effort. Your ob-

jective should be the improvement of your form during the approach and the futherance of coordination during the delivery strides and the final release. Master the niceties of form at this stage of your training. Increased distance will follow in due course.

7. Conclude this day's practice with 3 minutes of vigorous calisthenics, a sprint of 100 yards, and a jog of 150 yards. Analyze your weight chart for the week.

Midseason. Customarily, competition is held at least once each week during midseason. Practice activities are suggested for 4 days, semirest for 1 day, and competition for 1 day. Provided the athlete has demonstrated adequate skills in other track and field events, he may be called upon to provide supplemental point scoring for his team by competing in additional events.

Monday

1. Begin with a jog of 250 yards, a walk of 50 yards, a run of 25 yards, and a sprint of 25 yards.
2. Execute 5 to 10 minutes of gymnastic feats such as trunk bends, trunk twists, handstands, handsprings, the wood-chopping exercise, and tumbling.
3. Begin with easy jabbing into the ground at a spot 20 feet away and gradually increase the force applied with each succeeding trial. A total of 15 to 20 trials is indicated.
4. Run through the approach 3 times to verify the speed of the run, the accuracy of the checkmarks, and the timing of the delivery. Release the javelin but apply only ½ your best throwing effort. An observer or your coach will note whether or not the actions in the javelin carriage coordinate with the leg movements. In practice, vary the type of footing in the approach so that you will become ac-

customed to a runway of long turf, short turf, firm cinders, loose cinders, loam, or all-weather surface.

5. Throw the javelin 6 or 7 times using the running approach but exert only ½ effort on the early throws. Gradually increase their intensity to ¾ your greatest effort. An observer or your coach will report on the path of the javelin during the delivery, especially noticing the angle formed by the javelin and the ground at the instant of release. Furthermore, the thrower should keep in mind the part played by the legs and the trunk during the final effort. Since Tuesday's practice will include a few throws at $\frac{9}{10}$ effort, Monday's work should not be strenuous.

6. Complete the day's practice with 15 to 30 minutes of weight-training exercises, provided you have found them to be beneficial.

Tuesday

1. Warm up as you would on the day of competition. In case your past experience is insufficient to guide you, the following exercises are suggested in preparation for a day of vigorous throwing
   a. Jog 250 yards, walk 50 yards, and run 100 yards at gradually increasing speed.
   b. Spend 5 to 8 minutes on varied exercises, including moderate stretching, bending, trunk twisting, leg swinging, and arm swinging.
   c. Stand 20 feet from a landing area and jab the javelin into it 10 to 15 times. The feet are not together when the delivery is made since one forward stride is taken with the left foot. Try to achieve good form in your jabbing practice. This means to duplicate the arm, the trunk, and the leg action and to maintain the same javelin path

that you would when throwing for distance.
   d. Remove with a towel any excess body perspiration which has been induced by exercising in a training suit. This prevents a rapid cooling of those parts of the body exposed to the wind, especially the throwing arm.
   e. Run through the approach to assure yourself of the correct placement of your checkmarks and the proper amount of speed between them. Repeat twice while carrying the javelin, but without throwing.
   f. Throw the javelin at ⅔ effort, using the recommended plan of running approach. Repeat twice. The competitor should feel out the timing of the footwork with the action of the throwing arm. He should get the sensation of an effective delivery stance conforming to the laws of body mechanics and a release that includes the summation of forces developed by legs, trunk, and arm.
   g. Throw the javelin 2 or 3 times at ¾ effort, using the running approach. These exercises should produce a feeling of body warmth and relaxation so that the athlete is in readiness to add force to his throws.

2. Throw the javelin for distance, applying slightly less than full effort. Repeat 3 or 4 times. The coach or observers assigned to specific activities will report on the accuracy and speed of your run, the timing of your delivery strides, the backward extension of the throwing arm, the path of the throwing elbow, the leading action of the right hip, the height at which the spear is released, and its angle of trajectory. Bear in mind, do not throw with maximum vigor today; $\frac{9}{10}$ effort is sufficient. Champion javelin throw-

ers report that their longest throws seemingly are achieved with little effort. This statement bears out the contention that a throw which coordinates properly the sources of force will be devoid of shock, yet most effective. Compare the distances made in each trial and draw your own conclusions regarding the amount and intensity of the warm-up performed that day.

3. Throw the javelin 4 or 5 times at ⅞ effort, measuring the distance. Experiment with various angles of the javelin at the instant of release. Note the most effective angle when throwing into a head wind, a wind quartering from the right, a wind quartering from the left, or a wind at the back.

4. This completes the most strenuous throwing of any day during a week in midseason whenever competition is scheduled for Saturday. It is pointed out, however, that there are some successful javelin throwers who vary this plan by throwing moderately hard on both Monday and Wednesday and lightly on Tuesday and Thursday.

5. End the day's schedule by jogging 150 yards, walking 50 yards, and sprinting 100 yards.

Wednesday

1. Limber up with a jog of 250 yards.
2. Join the sprinters and after a thorough warm-up take 2 starts of 35 yards. Speed is definitely a factor in the javelin throw, especially in the Finnish style.
3. Take 6 or 7 trials in the running high jump at gradually increasing heights, taking off alternately from the left foot and then the right foot. Note the amount of leg drive exerted in the javelin throw (Fig. 14-4, E and F).

4. Expose the body to the sun for 10 minutes.

5. Jab the javelin into the ground 8 to 12 times, increasing the effort with each succeeding throw. Vigorous jabs without the run may be executed without fear of arm injury, because the thrower usually has correct balance at the instant of release. The addition of the run presents a hazard to perfect poise at the onset of the delivery. It has been stated previously that imbalance of the body at the instant of starting the throw results in an incorrect stress on the arm, frequently causing strain.

6. Deliver the javelin at ¾ effort, experimenting with various rates of speed during the approach. Again note the amount of force supplied by the muscles of the trunk.

7. Engage in weight-training exercises. Either increase or reduce the intensity of these exercises depending on their effect on your javelin-throwing performances.

Thursday

1. Begin by jogging 220 yards, hopping and bounding 25 yards, running 50 yards, and sprinting 35 yards.

2. Prepare for the long jump by adjusting checkmarks and take 2 or 3 jumps for distance. Latent ability in this event may be uncovered. Frequently, javelin throwers are proficient jumpers. Both the high jump and the long jump combine well with javelin throwing.

3. Experiment with javelins that balance at varying points. Some throwers prefer the center of gravity at a point in the grip farthest from the metal tip. Others select shafts whose balance is midway of the corded grip, and still others will give first choice to the spear that balances at a point in the corded part well to-

ward the metal tip. Release the javelin 4 or 5 times, applying approximately ½ your best effort.

4. Become accustomed to the feel of a substitute or a reserve javelin. Champion throwers familiarize themselves with 2 or more spears, labeling them in the order of first, second, and third choice. In competition such as the Olympic games the athlete may use only those implements provided by the games committee. Therefore, the smart athlete will know how to select his implement and how to test it quickly and will be in readiness when called on to compete. Although a javelin thrower should take pride in and give care to his shafts, he should not become so wedded to one particular spear that its loss would shock him to the degree of lowering his morale. Throw 5 or 6 times at ⅔ effort, testing out 2 or more javelins.

5. Vary the practice by participating in a contest such as medicine ball passing, walking on the hands, sprint relay (50 yards each), or the standing long jump.

6. Conclude the day's schedule by running 200 yards, negotiating the last 30 yards at 9/10 sprinting effort.

Friday

1. Check your implements to make certain that they conform to the specifications found in the rule book. Of greatest importance is the minimum weight (800 grams) and the minimum length (260 centimeters). Good competitors upon presenting their javelins at the implement inspection booth have been surprised to see their shafts rejected because of underweight or underlength. Force continually applied to the point when striking the ground frequently jams the metal tip farther onto the wooden shaft, thus reducing the overall meas-

urement. A javelin once weighing 800 grams may weight less at a later date for a number of reasons, chiefly, the evaporation of moisture in the wood. Become a handy man to the extent of being able to remedy such imperfections. Underweight in the javelin may be corrected by removing the metal point, inserting bird shot or lead foil of the required amount, and replacing the metal point accurately.

2. Study the conditions under which you will compete on Saturday. Note the composition of the approach and the direction and velocity of the prevailing winds.

3. Do no javelin throwing today.

4. Follow the advice of your coach on the matter of Friday's routine. Some coaches prefer that their athletes dress in competition suit and limber up lightly. Others recommend complete absence from the practice field.

Saturday

Since Saturday is competition day, adjust your program, including meals and rest so that your efficiency is at its highest point. Conserve both physical and nervous energy but otherwise carry on the usual daily routine.

1. Present the implements to the official responsible for their inspection.

2. Warm up according to a plan which, in the light of past experience, has proved the most effective.

3. Begin the arm exercises with easy jabbing, then firm jabbing, and then forceful jabbing, repeating several times.

4. Throw the javelin (with a full run) at ½ effort, then ⅔ effort, and finally ⅞ effort. Repeat until you feel in readiness for vigorous action.

5. Set an objective in distance and, with your thought on executing a smoothly

coordinated delivery, unleash your supreme effort.

6. Protect the arm between throws. In case your throw was creditable, indicating a proper warm-up, omit intense practicing during intervals between your official trials. In case you find that your warm-up was insufficient, you may increase safely the intensity of a few more practice throws. Select an observer to note your sequence of movements from the initial stance to the recovery stride. Should you lead the field in the first round, figure out how you can improve. Should you trail the field in the first round, constructively map out a plan that will place you among the leaders in the second round. Concentrate on the early throws. A survey of officials' scoring charts for the javel throw reveals that the winning effort was made on the second trial more frequently than on any other of the 4 preliminary and 3 final trials. Next in the frequency distribution came the first trial, and next in prevalence came the third trial.

7. Regardless of the fact that one is permitted a specified number of preliminary and final throws, he need not avail himself of this privilege. Since he is credited solely with the one best effort, there are times when good judgment calls for no more than 3 or 4 throws applying maximum effort. True enough, javelin contests have been won dramatically on the last throw in the final round. However, such achievements are the exception, and it is strongly recommended that the athlete set himself mentally and physically to deliver the spear the maximum distance in the early trials. Furthermore, injuries are less prevalent when the arm and trunk muscles are not fatigued. The thrower is more susceptible to injury during the later trials than during the first, second, and third trials. These precautionary measures should not cause the athlete to become javelin-shy or induce a phobia that he is a "brittle bone." To the contrary, by intelligent conservation of energy and by precision in body mechanics, he can assume his initial stance fearlessly, speed down the approach, and forcefully whip out the spear with all the force at his command.

Late season. In this season the calendar calls for the most important contests of the track and field year. If the javelin thrower has been competing in additional track or field events during midseason, during late season he frequently discontinues competition in those events in which he is least proficient. He then specializes in his major events. He may have experimented on various forms during early season and may have made a few changes during midseason. In late season he should make no radical departure from his midseason style. Many coaches recognize the improvements resulting from evolutions in form, but they likewise are cognizant of the fallacy of shopping around promiscuously. In other words, the thrower who tries to copy the delivery style of one champion this week and that of another next week may confuse an otherwise well-ordered plan of procedure. Random imitation is as illogical as the random selection of pills to alleviate a body ailment.

Hence, if the style of throwing arrived at after early season experimentation was selected soundly, no basic changes from this style are desirable during late season. Even though the athlete is aware of certain imperfections that respond slowly to correction, he will be better off to continue the same style rather than to inaugurate a new system during late season.

Possibly after one year of competition, conditions may arise that warrant the javelin thrower's adopting a different style. However, any fundamental changes should be made during the next year's preliminary season and early season schedules of practice, not during the period of important competition.

In late season the practice periods are designed to add finesse to the thrower's technique and to perfect his physical and mental responses. The competitor is occupied in self-analysis and advanced study of the event. Many times the only perceptible characteristic distinguishing a champion from an ordinary thrower is his ability to master details. If the knack of self-diagnosis and self-correction does not come naturally, the novice should cultivate it. A well-known coach repeatedly tells his squad that if they relied solely on the knowledge that he imparted to them they would never be top-flight competitors.

The daily routine is highly individualized during late season. For example, as a group of javelin throwers begins practice at the start of the year, their individual practice schedules might be quite similar during early season, less alike during midseason, and quite different in late season.

Monday

Analyze in detail the activities of the previous Saturday's competition. For example, was the previous week's throwing schedule of the right type? Was the rest period sufficient? Could the timing of the warm-up be improved? Were the longest throws made before competition started, in its early stages, in its late stages, or after competition had been concluded? Was there any sign of pressing or trying too hard? Was the speed of the run properly cumulative? Was there correct timing of the footwork and the action of the throwing arm? Did the legs and the trunk contribute their share to the force in the delivery? Was the javelin point elevation too high or too low at the instant of release? Were any long throws invalidated because of stepping on or over the restraining arc? If the trunk muscles or the throwing arm felt weary or lacked snap, at what stage of the contest did these symptoms of fatigue appear? Are there any physical or mental effects of Saturday's competition present Monday? Will therapy such as massage or the infrared ray be desirable? The advice of a coach or an observer is necessary to get information on these and additional questions that arise.

1. Warm up by jogging, running, and sprinting.
2. Perform 5 minutes of exercises, varied in character and designed to provide development where it is most needed.
3. Jab the spear into the ground with gradually increasing vigor 10 to 12 times. Assisted by a coach or observer, correct any errors in your delivery form. If you are feeling fit, prepare for throwing the javelin at $\frac{1}{2}$ effort, using the full approach. If the arm feels tired or lacks snap, refrain from further jabbing and throwing.
4. Verify the checkmark adjustments and the speed of approach by running through twice, releasing the javelin with only a small amount of effort.
5. Throw 5 or 6 times with $\frac{3}{4}$ effort, concentrating on that phase of your form that needs your attention most urgently. Tuesday's schedule includes a few throws at nearly full effort. Monday's workout should not be strenuous.
6. If weight-training exercises have proved beneficial, continue them.

Tuesday

Obtain the advice of a physician whenever in doubt on the matter of injury. Furthermore, seek his counsel on the use of such devices as the ultraviolet ray, diathermy, and the infrared ray. Massage and hydrotherapy are frequently valuable to the competitor before he begins his daily practice and at its conclusion. On the other hand, there are a number of first-class throwers who believe that they require neither massage nor therapeutic ministrations.

1. Note the changes in your body weight as the season progresses and determine your most effective poundage.
2. Warm up with jogging, bounding, running, and sprinting.
3. Prepare the arm for throwing according to the plan best suited to your needs. This may include swinging, jabbing, or tossing activities.
4. Deliver the javelin 3 or 4 times, employing the usual approach, with gradually increasing effort. Station one or more observers and assign specific movements to report on. The next step is throwing the javelin under conditions quite similar to those of competition, except that the competitor holds something in reserve.
5. Set a target on the ground in front of the restraining arc at a spot that is 10 to 20 feet short of your best distance. The target may be either directly in line with the center of the restraining arc or slightly to the thrower's right. Execute a few throws, staying well within the limit of your ability, fixing your attention on that section of the event requiring polish. Your own experience will guide you in the number of such trials, but you should try no more than 3.
6. Take a sun bath for 5 or 6 minutes.
7. Conclude this, the most strenuous practice day of the week in late season, with a jog of 200 yards, a walk of 50 yards, and a sprint of 25 yards.

Wednesday

The attention of the novice again is called to the fact that many successful javelin throwers depart from this procedure by practicing lightly on Tuesday and Thursday. They engage in moderately strenuous throwing on Monday and Wednesday.

1. Weigh and measure the javelins so that any adjustments needed can be made before competition Saturday.
2. Begin the workout with the usual jogging, walking, running, and gymnastic feats. The competitor will lessen the intensity of such exercises during this period of his training.
3. Participate in a game or contest, so as to vary the practice procedure.
4. Perform an optional amount of jabbing or throwing with moderate effort.
5. Join the long jumpers and take 2 or 3 trials each of the standing long jump and the long jump.
6. If weight-training and tension exercises have aided the improvement of your javelin throwing, spend 15 to 30 minutes on these exercises.

Thursday

1. Get a massage, especially emphasizing work on the muscles of the throwing arm and the trunk. The athlete should be able to judge the quantity and type of massage that best meets his requirements. If you are one who feels better without massage, disregard this suggestion.
2. Expose the body to the sun's rays for a period of 5 to 10 minutes. The novice will note that the sun bath is not recommended on those days when he throws for distance. On days of competition, before your event is called, likewise avoid prolonged exposure to direct sunlight. Athletes report that they become sluggish or drowsy after lying in the hot sun for a period of 15 to 30 minutes.
3. Limber up with jogging, walking, running, and sprinting.
4. Jab the spear into the ground 10 to 15 times.
5. Verify the checkmarks and the speed of the run, throwing the javelin with reduced effort 3 or 4 times. Empha-

size your stance at the time of delivery.

6. Either take an optional number of throws at ¾ effort or omit entirely any further practice with the javelin for this week. The mental and physical build-up for Saturday's important competition should begin Thursday.

7. Execute a few minutes of optional calisthenics and end the day's practice.

Friday

It has been pointed out previously that some coaches advise their throwers to stay away from the athletic environment on Friday. These contestants neither dress in competition suits nor come near the practice field. Other coaches believe in maintaining the daily practice routine, asking the men to dress in competition clothing, to limber up lightly, and to get a massage.

If the contest is held on a foreign field, the javelin thrower may obtain valuable information by inspecting the site of the competition on Friday. For example, he may have to adjust the length of spikes worn, a matter often requiring more than 10 or 15 minutes.

Regardless of whether or not the athlete appears in competition suit, Friday is a rest day. A feeling of optimism or confidence will pervade that athlete who has completed the training routine conscientiously, and without needlessly expending nervous energy he will be in readiness for Saturday's contest.

Saturday

1. Report to the implement inspector with your javelins unless the rules specify that only those furnished by the games committee may be thrown.

2. Become familiar with the javelins provided.

3. Have massage and heat treatment if that is a part of your routine.

4. Warm up with that definite plan which you have tested and accepted. Time the warm-up so that you conclude all preparations 5 minutes in advance of the actual competition.

5. Try out the approach, adjust your checkmark flags (distinctively painted ice picks), and reassure yourself of the speed and accuracy of your run.

6. Throw the javelin with increasing effort until you are positive you have reached the correct stage of the warm-up.

7. Competition. Aim to obtain your best throw early in the contest, bearing in mind that one supreme effort is more valuable than several mediocre trials. The suggestions given for Saturday competition in midseason are applicable for Saturday competition in late season. Consider your body weight fluctuations in the adjustment of your practice schedule.

REFERENCE

1. Ohls, R.: Throwing the javelin, Sport Articles, 1932, Los Angeles, Calif.

Chapter 15

Contributions of experimental research to track and field athletics

Progress in track and field techniques is acquired only through diligent research. During the past years a number of problems dealing with track and field techniques have been studied in our laboratory. The results of these experiments not only furnish material that will improve performance but also serve to settle controversial questions and provide exact knowledge of the sport. For a comprehensive index of completed research in track and field athletics, see "A Compilation and Analysis of Classified Indexed and/or Completed Research in Track and Field Athletics, 1900-1963, Inclusive" by John T. Powell, *The Royal Canadian Legion's Coaching Review*, June 1967, Legion House, Ottawa, Ontario, Canada.

STARTING TIME

One of the essentials in running a good race is being able to get a fast start. There are different methods of starting which have been used successfully by sprinters. Obviously, there are certain merits in each method. In order to learn the advantages of each, the various methods are compared to determine which yields the fastest start. It might be argued that the best start is not necessarily the fastest one, but certainly, everyone will agree that a fast start which gets a sprinter off in good, well-balanced, and coordinated fashion is to be preferred to a good, slow start.

Before proceeding with this discussion, a definition of the term "starting time" must be given. There are a number of ways in which the term may be defined. Some may contend that whenever the sprinter makes the first move after the pistol is fired, he has started, whereas others might wish to define starting time as the instant that the last contact with the mark is broken. Thus it can be seen that the definition of starting time becomes a matter of choice.

In studying problems involving the start of the sprint, it was necessary to adopt some uniform standard definition of the start. Investigation revealed that the first movement which all sprinters make after the pistol is fired is a settling back of the body before any contacts with the blocks are broken. Following the settling back of the body, the right-handed sprinter proceeds to leave the mark by lifting his left hand and then his right hand.[1] This sequence is continued by driving off with the right leg and then the left leg. Since the movement pattern in the start of the sprint consists of five distinct movements, one may define starting time as the interval between the firing of the pistol and the beginning of the execution of any of the movements just described.

Method employed for measuring starting time. In the experiments of Bresnahan and Tuttle reported here, starting time was defined as the interval elapsing between the firing of the pistol and the lifting of the right foot (right foot back) from the back block. Starting time may be measured by means of any type of chronoscope that records time in 0.001-second intervals. The instrument used by Tuttle and Bresnahan[2] was arranged so that when the pistol was fired, a dial hand began to turn, and as soon as the sprinter left his mark, it stopped instantly. Time is read directly from the chronoscope dial in milliseconds (0.001

second). The accuracy of the method has been tested and found to be adequate for measuring starting time.

Effect of the caliber of the pistol on starting time. A study of the caliber of the guns used in the various parts of the United States as well as in other countries reveals that there was an almost complete lack of uniformity in the calibers used. In the United States, the availability of pistols and the preconceived ideas of officials seemed to determine the size and type used.

It became a matter of interest whether or not there is an optimum caliber of guns for starting races or whether the type and size have any bearing on the speed of the start.

An experiment was devised by Carson[3] for determining the effect of the caliber of the gun on starting time. Four different types and sizes of guns were used for this purpose. They consisted of the regular 0.32 caliber pistol, the automatic flash pistol, a toy cap pistol, and the Scotch gun. The latter is not a firearm, but a device which consists of two boards hinged at one end so that they can be clapped together, thus producing a report. The intensity of the sound of these guns was measured and, on the basis of loudness, ranked in the order in which they are described. A comparison of 500 starting times with each gun recorded from 25 trained sprinters showed that the intensity of the sound has no significant influence on the speed of the start.

Optimum time for holding a sprinter on his mark. The variations in the time that the different officials throughout the United States held sprinters on their mark continued to be a question of controversy until the National Collegiate Athletic Association track rules committee recommended that this time be approximately 2 seconds after the command "set" is given. In track some officials fired the pistol immediately after the command "set," whereas others held sprinters on their mark for what seemed to be an unnecessarily long time.

A psychological analysis of the situation throws some light on the question. It requires a little time for a sprinter to adjust himself in the set position. Then, it takes a little time for the attention of the sprinter to reach its peak. If the best possible start is to be executed, the peak of attention and the sound of the pistol must coincide. Attention has been proved to be a fluctuating phenomenon, reaching a peak, then subsiding, and then returning to its peak again. If the pistol is fired before or after the peak of attention is reached, the start will be slower than if the peak of attention and the sound of the pistol coincide. Evi-

dentally, within rather narrow limits, there must be an optimum time for holding the sprinter in the set position.

The problem of holding time was experimentally studied by Walker and Hayden.[4] Starting time was investigated for six different intervals. In this experiment, the holding time was defined as the interval that elapses between a position of momentary steadiness in the set position and the firing of the pistol. The series of holding times investigated was 1 second, 1.2 seconds, 1.4 seconds, 1.6 seconds, 1.8 seconds, and 2 seconds. Twenty-seven sprinters performed the series of 728 times, making a total of 4,368 starts. The data showed that the interval from 1.4 seconds to 1.6 sec-

Table 15-1. A distribution of the fastest starts for the series of holding times as indicated

Subject	1.0 Sec.	1.2 Sec.	1.4 Sec.	1.6 Sec.	1.8 Sec.	2.0 Sec.
1	1	2	8	10	2	5
2	5	3	6	7	4	3
3	4	3	6	8	4	3
4	0	2	8	10	3	5
5	1	1	9	13	2	2
6	3	4	8	6	2	5
7	2	5	4	10	2	5
8	1	7	5	9	4	2
9	6	3	7	5	4	3
10	3	3	6	13	0	3
11	3	2	4	15	3	1
12	5	0	10	4	3	6
13	0	2	7	11	5	3
14	2	4	8	7	5	2
15	2	2	9	9	5	1
16	6	4	5	6	4	3
17	2	3	11	8	4	0
18	3	2	10	8	3	2
19	3	6	7	7	5	0
20	3	1	10	10	2	2
21	4	1	10	5	5	3
22	4	4	11	2	4	3
23	1	5	7	9	2	4
24	3	2	7	7	4	1
25	2	3	8	8	3	0
26	1	4	8	1	3	3
27	0	2	6	7	1	0
Totals	70	80	205	215	88	70

onds yielded significantly shorter starting times that any of the other intervals. The intervals of 1 second and 2 seconds gave the slowest starting times. The distribution of the fastest starts among the various holding times is sufficiently interesting to be reproduced (Table 15-1).

Effect of the position of the hips on starting time. The hip position that a sprinter should assume in the set position is one of the points about which there is a difference of opinion. By casual observation one will find that the natural position which most trained sprinters assume in the set position is one in which the hips are significantly higher than the shoulders. With the shoulders as a point of revolution, the range is usually from 5 to 25 degrees.

In order to determine just what type of hip position yields the fastest starting time, the problem was experimentally studied by White.[5] The experiment consisted of measuring and comparing starting times from three angles of hip elevation. The technique consisted of having the sprinter start first from his natural position, next from a position in which the hips were carried lower than normal, and then from a position in which the hips were carried higher than normal. It is worthy of note that when a sprinter was asked to assume a position with his hips voluntarily placed lower than he normally held them, the position was never more than 9 degrees lower than the shoulders. However, when he was asked to keep his hips higher than usual, he assumed a position in which they were as much as 32 degrees higher than his shoulders. Apparently, a high hip elevation is more natural for a sprinter in the crouch position than is a low one. Of course, in this investigation the foot spacing was kept constant.

Measurements of 502 starts for each angle of elevation were made on 24 trained sprinters. The data showed that on the basis of starting time, a high hip elevation yielded the best getaway.

Foot spacing and starting time. Available treatises and opinions dealing with the most effective foot spacing point to considerable controversy on the question. The spacings of starts most frequently discussed are as follows.

Elongated spacing. In elongated spacing, the sprinter, upon assuming the on-your-mark position, places the knee of the back leg opposite the heel of the front foot.

Medium spacing. In medium spacing, the sprinter, while in the on-your-mark position, places the knee of the back leg opposite the ball of the front foot.

Bunch spacing. To assume this type of starting position, the sprinter, while in a standing position, places the toe of the back foot opposite the heel of the front foot.

On the basis of 832 starts made from each position by 26 trained sprinters Dickinson[6] found that the bunch spacing yielded a significantly faster starting time than any of the other positions. The medium spacing yielded the next fastest time, and the elongated position gave the slowest.

Using 30 inexperienced college students as runners, Menely and Rosemier[7] compared the mean elapsed times over distances of 10 yards and 30 yards for 4 sprint starting positions: the bunch start, the medium start, the elongated start, and the hyperextended start. The bunch, medium, and elongated starts were executed as described previously. The position for the hyperextended start was the same as for the medium start, except in the hyperextended start the hands and front foot were placed as close to the starting line as feasible. The mean times for 3 starts from each of the 4 starting positions for each of the 2 distances were obtained for each of the 30 subjects. The data were subjected to Scheffé tests, and the starts from the hyperextended position were found to be significantly faster for both distances (lower elapsed times) than the starts from the other 3 positions.

DISTRIBUTION OF THE FORCE EXERTED BY THE LEGS IN DRIVING OFF THE MARK

One point of interest in starting the sprint is the distribution of the driving force off the mark. About the only approach to the solution of this problem is to ascertain by actual measurement the distribution of the force exerted by expert sprinters. Such an experiment was made by Kistler.[8]

Two sets of spring scales were modified so as to measure the force exerted against the blocks by trained sprinters. The scales were equipped with adjustable starting blocks in order to fit the sprinter in the same manner as in competition. The scales were arranged so that they recorded in pounds the backward force exerted on the blocks.

Since there is no uniformity among sprinters as to the type of start used, it was necessary to investigate the various types of foot spacings. The sprinter was required to start from three different spacings: the bunch, the medium, and the elongated.

On the basis of 300 starts from each spacing made by 30 trained sprinters, the following facts relative to the force exerted by the legs on the blocks in the start of the sprint were established:

1. The drive was executed by both legs regardless of the type of spacing used.
2. The force of the drive against the front block was relatively constant regardless of the foot spacing (190 pounds to 196 pounds).
3. The force exerted against the back block varied directly with the distance between the feet (151 pounds for the bunch spacing, 196 pounds for the medium spacing, and 208 pounds for the elongated spacing).
4. At a front-back foot spacing of approximately 20 inches, the distribution of the drive against the blocks was about equal (front, 190 pounds; back, 196 pounds).
5. The total force exerted by a sprinter against the blocks increased as the front-back distance between the blocks increased (bunch, 346 pounds; medium, 386 pounds; elongated, 404 pounds).

PHYSICAL MEASUREMENTS AND FOOT SPACING

The wide variation in the height of sprinters and, obviously, in leg, trunk, and thigh length makes a definition of the different types of starts in terms of exact measurement impossible. Actual measurements made by Dickinson[6] showed that the distances behind the starting line at which sprinters place the blocks depends on the height of the individual, regardless of the type of spacing used. For example, an athlete 5 feet 8 inches in height placed the front block 11, 13, and 18 inches from the starting line for the elongated, the medium, and the bunch spacings, respectively. An athlete 6 feet 1 inch in height placed the front block 14, 16, and 21 inches from the starting line for the same series.

The distance from the starting line at which the back block is placed for the various types of starts also was found to vary directly with the height of the sprinter. For example, an athlete 5 feet 8 inches tall placed the back block 37, 33, and 28 inches from the starting line for the elongated, the medium, and the bunch spacings, respectively. An athlete of 6 feet 1 inch placed it 42, 37, and 32 inches from the starting line in the order previously mentioned.

The front-back distance between the starting blocks varies only slightly among large and small individuals, since, by definition, either the size of the foot or the length of the leg is the determining factor. This distance seldom varies more than 2 inches in any of the starting positions.

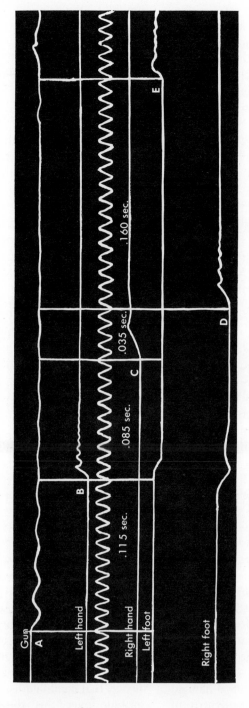

Fig. 15-1. A record showing the sequence of movements at the start of the sprint. Time is recorded in 0.01 second. **A,** Shows where the pistol was fired. **B,** Left hand up. **C,** Right hand up. **D,** Right foot off. **E,** Left foot off. This is a kymograph record.

MOVEMENT PATTERN OF THE SPRINTER STARTING FROM THE MARK

In the crouch start, a sprinter makes four contacts with the track in the set position. Since these contacts are broken involuntarily, it is of interest to know whether, through practice, he has established a reflex pattern of regular sequence. This problem was investigated by having a number of trained sprinters start from blocks that were arranged for recording the sequence of the breaking of contacts with the track (Bresnahan[1]) (Fig. 15-1).

A total of 495 movement patterns were recorded for 28 right-handed sprinters, 1 left-handed sprinter, and 4 mixed-handed sprinters. A study of these records revealed that the contacts with the track were broken in the following order:

Right-handed sprinters	Left-handed sprinter
1. Left hand	1. Right hand
2. Right hand	2. Left hand
3. Right foot	3. Left foot
4. Left foot	4. Right foot

Mixed-handed sprinters. In addition to the pure-dominant sprinters, 4 mixed-handed sprinters (w, x, y, and z) executed 14 starts each.

Subject w assumed a starting position with the left foot back. Six times his right hand came up first, 6 times his left hand came up first, and twice both hands came up simultaneously.

Subject x started with his right foot back. His right hand came up first 6 times, his left hand came up first 7 times, and both hands came up simultaneously once.

Subject y started with his right foot back. Six times his left hand came up first, and 8 times his right came up first.

Subject z, although seemingly left dominant, started with his right foot back. In 10 of his 12 starts his right hand came up first, and in 2 starts his left hand came up first.

The data revealed that the mixed-handed subjects employed variable sequences of movement when starting from the mark.

By studying the records, it was found that the sequence of movements previously described seems to be reflex in character, similar to the sequence of movements in walking.

TIME RELATIONSHIPS IN THE SEQUENCE OF MOVEMENT IN STARTING FROM THE MARK

The data presented by Bresnahan[1] showed that the mean times elapsing between the firing of the pistol and the breaking of the 4 contacts with the track by purely right-dominant sprinters were as follows:

1.	Left hand	0.17 sec.
2.	Right hand	0.22 sec.
3.	Right foot	0.29 sec.
4.	Left foot	0.44 sec.
	Total	1.12 sec.

For left-dominant sprinters, that is, those who place the left foot back, the relative relationships are the same.

It should be noted that the figures presented are based on the use of starting blocks.

RELATION OF STARTING TIME TO SPEED IN SPRINTING

It is recognized that the speed at which a runner is able to run down the track after he is off his mark and into stride depends on various factors other than his starting time. We believe, however, that other factors being equal, the sprinter who is off his mark and in stride first will win the race. Investigations were carried out to throw some light on this question.

By using a number of the variables which were proved to be influencing factors in starting time, the time spent by a sprinter in reaching a point 7½ feet in front of the mark was measured by Hayden and Walker.[2] It was found that any device that facilitated a fast start got the sprinter over this distance significantly faster.

In a more elaborate experiment, starting time was correlated with the time required for a sprinter to reach a point 15 feet from his mark. A high positive correlation was found, which is good evidence that a fast start is conducive to running a fast sprint race.

RELATIONSHIP OF SPRINTING VELOCITIES TO STARTING TIME

A study of the velocities of 9 university sprinters, from the instant of leaving the starting blocks to distances up to 35 yards, was undertaken by Sills and Pennybaker.[9] They utilized microswitches attached to strings stretched across the running track at 5-yard intervals and a cathode ray oscillograph to provide a photographic record of readings at each 5-yard interval. Repeated experiments indicated that no increases in velocities occurred beyond a distance of 30 yards. Among their conclusions are the following:

1. The mean time at the end of the first 5 yards was 1.05 seconds.
2. The mean time of the total time (for 35 yards) was 4.23 seconds.
3. Two of the 3 subjects who had recorded the fastest total time (for 35 yards) were below (faster than) the mean time at the end of the first 5 yards.
4. The 3 subjects who had recorded the slowest total time (for 35 yards) were above (slower than) the mean time at the end of the first 5 yards.
5. One of the 9 subjects attained maximum velocity between 25 and 30 yards.
6. Three of the 9 subjects attained maximum velocity between 20 and 25 yards.
7. Five of the 9 subjects attained maximum velocity between 15 and 20 yards.

Sills and Pennybaker's experiment indicates that there is a close relationship between fast sprinting times and fast starting times.

In a second experiment, Sills and Carter[10] studied the velocities of sprinters utilizing three types of foot spacing. The techniques used were similar to those of Sills and Pennybaker. Nine varsity sprinters were employed as subjects. The foot positions were the bunch spacing, the free-choice spacing, and the medium spacing. The data showed the following:

1. The subjects attained their maximum velocities between the 20-yard distance and the 25-yard distance from the starting line.
2. Maximum velocity at each 5-yard interval, up to 30 yards, was obtained more frequently with the bunch spacing than when they used the medium spacing.
3. The subjects covered 30 yards faster when they used the bunch spacing than when they used the medium spacing.
4. There is a high positive correlation between the velocity obtained by these subjects during the first and second 5-yard intervals. There is a low correlation among the velocities attained by the subjects for the first 5 yards and successive 5-yard intervals beyond 10 yards.
5. There is a high positive correlation between the velocities for the first 5 yards and the cumulative velocities at 10, 15, 20, and 25 yards.

The conclusions of Sills and Carter support further the contention that the type of foot spacing that yielded the fastest starting time also yielded the fastest sprinting time.

BREATHING PATTERNS OF SPRINTERS DURING THE START

Those who are engaged in coaching are sometimes in a quandary as to exactly what to tell the runner relative to his breathing pattern during the start of a race. It seems reasonable that the best method for establishing the most satisfactory practice is to find out the patterns of trained sprinters.

The breathing patterns of 24 trained sprinters were studied by Felkner[11] in order to see if there was any tendency toward uniformity during the start of a race. It was found that during the time elapsing between the commands "on your mark" and "set" the trained sprinters breathed normally. At the command "set," it was observed that they completed normal inspiration and held the breath in this phase of the respiratory cycle until the pistol was fired (Fig. 15-2).

The breathing patterns of 6 untrained sprinters during the start of a race were studied. During the first few trials of their practice in starting, these individuals had a tendency to breathe normally until they left their mark. However, in a short time each was found to be holding his breath at the command "set" in the same fashion as the trained group.

A psychologic analysis of breathing patterns strongly suggests that the respiratory adjustment during the start is not concerned with the problem of ventilation during the race. Instead, it is a part of the process of paying maximum attention while waiting for the pistol to be fired. The cessation of respiration also facilitates muscular fixation of the thorax, which is important in the acquisition and maintenance of a steady position. In fact, this is the customary behavior during the performance of any act of steadiness and precision in which one wishes to give maximum attention. It must be remembered that breathing during the start of the sprint is only a part of the story. Other phases of respiration are discussed elsewhere.

RELATION OF REFLEX TIME TO SPEED IN SPRINTING

Reflex time is defined as the interval elapsing between a stimulus and the beginning of an involuntary response, that is, one which is not under the control of the will. When the patellar tendon is struck a sharp blow, the leg extends. This is an illustration of a reflex movement known as the knee jerk. The time elapsing between the blow and the beginning of the jerk is designated as the reflex time of this movement.

When a sprinter hears the command "on your mark," he voluntarily takes the customary position. When the command "set" is given, he voluntarily assumes the set position. But when the pistol is fired, the sprinter does not start voluntarily. Instead, he leaves his mark reflexively in a fashion

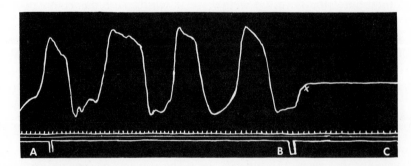

Fig. 15-2. Respiratory response of a trained sprinter. **A,** "On your mark." **B,** "Set." **C,** The pistol. Note that at x the sprinter began holding his breath in inspiration after releasing a little air. The breath was held until after the sprinter left his mark.

that parallels his responses to a blow on the patellar tendon.

Since it has been proved that there are individual differences in ability to respond involuntarily to stimuli, it seems reasonable to assume that the individual who responds the more quickly will be able to get away from his mark faster. Then, if other factors are equal, the sprinter with the faster reflex time should be able to run a faster race. Investigation has thrown some light on this question.

The relation of reflex time to speed in sprinting was studied by Lautenbach and Tuttle[12] who compared the reflex times of a group of trained sprinters and runners with their elapsed times in running a short distance. The group included national and Big Ten champions, varsity sprinters, varsity middle distance runners, and varsity distance runners. The entire group was well trained in running short distances. The evidence showed that there was a high positive correlation (0.815) between the reflex times of this group and the speed at which they were able to sprint 75 yards. This is evidence that a short reflex time is conducive to fast sprinting.

Tipton and Karpovich[13] measured the influence of exercise on changes in patellar reflex time. They found that mild exercise of a short duration (5 minutes) was associated with faster reflex times. On the other hand, they found that as the duration and intensity of exercise increased, reflex times became longer. One can extrapolate from these findings that a warm-up is desirable before competing in an athletic event and that a coach cannot expect a tired runner to have fast reflexes.

RELATION OF REACTION TIME TO SPEED IN SPRINTING

Reaction time is defined as the interval that elapses between a stimulus and the beginning of a voluntary response. The relation of speed in sprinting to reaction time was studied by Westerlund and Tuttle.[14]

The reaction time of a group including national champion sprinters, varsity sprinters, varsity middle distance men, and varsity distance men was compared with their ability to run a short distance. Here, again, the group was well trained in running short distances. The data showed a high positive correlation (0.863) between reaction time and speed in sprinting. This is good evidence that a short reaction time is an asset to sprinters.

It appears that both reflex time and reaction time are determining factors in running as well as in getting off the mark.

RACIAL DIFFERENCES— CONTRIBUTING FACTORS TO SPEED

As one looks over the list of immortal track and field athletes, he finds that on the basis of population the percentage of Negro champions far exceeds that of the white race. It seemed possible that perhaps the Negro athlete possesses some characteristic peculiar to his race which might account for his success. An experimental investigation of this subject was carried out by Brown.[15]

On the basis of a comparison of 4,100 patellar tendon reflex times taken from 82 white subjects and 4,050 patellar tendon reflex times taken from 81 Negroes, it was found that the Negro group had a reflex time significantly shorter than the white group. For the purpose of making accurate comparison, the groups were selected so that the average age, height, and weight were practically the same. On the basis of what is known about the relation of the reflex time to speed in sprinting, this finding may point out one reason for the marked success that Negro sprinters have. It is recognized that this is only a small bit of evidence, and no claim is made that it offers a complete answer.

THE STOP WATCH

Stop watch versus mechanical timing. There is considerable discussion continually going on concerning the use of the stop watch for timing races. By comparing stop watch time with that recorded by means of mechanical devices, one observes that there is a significant difference. This fact has stimulated investigation in order to make mechanical devices that are practical for timing races.

It is obviously the human element of reaction time that makes stop watch and mechanical times differ. A number of investigations have been completed which show some facts of interest. When the pistol is fired, some time is lost in getting the watch started because of the reaction time to the flash of the pistol. When the sprinter crosses the finish line, again time is lost in getting the watch stopped. However, it is obvious that if the neurophysiologic loss at the start and at the finish of a race were the same the difference in reaction times of the timer would cancel out. This is not the case, since stop watch time is usually shorter than time recorded by mechanical means.

In order to ascertain just what difference one should expect to find between mechanical and stop watch time, a comparative study was made by Graflund.[16] Five of the shorter running events (the 45-yard low hurdles, the 50-yard low hurdles, the 60-yard low hurdles, the 50-yard dash, and the 60-yard dash) were included in the study. In each event, times were recorded simultaneously by the stop watch and by a mechanical timing device. Not less than 60 races were timed in each event. The information secured in this manner provided 300 stop watch times and a like number of mechanical times, which were compared.

A group of expert timers who had wide experience in timing races in Big Ten competition was used in obtaining the official stop watch time for each race. The procedure for timing these races was that commonly employed in timing such events. The experiment showed that the stop watch times were consistently shorter than the mechanical times, the mean difference being 0.1 second.

This experiment immediately raises the question of why the reaction time at the start failed to be canceled out by the reaction time at the end of the race. This problem was investigated by Cunningham.[17] In order to answer the aforementioned question, the reaction time of a group of expert timers to the flash of a pistol was measured 1,000 times. The timing group consisted of 10 men; thus each responded 100 times. The experiment was repeated at the finish line. When the results were compared, it was found that for the group as a whole the mean reaction time in stopping the watch at the finish line was 0.1 second shorter than the reaction time in starting the watch at the flash of the pistol.

The next question to be answered is, "Why does a discrepancy between these reaction times exist?" The response to the flash of a pistol represents what is commonly called simple reaction time since there is a single, clear-cut stimulus. The response at the finish is what may be termed an anticipated reaction time, since there is not a single clear-cut stimulus. Instead there is a combination of more or less blurred stimuli, the strongest phase obviously being the approaching runners. What evidently happens is that the timer, while attempting to watch the finish line, consciously or unconsciously follows the approaching competitors. In most cases the contact with the line by the winner is not a clear-cut stimulus, and the timer anticipates the finish, stopping the watch too soon. Another reason for believing that this is the correct explanation is that timers actually stopped their watches before the runners reached the line. Other experiments have shown that inexperienced timers respond less consistently, thus yielding running times that are extremely variable. Although the experiment in question requires sampling, the results seem reasonable.

Use of the stop watch. Because mechanical devices for timing races are so expensive and present some difficulties, they may not meet the popular demand for some time. This fact warrants a discussion of the proper manipulation of the stop watch since it is the common instrument used. The correct use of a stop watch requires instruction and practice.

The first consideration is the personnel of the timing team. It is bad practice to select timers indiscriminately. Where meets are held regularly, a group of individuals who are willing to devote their time should be instructed and provided practice in the use of the watch. This practice and instruction will not eliminate the source of error in stop watch timing, but it will reduce the errors to a minimum.

The timer should be in such a position that he can see the flash of the pistol distinctly. He must learn to discriminate between sound, smoke, and flash. The timer must take a position where he can see not only the flash of the pistol but also the finish of the race. By the selection of proper positions, the timers can eliminate considerable confusion.

When the finish occurs, the timer should be at right angles to the runners, looking along the finish line. He should pay as little attention as possible to the contestants coming down the track and should be ready to stop the watch when, in his judgment, the runner's torso reaches the line. This will help to avoid anticipating the finish. Uniformity in these details makes for uniformity in the times recorded. Data collected from a large number of races support this contention. The timer should never be between the finish line and the start, nor should he stand in front of the finish line. Experience has shown that these positions are conducive to wide variations in time readings.

Errors in handling the watch may be ob-served at any race where inexperienced timers are employed. The watch should be grasped firmly so that it can be started by the index finger without any extraneous movements of the arm or hand. One who is a member of a timing team always should use the same watch so as to become familiar with it. If there is slack in the stem, this slack should be removed before the time to start or stop the watch occurs. A watch is like a gun. To know its peculiarities makes for efficiency in handling it.

Care of the stop watch. The first prerequisite to good timing is a good watch. It should be remembered that the stop watch, like any watch, requires cleaning and adjusting. For the timing of competitive events it is best to have watches that are reserved for meets only. They must be kept in condition so that they will be ready when competition occurs. Each watch should be numbered and assigned to the same timer at every meet. Those officials who consistently miss times are prone to blame the watch. The proper care of the watch will help to eliminate such alibis.

DESIGN OF THE HIGH SCHOOL DISCUS

Although discus throwing had been practiced in the high schools as a competitive sport for years, no successful attempt had been made to design an implement entirely suitable for high school boys until 1938. Previous to this time the collegiate discus was employed in spite of the admission that it was unsuited as a high school implement.

In 1938, at the request of the officials of the National Federation, Tuttle, Bresnahan, and Canine[18] designed a discus suitable for use by high school boys. In 1939 this implement was declared official by the National Federation of State High School Athletic Associations.

The problem involved in designing the new discus was to determine the proper size and weight of the implement. The assumption was made that the collegiate discus met the weight and size requirements of college men. It was logical to conclude that a discus suitable for use by high school boys should have the same size and weight relationship to the collegiate discus as the size and strength of high school boys had to the size and strength of college men. In order to obtain this relationship relative to weight, a strength index was established for college men and for high school boys. Substituting the strength index of college men (1,648) and high school boys (1,334) in the formula

$$\frac{\text{Strength index}}{\text{Strength index}} = \frac{\text{weight of college discuss}}{\text{weight of high school}}$$
$$\frac{(\text{college men})}{(\text{high school boys})} = \frac{(4.4\ \text{pounds})}{\text{discuss (X)}}$$

we have:

$$\frac{1,648}{1,334} = \frac{4.4}{X}$$

X = 3.56 pounds (3 pounds 9 ounces) weight of high school discus

By applying the same reasoning as employed in determining the weight of the high school discus, the diameter, thickness at the center, and thickness at the rim were found. On the basis of a comparison of the size of the hands of high school boys with that of college men, an index of hand size was calculated. The relative size of the high school discus was determined on the same principle as that used in determining its weight.

On the basis of the investigation reported above, the official high school discus is described as follows:

Diameter	8¼ inches
Center thickness	1.67 inches
Thickness ¼ inch from rim	0.48 inch
Weight	3 pounds 9 ounces

RELATIONSHIP BETWEEN TIME SPENT IN THE SPRING AND THE HEIGHT OF A JUMP

Although the importance of the time spent in the spring and the height attained by a running high jumper has been recognized for a long time, data were not available on this point until quantitative methods were adapted to the problem.

This problem was attacked by Lance and Tuttle[19] who had varsity jumpers spring from a platform equipped with contacts that started a chronoscope when the jumper landed on it and stopped the chronoscope when he left it. Beginning at low heights and progressing upward, it was found that the greater the height a jumper is attempting to attain, the less time he spends in executing the spring. It was shown also that, on the average, a jumper putting forth maximum effort spends 0.16 second in executing his spring.

Klissouras and Karpovich,[20] by means of electrogoniometry, made simultaneous recordings of the action of the hip, knee, ankle, and big toe joints during the execution of the high jump, the long jump, and the triple jump. Included in their analysis of data were evaluations of (a) the time spent in the spring and the distance or height of the jump and (b) the angle of the leg thrust at the moment of take-off. Their findings support the finding of Lance and Tuttle[19]; that is, performance (in terms of height or distance) was found to be inversely related to the time spent in springing for both the high jump and the long jump but not for the triple jump. During the spring for the high jump, the angle of the leg thrust was greater than 90 degrees; for the long jump and the triple jump, less than 90 degrees.

Utilizing a force platform and slow-motion movies, Hay[21] compared the overall efficiency (in terms of forces at take-off and heights cleared) of the straddle style of high jumping with the western roll style. He, too, found the time spent in springing to be inversely related to the height of the jump. His findings also indicate that for heights below 90 to 100 percent of the jumper's standing height, the western roll style of jumping is probably more efficient than the straddle style; for heights greater than the jumper's standing height, the straddle style is probably the more efficient of the two styles.

POLE VAULTING—FACTORS THAT INFLUENCE POLE-BEND

Hay[22] investigated the relative influence of five factors (angle of take-off, horizontal velocity at take-off, vertical velocity at take-off, distance between the vaulter's hands at take-off, and the horizontal distance between the vaulter's top hand and his take-off foot at take-off) and the magnitude of the pole-bend obtained in vaulting with a fiber glass pole. Slow-motion movies and a chronoscope calibrated in one-hundredths of a second were the means by which data were collected. Hay concluded that of the five factors investigated the horizontal velocity of the vaulter at take-off makes the principal contribution to the pole-bend.

PHYSIOLOGIC EFFECTS OF ABDOMINAL COLD PACKS

Happ,[23] who was a pilot in the European Theater during World War II, learned while in England that the German Air Force was making use of cold hip baths in an attempt to alleviate fatigue. This same information was reported by Counsilman,[24] who was also a member of the Air Force.

Happ, Tuttle, and Wilson[25] investigated the German idea by applying ice packs to the midsection of the human body to ascertain if "cold" was a useful device for promoting recovery from fatigue. Instead of spraying cold water on the hips and midsection as the Germans did, Happ conceived the idea that, if "cold" produced physiologic changes, these effects would be more pronounced if ice packs were applied to the abdominal region. It was concluded from the study that recovery from fatigue resulting from strenuous exercise is facilitated by the application of "cold" to the abdomen. Numerous reports have been made substantiating the idea that ab-

dominal ice packs have been effective as an aid in recovering from fatigue during the half-time intermission in both football and basketball. The effect of spraying cold water on the abdominal region of track athletes was investigated by Rosen.[26] He found that in repeat performances of the 440-yard race, the mean time of the runners was always faster following the application of the cold spray as compared to their mean time when the cold spray was omitted. It was observed, however, that the use of a cold spray on the abdomen was not advantageous to all runners.

TRAINING METHODS

Glincki[27] attempted to unravel some of the confusion concerning the advantages of Fartlek, interval, and sprint training methods on performance times. Sixty-seven college students were randomly assigned to 1 of 3 groups (Fartlek training group, interval training group, and sprint training group) and trained for 8 weeks. The times to run 60 yards and 880 yards were measured before and after the training programs. The results indicated that all groups improved significantly in their ability to run 60 yards, but only the Fartlek and interval training groups made statistically significant improvements in the times required to run 880 yards.

Griffin[28] compared the effects of an interval training program and a modified Fartlek training program on the time required to run 440 yards. The results showed that neither training program had any superiority over the other in improving performance times. Using a similar approach, but differing in details, Merwald[29] compared the Swedish and Oregon systems of training with respect to improvements in the times required to run 1 mile. The subjects using the Swedish program reduced their mean mile-run times by 21.0 seconds, whereas the subjects using the Oregon program had a mean reduction of 20.2 seconds. These and similar studies indicate that both types of training programs are equally effective in producing significant changes.

MEASUREMENT OF CAPACITY TO DO WORK

Following a discussion of each track and field event, schedules of practice are presented not only to improve the technique of the events but also to increase the physical capacity of the athlete. It is of distinct advantage to both the coach and the athlete to have quantitative information on the progress being made in both. As the athlete continues strenous work week after week, it is expected that his capacity to do work increases. Whether or not this is true can be demonstrated by the proper use of a bicycle ergometer. A bicycle ergometer is shown in Fig. 15-3. The details of its construction, calibration, and use have been made available by Tuttle and Wendler.[30] At the present time many exercise physiology laboratories are using the bicycle ergometer manufactured by the Monarc Company of Stockholm, Sweden.

STRENGTH

Considerable research has been done in an attempt to relate strength to health, physical condition and efficiency, and athletic performance. The need for further study in this area prompted the design and construction of a dynamometer. This instrument provides for a quantitative measure of strength endurance as well as maximum strength. The features of the dynamometer are that it provides for (1) quantitative measurements, (2) quick calibration, (3)

Fig. 15-3. A bicycle ergometer for measuring capacity to do work. For an explanation of the construction and operation of such an instrument, see Tuttle, W. W., and Wendler, A. J.: J. Lab. & Clin. Med. **30**:173, 1945.

measurement of strength endurance, (4) measurement of isometric muscular movement, and (5) recording both maximum strength and strength endurance.

Two types of dynamometers have been devised and constructed, the one for grip strength and the other for back and leg strength. These instruments and their application to strength problems have been described by Tuttle, Janney, and Thompson[31] and Tuttle, Janney, and Salzano.[32] These dynamometers, based on electronic principles, lend themselves to the accurate measuring and recording of both maximum strength and strength endurance.

Winningham[33] studied the influence of ankle weights on the ability of 120 college students to run an experimental maze. Four groups of 30 students each were used. One group was the control; the remaining 3 groups were trained to run with ankle weights of 0, 2, and 5 pounds respectively. The investigator found that after 6 weeks of training all groups ran faster than before but that the presence of weights alone had no significant effect on performance times. These findings suggest that use of ankle weights while training has limited value.

Schultz[34] utilized a weight training group and a repetitive sprinting group in his study of motor performance. His subjects were 120 college freshmen. One of his test items was the 60-yard dash. From his results Schultz concluded that practice in underdistance repetitive sprinting would improve the time to run the 60-yard dash. However, weight lifting per se had no appreciable influence on 60-yard dash times, and he believed that this practice should be avoided as a training technique.

NUTRITIONAL CONSIDERATIONS AND RUNNING PERFORMANCE

In recent years Swedish investigators[35,36] have been measuring the relationship between endurance events and muscle glycogen levels. From their findings they have concluded that muscle glycogen is indis-

pensable for heavy and continued work. In addition they found that after severe exercise muscle glycogen was replenished to a higher level than before exercise. Several days were needed for this change to occur. To facilitate this change a diet rich in carbohydrates was provided. The authors have recommended that athletes physically exhaust themselves several days in advance of competition and then recover on a diet high in carbohydrates. Time will verify if this approach is valid.

Youmans, Alley, and Tuttle[37] investigated the effects of eating a light meal consisting of cereal and milk, toast, butter, and sugar, which provided approximately 500 calories, at various time intervals before sprinting. The distances run were 50 yards and 100 yards. The meal was eaten at six different time intervals—½, 1, 1½, 2, 2½, and 3 hours previous to sprinting. The purpose was to provide a meal that was easily digestible.

An electronic apparatus that was adequate for measuring both starting and sprinting times was designed. The conclusions were based on the average of the results from 15 male subjects 17 to 24 years of age who ran the distances ten times after each time interval.

The data collected showed no statistically significant effect on starting and sprinting times, regardless of the time between eating and sprinting.

In another experiment, Asprey, Alley, and Tuttle[38] studied the effects of eating the same meal described by Youmans, Alley, and Tuttle[37] at various time intervals between the meal and running 440 yards and 880 yards. The time intervals in this experiment were ½, 1, and 2 hours.

Sixteen male subjects, ranging in age from 17 to 21 years, participated in the experiment. Fourteen of the subjects had participated in interscholastic competition as members of high school track teams. The remaining two had participated in the required program of physical education at a university. Eight subjects ran ten times at the 440-yard distance, and 8 other subjects ran nine trials at the 880-yard distance at the prescribed interval between eating and running. Each subject also ran the 440-yard distance and 880-yard distance the same number of times, following the same running pattern when there was no food involved. These data served as controls. In both runs, the means of the times were computed for each eating time interval and likewise for the control group when no food was eaten before the runs. These means were taken as the subject's criterion score and were used to compute the general means for all subjects. The data were subjected to an analysis of variance. There was no evidence that suggested that eating had any adverse effect on performance times.

Using the same experimental design in two recent studies Asprey, Alley, and Tuttle[39] utilized 8 subjects, each of whom ran ten trials of the 1-mile run for each of three time intervals ($\frac{1}{2}$, 1, and 2 hours) between eating and running and for a control run (no eating for at least 3 hours before running) and 8 additional subjects, each of whom ran eight trials of the 2-mile run for each of the time intervals and the control run. The data were analyzed in the same manner as in the earlier studies.

The data justify the conclusion that eating a meal which provides quick and lasting energy (cereal and milk, toast, butter, and sugar) had no adverse effects on the 440-yard, 880-yard, 1-mile, and 2-mile performances after any of the time intervals included in the study. Furthermore, none of the subjects experienced adverse effects in the form of either stomach cramps or nausea during or after the runs.

RUNNING VELOCITY: BODY RISE AND STRIDE LENGTH

Rapp[40] investigated the effects that changes in running velocity have on the stride length and body rise of runners. Eighteen subjects from the Big Ten cross-country champion team and the freshman track team at the University of Iowa participated in this experiment.

An Athletic Performance Analyser, which is a type of electronic timer, was used to time two strides of each trial run. A Bolex 16 mm. motion picture camera was used to photograph the two strides that were timed. A steel tape was employed to measure the length of the two strides.

Each subject was required to execute 9 trial runs. In 3 of these the subject exerted minimum effort, in 3 he exerted moderate effort, and in the remaining 3 he put forth maximum effort.

Data from a 2-stride segment of each trial run was measured to gain the following information:

1. The amount of body rise in each stride. This was measured photographically.
2. The velocity of the runner. This was determined by finding the sum of 2 stride lengths and dividing this sum by the time required to take the strides.
3. The stride lengths. This was found by measuring the distance between the imprints made by the runners feet.

The data justified the following conclusions:

1. Changes in velocity of runners resulted in statistically significant changes in body rise, which are in inverse relationship to the velocity changes.
2. Changes from a slow to a moderate pace result in an increased stride length and decreased body rise. In increasing from a moderate pace to a sprint, a decrease in body rise is the only significant change in running form.

PREDICTING DESIRABLE WEIGHT OF INDIVIDUALS

Research findings from the Minnesota Study on Starvation have clearly shown that a weight loss of 10 percent or more below normal weight will markedly influence the performance level of the individual losing the weight. Because weight loss is fairly common during a competitive season, it is important that each competitor know his desirable weight. There are several scientific methods for accomplishing this task, but many of these methods require a large amount of time, equipment, space, and personnel. An exception is the anthropometric method developed by Hall.[41] During the past 25 years, more than 30,000 Illinois boys and girls between the ages of 10 and 18 years have been measured in accordance with his procedures. The finding from these measurements have been condensed into tabular form for use in predicting weights.

The equipment needed is a sliding caliper (Naragansett Co., Moberly, Missouri), a steel tape (L. S. Sarrett Co., Athol, Massachusetts), and a weighing scale with a rod to measure standing height.

Recently this method was used to predict the weight of more than 280 junior and senior high school wrestlers. It was found that the group difference between actual and predicted weights was less than 2 percent. These results prompted the Iowa Medical Society to recommend its use by the members of the Iowa High School Athletic Association. This method would be equally effective for predicting the weight of individuals training for track and field events.

To take the necessary measurements, a minimum amount of clothing should be worn. The procedures for obtaining these measurements are as follows:

1. Standing height. Stand erect with head high. Place the hands on hips and record height measurement to nearest 0.25 inch during the inspiratory phase of breathing.
2. Chest width. Calipers are inserted near the axillary region at the level of second or third rib. Care must be taken to exclude the pectoralis muscle group. Press calipers firmly against the ribs and record to nearest 0.1 inch during the end of the expiratory phase of breathing.
3. Chest depth. Calipers are placed on xyphoid process of sternum (lowest point of chest) and on the back near spinal column. Measurements are read to nearest 0.1 inch and obtained during the end of the expiratory phase of breathing. As in previous measures, a firm pressure is exerted when calipers are used.
4. Hip width. Place calipers on hips at level of the iliac crest. Press firmly and read to nearest 0.1 inch.
5. Thigh circumference. Have the subject stand with his feet 12 to 18 inches apart and his weight equally distributed over both feet. Place steel tape around thigh at approximate midpoint between the knee and hip. Record result to the nearest 0.25 inch.

With a little practice these measurements can be obtained in less than 2 minutes. Once they have been tabulated, use the numbers in Table 15-2 to predict the desirable weight of an individual. The following example will illustrate the procedure to follow.

Measurement	Result	Weight contribution
Standing height	68.0 in.	63.8 lbs.
Thigh circumference	19.0 in.	14.6 lbs.
Hip width	11.0 in.	12.3 lbs.
Chest width	11.6 in.	36.6 lbs.
Chest depth	7.6 in.	19.2 lbs.
Predicted weight		146.5 lbs.
Actual weight		143.2 lbs.
Percent difference		2%
		(approximately)

This method is very reliable with individuals who weigh between 90 and 155 pounds. Individuals who weigh more than this amount should know that their predicted weight will be 5 to 6 percent lower than should be the case. As a general rule, the actual and the predicted weights should agree within 2 to 4 pounds.

Table 15-2. Hall method for calculating predicted weight*

Measurement 1		Measurement 2		Measurement 3		Measurement 4		Measurement 5	
Height	Add	Thigh circum.	Add	Hip width	Add	Chest width	Add	Chest depth	Add
(In.)	(Lbs.)	(In.)	(Lbs.)	(In.)	(Lbs.)	(In.)	(Lbs.)	(In.)	(Lbs.)
50	19.0	13.0	2.1	8.0	2.1	7.6	15.3	5.0	4.1
51	21.4	13.5	3.1	8.2	2.8	7.8	16.4	5.2	5.2
52	24.0	14.0	4.1	8.4	3.5	8.0	17.5	5.4	6.4
53	26.5	14.5	5.2	8.6	4.2	8.2	18.5	5.6	7.6
54	28.9	15.0	6.2	8.8	4.9	8.4	19.6	5.8	8.7
55	31.4	15.5	7.3	9.0	5.5	8.6	20.6	6.0	9.9
56	33.9	16.0	8.3	9.2	6.2	8.8	21.7	6.2	11.0
57	36.4	16.5	9.4	9.4	6.9	9.0	22.8	6.4	12.2
58	38.9	17.0	10.4	9.6	7.6	9.2	23.8	6.6	13.4
59	41.4	17.5	11.4	9.8	8.3	9.4	24.9	6.8	14.5
60	43.9	18.0	12.5	10.0	8.9	9.6	25.9	7.0	15.7
61	46.4	18.5	13.5	10.2	9.6	9.8	27.0	7.2	16.9
62	48.9	19.0	14.6	10.4	10.3	10.0	28.1	7.4	18.0
63	51.4	19.5	15.6	10.6	11.0	10.2	29.1	7.6	19.2
64	53.9	20.0	16.6	10.8	11.6	10.4	30.2	7.8	20.3
65	56.4	20.5	17.7	11.0	12.3	10.6	31.3	8.0	21.5
66	58.9	21.0	18.7	11.2	13.0	10.8	32.3	8.2	22.7
67	61.3	21.5	19.8	11.4	13.7	11.0	33.4	8.4	23.8
68	63.8	22.0	20.8	11.6	14.4	11.2	34.4	8.6	25.0
69	66.3	22.5	21.8	11.8	15.0	11.4	35.5	8.8	26.2
70	68.8	23.0	22.9	12.0	15.7	11.6	36.6	9.0	27.3
71	71.3	23.5	23.9	12.2	16.4	11.8	37.6	9.2	28.5
72	73.8	24.0	25.0	12.4	17.1	12.0	38.7	9.4	29.6
73	76.3	24.5	26.0	12.6	17.8	12.2	39.7	9.6	30.8
74	78.8			12.8	18.4	12.4	40.8	9.8	32.0
75	81.3			13.0	19.1	12.6	41.9	10.0	33.1
76	83.8			13.2	19.8	12.8	42.9	10.2	34.3
77	86.3			13.4	20.5	13.0	44.0		
78	88.8			13.6	21.1	13.2	45.1		
						13.4	46.1		
						13.6	47.2		
						13.8	48.2		
						14.0	49.3		
						14.2	50.4		
						14.4	51.4		
						14.6	52.5		
						14.8	53.5		
						15.0	54.6		

*Hall, D. M., Cain, R. L., and Tipton, C. M.: Keeping fit: an evaluation of the fitness of Illinois young people, Cooperative Extension Service, University of Illinois, Urbana, Illinois, p. 17.

SUMMARY

In order that the reader may have a condensed statement of the results of some of the scientific investigations dealing with track and field problems, a brief summary of the findings follows. Those who wish to know the procedures and techniques should consult the list of references at the end of this chapter.

1. The intensity of the report of the pistol that an official uses to start a race has no significant influence on starting time.

2. The optimum time for holding a sprinter on his mark in the set position (as soon as a state of momentary steadiness is reached) lies between 1.4 and 1.6 seconds.

3. A relatively high hip position permits faster starting time than a low hip position.

4. The distribution of the force exerted on the blocks at the start of a race depends on the type of start used. Although there is force exerted by both legs, the force exerted against the front block is relatively constant. As the front-back distance between the blocks is increased, the force exerted against the back block is increased.

5. When the foot in front is placed as close to the starting line as is feasible, the bunch spacing yields significantly shorter starting times than either the medium or elongated foot spacings.

6. The distance at which a sprinter places the blocks from the starting line depends on the height of the runner.

7. The sequence of movements in the start of the sprint is a reflex phenomenon, and thus it is common to both the trained and the untrained runner.

8. There is a high positive correlation between starting time and sprinting time; therefore, a fast start is conducive to a fast race.

9. The breathing pattern of a sprinter at the start of a race is related to attention and muscle fixation rather than to ventilation. The sprinter holds his breath between the command "set" and the firing of the pistol.

10. There is a high positive correlation between reflex time and speed in sprinting. This is true also of reaction time and speed in sprinting. This is evidence that sprinters with both fast reaction and reflex times are at a distinct advantage.

11. Warm-up can result in faster reflex times.

12. The apparently faster reflex time of Negroes may be one of the factors responsible for their success as sprinters.

13. Stop watch times are consistently 0.1 second shorter than those obtained by mechanical devices.

14. The discrepancy between stop watch time and mechanical time is due to an error on the part of the timer. The time lost in starting the watch is not balanced by that lost in stopping it, because the runners reaching the line do not present a clear-cut stimulus and the finish is anticipated.

15. On the basis of the strength and size of high school athletes, a discus was designed which is accepted as the official implement of the National Federation of State High School Associations.

16. In the running high jump and the long jump, the greater the height or distance jumped, the shorter is the time spent in the spring.

17. During the spring for the high jump, the angle of the leg thrust is greater than 90 degrees; for the long jump and the triple jump, less than 90 degrees.

18. The western roll style of high jumping is probably more efficient than the straddle style for heights less than the jumper's standing height. For heights greater than the jumper's standing height, the straddle style is probably more efficient than the western roll style.

19. Other things being equal, the greater the horizontal velocity of the pole vaulter at take-off, the greater the bend produced in the pole.

20. The Fartlek training program and the interval training program are equally effective in producing significant improvements in running times for distance runs (880 yards and 1 mile).

21. Dynamometers for measuring grip strength, leg strength, and back strength have been described. These dynamometers provide for (a) quantitative measurements, (b) quick calibration, (c) measurement of strength endurance as well as maximum strength, (d) measurement of isometric muscular contraction, and (e) recording both maximum strength and strength endurance.

22. The use of weight training to improve sprinting times is of limited value.

23. A bicycle ergometer for measuring capacity to do work is described.

24. Recovery from fatigue resulting from strenuous exercise was shown to be facilitated by the application of cold to the abdominal region.

25. In terms of improved performances, it might be advantageous for the endurance runner to physically exhaust himself several days before competing and then recover from the exhaustion on a diet high in carbohydrates.

26. Eating a 500 calorie meal, consisting of cereal, toast, butter, sugar, and milk, ½, 1, 1½, 2, 2½, or 3 hours previous to sprinting 50 yards or 100 yards had no significant statistical effect, one way or another, on starting time and sprinting time, regardless of the time interval between eating and sprinting. In a similar experiment eating a 500 calorie meal ½, 1, and 2 hours before running the 440 yard, the 880-yard, the 1-mile, and the 2-mile runs had no statistically significant effect, at any interval, on starting time and elapsed time in running these distances. Also, it was found that none of the subjects reported adverse effects in the form of nausea or stomach cramps either during or after the runs.

27. A study of running velocity, body rise and stride length in running, leads to the conclusion that changes in velocity of runners resulted in statistically significant changes in body rise, which are in inverse relationship to the velocity changes. Furthermore, it was found that changing from a slow to a moderate pace resulted in an increased stride length and decreased body rise. In increasing from a moderate pace to a sprint, a decrease in body rise was the only significant change in body form.

28. A weight loss of 10 percent or more below normal weight will markedly impair performance. A relatively simple scheme for determining what the nomal weight of a given athlete should be is provided.

REFERENCES

1. Bresnahan, G. T.: A study of the movement pattern in starting the race from the crouch position, Res. Quart., Am. A. Health, Phys. Ed. & Rec. 5(supp. 1):5, 1935.
2. Tuttle, W. W., and Bresnahan, G. T.: An apparatus for measuring starting time in foot races, Res. Quart., Am. A. Health, Phys. Ed. & Rec. 4:110, 1933.
3. Carson, G.: The effect of the intensity of the

stimulus on starting time, Athletic J. **15**:13, 1935.

4. Walker, G. A., and Hayden, T. C.: The optimum time for holding a sprinter between the "set" and the stimulus (gun shot), Res. Quart., Am. A. Heath, Phys. Ed. & Rec. **4**:124, 1933.

5. White, R. A.: The effect of hip elevation on starting time in the sprint, Res. Quart., Am. A. Health, Phys. Ed. & Rec. **5**(supp. 1):128, 1935.

6. Dickinson, A. D.: The effect of foot spacing on starting time and speed in sprinting and the relation of physical measurements to foot spacing, Res. Quart., Am. A. Health, Phys. Ed. & Rec. **5**(supp. 1):12, 1934.

7. Menely, R. C., and Rosemier, R. A.: Effectiveness of four track starting positions on acceleration, Res. Quart., Am. A. Health, Phys. Ed. & Rec. **39**:161, 1968.

8. Kistler, J. W.: A study of the distribution of force exerted upon the blocks in the starting of the sprint from various starting positions, Res. Quart., Am. A. Health, Phys. Ed. & Rec. **5**(supp. 1):27, 1934.

9. Sills, F. D., and Pennybaker, D. A.: A method of measuring the velocity of speed of movement with a cathode ray oscillograph, Proc. Twenty-Second Ann. Convention, Central District, Am. A. Health, Phys. Ed. & Rec., Res. Sect. pp. 24-36, 1956.

10. Sills, F. D., and Carter, J. E. L.: Measurement of velocity for sprint-start, Proc. Seventy-Fourth Ann. Convention, Am. A. Health, Phys. Ed. & Rec. Res. Sect., p. 19, 1959.

11. Felkner, A. H.: A study of the respiratory habits of sprinters in starting a race, Res. Quart., Am. A. Health, Phys. Ed. & Rec. **5**(supp. 1):20, 1934.

12. Lautenbach, R., and Tuttle, W. W.: The relation between reflex time and running events in track, Res. Quart., Am. A. Health, Phys. Ed. & Rec. **3**:138, 1932.

13. Tipton, C. M., and Karpovich, P. V.: Exercise and the patellar reflex, J. Appl. Physiol. **21**:15, 1966.

14. Westerlund, J. H., and Tuttle, W. W.: Relationship between running events in track and reaction time, Res. Quart., Am. A. Health, Phys. Ed. & Rec. **2**:95, 1931.

15. Brown, R. L.: A comparison of the patellar tendon reflex time of whites and Negroes, Res. Quart., Am. A. Health, Phys. Ed. & Rec. **6**:121, 1935.

16. Graflund, F. A.: The correlation between mechanical and stop-watch timing, Athletic J. **17**:15, 1936.

17. Cunningham, G.: Discrepancy between stopwatch and mechanical timing, Athletic J. **17**:36, 1936.

18. Tuttle, W. W., Bresnahan, G. T., and Canine, H.: Designing the new high school discus, Scholastic Coach **2**:7, 1938.

19. Lance, J. R., and Tuttle, W. W.: An informative article on the relationship existing between the time spent in executing the spring and the height of the jump, The Athlete **1**:41, 1937.

20. Klissouras, V., and Karpovich, P. V.: Electrogoniometric study of jumping events, Res. Quart., Am. A. Health, Phys. Ed. & Rec. **38**:41, 1967.

21. Hay, J. G.: An investigation of mechanical efficiency in two styles of high jump, Doctorate Thesis, University of Iowa, 1967, Iowa City, Iowa.

22. Hay, J. G.: Pole vaulting: a mechanical analysis of factors influencing pole-bend, Res. Quart., Am. A. Health, Phys. Ed. & Rec. **38**:34, 1967.

23. Happ, W. P., Jr.: Personal communication.

24. Counsilman, J. E.: Personal communication.

25. Happ, W. P., Jr., Tuttle, W. W., and Wilson, M.: The physiologic effects of abdominal cold packs, Res. Quart., Am. A. Health, Phys. Ed. & Rec. **20**:153, 1949.

26. Rosen, M.: The effect of cold abdominal spray upon a repeat performance in the 440-yard run, Res. Quart., Am. A. Health, Phys. Ed. & Rec. **23**:226, 1952.

27. Glinski, J. V.: A comparative study of Fartlek, interval and sprint training, P.E.D. Thesis, Indiana University, 1967, Bloomington, Indiana.

28. Griffin, J. M.: A comparison of two methods of training: the conventional method and the interval method, Ph.D. Thesis, New York University, 1961, New York, New York.

29. Merwald, R. L.: A comparison of the effectiveness of training middle-distance runners by the Swedish system and the Oregon system, M.S. Thesis, University of Oregon, Eugene, Oregon, 1965.

30. Tuttle, W. W., and Wendler, A. J.: The construction, calibration and use of an alternating current electrodynamic brake bicycle ergometer, J. Lab. & Clin. Med. **30**:173, 1945.

31. Tuttle, W. W., Janney, C. D., and Thompson, C. W.: Relation of maximum grip strength to grip strength endurance, J. Appl. Physiol. **2**:663, 1950.

32. Tuttle, W. W., Janney, C. D., and Salzano, J.: Relation of maximum back and leg strength to back and leg strength endurance, Res.

Quart., Am. A. Health, Phys. Ed. & Rec. **26:**96, 1955.

33. Winningham, S. N.: Effect of training with ankle weights on running speed, Ph.D. Thesis, University of Southern California, 1966, Los Angeles, California.

34. Schultz, G. W.: The effects of direct practice, repetitive sprinting and weight training on selected motor performance tests, P.E.D. Thesis, Indiana University, 1964, Bloomington, Indiana.

35. Hultman, E.: Physiological role of muscle glycogen in man with special reference to exercise, Circulation Research **20**(supp.1):99, 1967.

36. Astrand, P. O.: Physical activity and health, Canad. Med. Assoc. J. **96:**718, 1967.

37. Youmans, E., Alley, L. E., and Tuttle, W. W.: Effect on eating at various times upon sprinting performance, Scholastic Coach **30:**3, 1960.

38. Asprey, G. M., Alley, L. E., and Tuttle, W. W.: Effect of eating at various times on subsequent performances in the 440-yard run and the 880-yard run, Res. Quart. **34:**267, 1963.

39. Asprey, G. M., Alley, L. E., and Tuttle, W. W.: Effect of eating at various times on subsequent performances in the 2-mile run, Res. Quart. **36:**233, 1965.

40. Rapp, K. E.: Running velocity: body rise and stride length, M.A. Thesis, State University of Iowa, 1963, Iowa City, Iowa.

41. Hall, D. M., Cain, R. L., and Tipton, C. M.: Keeping fit: an evaluation of the fitness of Illinois young people, Cooperative Extension Service, University of Illinois, Bulletin ES-1759, Urbana, Illinois.

Chapter 16

The responsibilities for the conduct of a track and field meet

Games committee
Athlete
Coach
Referee
Clerk of course
Starter (pistol firer)
    Equipment
    Position
    Commands
        "Remove sweat clothes"
        "Timers and judges ready"
        "Starters ready"
        "Get on your mark"
        "Set"
        Pistol shot
Judges of the finish
Timers
Inspectors
Judges of the pole vault
Judges of the high jump
Judges of the long jump
Judges of the shot put
Judges of the javelin throw
Judges of the discus throw

Because of the large number of details requiring attention if a track and field meet is to be staged successfully, it is essential that the task of each individual be clearly set forth. These duties are discussed under the following headings: games committee, athlete, coach, referee, clerk of course, starter (pistol firer), judges of the finish, timers, inspectors, judges of the pole vault, judges of the high jump, judges of the long jump, judges of the shot put, judges of the javelin throw, and judges of the discus throw.

GAMES COMMITTEE

In selecting a games committee, individuals should be obtained who not only have an adequate knowledge of the events and a keen interest in the sport but who also are willing to devote an adequate amount of time to set up a smoothly functioning organization. The following duties are the responsibilities of the games committee:

1. Formulate plans for the contest sufficiently far in advance and mail out adequate information sheets, including special regulations or eligibility rules.
2. Provide suitable running track, landing areas, runways, weight circles, locker space, and spectator facilities (see pp. 286 to 294).
3. Supply unbiased officials for their respective posts. Excerpts of the rules pertaining to the particular officials' tasks should be provided.
4. Invite as honorary officials the executive or administrative leaders of the institution, post, base, or governmental division.
5. Supervise the field and grounds equipment to the end that the prearranged time schedule and order of events can be adhered to.

6. Order in advance the official implements required in the contest (see pp. 297 and 298).

7. Provide the press with suitable photographs, matrices, or copy at intervals ahead of the date of the contest.

8. Obtain in advance the ribbons, medals, or trophies to be awarded the winners and arrange for their appropriate presentation.

9. Consider the advisability of including items of pageantry or special music.

10. Strive to keep the spectators fully informed of the progress of the various events by timely announcements. Anticipate and remove possible obstacles to a smoothly conducted contest.

11. Delegate the officials to accept the entries, edit the program, conduct the drawings for heats and lanes, certify the implements submitted by contestants, and assume responsibility for equipment.

12. Designate the officials who will serve as head field judge, head finish judge, head inspector, referee, starter, and head timer.

13. Nominate one individual as meet manager. This individual will coordinate the work of the various committees.

14. Consider the selection of a finance chairman to formulate plans for receipts and disbursements.

15. Determine the policy of recording the meet in pictures, either still or motion. Frequently a closely contested race requires the aid of motion pictures to determine the place winners.

16. Initiate any claim for a record that may arise, and upon proper certification by the meet officials submit it to the chairman of the records committee (see Official Track and Field Rules, Claim for Record).

ATHLETE

One of the duties of the coach, in addition to training the athlete for his special event, is to develop the proper attitude of team members toward the meet itself. Telling the athlete what his attitude should be just prior to a meet is not enough. By precept and example such attributes as promptness, courtesy, and respect for others must be instilled into him. This is just as important as the development of the will to win. The more important responsibilities of the athlete are as follows:

1. Report promptly to the clerk of course for track events or to the judges of the field events.

2. Do not cause needless delay to officials or to the contestants.

3. Wear presentable and acceptable clothing.

4. Conduct yourself as a true sportsman whether as a winner or a loser.

5. Know the rules of your event which include both your rights and your obligations.

6. Accept the decision of the appointed officials. If an official makes a decision believed to be contrary to rules, means are provided for courteously requesting an appeal. One should not question the official's judgment of fact.

7. Respect the ownership of certain implements in the field events not furnished by the games committee. Permission for their use is required.

8. Take no undue advantage in breaking for the pole position nor in stepping in front of an opponent who has been leading.

9. Boxing, pocketing, elbowing, seesawing the pace, and beating the gun are not a part of accepted track strategy.

10. Strive to retain physical control even at the end of a fatiguing contest and leave the field under your own power. Physical recovery is speeded by moderate jogging; it is retarded by slumping to the ground or sup-

porting one's weight on the shoulders of others.

11. Have consideration for spectators and officials. Take a seat in the proper area so that you do not impede the view of the spectators.

12. Return in your own lane at the finish of races so that you may be identified properly by the officials.

13. Carry out conscientiously all reasonable tasks assigned by the coach.

COACH

The coach must of necessity keep in mind most of the details in preparing for a track and field meet. In addition to his duties of coaching the athletes in the various events, he can add much to a meet by promoting good will among school officials, contestants, and spectators. Some of the items that require his attention are listed as follows:

1. Instruct athletes to strive to win, but only by fair and accepted means.

2. Teach the athletes the rules of the contest so that they may compete intelligently and without debate.

3. Agree in advance with opponents on controversial items not particularly covered by the official rules.

4. Aid the opponents visiting your community in making arrangements for housing, meals, transportation, and similar matters about which they have limited information.

5. Cooperate fully with the academic and athletic authorities in carrying out established policies on a high plane.

6. Stimulate a wholesome attitude toward opponents.

7. Complete your coaching tasks in advance and omit instruction while the contest is under way.

8. Discourage the practice of athletes rushing to the finish line and proffering their services in carrying a tired competitor off the track.

9. Recommend or administer no stimu-lants except on the advice of a physician.

10. Accept for membership on the squad only those who have been approved after a physical examination.

11. Strive by both teaching and example to uphold the code of amateur athletics.

12. Encourage the less talented athletes on the theory that benefits accrue to all if the habit of "right living" is a part of the training program.

13. Teach the squad to win graciously and accept defeat in a sportsmanlike manner.

14. Recommend the purchase of adequate athletic supplies to protect the competitor from injury and to improve his performance.

15. Place the welfare of the athlete before the desire for winning points. Protect his health.

REFEREE

Since the referee is the final authority in deciding all questions relative to a track and field meet, he must merit the respect of coaches, athletes, and spectators. He can do this only if he is an earnest student of the rules and has had adequate experience in the conduct of a meet.

The referee is the active administrator on the track and field. He decides all questions of rules interpretations and is responsible for the prompt and efficient handling of the meet.

The referee should confer with the starter, clerk of course, head judge of finish, head field judge, head inspector, and head timer in advance of the first event on the program. He should review the specific duties with each of the above officials.

The referee should delegate one timer to announce the time by laps and one official to notify the contestants of the number of laps remaining. He may, on his own volition or through a report of other officials, disqualify a contestant for infraction of rules.

Whenever the performance of the athlete betters the previous record, the referee shall assume leadership in obtaining certification from the judges, timers, measurers, surveyor, and starter (pistol firer).

CLERK OF COURSE

The clerk of course has the task of coordinating the activities of the athletes and the officials. The smoothness and orderly sequence of contests rests largely with him.

The clerk of course should be a member of the drawings committee and should take an active part in the seeding (see suggestions in Official Rules), heat selection, and assignment of lanes. Additional copies of the clerk of course's record list should be made available to the head judge of finish, the referee, and the announcer. Each of these officials should have a record of the heat and lane of every competitor.

He will require all contestants in a given race to report at the starting post no less than 5 minutes in advance of the starting time. He will assign the lanes and allow the athletes a reasonable time to try starting blocks before relinquishing control to the starter. The clerk of course, on authorization from the referee, may alter the personnel of heats and redraw whenever the number reporting is insufficient to warrant the number of heats originally determined.

The clerk of course will require, in straightaway races, that the competitor run in the lane drawn. Exception: the clerk, with the approval of the referee, may make adjustments in lanes when unusual conditions make the original lane assignments unfair to one or more participants.

If a competitor does not report in a race around the oval track, the clerk should move poleward, in order, all the remaining contestants so that the inner lanes are occupied.

The clerk of course is advised to permit no delay in starting an event because of a tardy contestant. A track event has preference over a field event in case a competitor's turn is called simultaneously in a track and a field contest. The competitor is responsible for obtaining permission from the head judge of the field event for his temporary absence.

The clerk shall assign such duties to his assistants as he may see fit.

STARTER (PISTOL FIRER)

The starter alone assumes control of a trial or final heat of competitors immediately after the clerk signals that the roll has been called and the men have been assigned to the lanes drawn.

The starter's task consists of getting the contestants off to an even start. Through his tone of voice, his poise, or demeanor, he will merit the confidence of the competitors. As the contestants are called to the mark, the starter will require that all persons in the area remain silent and motionless.

Equipment. The starter will be provided with a suitable pistol with whose touch or mechanism he is familiar. The official rules of the Amateur Athletic Union of the United States of America and the National Collegiate Athletic Association of the United States of America specify that the caliber of the pistol employed in starting races shall be not less than 32. The powder in the shells shall yield a distinct flash that provides a clear-cut stimulus for the timers.

It is considered good policy to remove all discharged shells so that the cylinder is filled with fresh ammunition for each race. He will have a whistle to signal both the competitors and officials.

A loaded reserve pistol carried by either the starter or the assistant starter is a safeguard against failure of the repeating mechanism of the No. 1 pistol.

The successful pistol firer will not advise the athletes that he will hold (1.4 to 1.6 seconds after hip steadiness) and then surprise them with a pistol shot at a much shorter interval. Neither will he overhold

(2.0 seconds after hip steadiness) because the peak of attention has passed and the contestants may become unsteady.[1]

If any competitors are unsteady on the mark or if they have not responded to the commands in unison, he will say, "Stand up."

Position. The starter will assume a position on the track that provides him the best view of the line of competitors for the purpose of detecting any unsteadiness. He may stand a few yards to the rear and to one side of the track, keeping his vision on a line of hips. If he chooses, he may stand 5 to 10 yards in front of the starting line and to one side of the track. He fixes his vision on either the line of hands or the line of shoulders of the contestants. The latter position is more commonly taken. He will consider both the spectators in the stands and the timers at the finish line who are required to see the flash from the pistol which is the stimulus to start their watches. A colored sleeve and a black screen background are visual aids for the timers.

Commands. The following commands are used:

"Remove sweat clothes." This command is superfluous when weather conditions are favorable enough to omit the wearing of sweat clothes. The starter is responsible that no competitor needlessly delays removal of his clothing so that his prompt opponents are inconvenienced.

"Timers and judges ready." In case the timers are at some distance from the starter so that this command is inaudible, the starter will sound one blast on his whistle. The head judge (when all is in readiness) will respond with two blasts on his whistle.

"Starters ready." Upon hearing this command, the competitors will take positions in their individual lanes, standing 1 or 2 yards behind their starting blocks.

"Get on your mark." The competitors will come to a kneeling position, hands behind the starting scratch line, feet braced against the starting blocks. The starter will permit a period of 10 to 15 seconds for personal body adjustments. He will raise the pistol above his head prior to the next command.

"Set." The competitors elevate the hips, raising both knees so that there is a four-point contact with the track (both feet and both hands). An interval of no less than 1 second (after momentary hip steadiness) nor more than 2 seconds has been determined experimentally as the range for holding athletes in the set position.

Pistol shot. After the athletes have held for about 2 seconds after the set command, the pistol may be fired. If one or more contestants start before the pistol is fired, the starter is required to assess one false start against each offender. If the pistol is fired but one or more contestants gain an undue advantage, the pistol is fired again, the athletes return to their marks, and one false start is assessed against each offender. The starter will warn them that disqualification is the penalty for a second false start. The reader is advised to refer to the rules governing his specific level of competition.

JUDGES OF THE FINISH

The head judge of the finish serves in close relationship to the starter and clerk of course.

The head judge of the finish should be supplied with a whistle to signal the starter that the officials are ready, a copy of the program containing the drawings for lanes, and a packet of mimeographed cards on which to note the names of the place winners. He should have a number of judges assigned him, no less than 1 and, preferably, 2 judges for each place scored in the race. Each judge should be given the task of picking one place winner. They should take positions on elevated steps at the finish line that are placed at least 20 feet from the track.

A competent judge of the finish, upon hearing the warning "gun up," turns to watch the start of the race and keeps the runners in his view until they are about 5 to 10 yards from the finish yarn. If he has been assigned the task of picking the third-place competitor, he will sift out the first and second runners and then turn his vision on the finish yarn. He will base his decision on the order in which the torso of each runner crosses the finish line. Each judge of finish will record on a card his independent selection, listing the competitor's number and order of finish, and hand his card to the head judge of the finish. The head judge will compile the official order of finish, obtain the official time from the head timer, enter the results on the clerk of course's record, and hand the completed data to the official scorer.

Competent judges seldom decide that two or more athletes have tied for positions at the finish, because sharpness of vision enables them to determine intervals of space between the runners. Motion pictures recording the finish of races are utilized to establish the order of placement.

TIMERS

The head timer shall assign 3 timers and 1 alternate timer for each running event. Additional timers are optional, and one of these may be assigned to call out the time by laps on races on the oval track.

All timers should be supplied with tested $\frac{1}{10}$ second watches. The timer, through manipulation, should acquaint himself with the spring tension of the starting mechanism of his watch.

The pattern of the stimulus in starting the watch is clear-cut—the flash of the pistol in the starter's hand. The order of stimuli are (1) flash, (2) smoke, and (3) sound. The pattern for the stimulus in stopping the watch is not clear-cut, since a group of surging competitors strive to cross a finish line on the ground. As an aid to the officials, a piece of yarn is stretched above the finish line at chest height. The timer will press the stop watch stem at the instant the athlete breasts the finish yarn.

There is a difference of opinion regard-ing the use of the forefinger or the thumb in pressing the start or stop mechanism, but the majority prefer the forefinger technique.

A competent timer will hold the watch steady at both the start and the finish and make no sweeping or swinging motion of the arm.

Each timer will write on an individual card the reading of his watch, sign his name thereto, and hand it to the head timer. He will retain his watch reading until it has been checked by the head timer and referee and then press the release.

Laboratory tests on hand timing versus mechanical timing reveal that human watch handlers credited the athlete with performances $\frac{1}{10}$ second faster than the automatic devices.[2] Further investigation showed that the error rested with timers who anticipated the finish—thus stopping their watches before the athlete reached the finish yarn.

An efficient timer will be alert for the warning "gun up," fix his vision on the pistol point, take up any slack in the watch stem by pressing the forefinger, and start the watch with the flash of the pistol. He will keep the competitors in his view until 5 to 10 yards from the finish line, then fix his vision on the finish yarn, and finally press the stop button as the contestant's chest contacts the yarn.

INSPECTORS

The head inspector should be assigned three inspectors so that the complete area of a given race is supervised adequately. Inspectors will be alert to anticipate and ward off potential infractions that may lead to disqualification. They will see that each athlete runs in his own lane in the hurdles and sprints and that he hinders no opponent when passing on the curve.

Whenever cases of alleged jostling, elbowing, or cutting-in occur, the inspector shall report to the head inspector and the referee and to no one else. The inspector will report an infraction, but he cannot disqualify the offending athlete. Penalties may be assessed by the referee only.

For shuttle hurdle relay races the rules committee has recommended that a touch-off inspector be assigned each runner.

In the shuttle hurdle relay it is recommended that two lanes of hurdles be provided each team and that the athlete runs in the left lane.

JUDGES OF THE POLE VAULT

The head judge of the pole vault should be supplied with the pole vault record sheet which contains each competitor's name, number, and order of competing. The drawings chairman of the games committee should supply the order of vaulting together with the stipulated starting height and each succeeding height thereafter. The committee will establish the plan after determining the ability of the vaulters, the number of competitors, and the weather.

The judges of the pole vault will permit practice vaulting in advance of the established starting hour.

During competition, the judges will permit each vaulter to move the standards and crossbar forward or backward as he chooses. The judges shall set a reasonable time limit of 2 minutes for the completion of each athlete's trial so that delay may be avoided.

The head judge of the pole vault shall excuse temporarily a vaulter who desires to compete in a track event. He shall assign one official to catch the vaulting pole after each trial.

It is recommended that the pole vault official keep the event progressing smoothly by calling up competitors in threes as: "Adams, up"; "Brown, on deck"; "Charles, in the hole."

JUDGES OF THE HIGH JUMP

The head judge of the high jump should be provided with the high jump record sheet which contains each competitor's name, number, and order of competing. The drawings chairman of the games committee should supply the order of jumping, together with the stipulated starting height and each succeeding height thereafter. The committee will set the plan on the basis of the ability of the jumpers, the number of competitors, and the weather.

The judges of the high jump will permit practice jumping in advance of the starting hour. They will not permit the jumper to move the standards forward or backward as is the case in the pole vault. The difference is attributed to the fact that the high jumper is free to select his take-off spot whereas the pole vaulter is restricted to one take-off spot—the pole plant trough.

The head judge of the high jump shall excuse temporarily a high jumper who desires to compete in another event. He is responsible for the prompt and orderly conduct of the event by notifying each competitor sufficiently far in advance of his approaching trial.

JUDGES OF THE LONG JUMP

The head judge of the long jump should be supplied with a long jump record sheet which contains each competitor's name, number, and order of competing. The drawings committee should provide the order of jumping. The head judge of the long jump shall excuse temporarily a long jumper who desires to compete in another event. He will permit the jumper to place a target or marker adjacent to the landing area as an incentive or goal.

The judges of the long jump shall be familiar with the rules governing the specifications of the take-off board and its appendages at the appropriate level of competition—either high school, college, or Olympic.

The judges of the long jump should permit the jumper to measure, establish, and mark distances from the take-off board in adjusting his run.

In measuring the jump, the judge shall hold the measuring tape at a right angle with the front edge of the take-off board or take-off board extended. The zero end should be held at the spot where the competitor broke ground so that the reading is made at the take-off board or take-off board extended.

Frequently the long jump is started 30 minutes or more in advance of the track events, thus allowing a wider time range of competition and permitting an earlier completion of the event.

JUDGES OF THE SHOT PUT

The head judge of the shot put should be provided with the shot put record sheet which contains each competitor's name, number, and order of competing. The drawings chairman of the games committee should supply the order of competing.

The head judge of the shot put shall be responsible for checking the shots used by the competitors. By agreement, when the games committee supplies one of each type of shot, the competitor is not permitted to use his personal implement. In cases where the competitor is permitted to use his own shot, the head judge will be responsible for seeing that it conforms to the official rules. He will check to see that there is affixed a seal on the shot as evidence that it has passed inspection.

The judges of the shot put will permit each contestant a reasonable number of practice trials or warm-up puts in advance of the hour of starting competition. They will require the athlete to compete promptly after his name has been called.

The head judge of the shot put shall excuse temporarily a contestant in the shot put who is called to compete in another event.

The judges will require the contestant in the shot put to remain within the circle until his effort has been marked. The athlete may, by rules, leave the circle while the distance of the put is being measured, but he must leave from the back half of the circle.

JUDGES OF THE JAVELIN THROW

The head judge of the javelin throw should be supplied with the javelin throw record sheet containing each competitor's name, number, and order of competing. The drawings chairman of the games committee should supply the order of competing.

The head judge of the javelin throw shall be responsible for checking the javelins used by the competitors. By agreement, when the games committee supplies one of each type of javelin, the competitor is not permitted to use his personal implement. In cases where the competitor is permitted to use his own javelin, the head judge will be responsible for seeing that it conforms to the official rules. He will check to see that there is affixed a seal on the javelin as evidence that it has passed inspection.

The judges of the javelin throw will permit each contestant a reasonable number of practice throws in advance of the hour of starting the competition. They will require the athlete to compete promptly after his named has been called.

The head judge of the javelin throw shall excuse temporarily a contestant who has been called to compete in another event. He shall be responsible also for the prompt running off of the event. It is recommended that to add interest for the spectators the javelins be allowed to remain where thrown until the next flight of contestants is called up.

JUDGES OF THE DISCUS THROW

The head judge of the discus throw should be provided with the discus throw record sheet which contains each competitor's name, number, and order of competing. The drawings chairman of the games committee should supply the order of competing.

The head judge of the discus throw shall be responsible for checking the discuses used by the competitors. By agreement, when the games committee supplies one of each type of discus, the competitor is not permitted to use his personal implement. In cases where the athlete is permitted to use his own discus, the head judge will be responsible for seeing that it conforms to the official rules. He will check to see if there is affixed a seal on the discus as evidence that it has passed inspection.

The head judge of the discus throw shall excuse temporarily the competitor who has been called to compete in another event.

It is recommended that whenever the number of competitors is large the contestants be divided into flights of 2, 3, or 4 athletes. Each flight will complete its series of trials before the succeeding flight is called up. This recommendation for flights applies as well to the long jump, shot put, and javelin throw.

REFERENCES

1. Walker, G. A., and Hayden, T. C.: The optimum time for holding a sprinter between the set and the gun shot, Res. Quart., Am. A. Health, Phys. Ed. & Rec. 4:124, 1933.
2. Cunningham, G.: Discrepancy between stop watch and mechanical timing, Athletic J. 17:36, 1936.

Track and field construction

One of the first things to consider in track and field planning is the accessibility of the location. Proximity to the gymnasium and dressing quarters is important to the athlete. Accessibility to automobile driveways and parking spaces and to public transportation is important to the spectator.

Whenever possible, the services of an engineer or architect, experienced in track and field construction and layout, should be obtained.

The size of the area depends on the scope of the recreational and sports program contemplated. Administrators seldom complain that the sports area is too large. More frequently they express regret that a larger space was not provided.

Another point to consider in connection with the track and field layout is adequate drainage by means of storm sewers and sumps. Also, water mains are required for use in sprinkling and for drinking water supply.

In addition, since wind velocity affects both running and field events, an area protected from excessive wind is desirable. Even though tracks are laid out in stadiums of height, there may be problems in wind effects. A track and field layout is shown in Fig. 17-1. The items discussed here include: running course, long jump landing area and runways, pole vault landing area and runways, running high jump landing area and approach, and weight circles.

RUNNING COURSE

In laying out the running course, the things to be considered are shape and dimensions, materials and construction, maintenance, and the all-weather track.

Shape and dimension. Running tracks are planned either oval in shape or oval with a 220-yard straightaway. In width the range is from 21 to 40 feet. A lane 48 inches in width permits the use of a hurdle 48 inches wide, thus requiring 25 feet for 6 lanes or 37½ feet for 9 lanes.

The length of the oval track is usually 440 yards (¼ mile), although a few courses measure 293⅔ yards (⅙ mile). Measurement of the oval track is taken on a line 12 inches outside the inner curbing (pole) on the theory that the average runner traverses the circuit on that path.

Materials and construction. Materials must be selected and arranged so that adequate drainage is assured. Also, the quality of the surface of the track must be satisfactory, and it must lend itself to upkeep with a minimum amount of attention. The points to consider are subsurface drainage, rough fill, screened cinders fill, top dressing, surface drainage, curbing, and water supply. Fig. 17-3 shows the type, relative amounts of materials, and drainage commonly used in track construction.

Subsurface drainage. Water seeping through the surface of the track should find an outlet in a storm sewer or a sump or a cistern.

Rough fill. The rough fill may consist of (1) crushed rock leveled and rolled to grade, 6 to 8 inches in thickness, (2) boiler run coarse cinders leveled and rolled to grade, 6 to 8 inches in thickness, or (3) cinders screened through ¼-inch mesh leveled and rolled to grade, 6 to 8 inches in thickness.

Drain tile frequently is laid in herringbone pattern at intervals of 50 feet. Care should be taken that the tile is adequate to support the weight of the power machinery which subsequently will be used in grooming the track.

Screened cinders fill. This is the middle layer of the track and frequently consists of cinders screened through a ¼-inch mesh. Ordinary boiler run cinders having only a few clinkers are acceptable. The thickness of this layer after leveling and rolling to grade is 3 to 5 inches. In a few cases such

material as sawdust, woven fiber matting, or peat has been added to the middle layer. It was claimed that these organic substances provided resiliency, helped to retain a fair degree of moisture, and yet permitted seepage of surface water.

Top dressing. The top dressing is the upper of the three layers and ranges from 1½ to 4 inches in thickness. If the top dressing consisted only of cinders screened through a ¼-inch mesh, the track might not hold up under the drive of the spikes. Most running tracks require some material added to the cinders as a binder. Clay is commonly used, but care must be taken to prevent the formation of a nonporous sheet. This error results in a sealed track.

Aside from serving as a rubber blanket to prevent downward seepage, the nonporous sheet of clay cinders becomes brittle in dry weather and flakes out under the impact of running shoes.

Loam or clay loam instead of clay serves to bind the cinders and yet permits drainage. Certain types of peat have been used as top dressing with good results. The advantage of its use lies in the fact that it requires no mixing with loam, cinders, or clay.

It is the opinion of many authorities that there is no need for heavy rolling with equipment that weighs 3 to 5 tons. They believe that the resiliency, or life, is squeezed from the track by a 3-ton roller and instead recommend a tennis court roller of ½ ton.

Surface drainage. In the north temperate zone the greatest amount of rains falls in April and May, two important months in the track season. Running tracks differ from tilled land in that very little rain water is desired on the cinder oval, and the excess should be drained off at once. One plan is to build the top surface of the running track several inches higher than the surrounding terrain. Outlets in the curbing at frequent intervals permit surface runoff without the washing of gulleys in the cinder surface. It

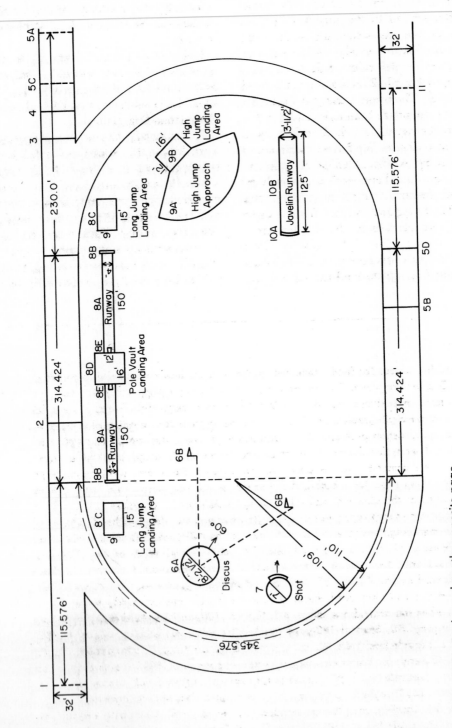

Fig. 17-1. For legend see the opposite page.

is claimed that a slight grade or fall from the pole position to the outer curb would drain the rainfall to the outside edge and away from the most-used lane of the oval.

Curbing. The inner edge of the track as defined by official rules shall be a solid curb approximately 2 inches above the level of the track. The upper surface of this curb should be rounded. Materials used for the curb are creosoted wood, 2 inches by 6 inches, or concrete. We have experimented with curbing of discarded steel rails obtained from an abandoned steam railway line and found it satisfactory. The rails were 30 feet long and weighed 60 pounds to the yard. At intervals of 15 feet a concrete pillar was sunk 4 feet in the ground. Bolts set in the fresh concrete permitted the attachment of flanges to hold the rail secure.

Two workmen using a manual rail bender did a satisfactory job on the arc at each end of the oval. No heating of the steel rail was required.

Holes were burned through the rail at intervals of 5 feet at the level of the surface of the track for the purpose of speedy drainage. The track surface was 6 inches above the surrounding ground.

Water supply. Whenever the drainage of a track is rapid, provision should be made to supply an even amount of moisture. Water lines with convenient taps should be provided along the straightaway and the oval tracks. More elaborate installations include fixed sprays which, when the valve is opened, sprinkle a considerable area. Prolonged windstorms are a hazard to cinder tracks, because if the weather is hot and

---

Fig. 17-1. This layout for field events within the oval obviously is not drawn to scale. Runways and landing areas for the long jump, running high jump, and pole vault can be constructed in positions that do not interfere with a regulation football feld. The radius of the semicircle (depicted as 110 feet in the diagram) can be adjusted in order to meet given construction problems. If the radius is shortened, the straightaway distance must be lengthened; thus the curve will be sharp. If the radius is lengthened, the straightaway must be shortened; thus the curve will be gradual. Since most construction plans include a playing area for football, the location of the equipment used for the field events, as well as the dimensions of the running track, must be considered. **1,** Finish of the 220-yard events that are run on the straightaway and the 180-yard low hurdles that are run on the straightaway. **2,** Start and finish of the 440-yard, 880-yard, 1-mile, and 2-mile events; finish of the 100-yard and 120-yard events; finish of the 220-yard dash and 180-yard low hurdles whenever either race is run around a curve. **3,** Start of the 100-yard events. **4,** Start of the 120-yard events. **5A,** Start of the 220-yard dash (straightaway); start of 440-yard events that are run around one curve. **5B,** Start of 220-yard dash when run around one curve. **5C,** Start of 180-yard low hurdles when run on the straightaway. **5D,** Start of 180-yard low hurdles when run around one curve. **6A,** Discus circle (see rule book). **6B,** Discus sector (60 degrees); flags. **7,** Shot circle (see rule book). **8A,** Runways for both the long jump and the pole vault. **8B,** Take-off boards for the long jump (see rule book). **8C,** Landing areas for the long jump. **8D,** Landing area for the pole vault. **8E,** Troughs for planting the vaulting pole. **9A,** Approach for the running high jump. **9B,** Landing area for the running high jump. **10A,** Restraining arc for the javelin throw (see rule book). **10B,** Runway for the javelin throw. **11,** Finish of races of 440 yards (or multiples thereof) whenever the start is made at **5A**.

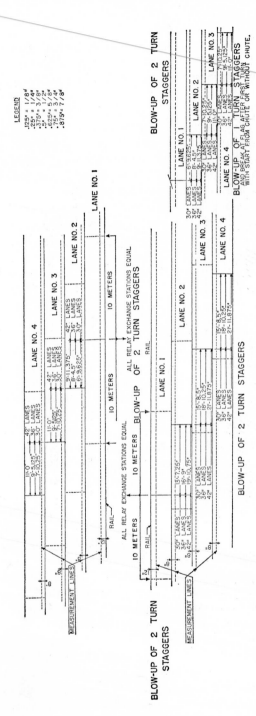

Fig. 17-2. A guide for measuring turn staggers for track lanes. (Reproduced by permission of the National Federation of State High School Athletic Associations.)

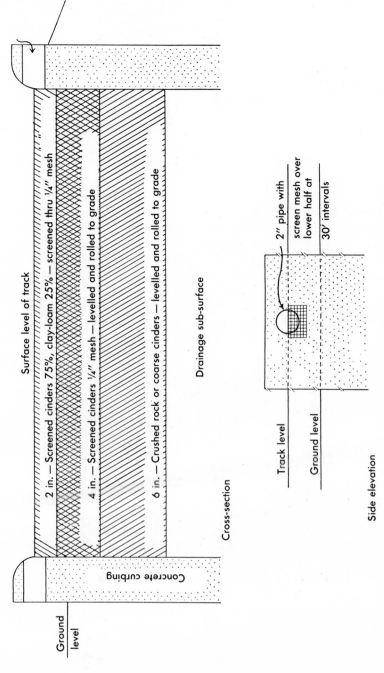

Surface level of track

2 in. — Screened cinders 75%, clay-loam 25% — screened thru ¼" mesh

4 in. — Screened cinders ¼" mesh — levelled and rolled to grade

6 in. — Crushed rock or coarse cinders — levelled and rolled to grade

Drainage sub-surface

Concrete curbing

Ground level

Cross-section

2" pipe with screen mesh over lower half at 30' intervals

Track level

Ground level

Side elevation

Fig. 17-3. Track construction showing the type and relative amount of materials and drainage.

dry, the valuable top dressing is carried skyward. Sprinkling the track with water and applying calcium cloride are two means of retaining the top dressing.

Maintenance. The upkeep of the running track is necessary if it is to continue to be level and resilient and to retain the correct texture.

The holes should be filled daily and the track brushed, leveled, and sprinkled lightly. Some tracks may require a light rolling, but as was pointed out earlier in this discussion, many authorities keep track rolling at a minimum.

A fiber brush 36 inches wide dragged frequently around the track keeps the small holes filled. If a small motor truck is available, a metal doormat 6 by 6 feet hooked on will permit a speedy job of leveling. For indoor tracks and on some outdoor cinder ovals an application of sawdust might be beneficial.

Cinders should be renewed a little each year because they become crushed and lose their resiliency. A thin layer worked into the surface assures a track that provides bounce or spring.

Once the track has been placed in readiness, the next items to consider are the jumping and vaulting runways, the landing areas, and the weight circles.

All-weather track. For a number of years, runways for the various field events have been constructed of all-weather surfacing materials and have proved very effective. This type of surfacing is known by a number of names, but the majority of materials are asphalt or other bituminous derivatives.

Recently, all-weather tracks of various materials have been construced at many high schools, colleges, and universities. In addition to their utility, these tracks reduce the costs of maintenance and are suitable for permanent markings that designate the start and finish lines, the lanes for each runner, the hurdle stations, the baton passing zones (indicated by different colors)

for the relays, and the lanes or lines necessary whenever races are run around curves that require echelon (staggered) measurements.

LONG JUMP

The items to consider in the layout of the long jump are runway, take-off board and joist on which it rests, and landing area.

Runway. The runway should be 125 to 150 feet long and from 4 to 5 feet in width. The length should be sufficient to accommodate the athlete requiring considerable distance in generating the speed of his run. The width of the path depends on the equipment used to condition it but should be wide enough to permit use of a power roller, drag, leveler, or brush.

The same plan for drainage and three layers of building material as used on the running track seem adequate for the long jump runway. The coarse layer at the bottom and the screened cinder middle stratum permit drainage. It is recommended that the top surface of the runway be 3 to 5 inches higher than the adjacent ground.

Daily attention to such tasks as filling holes, leveling, brushing, and sprinkling result in a presentable path.

In some cases the top of the curb bears a scale in feet, from 0 at the take-off board to 150 feet at the start, so that competitors may lay out the checkmarks used in the run.

All-weather runways are currently widely used and are recommended.

Take-off board. The take-off board as defined in the collegiate rules "shall be a joist 8 inches wide and at least 4 feet long which shall be set firmly in and on the same level as the ground." For technical information on the construction of the long jump take-off board and its appendages, the reader is urged to consult the official rules at the various levels of competition—high school, college, or Olympic.

The take-off board requires replacement because of continued chipping by jumping spikes. To facilitate taking up the old and setting down the new plank, a heavy beam or railroad tie sunk 2 inches below ground level is recommended. Four spikes are sufficient to secure the take-off board to the permanent beam.

Landing area. The landing area should be not less than 9 feet wide and of a length adequate to accommodate the most proficient of the jumpers using it. The landing area may extend from a point 10 feet in front of the take-off board to a point 15 to 25 feet farther on.

Ordinary builder's sand is preferred as a filler for the landing area and is most satisfactory when slightly moist. The depth of the landing area ranges from 12 to 18 inches.

A straight edge or curbing along the landing area is frequently marked off in feet and inches to aid in determining rapidly, without a tape measure, the length of the jumps.

POLE VAULT

The planning for construction of facilities for the pole vault include runway, pole plant box, standards, and landing area.

Runway. The runway should be 150 feet long and approximately 4 feet wide. As in the long jump, the runway should be long enough to satisfy those competitors requiring a large number of strides in gaining speed. The width of the runway may be increased to permit power machinery for dragging, leveling, and rolling.

It is common practice to construct a runway from two opposite directions (Fig. 17-1) so that weather or wind conditions may be met satisfactorily.

The three-layer plan for building a pole vault runway is similar to that suggested for both the running track and the long jump path. Again, it is recommended that the top surface of the runway be 3 to 5 inches higher than the surrounding terrain. All-weather runways are recommended for the pole vault and are widely used.

Pole plant box. Official rules call for a wooden or metal box. A diagram showing detailed measurements for the plant box is included in each issue of the official rules. The competitor may toss shavings or sawdust in the pole plant box for the purpose of lessening the shock.

Standards. The chief consideration in the selection of vaulting standards is their size and durability. Since the life of this item is unlimited, it is wise to purchase the best quality. One must consider that vaulting standards remain outdoors several months of the year and must withstand weathering. Again they should be manipulated readily and bear a measuring scale so that the height of the crossbar is immediately determined.

Landing area. Official rules designate a vaulting area of 16 feet in width by 12 feet in length, but a larger area (16 by 14 feet) is quite commonly constructed. Foam rubber (blocks or rectangles) has replaced shavings and sawdust in most built landing areas.

RUNNING HIGH JUMP

The items required in a high jump layout are approach and take-off area, standards, and landing area.

Approach. The approach is frequently constructed in a fan shape with a slope away from the landing area to provide a speedy runoff of rainfall. The customary three layers of strata used for the long jump runway apply in like manner to the high jump. However, all-weather material is now commonly used for the high jump approach. Such material has the qualities considered essential for the high jump. These qualities are firmness (does not disintegrate under spike pressure), resiliency (does not become too hard), and plasticity (can be reconditioned or smoothed readily). In the north temperate zone, high jumpers using an all-weather approach have been able to practice outdoors in a mild December and as early as March when the temperature was moderate. A clay or cinder loam approach on the same athletic field would likely be soft or mushy on a March day suitable for outdoor practice.

Standards. The suggestions offered in the section dealing with pole vault equipment applies to the high jump standards. Since the standards represent a long-term investment, the most efficient and sturdiest are recommended. They should provide speed in adjustment and clear visibility of the scale in feet and inches.

Landing area. The size of the landing area for the running high jump is specified in the official rules as 16 feet in width by 12 feet in length. Foam rubber (blocks or rectangles) in preference to shavings or sawdust has been selected for most landing areas.

WEIGHT CIRCLES

Weight circles having a diameter of 7 feet are prescribed for the shot put, the hammer throw, and the heavyweight throw. The heavyweight throw is contested with implements weighing 25 pounds (schoolboy), 35 pounds (college), or 56 pounds (A.A.U).

The discus is thrown from a circle having a diameter of 2.5 meters (8 feet 2½ inches).

Circles constructed of concrete or similar materials obviously require the use of shoes other than those constructed with conventional spikes. The discus must alight within a 60-degree sector.

Because the techniques of the hammer throw and the discus throw usually involve pivoting on the feet, one has to give careful consideration to both the texture of the circle material and the type of shoes worn. For this reason the top dressing is such that it does not impede the footwork so vital in both the discus and the hammer throw.

The three-layer plan used in constructing a running track has been applied to weight circles, except that the thickness of each layer was reduced to 3 or 4 inches. Subsurface drainage is of some importance, but protection of the surface from heavy rainfall is given greater consideration. Fortunately, the small size of the weight circle makes possible the use of waterproof material as a cover.

The outer edge of the circle for the shot put, hammer throw, heavyweight throw, or the discus throw should consist of a metal band.

Appendixes

Preparations for a track and field meet

If a meet is to proceed smoothly, the necessary items required must be at hand. In the following pages an attempt has been made to list the items pertinent to each event.

General equipment

1. Competitor numbers
2. Concessions—food and beverages
3. Dressing—locker and shower facilities
4. Parking area
5. Police
6. Press table
7. Prizes
8. Program (should include time schedule and list of records)
9. Public address system
10. Radio arrangements if the meet is to be broadcast
11. Rule book
12. Safety pins
13. Seats for officials
14. Score board
15. Scorers' record
16. Television arrangements if the meet is to be telecast
17. Ticket sellers and takers
18. Ushers

Track equipment

1. Anemometer—wind gauge for direction and velocity
2. Attendants—hurdle setters, starting block setters, baton custodians, and messengers
3. Batons for relay races
4. Cartridges
5. Clerk of course record, including heats and lanes
6. Elevated platforms (stair steps) for officials

7. Finish lines marked, finish posts, and finish yarn
8. Hurdles—10 for each lane
9. Hurdle stations marked
10. Judge of finished record cards
11. Kelly pool balls for drawing lanes
12. Pistols, 32 caliber; shells must contain powder that yields distinct flash, providing clear-cut stimulus for timers (see rule book)
13. Relay passing zones marked
14. Starting blocks—mallets or hammers
15. Startling lines marked
16. String to aid hurdle setters in correct alignment
17. Stop watches
18. Timers' record cards
19. Whistles for starter and head judge of finish

Field event equipment
General

1. Attendants returning implements and spading landing area for long jump
2. Instruments for measuring implements
3. Official seals to attach to approved implements
4. Scales for weighing implements
5. Weight circles, runways, landing areas so located that all events can be conducted simultaneously if so required

Long jump

1. Long jump score sheet, contestants' roll call with rules printed thereon
2. Brush to smooth runway if surface is soft
3. Colored pegs for contestant's individual checkmarks
4. Leveling board; straight edge for landing area
5. Loosened landing area—sand

6. Measuring tape, steel
7. Putty, molder's clay, soft earth, or plasticene (see rule book)
8. Putty knife
9. Take-off board painted white

Discus throw

1. Brush to smooth circle (see rule book, concrete circle plans)
2. Circle, 8 feet 2½ inches, metal
3. Discuses, official, either 3 pounds 9 ounces or 2 kilograms if supplied by games committee
4. Discus score sheet and contestants' roll call with rules printed thereon
5. Measuring tape, steel
6. Sector flags and boundary lines
7. Warm-up circle

Running high jump

1. Brush to smooth the area of approach if surface is soft
2. Crossbars
3. Hand tamper to pack take-off is surface is soft
4. High jump score sheet and contestants' roll call with rules printed thereon
5. Adequate landing area—sand, wood shavings, sawdust, or foam rubber (blocks or rectangles)
6. Measuring stick, accurate, 7 feet 6 inches
7. Standards

Javelin throw

1. Javelin score sheet and contestants' roll call with rules printed thereon
2. Javelins, official, if supplied by games committee
3. Markers on ground at 10-foot intervals from 175 feet upward

4. Measuring tape, steel
5. Restraining board arc (see rule book)
6. Sector, radial lines (see rule book)
7. Warm-up area

Pole vault

1. Brush to smooth away if surface is soft
2. Colored pegs for contestant's individual checkmarks
3. Crossbars
4. Forked stick for replacing bar
5. Adequate landing area—shavings or foam rubber (blocks or rectangles)
6. Measuring stick, accurate, 18 feet
7. Poles, extra—metal or fiber glass, 14 to 16 feet long
8. Pole plant box (see rule book specifications)
9. Pole vault score sheet and contestants' roll call with rules printed thereon
10. Standards
11. Step ladder

Shot put

1. Bangboard to check the roll of shot after alighting
2. Brush to smooth circle (see rule book, concrete circle plans)
3. Circle, 7 feet, flush with ground, metal
4. Limed arcs at 2-foot intervals from 46 feet upward
5. Measuring tape, steel
6. Sector markers (see rule book)
7. Shots, 12 or 16 pounds, if supplied by games committee
8. Shot put score sheets and contestants' roll call with rules printed thereon
9. Stopboard (see specifications in rule book)
10. Trough for returning shot
11. Warm-up circle

Journals and periodicals

A list of journals and periodicals is included in which appear from time to time articles dealing with all phases of track and field athletics. Contributions are made to these publications by the outstanding coaches and authorities of the world. Teachers and students of track and field events who wish to keep informed on the latest developments in teaching and coaching should have access to the authoritative literature which appears periodically.

Another prerequisite to good instruction, as well as to good performance, is familiarity with the rules governing track and field events. In this book, rules were discussed only briefly since publications are available that treat the subject adequately. For the convenience of those who wish to avail themselves of such material, a list of periodicals devoted to rules is likewise presented.

Although the importance of records in the various events is recognized, they are intentionally omitted since they are continually changing. The desired information can be gained by securing the publications as indicated in the lists which follow.

Journals

The Amateur Athlete. Edited by Tim Horgan, H. O. Zimman, Inc., 156 Broad St., Lynn, Mass. 01901. Monthly.

Athletic Journal. Edited by M. M. Arns, 1719 Howard St., Evanston, Ill. 60202. Monthly except July and August.

Journal of Applied Physiology. Edited by Sara F. Leslie, 9650 Rockville Pike, Bethesda, Md. 20014. Monthly.

Journal of Health, Physical Education and Recreation. Managing Editor, Nancy H. Rosenberg, 1201 Sixteenth St., N.W., Washington, D. C. 20036. Monthly September to April inclusive and bimonthly in May and June.

Journal of Sports Medicine and Physical Fitness. Edited by Giuseppe La Cava, Minerva Medica, Torino, Italy. Quarterly.

The Physical Educator. Edited by C. O. Jackson, 4000 Meadows Drive, Indianapolis, Ind. 46205. Quarterly.

Research Quarterly. Edited by Carolyn Bookwalter, 1201 Sixteenth St., N.W. Washington 6, D. C. Quarterly in March, May, October, and December.

Scholastic Coach. Edited by Herman L. Masin, 50 W. 44th St., New York N. Y. 10036. Monthly except July and August.

Research Journal of Physical Education. Edited by Japanese Society of Physical Education, Faculty of Education, University of Tokyo, Motofugi-cho, Bunkyo-ku, Tokyo, Japan.

Track and Field News. Edited by Cordner Nelson, P.O. Box 296, Los Altos, Calif. 94022. Monthly.

Track Technique. Edited by Fred Wilt, P.O. Box 296, Los Altos, Calif. 94022. Quarterly.

Periodicals (rules and records) published annually

Amateur Athletic Union (USA) Official Handbook (includes rules, records, etc.), 231 West 58th St., New York, N. Y. 10019. Price, $2.25.

National Collegiate Athletic Association Track and Field Guide (includes records), College Athletics Publishing Service, 349 East Thomas Road, Phoenix, Ariz. 85012. Price, $1.

National Federation of State High School Athletic Associations Track and Field Rules (includes records), 7 South Dearborn St., Chicago, Ill. 60603. Price, 65¢.

Glossary

A.A.U. Amateur Athletic Union.

abdomen that part of the body lying between the thorax and pelvis.

abscissa the horizontal coordinate axis in a graph.

acceleration a change of speed.

achilles tendon the strong tendon formed of the united tendons of the large muscles in the calf of the leg and inserted in the bone of the heel.

acute having a sharp and relatively short course; not chronic.

adhesion the abnormal joining of parts to each other.

algae a group of cellular fresh-water plants.

alkali reserve the amount of bicarbonate in the blood (or body) available for neutralizing acids.

ambidextrous ability to use both hands (or other opposite parts of the body) equally well.

anchor the fourth and last position on a relay team.

angle of delivery the angle at which a missile travels in relation to the ground as it leaves the hand of the thrower (same as angle of trajectory).

angle of trajectory see *angle of delivery*.

angular velocity speed generated by rotation.

anoxemia the lack of the proper amount of oxygen in the blood.

antagonistic opposite in action.

assimilation the transformation of food into living tissue.

ball-heel referring to a contact with the ground in which the ball of the foot strikes before the heel.

bar bell a piece of gymnastic apparatus resembling a dumbbell but having a long bar for a handle.

body whip a vigorous movement of the body.

bottom endurance; ability to repeat; reserve strength (see *stamina*).

bounding moving with a succession of springs or leaps.

breaking (start) the act of leaving the starting mark before the official has fired the starting pistol.

breasting the yarn the act of contacting the yarn with the chest at the finish of the race.

buck the forward trunk bend executed by a high hurdler almost simultaneous with the spring from the ground.

buttocks the protuberances at the back of the hips on which one sits.

cadence harmony and proportion in motion; rhythm; rate of locomotion.

calibration the determination of the graduation as of various standards or graduated instruments.

calisthenics the practice of bodily exercises to promote strength and gracefulness; light gymnastics.

calorie the unit of heat energy.

cardiac pertaining to the heart.

cardiorespiratory pertaining to the heart and respiration.

cast to throw; to shed.

caste class or division of society.

catapult (noun) a device used for hurling heavy missiles (or stones) with extreme force.

catapult (verb) to throw, drive, discharge, move, or launch by or as if by means of a catapult.

cathartic a medicine that quickens and increases the evacuation of the bowels.

center of gravity a center of gravitational attraction; hence that point in a body from or on which the body can be suspended or balanced in equilibrium in any position.

center of body weight see *center of gravity*.

centimeter (cm.) 1/100 of a meter, equivalent to 0.3937 inch.

centipede race a contest in which 3 or 4 athletes straddle a light pole 15 feet in length or longer, grasping it with their right hands; when running, the legs of the contestants move in unison like those of a centipede.

centrifugal force a force directed outward when a

body is constrained to move in a curved path.

chafing injury or irritation caused by rubbing; friction.

checkmark an aid to ensure accuracy of stride; usually a mark at the side of the runway.

choice reaction time the time required to react to a complex stimulus pattern.

chronic long continued; not acute.

chronoscope a standard scientific apparatus for measuring short intervals of time.

circumduction the active or passive movement of a limb.

collect to poise or adjust oneself both mentally and physically, especially just before the take-off in a jump or vault.

compensation the act of counterbalancing any defect of structure or function; alteration of function to meet a specific need.

compound tincture of benzoin a sticky rosinlike substance (see *tincture of benzoin*).

concentric muscle contraction extending out equally in all directions from a common center.

condiment a pungent and appetizing substance such as pepper and mustard.

connective tissue tissue that binds together; also tissues that support various structures of the body.

constipation a state of the bowels in which the evacuations are infrequent or difficult or in which the intestines become filled with hardened feces.

constrict to draw together; to render smaller or narrower.

contraction the shortening (accompanied by a thickening) of a muscle fiber or of a whole muscle in action.

coordination harmonious adjustment; the combination of muscular movements in harmonious action.

correlation a mutual or reciprocal relation; also the act of determining such relationship.

counter the upper leather part of the heel of the shoe.

criterion standard of judging.

crotch the angle formed by the parting of the legs.

cupped (1) a partially flexed position of the fingers; (2) a condition in which the track is dug out by the spikes in the toe of the shoe.

curl flexion of the arms at the elbows or flexion of the legs at the knees.

cut-down the speedy, shortened, downward leg action in the stride or in clearing a hurdle; also the shortening of the last stride in preparation for striking the take-off board.

danger line a theoretical line of demarcation between an athlete and his leading rival in the race; should the rival obtain an additional lead, the athlete will quite likely lose the race.

diagnosis the determination of the nature of a disease by its symptoms.

diarrhea abnormal frequency and liquidity of fecal discharges.

diastolic pressure the blood pressure in an artery during the relaxing phase of the heart cycle.

dilatation enlargement of a cavity; dilation.

debility lack or loss of strength.

defecation the discharge of fecal matter from the bowels.

deltoid a triangular-shaped muscle over the shoulder.

density the relation of mass to volume.

dermatology pertaining to diseases of the skin.

desquamation the shedding of skin in scales or sheets.

diametrical directly opposite.

diaphragmatic referring to the diaphragm.

diathermy local elevation of temperature in the tissues by electric current.

disinfectant an agent that destroys disease germs.

dominance the quality or state of exercising better control over either the left or right members of the body.

double float that period in running when both feet are off the ground.

driving muscles those muscles of the thigh and leg that furnish the force for propelling the body.

dynamometer an instrument for measuring strength.

dysentery an inflammation of the large intestine accompanied by nervous prostration and bloody fecal discharge.

echelon placement of athletes in a steplike position at the start of a race so that all competitors run an equal distance.

eczema an inflammatory skin disease in which there are a watery discharge and a development of scales and crusts.

elasticity (mechanical) responsiveness or adaptability to the requirement of changes in load; flexibility.

elimination the act of expelling waste material from the body.

emulate to strive to equal or excel in performance.

endurance stamina, ability to repeat muscular movements for a long time (see *bottom* and also *stamina*).

energy capacity for performing work.

enervate to deprive of nervous energy, strength, or force.

ergometer instrument that measures capacity to do work.

excised removed from the body.

exhalation the act of giving off vapor or other substances such as carbon dioxide from the lungs.

exigency emergency.

expiration expelling air from the lungs (see *exhalation*).

extensor any muscle that performs extension of a member of the body.

extraneous not essential or necessary; foreign.

Fahrenheit (F.) a scale used for measuring temperature on which the boiling point is 212° and the freezing point 32°.

Fartlek system (speed play) a plan of athletic exercises, semiformal in nature, whereby the athlete determines the type, intensity, and duration of his activity.

fen boggy land; a marsh.

feces the undigested residue of the food discharged from the bowels.

fiber an elongated, threadlike structure of organic tissue.

field the group of competitors engaged in athletic competition.

finesse subtle discrimination or cunnning in meeting situations.

flat without obstacles such as hurdles; level ground.

flat-footed a contact with the ground where both the heel and the ball of the foot strike simultaneously.

flex to bend a joint in such a direction as to approximate the two parts which it connects; opposite of extend.

flight the passage of a jumper over the landing area (see *transit*); also a group of individuals performing at the same time.

flush level or even with an adjacent surface.

focus point of concentration.

force (physics) the cause of the acceleration of the movement of material bodies.

free distance the distance gained in relay races by the backward extension of the receiver's arm and the forward reach of the passer.

free leg the leg which is not driving but the one that is swinging into position for the execution of the next drive.

function pertaining to the normal and special action of any part of a living animal.

fungus a class of vegetable organism of a low order of development.

gastric pertaining to the stomach.

gastrocnemius the large muscle in the calf of the leg.

gastrointestinal pertaining to the stomach and intestines.

gather same as *collect*.

germicide an agent that destroys germs.

glycogen sometimes called animal starch and is the form in which sugar is stored in the body.

gram (gm.) 1/28 of an ounce.

graphite native carbon, commonly used in lead pencils.

groin the lowest part of the abdominal wall near its junction with the thighs.

hamstring (muscles) referring to the muscles at the back of the thigh.

hand abduction an action by which the hand is drawn away from the midline of the extended arm.

hand adduction an action by which the hand is drawn toward the midline of the extended arm.

hand hammock a groove or bed in the hand supplying a natural cradle for the javelin.

head wind a wind that is blowing directly against the flight of a missile or directly in the face of a runner.

heel cup a protective device inserted in the shoe for the purpose of spreading the effect of shock on the athlete's heel.

hemorrhage an escape of blood either inside or outside of the tissue.

high bar same as *horizontal bar*.

horizontal bar a gymnasium apparatus, either fixed or adjustable, consisting of a single, firmly supported steel or wooden bar.

hydrotherapy the use of water in treating disease.

hygiene the science of health and its preservation.

I.A.A.F. International Amateur Athletic Federation.

idiosyncrasies habits or qualities of body or mind peculiar to an individual.

imbalance out of balance.

immobilization (immobilize) the act of making immovable.

impetus the property possessed by a moving body by virtue of its weight or its motion; the popular equivalent of momentum.

Indian wrestling a competitive game in which 2 athletes lie side by side on their backs, heads pointing in opposite directions, with their inner legs raised to a vertical position; at the command "go" they hitch legs and try to roll each other over.

inertia (physics) the property of matter by which it will remain at rest or in uniform motion in the same straight line or direction unless acted upon by some external force.

infected the communication of disease from without.

ingestion the act of taking substances such as food into the body.

inherent existing in something as a permanent attribute; inborn, native, or innate.

inhibition the act of holding back or in; self-restraint.

initial stance the position of stability, balance, or poise at the start of an event.

initiate to start; to begin.

inorganic matter other than animal or vegetable; not organic.

inspiration the act of filling the lungs with air.

intact inside the body in a natural position.

interdigital situated between 2 adjacent fingers or toes.

interscholastic between schools of secondary level; between high schools, academies, or similar intermediate institutions.

interval running practice exercises in which the athlete runs specified distances interspersed with intervals of jogging. The jogging assigned may be either a fixed distance or a fixed interval of time.

inverted running sometimes called inverted bicycle riding; an exercise in which the athlete, with his back on the floor, extends his legs in the air and executes a treading motion with the feet.

involuntary performed without conscious mental effort.

isolate to separate from surrounding objects; to pick out one thing or part and exclude all others.

isometric referring to the contraction of a muscle under circumstances that prevent it from shortening.

jogging traveling at an extremely slow cadence.

✗ *jumping leg* the leg that is in contact with the ground and that imparts force to the body.

jump-stick relay a relay in which 2 or more teams line up in columns; in each column the athletes are spaced by an arm's length; 2 members of each team grasp either end of a 6-foot-stick, hold it at knee height, and sprint down their column so that in succession each team member jumps the obstacle as it reaches him; the carriers of the stick are successively relieved by their teammates, so that each has had a trial in running with it; the team that first completes its full cycle wins the race.

key to prepare oneself by concentrated mental effort.

kilogram equivalent to 2.2 pounds; 1,000 grams.

kipping (the kip, gymnastics) a method or feat of raising the body when hanging or swinging by the arms, as for the purpose of mounting upon the horizontal bar; the legs are swung forward and upward by bending at the hips, then down again, thus giving upward impetus to the body.

kneading manipulating muscle by movements similar to those used by a baker in mixing dough.

kymograph an apparatus that revolves a drum upon which may be recorded physiologic responses.

laceration a tear; a wound made by tearing.

laity those who are not of a certain profession, such as medicine.

landing contacting the shock-reducing area at the end of the flight; also contacting the ground with the foot in running.

latent ability hidden ability.

lead-off competitor the athlete who runs the first sector of a relay race.

lesion a wound or injury.

lethargy a state of inaction or indifference.

lymphatic pertaining to lymph, a transparent, slightly yellow liquid of alkaline reaction, found in the lymph vessels and spaces.

malpractice wrongdoing; any practice that is not considered sound or desirable.

maneuver to change one's position so as to gain an advantage.

mark the line on the ground defining the start of running races (the pistol firer's command to the competitor is get on your mark).

masseur one who practices massage.

mat hurdling a stretching exercise performed on a gymnasium mat in which the athlete first assumes a sitting position, right leg extended forward, the left leg and foot forming 2 right angles; the trunk is moved to simulate the actions executed when clearing a hurdle.

maturation the process of acquiring full growth in size or ability.

mean average.

medial pertaining to the middle; toward the body.

✗ *medley* a race in which the various sectors are of unequal lengths.

mental hygiene that phase of hygiene dealing with the health of the mind.

✗ *meter* the metric equivalent to 39.37 inches.

metronome an instrument for marking exact intervals of time.

millimeter (mm.) 0.1 centimeter.

millisecond 0.001 second.

momentum the force possessed by a body in motion.

motor-minded a term designating a person who reacts reflexly or automatically to a stimulus.

movement pattern a sequence of movements, as, for example, leaving the mark at the start of a race.

musculature the muscles of an animal.

nausea sickness at the stomach; an inclination to vomit.

N.C.A.A. National Collegiate Athletic Association.

neuromuscular pertaining to muscles and nerves.

neurophysiologic pertaining to the physiology of nervous tissue.

neutral soap a soap neither acid nor basic in reaction.

N.F.S.H.S.A.A. National Federation of State High School Athletic Associations.

nitrogenous containing nitrogen.

noncompensated a condition in which the organs of the body fail to change their activity to meet the demands placed on them.

objective the goal or aim for which the athlete is striving; also used in reference to measuring accurately with specific physical devices.

optimum most efficient; most desirable.

ordinate the vertical coordinate axis in a graph.

organic pertaining to or derived from living organisms.

orthodox approved; conventional.

overstimulation a condition of excitement or nervousness.

pace rate of movement.

pace judgment the ability to estimate one's rate of speed.

panacea a cure-all.

parallel bars a gymnasium apparatus consisting of 2 firmly supported wooden bars, arranged horizontally and parallel to each other.

parasite a plant or animal living on or with another living organism at whose expense it gets its food.

passer a runner completing his sector of a relay race and in the act of handing the baton to his teammate.

passing zone the distance (20 meters) prescribed by relay racing rules within which the baton must be exchanged.

pasteurize to arrest or check fermentation by heat; to kill bacteria by heat.

patellar tendon the tendon that attaches the rectus femoris muscle in the thigh to the patella (kneecap).

pathologic pertaining to disease.

pawing a downward and backward action of the legs similar to the front leg movement of a quadruped, such as the horse.

pectoral pertaining to the breast.

peripheral referring to the outer edge.

perspiration sweat; a fluid excreted by glands in the skin.

philosophic pertaining to philosophy, the knowledge of phenomena as explained by and resolved into causes and reasons, powers, and laws.

phobia fear; aversion or extreme dislike, usually morbid in nature.

physiologic pertaining to the science dealing with the normal processes, activities, and phenomena of living organisms.

pike same as jackknife in athletics.

pinched off having both the forward and sideward paths blocked (applies to a runner).

plane a level surface, real or imaginary.

plumb line a line having a weight attached to one end and used to indicate a vertical direction.

postexercise after exercise.

potential hidden possibility; latent power.

power (physics) the rate of transfer of energy.

prognosticate to foretell; to prophesy; to predict.

prophylactic tending to ward off disease or injury.

propulsion the act of driving forward or away.

proximity a state of being near.

psychologic pertaining to the mind; mental.

pulled muscle an injury in which the fibers of a muscle are pulled apart.

pusher a chamois covering for the toes and ball of the foot.

putrefaction decomposition through the agency of microorganisms (germs).

pyogenic producing pus.

ramification (ramify) to branch out.

reaction time the interval elapsing between a stimulus and a voluntary response, such as pressing a telegraph key upon seeing the flash of a light.

receiver the runner receiving the baton in the zone of exchange in a relay race.

recovery leg the swinging leg during the running stride.

recovery phase that part of the running stride in which the leg is swinging forward into position for the oncoming drive.

rectilinear in a straight line.

red blood corpuscle one of the formed elements of the blood which has no nucleus; its chief function is to carry oxygen.

reflex refers to movements that involve chiefly the spinal cord (involuntary).

reflex pattern a sequence of movements which is executed involuntarily, such as the movements in leaving the mark when starting the sprint.

reflex time the interval elapsing between a stimulus and an involuntary response.

relax to make less firm, rigid, or tense.

research diligent investigation to ascertain facts.

resilience (1) an act of springing back; (2) the recoverable potential energy of an elastic solid body or structure due to its having been subjected to stress not exceeding the elastic limit.

respiration the act or function of breathing.

respite an interval of rest; a temporary intermission.

rhythm movements marked by regular recurrence; symmetry of movement.

ride to accept in a relaxed fashion the pace set by a rival who is leading by only a few yards.

rock-over a movement in which the athlete lands on one foot and through a continuous movement shifts the body weight to the other; also a movement in which a runner lands on the heel and shifts the weight to the toes through a rocking motion.

rock-up the action involved in shifting the body weight from an even distribution on the heel and ball of the foot to the ball of the foot.

roughage coarse substances in the diet, such as bran and whole wheat bread.

rubble broken stones of irregular sizes and shapes.

running leg the leg that is applying force during a stride (same as driving leg).

saline salty; containing a salt or salts.

sarcolemma a delicate elastic sheath covering a muscle fiber.

scarecrow dance a loose-jointed hopping and bounding exercise executed before a race for the purpose of relaxing the musculature.

schema a general representation but not with absolute exactment; a plan; an outline; a diagram.

scratch line the front edge of the take-off board.

scrotum the pouch that contains the testicles and their accessory organs.

sector (1) an area bounded by 2 radii and the included arc of a circle; (2) in relay racing, the distance traversed by a given runner.

sedentary a state of physical inactivity.

semicoast the slight decrease in effort just prior to reaching the take-off board; partial relaxation during a running event.

sensory pertaining to sensation.

settle down a slight lowering of the body, with only a momentary pause.

shift (1) to change, such as shifting the handhold in the pole vault; (2) in relay racing, moving the baton from one hand to the other.

shin-splint an injury resembling a chronic strain of the muscles in the region of the shin bone; another type is an inflammation of the covering of the shin bone; sometimes there is an inflammation of the tendons and joints of the foot.

shuttle hurdle a relay race in which a team of hurdlers (usually 4) race back and forth on the hurdle course.

side horse a gymnasium apparatus consisting of a leather-covered box firmly supported and containing 2 handles or pommels.

simulate to assume the mere appearance of; without the reality.

skeletal muscle the muscles attached to the skeleton.

skeleton dance same as *scarecrow dance.*

snapped a quick forceful movement.

sodden soaked, saturated, heavy with moisture.

sound key an electric switch that is opened or closed by sound vibrations.

spring the movement of the body off the ground, such as a leap or jump.

staggered same as *echelon.*

stall bars a gymnasium apparatus consisting of a series of closely spaced wooden bars fastened to a wall.

static-type contraction muscle contraction against a load it cannot move; no shortening of the muscle.

stop board a curved block of wood placed outside the front edge of the shot put circle as a restraining device.

stamina robustness of constitutional make-up; staying power.

stance a standing position.

steeplechase a race in which hazards such as hurdles, hedges, and water jumps are erected in the course of the runners.

stethoscope an apparatus commonly used by a physician for amplifying the sound of the heartbeat.

stimulus any agent that produces functional reaction in an irritable tissue.

strategy tactics or methods employed in executing an event.

stride a long step or the distance covered by a long step.

stride stand a standing position in which the legs are spread.

subcutaneous under the skin.

subjective purely psychical; mental observations contrasted to physical measurements.

summation the aggregation of a number of phenomena into a totality; the act of combining.

sump a pit, depression, reservoir, or tank serving as a receptacle for fluids.

superficial near the surface.

supporter an item of athletic equipment that is worn to protect the genitalia; commonly called the jock strap.

suspensory a type of supporter.

symmetrical having parts mutually well proportioned.

synchronized arranged to occur at the same time.

systolic pressure the arterial pressure during the contraction of the heart.

take-off the act of leaving the ground when executing a spring as in the high jump, the pole vault, and the hurdles.

take-off foot the foot from which the athlete drives off the ground.

take-off spot the spot from which the spring is executed for a jump, a vault, or a hurdle.

technique the form commonly used for the execution of an event.

tendinous pertaining to a tendon (a tough cord or band of dense inelastic white fibrous connective tissue).

tepid moderately warm; lukewarm.

therapeutic pertaining to the art of healing.

therapy the treatment of disease.

thigh the portion of the leg between the hip and the knee.

thorax that part of the body located between the neck and the abdomen.

thrust (verb) to exert force upon or against an object so as to move in a desired direction.

timing the proper relationship between 2 or more movements.

tincture of benzoin the balsamic rosin from a tree of the storax family (Styrax benzoin) found in Sumatra and Java.

tonus a state of elastic tension that keeps the tissue alert and ready to respond to a suitable stimulus.

torque that which produces or tends to produce rotation or torsion.

torso the trunk of the human body.

touch-off in some forms of relay races, especially shuttle relays, the baton is not used, and the oncoming runner touches the shoulder or outstretched hand of the relief runner.

transit passage over the landing area or bar (see *flight*).

transitional strides those running strides in the early stage of a race in which the runner gradually alters his form toward top-speed striding.

treading an action similar to riding a bicycle or walking.

trunk the body minus the head, legs, thighs, and arms; same as *torso*.

trunk tilt the inclination of the trunk from the vertical while in the act of running.

trunk twist a sudden rotary motion of the trunk used in various weight-throwing and jumping events.

tying up a condition brought on by fatigue in which the athlete overtenses certain muscles, thereby detracting from his performance.

urinate to discharge urine.

velocity time rate of motion; obtained by dividing the distance by the time.

vital alive.

vital volume the amount of air that is breathed out by the most forceful expiration after the deepest possible inspiration; respiratory capacity; breathing capacity.

vitamins a group of substances present in very small amounts in natural foodstuffs that are essential to normal metabolism and the lack of which causes deficiency diseases such as rickets.

voluntary refers to movements involving chiefly the cerebral cortex (brain).

whip (body whip, arm whip) a nimble and speedy movement of the body or arm.

wood-chopping exercise a stunt performed by assuming the stride-stand position, extending fully the clasped hands above the head and vigorously whipping them downward.

work—mechanical force (weight) times distance.

work—physiologic expressed as the caloric equivalent of the oxygen required to do work.

wrist roll a machine (gymnastic apparatus) offering varied resistance to the twist of the wrist.

zone of transfer in relay races the zone (20 meters) in which the baton must be passed.

Name index

Subject index

A

Abdominal cold packs, physiologic effects of, 267
Ache, side, 84
Adjustment, physical, for competition, 4
Aids, physical, 28
Alcohol, 26
Amateur Athletic Union of America, 299
Appetite, loss of, 25
Approach; *see* individual events
Athlete, responsibilities of, 278
Athlete's foot, 30
Athletic injuries, 33
Athletic supporter, 3
Attention, 42

B

Bath, 28
  duration of, 28
  purpose of, 28
  shower, 29
  temperature of, 29
  therapeutic value of, 29
  tub, 29
Baton, 98
  grasp, 101
  pass, 98
    arm position in, 100
    factors to be considered, 102
    hand position in, 100, 102
    variations in, 103
  passing zones, 99
  transfer, methods of, 99
    nonvisual, 102
    visual, 102
Benzoin, compound tincture of, 29
Bicycle ergometer, 268
Blisters, 30
Blocks, 36; *see also* Starting blocks
Body wastes, 21
Body weight charts, 23, 24
Breakfast, 16, 18, 19; *see also* Diet
Breathing, 41

C

Caliber of pistol, 42, 255, 280
Calisthenics, 11; *see also* Exercises
Calluses, 30
Caloric requirements, 20

Checkmark adjustments; *see* individual events
Cigarettes, 26
Circle
  discus, 213, 288, 294
  shot, 195, 288, 294
Clerk of course, 280
Coach, responsibilities of, 279
Coast, 47, 81
Command, starting, 43, 281
Common errors; *see* individual events
Competition
  comparative marks for
    long jump, 136
    discus throw, 214
    distance runs, 78
    high jump, running, 154
    hurdle races, 110
    javelin throw, 234
    middle distance runs, 62
    pole vault, 172
    relay racing, 98
    shot put, 196
    sprints, 136
  menus for, 19
  physical adjustments for, 4
  planning for, 7, 278
    cross-country, 90-91
    discus throw, 229, 232
    distance runs, 86, 88
    high jump, running, 168
    hurdle races, 134
    javelin throw, 249
    long jump, 149, 150, 152
    middle distance runs, 72, 76
    pole vault, 193
    relay races, 103
    shot put, 209, 211
    sprints, 56, 59
Competitors, types of; *see* individual events
Conditioning, 15
  diet, 15
  elimination, 21
  exercise, 22
  rest, 25
  sleep, 25
  staleness, 25
  tobacco, 26
  weight chart, 23, 24

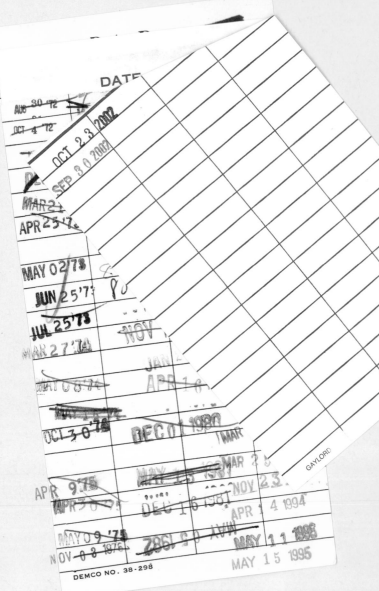